With more than 185 South-related titles, we have the area covered. Whether you're looking for the path less traveled, a favorite place to eat, family-friendly fun, a breathtaking hike, or enchanting local attractions, our pages are filled with ideas to get you from one state to the next.

For a complete listing of all our titles, please visit our Web site at www.GlobePequot.com. The Globe Pequot Press is the largest publisher of local travel books in the United States and is a leading source for outdoor recreation guides.

FOR BOOKS TO THE SOUTH

INSIDERS' GUIDE

FALCON GUIDES

Available wherever books are sold.
Orders can also be placed on the Web at www.GlobePequot.com,
by phone from 8:00 A.M. to 5:00 P.M. at 1-800-243-0495,
or by fax at 1-800-820-2329.

[Top] *Entrance to beach.* LABRANCHE PHOTOGRAPHY
[Bottom] *Bicyclers on beach.* LABRANCHE PHOTOGRAPHY

Dolphin statue at beach. LABRANCHE PHOTOGRAPHY

Day at the beach. LABRANCHE PHOTOGRAPHY

Surfers. LABRANCHE PHOTOGRAPHY

Baseball park. LABRANCHE PHOTOGRAPHY

Alltel Stadium. LABRANCHE PHOTOGRAPHY

Skyline by day. LABRANCHE PHOTOGRAPHY

Skyline by night. LABRANCHE PHOTOGRAPHY

Port at Jacksonville. LABRANCHE PHOTOGRAPHY

Shrimp boats on St. Johns River. LABRANCHE PHOTOGRAPHY

San Marco. LABRANCHE PHOTOGRAPHY

Lions at San Marco. LABRANCHE PHOTOGRAPHY

Gator at Jacksonville Zoo. LABRANCHE PHOTOGRAPHY

CONTENTS

CONTENTS

Directory of Maps

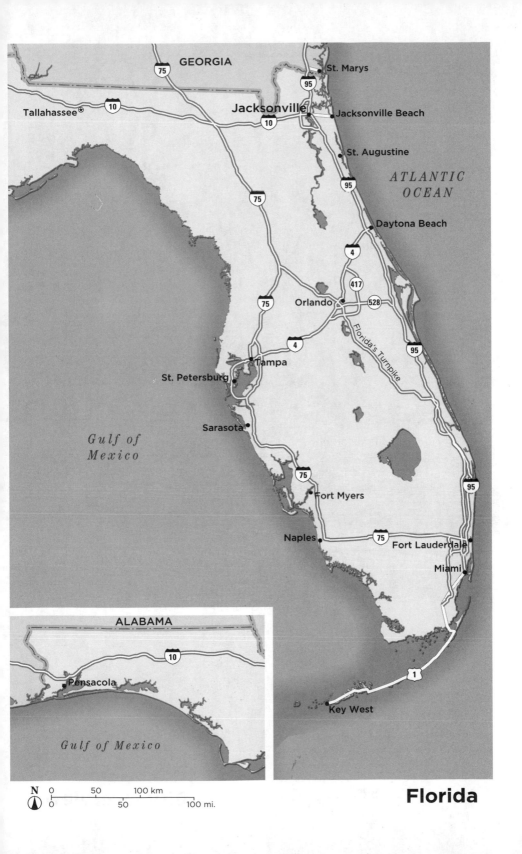

Florida

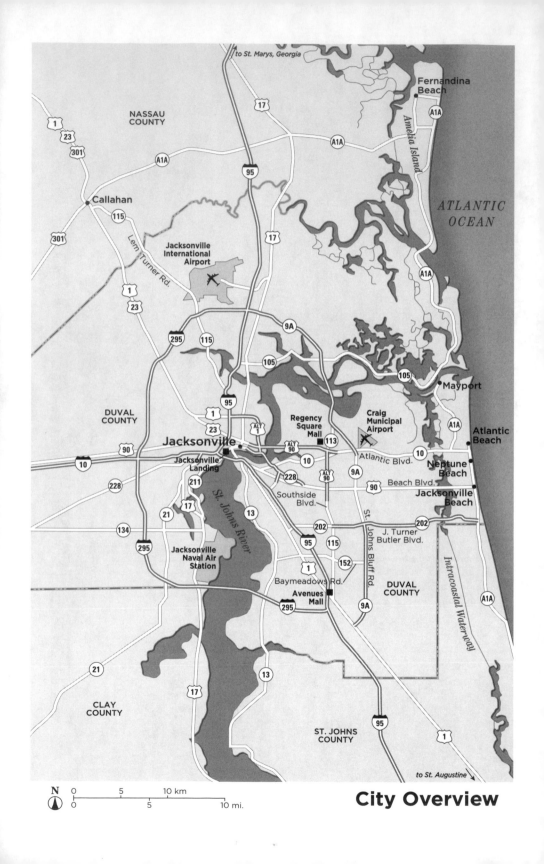

City Overview

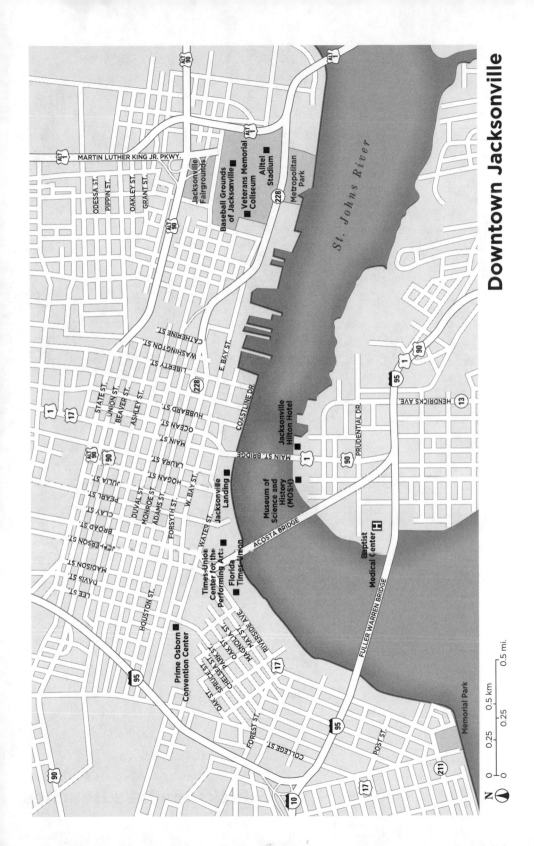

Downtown Jacksonville

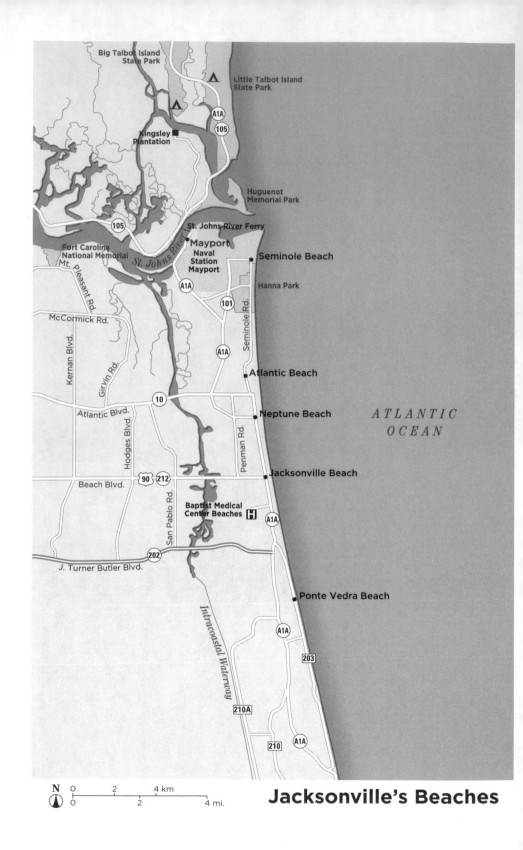

Big Talbot Island
State Park

Little Talbot Island
State Park

A1A

105

Kingsley
Plantation

Huguenot
Memorial Park

105

St. Johns River Ferry

Fort Caroline
National Memorial

Mt. Pleasant Rd.

St. Johns River

Mayport
Naval
Station
Mayport

Seminole Beach

A1A

Hanna Park

McCormick Rd.

101

Seminole Rd.

Kernan Blvd.

Girvin Rd.

A1A

Atlantic Beach

10

Atlantic Blvd.

Hodges Blvd.

Penman Rd.

Neptune Beach

ATLANTIC
OCEAN

90 212

Beach Blvd.

San Pablo Rd.

Jacksonville Beach

Baptist Medical
Center Beaches

H

A1A

202

J. Turner Butler Blvd.

Ponte Vedra Beach

Intracoastal Waterway

A1A

203

210A

210

A1A

N

0   2   4 km

0   2   4 mi.

Jacksonville's Beaches

PREFACE

As journalists we're constantly criticized for focusing only on the bad, for being negative, for never reporting any good news. Well we're happy to report that the news on the *Insiders' Guide to Jacksonville* is all good news. In fact, if it was bad news—a bad hotel or a restaurant with service that didn't deliver—we left it out. Omitted. Deleted. Outta here. (How we wish we could deal with daily news topics the same way!) Consequently, the hotels and restaurants and everything else listed in this guidebook are things we really like about our city and want you to know about.

Still, this is not meant to be an exhaustive guide to Jacksonville. If you want that, open the yellow pages. The purpose of the *Insiders' Guide to Jacksonville* is to tell you the best things about this city by the sea, the things we're most proud of after living here for a combined total of 30 years.

As you can see from the sheer size of this book, Jacksonville has an enormous number of places to see and things to do. But what you can't see is the great growth this city has gone through in the last four years. Jacksonville has a string of new libraries, including a new main library downtown. It also has a new baseball stadium, a new coliseum, a new federal courthouse, and a new county courthouse still under construction. There are new condos both downtown and at the Beaches, new roads, many new strip centers and subdivisions—the list goes on and on. One thing's for certain: Jacksonville is no longer the sleepy Southern city it once was. Jacksonville has been discovered.

We're excited to be the authors of this guidebook to Jacksonville. We're proud to be the ones to introduce you to this remarkable river city. Nevertheless, we cannot guarantee that the restaurants or hotels you visit will be the same as we found them to be. So we want to hear from you. Let us know the quality of your experiences in Jacksonville so that we can make this book its best guide. If you have comments, suggestions, or recommendations, e-mail us at editorial@Globe Pequot.com. Or write to us care of *Insiders' Guide to Jacksonville*, The Globe Pequot Press, P.O. Box 480, Guilford, CT 06437.

At press time some sections of Florida were still recovering from the effects of a hurricane. Please call ahead to check the status of restaurants, accommodations, and attractions listed in this book.

ACKNOWLEDGMENTS

It's an awesome responsibility to introduce your hometown to strangers via a guidebook. We've tried our best to be fun, fair, and informative, and to that end we had much assistance.

The authors would like to thank Stacy Badics, former communications manager with the Jacksonville and the Beaches Convention and Visitors Bureau, for her enthusiasm and support for this project. Ditto Marilyn Matejcek, the events and public relations coordinator for the City of Jacksonville Beach. Marilyn gave generously of her time and historical knowledge of the Beaches.

The authors would also like to thank the photographers at the *Florida Times-Union* whose photographs, unbeknownst to them, ended up in this book. We were able to share resources with the *T-U* because Jacksonville's main newspaper and The Globe Pequot Press are owned by the same corporation, Morris Communications. Additional thanks go out to Maryann Sterzel at the *Times-Union,* who can ferret out a photo in the newspaper's vast photo archives better than a hunter in search of wild turkey in the North Florida backwoods.

Many of the military photographs in this book came to us care of Nancy Crook, public affairs and communications officer at Naval Air Depot, Jacksonville. The navy is a big deal in this city, but in these security-conscious times it can be difficult to access. Nancy couldn't have made things easier. Plus, her department has some of the best Blue Angel photographs around, so we are doubly grateful.

Thanks, too, to the many others who walked that extra mile to help us: Laura Healan, Kathleen O'Brien, Jay Humphreys, Stacy Mosley, Robert Peek, Anthony Rieck, Susan Tucker Johnson, Peter Cassella, Teresa Eichner, Dan Dundon, David Delene, Bob Perry, and Jim LaBranche.

Our special thanks as well to Rona and Buford Brinlee, owners of The Book Mark in Atlantic Beach. We have learned that behind every successful publishing project lies at least one strong, independent bookstore.

Marisa would also like to thank her father, Al; her sister, Liz; and her brother, Rick, for all their love and support.

John dedicates this book to his mother, Betty, and the memory of his father, John R.

And finally, to Nick and Ana, always remember there's no place like home.

ACKNOWLEDGMENTS

HOW TO USE THIS BOOK

Rare is the guidebook that's read cover to cover. Rather, it seems, guidebooks are meant to fill a need: help you find a hotel, help you find a restaurant, help you find something to do. But we set out to change that in our *Insiders' Guide to Jacksonville.* We've packed this book full of useful information designed to make our city more accessible and, hopefully, more entertaining for you, the visitor. We put many hours and much thought into writing "Close-ups," stories designed to give you our insight into some of the people, places, and things that truly make Jacksonville unique. And we added tips throughout the book—Insiders' advice (marked with an **i**) designed to maximize your visit here and make it as safe and enjoyable as possible.

If you're on a plane heading to Jacksonville, sit back, sip a drink, and check out our chapter on getting around. It's full of tips on how to get from Jacksonville International Airport to downtown, the Beaches, or wherever you want to go in the River City. If you're still home and using this book to plan your vacation, our thorough chapters on accommodations will give you plenty of information on finding the hotel, motel, deluxe resort, or bed-and-breakfast that best suits your needs and your pocketbook. The maps will give you a good idea of where everything is located around town and the distances between them.

And be sure to bring this book along as you travel around Jacksonville. Think of us as your local friends who will constantly be at your side, helping you find the best places to shop, the best places to eat, the best places to go out at night. We're also a convenient reference if you have a quick question about local history or need an idea for something fun to do.

To help you gain an even greater appreciation for our town, we've included chapters on education, health services, child care, senior living, religion, local media, and the all-important job outlook for our city. If you're moving to Jacksonville, be sure to read our Relocation chapter to help you better understand the different parts of this city. It will also help you narrow down what can seem an overwhelming task when searching for the neighborhood that's right for you.

Above all, we hope this book will help enrich your visit to Jacksonville. We also hope it will help you decide whether Jacksonville would be a good place for you to live. If you've used other books in the *Insiders' Guide* series (and if you haven't, we hope you will), you'll find this book similar in terms of content.

Finally, we beg your indulgence if you find that phone numbers or addresses have changed since publication. Change is inherent in guidebooks. Businesses open and close, phone numbers change, restaurants change chefs—the list goes on and on. The changes are frustrating and difficult to keep track of. But in the end we've just had to accept that, like the weather, change is what keeps Jacksonville fresh and makes it an interesting place to live—and to visit.

NOTE: Unless otherwise indicated, all addresses in this book are in Jacksonville proper.

WHY JACKSONVILLE?

Chamber of commerce officials will tell you that Jacksonville is a fine place to live. And guess what? They're right. Jacksonville is a growing city that's managed to retain its small town, friendly feel. It's a place where you can accomplish what you want because there's still plenty of opportunity here, whether it's working for a big company, starting a business, or just enjoying the beauty of Northeast Florida.

At 841 square miles, Jacksonville is the largest city in terms of landmass in the contiguous United States. It's tucked away in the far northeast corner of Florida, about 30 miles south of Georgia. Spanish moss drapes the live oak trees, making the area feel more "Southern" than "South Florida." Contrary to Florida's reputation as a retirement haven, Jacksonville has a young population with a median age of 33. The winters are mild; the summers are hot. But a mild winter, or extended spring as some people like to call it, means it's hard to be a couch potato in Jacksonville. There are more than 60 miles of clean, wide, sandy beaches and more than 50 golf courses in the region. The St. Johns River flows through the center of downtown, giving Jacksonville its nickname, the River City, and provides a beautiful backdrop for many downtown events.

After years of nursing an inferiority complex, Jacksonville has finally come into its own. It used to be thought of as a sleepy Southern town with an odor problem. The smell of rotten eggs permeated almost every neighborhood, depending on how the wind blew. The odor came from several downtown paper mills, and in the early nineties city and federal officials launched an aggressive campaign to clean up the air. It worked. Some of the paper mills eventually closed; others installed high-tech equipment to eliminate the odors.

These days the air has never smelled sweeter in Jacksonville. The biggest boost to the city's image came in the mid-nineties when the National Football League awarded Jacksonville a football franchise. Without question, the Jacksonville Jaguars have put this city on the map. The Jags, as they're affectionately called, play home games at Alltel Stadium along the St. Johns River in one of the biggest stadiums in the NFL. And the city's new feel-good image was reaffirmed when the NFL selected Jacksonville to host the Super Bowl in February 2005.

The economy has continued to be strong. Big companies like Landstar realized the city's advantages and relocated here. Others, like Merrill Lynch and Johnson & Johnson, made major new investments in the River City. Jacksonville, long a financial center, is also headquarters for the state's biggest banks. And with two bases located here, the United States Navy is one of the city's biggest employers.

All this means that the city is growing like never before. Housing prices are rising, too, as new luxury communities sell big homes and relaxed lifestyles. In the late nineties the Jacksonville area reached a milestone when its population topped the one-million mark. And more newcomers arrive every year.

In 2000 city leaders, mindful of the impact torrid growth can have on the quality of life, asked Jacksonville voters to approve a sales tax increase to pay for an innovative $2.2 billion growth-management plan. The Better Jacksonville Plan built new roads and preserved new parkland and open green space. In addition the plan included construction of a new state-of-the-art downtown library, sports arena, baseball field, and county courthouse.

Jacksonville offers an active outdoor lifestyle for visitors and residents alike. Whether it's golfing on world-class courses, fishing in scenic marshes or the open ocean, playing tennis at ritzy resorts, or just walking on the beach at sunrise, Jacksonville's got it all. And for tourists who like to pick up a little history on their vacation, Northeast Florida will give you some great lessons. (Did you know that the first wine ever made in America was made right here—by Spanish priests in St. Augustine?) The area dates back to the days before Jamestown and Plymouth Plantation, when French and Spanish settlers landed on these shores and built the first fledgling

Expansion Management *magazine ranked Jacksonville the #1 hottest city in America for business relocation in January 2002.*

communities in what would one day become the United States of America.

Jacksonville's restaurants reflect its location. The city's two signature foods are fried Mayport shrimp and pork barbecue. Many Jacksonville residents are partial to all-you-can-eat family-style restaurants, but the city also boasts some of the best fine-dining establishments in Florida.

Regardless of where you stay in the area and for how long, we're confident you'll come to appreciate the city as much as we do. Enjoy!

Jacksonville Vital Statistics

Mayor: Republican John Peyton

Governor: Republican Jeb Bush

Population: 1.3 million

Average winter temperatures (high/low): January: 65/40

Average summer temperatures (high/low): July: 95/71

Average annual number of sunny days: 226

Government: City and county consolidated in 1968; now one mayor and 19 city council members represent everyone, including residents of Baldwin and the communities of Atlantic Beach, Neptune Beach, and Jacksonville Beach.

Land area: 841 square miles

Residents' median age: 33

Nickname: The River City

Mottos: "Bold New City of the South"; "Islanders: We never cross the ditch" (for Beaches residents)

River: The St. Johns River flows north for 310 miles and empties into the Atlantic Ocean near Mayport.

Major universities: University of North Florida, Jacksonville University, Edward Waters College, Flagler College in St. Augustine, Florida Coastal School of Law, Florida Community College at Jacksonville

Major area employers: United States Navy, CSX Transportation, Winn-Dixie, Bank of America

Average household income: $60,054

Average new home price: $199,327

Famous sons and daughters: Pat Boone, Rita Coolidge, David Duval, James Weldon Johnson, Chipper Jones, Lynyrd Skynyrd, Tim McGraw, A. Philip Randolph, Norm Thaggard, Slim Whitman

Bragging rights: The Dames Point Bridge is the longest concrete cable-stayed bridge in the Western Hemisphere. It's 2 miles long and supported by 21 miles of steel cables. It rises 175 feet above the St. Johns River.

Sales tax: 7.5 percent on almost everything except for medicine and certain foods

Military bases: Naval Station Mayport, Naval Air Station (NAS) Jacksonville, Coast Guard Group Mayport

Largest industrial employer in Northeast Florida: Located at NAS Jacksonville, the Naval Air Depot (NADEP), Jacksonville, employs 3,800 civilian employees who repair Navy aircraft and ground support equipment.

How busy is the port? Jaxport's three marine terminals handled 7.3 million tons of cargo in 2003, including almost 540,000 vehicles.

Annual event with the biggest economic impact: In 2001 the Players Championship generated $62.2 million for Northeast Florida. That translated into $1.1 million in sales tax for St. Johns County, where the golf tournament is held, and about $900,000 in tax revenue for Jacksonville.

Largest daily newspaper: *Florida Times-Union,* daily circulation 185,000; Sunday circulation 250,000

Weather number: (904) 741–4311

Jacksonville and the Beaches Convention and Visitors Bureau:
     550 West Water Street
     Jacksonville, FL 32202
     Phone: (904) 798–9111 or (800) 733–2668
     (U.S. and Canada)
     www.visitjacksonville.com

Direct impact of travel and tourism on Northeast Florida: In 2002, 5.14 million tourists pumped $3.6 billion into the local economy.

Number of lighthouses: Three: Amelia Island, Mayport, and St. Augustine

Jacksonville's favorite foods: Fried Mayport shrimp and pork barbecue

GETTING HERE, GETTING AROUND

If a Northeast Floridian has heard it once, he or she has heard it a dozen times—that vague response to a mention of Jacksonville, Florida. The conversation often goes something like this: "Jacksonville? Isn't that near St. Pete? Is it on the Atlantic or Gulf of Mexico side of Florida?" The response is generally: "Jacksonville is located in the northeast corner of the state, just south of the Florida-Georgia border, thank you very much."

Thank goodness that kind of exchange is occurring less frequently these days, partially due to a growing population—more than one million residents in the Jacksonville area—and to the national attention brought on by the city's NFL team, the Jacksonville Jaguars.

In fact, the city's growth has made getting here much easier as more and more airlines offer direct service. Unfortunately, getting around town has become more difficult because of congested roads. A major overhaul of the city's roadways and bridges, begun in 2001, is expected to alleviate the problem.

GETTING HERE

By Air

Jacksonville International Airport (JIA) is located 12 miles, or about 15 minutes, from downtown. After years of trying to get better air service, JIA now has something to brag about: With 19 airlines making 206 daily arrivals and departures, direct service is available from most of the nation's metropolitan areas. Travelers now have more options for direct flights to cities such as Philadelphia, Washington, D.C., New York, Dallas, and Detroit.

As it has done in other cities, the arrival of discount carrier Southwest Airlines in Jacksonville in 1997 spurred more service and lower fares. Southwest is now the leading carrier at JIA with 20 daily flights. Delta Air Lines, once the city's longtime leader, is the next busiest with 12 daily flights. US Airways, with 10 daily flights, is No. 3.

Here are the major air carriers serving JIA, along with their toll-free reservation numbers:

AirTran Airways, (800) 247–8726
American Airlines, (800) 433–7300
Continental, (800) 523–3273
Delta Air Lines, (800) 221–1212
Northwest Airlines, (800) 225–2525
Southwest Airlines, (800) 435–9792
United Airlines, (800) 241–6522
US Airways, (800) 428–4322

Once you arrive at JIA, you'll enjoy a newly renovated airport that recently completed a 15-month, $230 million expansion project. The facelift added ticketing counters and badly needed baggage handling space. It also included a newly expanded parking garage, which added 4,700 parking spaces to the airport, bringing the total number to more than 12,000. The airport also built a 200-foot moving sidewalk and two escalators to help travelers get from the garage to the ticket counter level of the terminal.

The terminal itself underwent a $25 million expansion that added 40,000 square feet of public courtyard space. This means there are now more shops and eateries for airport patrons to enjoy as they wait for connecting flights or for passenger arrivals and departures.

The airport is also proud of its state-of-the-art baggage security system. JIA was the first airport in the nation to install a CTX2000, which is an X-ray device that can detect everything from bombs to chemical weapons packed away in checked bags. Once you turn over your luggage to an airline, it takes a long and windy trip via conveyer belt to your plane. Along the way, teams of federal agents sitting in front of huge computer screens carefully assess what's inside your suitcase. If there's anything that seems suspicious, the agents call for a luggage check. This means a federal agent may actually open your suitcase to see what's inside. So here's a big tip: Do not lock your luggage. Although the agents have big key rings with all types of luggage keys on them, their first priority is to check your baggage. If they can't find the correct key, ultimately they will rip open your bags if they must.

Despite all the recent updates to JIA, more are planned. Another expansion project is on the drawing board that includes larger gate concourses This expansion will be done to enable the airport to handle a projected eight million passengers by 2010. Currently, JIA serves about five million passengers annually.

City leaders believe improvements to air travel are key components to the future of Jacksonville's economy, and perhaps the most important component if the city wants to lure international companies to do business here. For more information about JIA, call the airport's automated operator at (904) 741–4902 or check out JIA's Web site at www.jax airports.org.

REGIONAL AIRPORTS

The following airports located within the greater Jacksonville area serve the corporate and private plane travelers.

Craig Airport
855–11 St. Johns Bluff Road
(904) 641–7666

Centrally located near Jacksonville's suburban business centers, Craig Airport is a general aviation field perfect for busy corporate executives and ideally situated for quick access to the city's beaches, downtown business district, and Jacksonville Jaguars football games at nearby Alltel Stadium. In 2003 Craig reported 170,643 takeoffs and landings.

The cheapest way to get from the airport to downtown or the Beaches is by Gator City Shuttle Service. Charges are about $21 for four people to downtown and about $38 for four people to the Beaches. Call (904) 353–8880 for information/reservations.

Herlong Airport
9300 Normandy Boulevard
(904) 783–2805

Located on the city's west side, Herlong Airport serves as a general aviation field and prime recreational site for small private planes, hot air balloons, gliders, and similar craft. It covers 1,434 acres of land, houses approximately 140 aircraft, and features 3,500- and 4,000-foot runways. Single- and twin-engine aircraft, gliders, helicopters, ultralights, and an increasing number of corporate jets and turboprop aircraft use this airport, which is located about 11 miles southwest of downtown Jacksonville.

St. Augustine/St. Johns County
Municipal Airport
4794 U.S. Highway 1, St. Augustine
(904) 825–6860
www.staugustineairport.com

St. Augustine/St. Johns County Municipal Airport is the closest private, noncommercial airport for general aviation and corporate air travel to historic St. Augustine and the World Gold Village. It has three paved runways (longest is 7,000 feet), two lighted runways, and full-service fixed-based operations.

By Train

Amtrak
3570 Clifford Lane
(904) 766-5110, (800) USA-RAIL
(reservations)
www.amtrak.com
Arriving by train is an affordable option. Amtrak has daily service to Jacksonville's station, located on the city's north side, about 7 miles from downtown. City buses and taxis are available at the station for local transportation.

By Bus

Greyhound Bus
10 North Pearl Street
(904) 356-9976, (800) 231-2222
(fare and schedule information)
www.greyhound.com
For those traveling on a limited budget, Greyhound Bus is the most affordable way of getting to Jacksonville. The bus line's main terminal is located in the heart of downtown Jacksonville, where transferring to public transportation or grabbing a taxi is a snap.

By Car

Reaching Jacksonville from the Northeast or Mid-Atlantic states couldn't be much easier: Hop on Interstate 95 and head south. I-95, the major highway running along the East Coast, runs right through downtown Jacksonville.

As you travel south on I-95, you'll know you're getting close to Jacksonville

Taking a cruise? Gator City Shuttle Service will take two people from the airport to Jaxport's Cruise Terminal for about $22. Call (904) 353-8880 for reservations/information.

when you cross the Georgia-Florida border. If your destination is downtown Jacksonville, one of the surrounding neighborhoods, or the south side of town, continue on I-95. However, if you're headed to one of Jacksonville's beaches—Atlantic, Neptune, or Jacksonville—you'd be better off taking State Road 9A.

The exit for SR 9A and the Beaches is the first one after the exit for Jacksonville International Airport. Head south. As you drive over the St. Johns River on the majestic Dames Point Bridge, directly to the left you can see the Jacksonville Port Authority's busy shipping terminal. To the right, off in the distance, is downtown Jacksonville. Continue on SR 9A to the Atlantic Boulevard exit and head east to the Beaches.

If you're coming from the Midwest or other parts of the South, such as Atlanta, take Interstate 75 south to Interstate 10 and head east. Like I-95, I-10 is a direct shot to Jacksonville. I-10 connects with I-95 within sight of downtown Jacksonville, where you can head north or south on I-95. Other routes include U.S. Highway 1, which runs the length of the East Coast, and U.S. Highway 17 from the west.

GETTING AROUND

Now that you're here, it's time to explore Jacksonville's diverse surroundings. Grab a street map and your *Insiders' Guide,* and let's go.

It wasn't too many years ago that getting around Jacksonville could lighten your wallet considerably. Traveling along I-95 through Jacksonville was often a nightmare, with agonizingly long backups caused by the St. Johns River tolls.

In 1988 then Jacksonville mayor Tommy Hazouri led the campaign to eliminate tolls on the city's bridges and newest expressway—Butler Boulevard—and replace them with a half-cent sales tax. The tax now provides an ongoing revenue source for road and bridge construction in Duval County and bus system improvements.

The St. Johns River

In Jacksonville "a river runs through it" refers to the wide St. Johns River, which runs through the heart of the city like blood coursing through a body. The St. Johns was once a major commercial artery, but with the advent of the automobile, it became more of a headache to cross than a way to get around. Jacksonville started to take its river for granted and allowed years of pollution to take its toll. Fortunately a river revival began in the nineties, and the river began to be celebrated as a natural resource that contributes to our city like nothing else.

In 1998 the St. Johns River was named an American Heritage River, one of only 14 in the country. This makes it eligible for federal funding to help build trails along the river or buy key pieces of riverfront property for preservation. There's also a St. Johns Riverkeeper now, who's paid to be a full-time advocate for the river. Mike Hollingsworth travels up and down portions of the St. Johns almost daily, keeping abreast of the stresses and successes that affect this 310-mile waterway.

Tangible signs of river revival are evident in downtown Jacksonville, where expensive riverfront condominiums and town houses are under construction. The city also bought riverfront property to extend the Northbank Riverwalk a total of 3 miles from Alltel Stadium to Riverside.

The St. Johns River starts just west of Vero Beach and ends at the Atlantic Ocean. It drops just 30 feet during that journey, making it one of the laziest rivers in the world. The St. Johns also changes a lot from its swampy start to its saltwater end. The first 150 miles are marked by small towns, fish camps, and parks like Blue Springs State Park near DeLand. The springs, which feed the St. Johns, are 72 degrees Fahrenheit year-round and draw manatees in the winter, swimmers and tubers in the summer.

Around Palatka the St. Johns turns into a wide "river of lakes," or "Welaka," as the Timucuan Indians called it. As you head toward Jacksonville, expensive homes line the riverbank, and riverfront lots, if you can still find one, start at half a million dollars. In Jacksonville the river gets industrial—or, as some prefer, downright ugly. Hundreds of huge container ships use the river as a highway every year to deliver their cargo to the docks at Talleyrand and Blount Island. Often the cargo is new cars from Japan and Germany, which are unloaded here then trucked to their final destinations. Boating seems to be the greatest common denominator along the entire length of the St. Johns River. Everything plies these waters—kayaks to container ships, sailboats to shrimp boats, pontoons to powerboats.

Naturalist William Bartram traveled the St. Johns River in a canoe in the 1700s and was one of the first to write about the river's clear water and colorful fish. Today Bill Belleville's book about the St. Johns, *River of Lakes: a Journey on Florida's St. Johns River,* discusses one of its major stressors: storm water runoff, which carries lawn chemicals and highway dirt into the river. But, says Belleville, there are still places along the St. Johns nearer its headwaters where the water is as clear as it was in Bartram's day. Belleville is optimistic that the new appreciation and awareness of the St. Johns River will only add to its health in the future.

By Taxi

Jacksonville International Airport is located about 12 miles north of downtown, just off I-95. Travel into the city isn't difficult, as long as you aren't planning to take public transportation—there isn't any. The Jacksonville Transportation Authority experimented with bus service from the airport to downtown and Jacksonville's beaches, but there wasn't enough demand to support the service. There is, however, reliable taxi and limo service (though the shuttle service mentioned on page 7 is cheaper). If you want to take a taxi at the airport, you have one option. Gator City Taxi has the exclusive contract to serve the airport. Charges are about $27 to downtown Jacksonville and about $50 to Jacksonville's beaches. Call (904) 249-6289 for the Gator City Taxi Beaches location. Service is available at the entrance to JIA, or call Gator City Taxi at (904) 741-0008 or (904) 355-8294. Gator City accepts all major credit cards.

If you'd prefer to travel in style, say a Lincoln Town Car or stretch limousine, several limousine and transportation companies serve the airport. The cost will run about twice as much as the taxi. For example, Carey Jacksonville charges about $70 to transport two passengers from the airport to the Beaches.

Beaches Limousine, (904) 221-5466
Dana's Limousine, (904) 744-3333
Carey Jacksonville, (904) 992-2022

When traveling around downtown Jacksonville, take the Trolley. It's free. The Trolley—a motorized, air-conditioned replica of a trolley car—loops around downtown, from the Sports Complex to the Jacksonville Transportation Authority's passenger transit center. Service to a dozen stops operates every 10 minutes from 6:30 A.M. to 7:00 P.M., Monday through Friday.

By Car

Jacksonville is a big city. So big, in fact (841 square miles), it ranks as the biggest city in the contiguous United States. Because of the city's size, a car is the best way to get around.

Whether you're arriving by car or you plan to pick up a rental at the airport, be prepared for extensive road work. Jacksonville is undergoing a massive overhaul of its roadway system as part of a $2.2 billion Better Jacksonville Plan. Started in 2000, construction is expected to greatly improve Jacksonville's congested roadways. But for the next few years, construction will cause its own problems. The project includes a new Beach Boulevard bridge across the Intracoastal Waterway, the widening or building of 11 roads and highways, and construction of 12 interchanges at some of Jacksonville's most heavily traveled intersections.

If you're traveling to Jacksonville's beaches, you've got through routes—Atlantic, Beach, or Butler Boulevards. During morning and evening rush hour, all three roads are very congested. Your best bet is to travel to the Beaches during non-rush hours.

CAR RENTALS

Call for rates and availability. The following car rental companies operate at JIA.

Alamo Rent A Car, (800) 327-9633;
www.goalamo.com

Avis, (904) 741-2327, (800) 831-2847;
www.avis.com

Budget, (800) 527-0700; www.budget
rentacar.com

Dollar Rent A Car, (904) 741-4614,
(800) 800-4000; www.dollarcar.com

Hertz Corp., (904) 741-2151, (800)
654-3131; www.hertz.com

National Car Rental, (904) 741-4580, (800) 227-7368; www.nationalcar.com

To return an airport rental car, drive directly into the ground floor of the parking garage, which is adjacent to the terminal building.

Public Transportation

Jacksonville Transportation Authority (JTA)
(904) 630-3100
www.jtaonthemove.com

The Jacksonville Transportation Authority operates the city's bus system and the Skyway Express monorail, and it's responsible for maintenance and expansion of some of Jacksonville's vast network of roadways and bridges.

The bus system serves all Duval County, from the Beaches west to Orange Park. The system connects with the Skyway Express downtown. **NOTE:** There is currently no bus service to Jacksonville International Airport. Special JTA shuttle buses have served the airport in the past; if you're arriving by plane, inquire to see if public bus service to downtown Jacksonville has resumed.

Every JTA bus stop displays a black-and-white graphic of a bus. To find your closest bus stop, first check your route map, available online or by phone at (904) 743-3582. It will tell you which streets your bus travels. Then look for the bus stop signs located every few blocks along the route.

Bike racks have been installed on 53 JTA buses. Each lightweight rack holds two bicycles and is easy to use. Bike space is available on a first-come, first-served basis. If the rack is full, you will need to wait for the next bus (bicycles are not permitted inside JTA buses). To use the bike racks, you buy a permit for $3.00.

Regular bus fare is 75 cents, and exact change is required. Long trips cost more. Service from the Beaches to downtown is

Jaxport's Cruise Terminal is located about 10 minutes from the airport just off Heckscher Drive. If you're driving, take I-95 to SR 9A heading south and exit onto Heckscher just before the Dames Point Bridge.

$1.35; the fare from Orange Park to downtown Jacksonville is $1.50. Senior citizens (60 and older) ride free with a pass.

Buses equipped with wheelchair lifts are available on many routes. Check the schedule cover for the wheelchair symbol, or call bus information at (904) Ride-JTA (743-3582) to find out which routes provide this service. Priority seating for senior citizens and the disabled is available at the front of every bus. Wheelchair tie-downs are available on about 40 percent of JTA's bus fleet.

THE SKYWAY EXPRESS

The Skyway is a state-of-the-art elevated, electrified monorail transit system with eight stations serving both sides of the St. John's River.

The Skyway operates Monday through Friday from 6:00 A.M. to 11:00 P.M., Saturday from 10:00 A.M. to 11:00 P.M., and Sunday only for special-event service, such as Jaguars football games. Stations are continually monitored by closed-circuit television, and all vehicles have two-way voice communications with interior video recordings. Stations and vehicles are fully accessible to the disabled.

While downtown you can ride the Skyway Express to visit the Prime Osborn Convention Center and the Hemming Plaza (City Hall and federal courthouse). Cross the St. Johns River to San Marco Station, where it's an easy walk to the River City Brewing Co. restaurant, the Museum of Science and History (MOSH), and Friendship Park Riverwalk. There's also a stop near the Hilton Hotel, Hampton Inn, and Extended Stay. The final stop provides easy access to the Radisson

If you forget something on a JTA bus, call (904) 630-3189 for help locating that lost article.

Hotel and Crawdaddy's and Charthouse restaurants.

On Jaguar game days, the Skyway is free for the three hours before kickoff and two hours after the game. The Skyway fare for nonmonthly commuters is 35 cents; 10 cents for the elderly and disabled.

RIVER TAXI

SS Marine Taxi
3189 East Old Port Circle
(904) 733-7782
www.jaxwatertaxi.com
Jacksonville offers one mode of transportation unique to the River City: river taxi service available for short hops across the St. Johns to Alltel Stadium or to points downtown or on the Southbank

Riverwalk. You can pick up a river taxi at the Jacksonville Landing on the Northbank or on the Southbank Riverwalk near the Hilton Hotel.

The river taxi is a nice way to travel if you're staying at a hotel on the Southbank and want to get across the river to go to the Landing or a jazz club. Conversely, if you're staying at a hotel on the Northbank, like the Omni or Adams Mark, and want to cross the river to eat at a nice restaurant, don't drive across the Main Street Bridge. Take a water taxi.

Daily service operates from 11:00 A.M. to 9:00 P.M. weekdays and 11:00 A.M. to 11:00 P.M. weekends. The fare can be purchased for one-way or round-trip service, and prices range from $3.00/adult one-way to $5.00/adult round-trip. Stadium prices vary.

Plan to wait about 20 minutes to get on your water taxi, then about 20 minutes more for the trip itself. We think it's worth the extra time to experience Florida and Jacksonville from the water.

HISTORY 🏛

Almost every history of Jacksonville and coastal Northeast Florida begins 4,000 years ago with the Timucuans, Native Americans said to have worn hand-painted fish bladders as earrings. We know that the Timucuans ate large amounts of oysters because archaeologists have found huge oyster-shell mounds in their ancient villages in places like Guana State Park off Highway A1A near St. Augustine.

EARLY EUROPEANS

Historians believe that Timucuans befriended Jacksonville's first European settlers, the French Huguenots (Protestants) who built a settlement on the St. Johns River in 1564 and named it Fort Caroline. This settlement angered the Spanish, who had claimed "La Florida" as their own in 1513, when Ponce de Leon landed near Cape Canaveral in search of the Fountain of Youth.

In 1565 the Spanish sent Pedro Menendez de Aviles to wipe out the French at Fort Caroline. He also started a settlement, St. Augustine, and a Catholic mission, Nombre de Dios, firmly establishing Spanish rule in Florida, a dominion that would last some 200 years.

That dominion was not altogether peaceful. It was punctuated by repeated English attacks on St. Augustine lead by Sir Francis Drake and others. To protect themselves, the Spanish built a fortress, the Castillo de San Marcos, which was finished in 1695, just in time to provide shelter against attacks by the governor of South Carolina, James Moore, in 1702 and by General James Oglethrope of Georgia in 1740. In 1763 the Spanish ceded La Florida to England.

The British reign in Florida was short, 20 years, but significant. During that time the British constructed a road from St. Augustine to Savannah called The King's Road. It crossed the St. Johns River at a narrow stretch called Cowford, a popular crossing with farmers who needed to get cows across the river. Cowford, located about where the Adams Mark Hotel stands today, is considered the humble beginnings of a settlement that would later become the city of Jacksonville.

Following the American Revolution, England gave Florida back to Spain in 1783 for another 37 tumultuous years. During these years "patriots" secretly sanctioned by the United States government repeatedly attacked Florida, trying to oust the Spanish. In 1821 Spain could hold on no longer, and it ceded Florida to the United States.

GETTING STARTED

Once Florida became a U.S. territory, settlers quickly arrived, many via The King's Road. Cowford started to grow, and by 1822 surveyors had measured out a town on the north bank of the St. Johns River. Settlers named it Jacksonville for General Andrew Jackson, a champion of the patriots and fighter of the Seminoles. Logging was a big early industry, in part because the St. Johns River was a good way to transport logs. Shipping was big, too, because of the town's location near the Atlantic Ocean. Florida became a state in 1845.

THE CIVIL WAR

Jacksonville's growth stopped in 1861 when Florida seceded from the United States of America and joined the Confederacy. Through the course of the war, Union troops burned down most of the

 CLOSE-UP

Jacksonville Beach

Jacksonville Beach sits on a barrier island along with several other beach communities, but for centuries before these communities began, the barrier island was simply wild land. It was the sole domain of hunters and fishermen and Native Americans, who collected shellfish along the shore. By 1885 a tiny hamlet, Ruby Beach, had taken root. It wasn't much more than a post office and a few tent homes, but in short order a railroad arrived bringing tourists from Jacksonville. An early railroad depot, along with a locomotive that carried many people out to enjoy the fresh ocean air, is now part of a history museum in Jacksonville Beach.

With the railroad came big progress. Ruby Beach was renamed Pablo Beach, and a half dozen luxury resorts were built along the ocean to serve all the tourists coming out from Jacksonville. The first resort, Murray Hall, boasted 192 rooms, an elevator, a steam heating system, hot and cold running water, sulfur baths, a bowling alley, and 58 fireplaces to ward off the winter chill. Sadly, there's no trace of Murray Hall left in Jacksonville Beach today. Built totally of wood, it burned to the ground just four years after opening in 1886.

As Pablo Beach grew, residents built themselves a city hall and a home for the very first American Red Cross Volunteer Life Saving Corp. Those lifeguards were badly needed in Pablo Beach because tourists were drowning at an alarming rate. A boardwalk soon followed so that tourists could promenade, enjoy restaurants and shooting galleries, and dance in pavilions at night.

By 1925 Pablo Beach residents wanted a change and voted to rename their community Jacksonville Beach. It was better to be associated with Jacksonville, they said. During the sixties, seventies, and eighties, much of the oceanfront area in Jacksonville Beach fell into disrepair, and Jacksonville Beach was no longer the tourist mecca it once had been. In the nineties, city leaders made a concerted effort to attract businesses back to the beach. They also built anchors, such as a new city hall in the heart of town and a new outdoor band shell on the ocean. Redevelopment has caught on, and Jacksonville Beach is enjoying a renaissance. Old beach shacks are being torn down to make way for new high-rise oceanfront condominiums as well as new restaurants, nightclubs, and hotels.

city on three separate occasions. Still, Florida became the breadbasket of the Confederate Army, providing the produce and cattle that fed Southern troops during the war.

The Battle of Olustee on February 20, 1864, was an unsuccessful effort by Union forces to cut off those Confederate supply lines. The South prevailed, inflicting heavy losses on hundreds of Union soldiers, many of them former slaves. The Battle of Olustee was the only major battle fought in Florida during the Civil War. Every anniversary, thousands of people watch a re-creation of the battle at the Olustee Battlefield, 90 minutes west of Jacksonville. On the weekend of the reenactment, Friday is always full of schoolkids. Saturday is the least crowded and, we think, the best day to go. Sunday is the formal scripted program, which is crowded. You can get a good feel for the reenactment during Saturday's dress rehearsal.

TOURISM

After the Civil War Jacksonville started to come into its own. It became a popular tourist destination for Northerners seeking warmer winter weather. Renowned author Harriet Beecher Stowe bought an orange grove on the St. Johns River in Mandarin and wintered here for many years. She also wrote what would become the region's first guidebook, a bestseller called *Palmetto Leaves*. (See the Close-up in this chapter.)

But prosperity went up in flames on May 3, 1901, when nearly 150 blocks of downtown Jacksonville burned to the ground in what has become known as the Great Fire. Ten thousand people were left homeless. The fire was so massive that Savannah residents reported watching it glow on the horizon. (See the Attractions chapter for more on the Great Fire.) Three days after the biggest blaze in the South, Jacksonville started to rebuild.

By 1908 a new industry had taken hold here: motion-picture production. Since the city could offer plenty of sunshine and a warm winter for moviemakers, Jacksonville was soon competing with Los Angeles for films. Oliver Hardy got his start here, George M. Cohan starred in his first movie here, and Lionel Barrymore filmed a movie in Atlantic Beach.

Moviemaking faded to black for several reasons. First, many Jacksonville residents became fed up with the business. In his book *Old Hickory's Town,* James Robertson Ward explains why: "The opponents became more outraged when other

For the centennial of the Great Fire in Jacksonville, the city commissioned a 48-foot stainless steel spire by artist Bruce White. The Great Fire Memorial Sculpture sits at the intersection of Market and Bay Streets, where many people jumped into the river and drowned trying to escape the flames.

producers made false fire alarms to get the fire trucks their scripts called for, filmed bank robberies during Sunday worship hours, and in one instance, placed a misleading advertisement in a newspaper to draw a crowd to avoid paying extras." Second, efforts to start a major film production center here with badly needed indoor production studios collapsed. Finally, World War I began, and Jacksonville found prosperity elsewhere.

SHIPS AHOY

By 1940 Jacksonville's long association with the United States Navy had begun. The navy opened an aviation training facility, Naval Air Station Jacksonville. Naval Station Mayport, home port to destroyers and aircraft carriers, soon followed. Downtown shipyards built ships for World War II, and one of the city's beach suburbs was invaded by German terrorists. In June 1942 four Nazi soldiers, under direct orders from Hitler himself, landed in Ponte Vedra Beach. Their assignment: Blow up power plants, factories, train terminals, and

The city is trying to create a silent-film museum at the old Norman Film Studios in Arlington. That's where Richard Norman, a white silent-film director in the 1920s, found his niche making serious dramas with all-black casts that were not the derogatory films then the style of the day.

CLOSE-UP

Harriet Beecher Stowe

Harriet Beecher Stowe was an original Florida snowbird. She began wintering in Jacksonville in 1867 after buying a 30-acre orange grove in Mandarin. More than anything else, Stowe enjoyed the freedom Florida offered from winters back home in Connecticut. She greatly appreciated "to be able to spend your winter out of doors, even though some days be cold; to be able to sit with windows open; to hear birds daily; to eat fruit from trees; and pick flowers from hedges, all winter long."

Stowe spent up to six months a year in Mandarin with her husband and twin daughters. She shared her enthusiasm for her relaxed lifestyle on the St. Johns River in a volume of sketches called *Palmetto Leaves*. Each chapter describes the simple things Stowe so appreciated, such as a picnic up Julington Creek, which involved catching fish, cooking it in a hole lined with leaves, and eating it the moment it was done. She gives advice on how to buy land, start a farm, and grow and sell oranges. She waxes poetic about the St. Johns River, "the great blue sheet of water [that] shim-mers and glitters like so much liquid lapis lazuli." Tourism increased almost overnight in Jacksonville once *Palmetto Leaves* was published. In fact, steamboats began pulling up at the Stowes' riverfront home so that tourists could see the woman who wrote not just *Palmetto Leaves,* but also *Uncle Tom's Cabin.*

While living in Mandarin, Stowe did not abandon her political beliefs. She helped raise money to build a school for freed slave children, which was also used as a church on Sunday. When the schoolhouse mysteriously burned down one night, Stowe, undaunted, helped raise money to rebuild it.

The Stowes enjoyed 17 winters in their Mandarin home, until 1884, when Dr. Calvin Stowe, Harriet's husband, became too sick to travel. Nothing remains of the Stowe homestead on Mandarin Road except, perhaps, some majestic oak trees trimmed in Spanish moss. If those ancient trees could talk, oh, the stories they might tell of the early days in Mandarin and the charming woman named Harriet Beecher Stowe who so loved the land.

department stores anywhere in the United States. Luckily, the German operatives were caught in New York and Chicago after another German operative turned them in before they could do any damage.

MILESTONES

In 1968 Jacksonville residents greatly simplified their local government, voting to consolidate 133 elective offices in Jacksonville, Duval County, the Beaches, and Baldwin. No longer would there be multiple tax and property appraisers; instead there would be one government encompassing the entire county, with one mayor, city council, and police force. This consolidation also meant that the city became huge in terms of area: 841 square miles. Jacksonville residents were so proud of their efforts that they gave the city a new nickname, The Bold New City of the South.

This bold new city really popped its buttons in 1995 when the Jacksonville Jaguars played their first game in the city's new NFL-worthy football stadium. Many credit the Jaguars with putting the city on the map. And with the 2005 Superbowl on our turf, Jacksonville prepared for game day by widening roads, constructing buildings, and lining up cruise ships to serve as floating hotels for all the fans who flocked here for the sports spectacular.

HOTELS AND MOTELS

Like most American cities, Jacksonville has a strong representation of hotel chains, providing a grand total of 21,000 rooms. That's how many rooms we promised the NFL for the 2005 Super Bowl. (In addition to all those hotel rooms, more than 5,000 Super Bowl tourists planned to stay on luxury cruise ships docked along the St. Johns River near downtown.)

Jacksonville has four main "hotel hubs." We've tried to pick a good cross section of hotels in these hubs in order to give you a range of options and prices to choose from when booking your stay. It would be impossible to include every hotel in Jacksonville in our guide, and we apologize in advance to the many fine hotels we had to leave out.

The Beaches is generally the most popular (and expensive) place for travelers to hang their hats. Downtown is a close second, especially during big-event weekends like the Gator Bowl.

North Jacksonville is starting to draw a lot of hotel guests, as evidenced by the number of new hotels on Airport Road off I-95. As the name suggests, Airport Road is the highway leading into and out of Jacksonville International Airport. With six new hotels in four years, Airport Road has been nicknamed Hotel Road. Helping to fuel this construction boom is an airport expansion. This is also where you will find the best values.

Another popular hotel hub is the Southpoint area at the confluence of two major arteries: I-95 and J. Turner Butler Boulevard. Southpoint is centrally located to the Beaches, downtown, and the Avenues Shopping Mall. Tinseltown, a growing entertainment and shopping area, is also nearby.

All these hotels have smoking and nonsmoking rooms, all have wheelchair-accessible rooms, and all take major credit cards. Finally a word about those oh-so-pesky hotel taxes that can add considerably to the cost of your room. In Duval County the bed tax is 13 percent with one exception—the Adams Mark Hotel downtown on the St. Johns River charges a 14 percent bed tax. The extra percent surtax goes to the city to repay the money the city gave to Adams Mark. In Nassau County (Amelia Island) and St. Johns County (Pointe Verda, St. Augustine), the bed tax is 9 percent.

PRICE CODE

Based on information available at the time of publication, we offer the following price code (average charge for double occupancy rates in peak season) as a general guide. Please note that fluctuations in price and availability occur frequently.

$	$45 to $69
$$	$70 to $99
$$$	$100 to $120
$$$$	$121 and up

DOWNTOWN

Adams Mark Hotel $$$–$$$$
225 Coast Line Drive East
(904) 633-9095, (800) 444-2326
www.adamsmark.com

With 966 rooms, this is Jacksonville's largest hotel. It makes its money on conventions and can accommodate groups of 10 to 4,300. The grand ballroom alone is 27,000 square feet. This 19-story hotel enjoys a fine location on the St. Johns River within walking distance of Alltel Stadium, Metro Park, Jacksonville Landing, and the Times-Union Center for the Performing Arts. Built in 2001, the rooms offer a fabulous river view or a so-so city view. They are decorated with a "Floribbean" feel; the colors are bright and the furniture is whitewashed rattan. Amenities include coffeemakers, irons/boards, hair dryers, HBO and Playstation, and a rooftop pool and fitness center. There are two restaurants in the lobby, including the casual Riverfront Cafe, which is popular for breakfast, and Bravo! Ristorante, an elegant Italian restaurant featuring a waitstaff that often breaks out in song at your table. There is also high-speed Internet access in 110 guest rooms on the hotel's 16th and 18th floors.

Hampton Inn Central   **$$–$$$**
1331 Prudential Drive
(904) 396–7770, (800) 726–6877
www.hampton-inn.com
Business travelers enjoy the convenient location of this Hampton Inn on the south bank of the St. Johns River in downtown Jacksonville. It's half a block from the Skyway Express, which will take you across the river to downtown's Northbank. It's also within walking distance of several fine restaurants and next door to Treaty Oak Park (see Parks) and the Museum of Science and History (see Attractions). The hotel offers 118 king and double rooms, five with spa tubs. Amenities include a free deluxe breakfast bar, HBO, *USA Today*, irons/boards, coffeemakers, free parking, and an outdoor pool. All local and "800" calls from your room are also free. A sundries shop in the lobby sells microwavable food and beer at prices that won't clean out your wallet. Guests also have free use of a health club located in an office building a block from the inn.

Hilton Jacksonville Riverfront   **$$$–$$$$**
1201 Riverplace Boulevard
(904) 398–8800, (800) HILTONS
www.jacksonvillehilton.com
Step out onto the balcony of your hotel room and enjoy the view of the St. Johns River from this 10-story riverfront hotel conveniently located on the south bank of the St. Johns. There are 292 rooms here, all featuring either river or city views. Guests often stroll on the Southbank Riverwalk, a 2-mile wooden boardwalk on

the river in front of the hotel, to nearby museums and restaurants. Amenities include HBO, coffeemakers, irons/boards, hair dryers, free credit-card and "800" calls, a fitness center, and a heated river-front pool. The hotel was extensively renovated in 2001, so there's not much left from the days when Elvis Presley used to rent a room year-round and rent an entire floor when he played a local concert. Gold records hang on the wall in Presley's suite, which now rents for $400 a night—no extra charge for the alarm clock, which will wake you up to the tune of "Jailhouse Rock." Ruth's Chris Steakhouse is located in the Hilton's lobby, as is The American Grill, which features a breakfast and lunch buffet. Airport and local transportation is available from the lobby for a charge. This hotel is popular with business travelers, who also like to take to the water on the hotel's yacht, *The Jacksonville Princess,* which is berthed out back. The weekend dinner cruises are a popular way to see some of the best views of the city... from the water.

The Omni Jacksonville Hotel   **$–$$$$**
245 West Water Street
(904) 355–6664, (800) 843–6664
www.omnihotels.com
Long a mainstay in downtown Jacksonville, the Omni enjoys a great location across the street from the St. Johns River, the Landing, and the Times-Union Center for the Performing Arts. It's also a short walk to the Skyway Express, Jacksonville's people mover, which will take you across the river for museums and fine dining, all within walking distance of the Riverplace stop. The Omni Jacksonville Hotel underwent a $4 million renovation in 2004. There are 348 rooms in this 16-story hotel, which features a wood-and-marble grand staircase and rooms with a river view especially designed for business travelers. Kids are also welcome here; in fact, upon check-in all children receive a suitcase (on rollers) chock-full of games and books and a list of the top-10 kids attractions in Jacksonville. All rooms feature Nintendo

Looking for a hotel near a movie theater? The Hilton Garden Inn in Deerwood Park is located about 100 yards from a 14-screen megaplex called Tinseltown. Call (904) 997-6600 for reservations.

64, coffeemakers, hair dryers, irons/boards, minibars, terry-cloth bathrobes, free newspapers including *USA Today,* and a fitness center and pool on the fourth floor. Pets are allowed with prior approval. An award-winning restaurant, Juliette's Bistro, is located in the hotel lobby, and a coffee shop and gift shop are located in an atrium the hotel shares with an office high-rise. Employees are justifiably proud that the Omni Jacksonville won the J. D. Power Award for hotel guest satisfaction in 2000.

Radisson Riverwalk Hotel $$$-$$$$
1515 Prudential Drive
(904) 396-5100, (800) 333-3333
www.radisson.com
If you like to walk, this is a great place to stay. The Radisson Riverwalk Hotel is located downtown on the south bank of the St. Johns River. Just outside the hotel's front door is a boardwalk along the river that stretches from the hotel to the Museum of Science and History, a distance of about a mile. It's a lovely walk and a popular place for people to exercise. The hotel offers 322 rooms, and well over half of them enjoy river views. The rooms were renovated in the late nineties, and they feature either a king-size or two double beds, a coffeemaker, an iron/board, a hair dryer, and high-speed Internet access. There's also free HBO in every room. In addition, the hotel offers a 24-hour fitness center, an outdoor swimming pool, and lighted tennis courts, which are hardly ever used. There's a restaurant in the Radisson called the River's Edge Cafe that's a nice place to eat breakfast. It also serves lunch and dinner, but don't feel like you have to eat every meal there. The Radisson sits within walking distance of

some of the city's best restaurants, including Morton's Steakhouse and bb's. (See our Restaurants chapter for more information about these and other restaurants in the Southbank area.) The Radisson is about a 25-minute drive to Jacksonville's new Cruise Ship Terminal, and because of that the hotel is offering something unique: a Cruise Package that lets you park your car at the hotel while you're away. This is not a bad deal since parking at the terminal costs $10 a day. The package includes transportation to the Cruise Ship Terminal and back to the hotel.

THE BEACHES

Best Western Mayport Inn
& Suites $-$$
2389 Mayport Road, Atlantic Beach
(904) 435-3500, (800) WESTERN
www.bestwestern.com
This Best Western opened in 2000 with 60 rooms, 12 of them suites. Five of the rooms have spa tubs. All rooms have queen- or full-size beds, HBO, coffeemakers, hair dryers, irons/boards, a microwave, and a minifridge. There's also a small fitness center, an outdoor pool, and free continental breakfast. The hotel is about 2 miles from Naval Station Mayport, so the clientele here is largely navy. It's also a mile or so from Hanna Park, one of the prettiest city parks in Jacksonville, with miles of unspoiled beaches and the area's best surf break.

Best Western Oceanfront $$$-$$$$
305 North First Street, Jacksonville Beach
(904) 249-4949, (800) 897-8131
www.jaxbestwestern.com
Imagine relaxing in a spa tub in your hotel room. The sliding glass doors are open, and you're watching the world unfold before you on the beach. There's a sea breeze blowing into the room, keeping things cool. When you finish relaxing in the tub, you sit on your private balcony and enjoy more of the ocean and the sea breeze. Such is the

ambience in this small 52-room ocean-front hotel in the heart of Jacksonville Beach, which seems to be a favorite with business travelers and couples. Some of the city's most popular nightclubs and restaurants are just a few blocks away. Many of the rooms have spa tubs; all have microwaves and refrigerators, cof-feepots, irons/boards, hair dryers, HBO, a deluxe continental breakfast in the lobby, and a free copy of *USA Today*. There's a heated outdoor pool and parking for hotel guests, an important amenity in the heart of Jacksonville Beach.

Casa Marina Hotel $$$-$$$$
691 North First Street, Jacksonville Beach
(904) 270-0025
www.casamarinajax.com

There's history in the halls of this ocean-front hotel, the name of which means "house by the sea" in Spanish (see the sidebar in this chapter). Built in 1925, the Casa Marina still sports a rare, original pecky-cypress ceiling in what is now the hotel's dining room. (Pecky cypress is wood pecked full of holes by birds trying to get at bugs.) The hotel has 23 rooms, 18 of them suites with sitting rooms and Mur-phy beds. Many of the rooms connect; in fact, a large group could actually book six connecting rooms. Prices vary depending on whether you get an oceanfront, ocean-view, or street-side room. All are extremely clean and functional, and smoking and pets are allowed in certain rooms. Guests can enjoy a continental breakfast at the mahogany bar or in the oceanfront court-yard, then head to the beach with hotel-supplied beach chairs and umbrellas. The hotel enjoys a great location in downtown Jacksonville Beach, within 6 blocks of many popular bars and restaurants as well as a city-owned beachfront band shell. Special rates are available for longer stays.

Comfort Inn Mayport $-$$
2401 Mayport Road, Atlantic Beach
(904) 249-0313, (800) 968-5513
www.mayport.com

The staff is extremely friendly and the rooms are extremely clean at this 108-room Comfort Inn, where the clientele is largely military or military related. The hotel is locally owned, so the owners are constantly updating and upgrading. Most rooms have two double beds. All have cof-feemakers, microwaves, refrigerators, hair dryers, irons/boards, HBO, and Nintendo. A free deluxe continental breakfast is served every morning in the breakfast room overlooking the pool. This hotel was one of three finalists for Comfort Inn of the Year in 1999. The inn is less than 2 miles from Naval Station Mayport; a block away from Fleet Landing, a popular retirement community; and 8 miles from the Mayo Clinic. Sorry, say the owners, but no pets.

Many off-ocean rooms at Beaches-area hotels still have ocean views. The views are not as sweeping, but the rooms are less expensive.

Comfort Inn Oceanfront $$-$$$
1515 North First Street, Jacksonville Beach
(904) 241-2311, (800) 654-8776
www.comfortinnjaxbeach.com

While not quite the "islands," this hotel has an island feel about it with its 120-foot heated swimming pool featuring four waterfalls that cascade down on you from large rock formations. More guests seem to use the pool than the ocean! The Kokomo Beach Bar is also a popular place to sip margaritas, listen to beach music, and enjoy karaoke on Friday night. All 180 rooms are either oceanfront or have ocean views. Every room has a security safe, iron/board, coffeemaker, hair dryer, and in-room movies. There's also a free deluxe continen-tal breakfast every morning. Golf, honey-moon, and fishing packages are available.

Days Inn Oceanfront Resort $$-$$$
1031 South First Street, Jacksonville Beach
(904) 249-7231, (800) 329-7466
www.daysinnjacksonvillebeach.com

Wake up early and watch the sunrise from the balcony of your oceanfront room, then

21

Legend of a Hotel

When relating the history of the Casa Marina Hotel, it's hard to separate fact from legend. Legend has it that the hotel was the hangout for silent-film stars back in the early days of film when Jacksonville, not Hollywood, was the country's movie mecca. Legend also has it that President Franklin Roosevelt stayed in the penthouse here, although proof of that is hard to find.

What's for sure is that the Casa Marina opened in 1925 at the height of the Roaring Twenties. Tin Lizzies, flappers, and speakeasies were the order of the day. Cars drove on the beach in front of the hotel, where there was also a boardwalk and a popular dancing pier. Photographs from this period hang on a wall in the hotel's bar. The Casa Marina was originally built with all the modern comforts, including 60 sleeping rooms with steam heat. Each room also had its own telephone and a connecting bath. When guests weren't sleeping, they lounged on rattan furniture in the hotel's lobby, now its dining room, where original floor tile from 1925 is still in place. During World War II the federal government used the hotel for military housing, and by the eighties the Casa Marina had been turned into an apartment building with a restaurant, tearoom, and vintage clothing store.

read a complimentary copy of the *Florida Times-Union,* which you'll find outside your door. Such could be your ritual at this popular hotel, where all 155 rooms face the ocean. All rooms were renovated in 1997 and have either double or king-size beds, a safe, and free HBO. There's also a complimentary shuttle (one trip daily) to the Mayo Clinic. Refrigerators, microwaves, and coffeemakers are available in your room for a small additional charge. Pets 20 pounds and under are welcome with a one-time, nonrefundable pet fee of $25. There's also a large oceanfront pool and a restaurant in the lobby.

Hampton Inn Ponte Vedra　　$$-$$$
1220 Marsh Landing Parkway
Ponte Vedra Beach
(904) 280-9101, (800) HAMPTON INN
www.hamptoninn.com
A blend of business and leisure travelers enjoy this 118-room, five-story, well-appointed hotel nestled under live oak trees. It's fast becoming an affordable option for Ponte Vedra travelers who don't want to pay resort prices. The hotel is extremely proud of its free deluxe continental breakfast featuring fresh fruit, biscuits with gravy, oatmeal, muffins—you name it—as well as 24-hour complimentary coffee and juice. There's a shady pool beneath the live oaks, and at the height of summer, that shade is a welcome relief. All the rooms have a desk with easy Internet access as well as a 27-inch color TV with 94 channels. The rooms also have coffeemakers and hair dryers, and some feature spa tubs. There are two meeting rooms, and business guests are known to take their free continental breakfast into a morning meeting. The hotel is close to the Mayo Clinic as well as shops and restaurants in both Ponte Vedra and Jacksonville Beach. If you're coming to the area for The Players Championship, book early. This is a popular place to stay.

Holiday Inn Sunspree Resort $$–$$$$
1617 North First Street, Jacksonville Beach
(904) 249–9071, (800) 590–4767
www.shanerhotels.com
Business travelers and families alike will
enjoy this oceanfront hotel, which has
local landmark status because of the huge
seven-story mother and baby whales
painted on the side of the building. There
are 143 rooms here, all with balconies;
90 are oceanfront, 53 are off ocean, and
12 are spacious suites. All rooms have a
refrigerator, microwave, coffeemaker,
phones with voice mail and dataports, hair
dryer, and iron/board. The rooms are
clean as a whistle and decorated in
Florida colors: pinks, peaches, and sea-
foam greens. There's an exercise room
and large oceanfront pool, where free kids
activities are often held in summer. There's
also a marketessen, a cross between a
market and a deli, in the lobby. You have
to buy your own breakfast here, but
there's a restaurant in the hotel that
serves breakfast and dinner. AAA gives
this hotel a three-diamond rating.

Quality Suites Oceanfront $$$$
11 North First Street
Jacksonville Beach
(904) 435–3535, (800) 294–2787
www.jaxqualitysuites.com
One of the best things about this six-floor
oceanfront hotel is its location. All 72
rooms face the ocean, and all are two-
room suites. Plus there's a lot to do here.
The hotel sits between the Jacksonville
Beach Lifeguard Station to the south and
the Jacksonville Beach band shell to the
north. The popular Sneakers Sports Bar is
across the street. So, in theory, you can
stand on your balcony, listen to a concert
while you watch the lifeguards working
the beach, then walk across the street to
watch a football game at Sneakers. This
hotel is popular with tourists and business
travelers, who enjoy meetings on the large
patio by the heated pool or in the hotel's
two large meeting rooms. There's a free
deluxe continental breakfast every morn-
ing and a manager's reception with com-

The Quality Suites Oceanfront in Jack-
sonville Beach does not allow smoking
in any of its rooms. However, smokers
may go out on their room balcony to
light up.

plimentary cocktails and nibbles in the
early evening.

Sea Horse Oceanfront Inn $$–$$$$
120 Atlantic Boulevard, Neptune Beach
(904) 246–2175, (800) 881–2330
www.seahorseresort.com
From the street this inn looks like an old
mom-and-pop Florida motel from the
fifties. But walk through a breezeway to
the back courtyard and you'll find a beautiful patio and oceanfront pool, perfectly
framed with sand dunes and sea oats. All
38 rooms here face the ocean, but if
you're on the first floor, you'll see more of
the dunes than the Atlantic. All rooms
were fully renovated in 2000–2001, with
coffeemakers, mini refrigerators, and HBO.
The rooms are large and so are the tiled
bathrooms. There's also a penthouse with
a kitchenette that has a great view of the
beach. You'll have to go out to get breakfast, but that's not a problem. The Sea
Horse is located in the heart of Town Center, a popular Beaches restaurant and
shopping district

Sea Turtle Inn on the Ocean $$$$
One Ocean Boulevard, Atlantic Beach
(904) 249–7402, (800) 874–6000
www.seaturtle.com
This luxury eight-story oceanfront hotel
was completely renovated in 2000. The
193 rooms are beautifully decorated in
grays and taupes and dark-wood furniture. All rooms have an ocean view, and
some are oceanfront with a balcony. All
have king-size or double beds, and there's
also a three-bedroom executive suite.
They all feature complimentary coffee and
tea, a refrigerator, guest robes, a newspaper Monday through Friday, HBO, iron/
board, hair dryer, laundry service, and

movie rentals. The hotel gets high marks with locals because during renovations it took extra pains to install "turtle windows," specially tinted windows that prevent light from the rooms from shining on the beach and luring hatching sea turtles away from the water. Tourists make up 60 percent of the clientele here; the other 40 percent are business groups. There's a lovely oceanfront pool and a highly rated restaurant, Plantains, on the premises. The hotel also enjoys a great location in the heart of Town Centre, within steps of some of the Beaches most popular restaurants, nightspots, and shops.

Surfside Inn   **$$–$$$**
1236 North First Street, Jacksonville Beach
(904) 246–1538
www.jaxsurfsideinn.com
Families enjoy this 32-room inn just across the street from the ocean. Free breakfast, featuring juice, cereal, and doughnuts, can be taken up to your room or eaten beside the large heated pool. The rooms are clean and well maintained and feature small refrigerators, microwaves, coffeemakers, hair dryers, and HBO. This is an older property with outside hallways that was fully renovated in 2000. Some of the rooms on the second floor even have a view of the ocean. It's in a great location near all the action in downtown Jacksonville Beach.

SOUTHPOINT

Inn at Mayo Clinic   **$$–$$$$**
4400 San Pablo Road
(904) 992–9992, (800) 228–9290
www.marriott.com
If you need to come to Jacksonville to visit the Mayo Clinic, this hotel is the place to stay. It's actually connected to the Mayo Clinic, so patients or their families don't have far to go. Be careful when booking your stay, however, because there is a second hotel, the Courtyard by Marriott at Mayo Clinic, that's about 150 yards away from the clinic itself, within walking

distance. The two are often confused. The Inn at Mayo Clinic is just that much closer, though, and the suites are perfect for an extended stay. There are 78 rooms on three floors, laundry facilities, and a complimentary continental breakfast for guests. Best of all, the Inn at Mayo Clinic is located just 5 miles from the beach, so guests can drive out there to walk on the beach or dine at Beaches restaurants.

Jacksonville Marriott Hotel   **$$$$**
4670 Salisbury Road
(904) 296–2222, (800) 584–2842
www.marriott.com
You get what you pay for, as the old saying goes, and you may pay a little more to stay at this 256-room suburban corporate hotel, but it's worth it. This Marriott was one of the first hotels in the Southpoint area. It's a beautiful full-service facility, sort of the Grande Dame of Southpoint. The lobby is beautifully decorated with natural stone floors. Art by local artists adorns the walls. The rooms are well maintained and well appointed with down pillows, down comforters, and large wooden armoires for the TV set. Amenities include coffeemakers with Starbucks coffee, hair dryers, irons/boards, terry-cloth bathrobes, free newspapers, small refrigerators in the rooms with living room suites, an indoor and outdoor pool, a sauna, and a fitness center. An award-winning restaurant, Banyan's Grill, and a popular lounge, Club Bimini, are both in the lobby. **NOTE:** Actually getting to this hotel can be tricky for guests not familiar with the area, so be sure to get good directions.

La Quinta Inn & Suites
off Butler Boulevard   **$$–$$$**
4686 Lenoir Avenue South
(904) 296–0703, (800) NU–ROOMS
www.laquinta.com
There's a lovely courtyard at this 136-room inn, which boasts a convenient location just off I-95 and J. Turner Butler Boulevard. In the summer the courtyard is a cool, green oasis, but it also gets plenty of use year-round because of the heated

outdoor pool and cabana with spa tub. Corporate travelers use this hotel a lot during the week; on weekends it serves more tourists. King-size rooms feature a microwave and small refrigerator; double-double rooms do not. Amenities in all rooms include HBO, coffeemakers, dataport phones, alarm clock radios, irons/boards, and hair dryers. There's a free continental breakfast in the lobby and a Cracker Barrel restaurant right next door. Pets 25 pounds or less are allowed.

Red Roof Inn Southpoint $$
6969 Lenoir Avenue
(904) 296-1006, (800) RED-ROOF
www.redroof.com

Affordable is the name of the game at this 127-room hotel located just off I-95 and J. Turner Butler Boulevard in Southpoint. The rooms are clean and functional, with either king-size or double beds. There's nothing fancy about the bathrooms, which have linoleum covering on the floors, but they, too, are clean and functional. Amenities include free *USA Today*, Showtime, and a light continental breakfast. Local calls are also free, and there's a heated outdoor swimming pool. AAA gives this hotel a three-diamond rating.

Residence Inn by Marriott–Butler Boulevard $$-$$$$
10551 Deerwood Parkway
(904) 996-8900, (800) 331-3131
www.marriott.com

This 120-room hotel is popular with corporate travelers who need to stay in Jacksonville for extended periods of time and with families relocating to the city. It's located off J. Turner Butler Boulevard near several large Southside office parks and a new branch of the Duval County Library. Most guests stay for five nights or longer, though one-night travelers also are welcome. The rooms are large with full kitchens, and if you need groceries, someone working at the 24-hour front desk will go to the store and buy them for you—with no service charge. (You pay only for the groceries.) Amenities include coffee-

makers, irons/boards, daily maid service, HBO, a free deluxe breakfast bar seven days a week, and an evening social Monday through Thursday that usually features enough food and drink to call it a meal. There's also a spa tub, an outdoor pool, and a small fitness center, or residents can use a full-service gym several miles away for free. Pets are allowed here with a $75 nonrefundable pet deposit.

Need a hotel near the Jacksonville Equestrian Center? The closest one is the Hampton Inn Westside on Chaffee Road, just 4 miles away.

StudioPLUS Deluxe Suites $-$$$
4699 Lenoir Avenue South
(904) 332-6512, (888) 788-3467
www.extendedstay.com

Business travelers and folks relocating to Jacksonville often stay at this StudioPLUS, conveniently located just off I-95 and J. Turner Butler Boulevard. Mayo Clinic patients have discovered it, too, because this facility is less than a mile away from Mayo's hospital, St. Luke's, and it's affordable for long stays. There are 73 rooms here, all either a queen or a queen deluxe. The queen deluxe is much larger and offers more living space and a more-separate kitchen. Both types of rooms have a complete kitchen with full-size appliances, microwave, coffeemaker, toaster, cookware, and utensils. Amenities include free local calls, free voice mail, a computer dataport, and free cable TV. There's also an outdoor pool and fitness center. No pets are allowed.

Wingate Inn Southpoint $$-$$$$
4681 Lenoir Avenue South
(904) 281-2600, (800) 228-1000
www.wingateinns.com

Computer users will appreciate it here because this hotel provides free high-speed Internet access in every room. The facility opened in February 2000 just off

J. Turner Butler Boulevard and I-95. All 102 rooms and 3 suites are decorated in shades of brown and gray with black accents. Amenities include a two-line desk phone and a cordless phone in every room that you can take poolside or to breakfast so that you don't miss important phone calls. Breakfast, by the way, is free thanks to a deluxe breakfast buffet in the lobby, but if you care to eat out, there's a Cracker Barrel restaurant directly across the street. There are coffeemakers in every room as well as hair dryers, a room safe, Nintendo 64, and irons/boards. The hotel also offers an outdoor pool, fitness center, and whirlpool. Business guests abound here, but families will appreciate it, too.

AIRPORT ROAD

**Clarion Hotel Airport
Conference Center $$-$$$$
2101 Dixie Clipper Road
(904) 741-1997, (800) 234-2398
www.jalaramhotels.com**
Talk about a diamond in the rough. This six-story facility comes chock-full of amenities and an extremely friendly staff that bends over backward to get you what you want. The location, though, is a bit less than desirable—just 1 block from Jacksonville International Airport. For airline pilots and crews this is a good thing, but for many travelers it's unthinkable. Think again. The 200 guest rooms are large, very clean, and well decorated and include spa suites, minisuites, and master suites. The bathrooms are tiled in marble. There's a free hot breakfast every morning, which includes an omelette station, and a lovely outdoor pool and spa for relaxing. There's also free 24-hour shuttle service from the airport, coffeemakers, hair dryers, irons/boards, bottled water, and current

---

ℹ *The most expensive hotel rooms in Jacksonville are at the Beaches; the best values are on Airport Road.*

Newsweek magazines in every room. Free *USA Today* newspapers are available in the lobby. There are 14 meeting rooms as well as interview rooms. An entire detached wing of the hotel, called the Lanai, is often rented for family reunions or weddings. Food options abound, with both a food court and a gourmet restaurant at either end of the lobby.

**Comfort Suites Airport $-$$$
1180 Airport Road
(904) 741-0505, (800) 228-5150
www.choicehotels.com**
This 59-room hotel was built in 2000, and everything still looks and feels very new. It's located on Airport Row, just five minutes from JIA. The rooms are large, with either king- or queen-size beds. All suites include coffeemakers, hair dryers, microwaves, and refrigerators. Plus the hotel serves up a deluxe complimentary breakfast that will start your day on the right foot. Additional amenities include an exercise room, a business center, an outdoor pool, and a free airport shuttle. The front desk staff is friendly and helpful and ready to make your stay here a satisfactory one.

**Courtyard by Marriott
Jacksonville Airport $$$-$$$$
14668 Duval Road
(904) 741-1122, (800) 321-2211
www.marriott.com**
There's a big bowl of free fresh plums in a basket at the front desk and a note nearby that reads: "We're plum crazy about our valued guests." That's the kind of hotel this is. Though the plums aren't always available, the friendly staff is. Located off Airport Road, five minutes from JIA, this 81-room Courtyard offers free airport transfers. There are coffeemakers, irons/boards, an outdoor pool and whirlpool, an exercise room, free newspapers, and HBO in every room. Spa suites featuring a microwave and small refrigerator are extremely popular with business travelers. There's a restaurant, which serves breakfast only, in the lobby.

Don't be surprised if you see a police car in the parking lot. There's a police STOP station in the lobby—which is a place designated by area businesses and the Jacksonville Sheriff's Office for beat officers to stop in and write police reports, make telephone calls, read the newspaper, whatever. The theory is that instead of hanging out at the local doughnut shop, they hang out here. STOP stations have been set up all over town, and citizens love them because they increase police presence in the community.

Fairfield Inn
Jacksonville Airport   **$$-$$$**
1300 Airport Road
(904) 741-3500, (800) 228-2800
www.fairfieldinn.com
Corporate travelers keep this hotel, located five minutes from Jacksonville International Airport, very busy. The 107 rooms are clean, the service is friendly, and the hotel serves up a free continental breakfast every day. Guest rooms come with a desk, dataport telephones, free HBO, and free local calls, and there's a free airport shuttle. There's also a heated outdoor swimming pool and a fitness center. Some larger rooms have a microwave and a refrigerator.

Hilton Garden Inn
Jacksonville Airport   **$$**
13503 Ranch Road
(904) 421-2700, (877) 924-2700
www.jacksonvilleairport.gardeninn.com
The sunny lobby of this hotel will bring a smile to your face. It's pretty, nicely decorated, even homey. Located five minutes from the airport, this 111-room hotel offers free airport transfers, refrigerators, microwaves, coffeemakers, hair dryers, and irons/boards in every room. An open cafe, The Great American Grill, in the

lobby serves breakfast, lunch, and dinner daily. If you want to eat in your room, no problem. The hotel's Pavilion Pantry is open 24 hours a day with microwavable and packaged food, drinks, and snacks. Guests also enjoy the outdoor pool and whirlpool, the fitness center, and the 24-hour business center with free Internet access. Most guests are business travelers, but families will also enjoy their stay here. There's no charge for children 18 and under when they occupy the same room as Mom and Dad or Gram and Gramps.

The closest hotel to the Jaxport Cruise Ship Terminal is the Holiday Inn Express, a mile away on New Berlin Road. Call (904) 696-3333 for reservations.

Holiday Inn Airport   **$$$-$$$$**
14670 Duval Road
(904) 741-4404, (800) HOLIDAY
www.holiday-inn.com
When you walk into the atrium lobby of this large hotel, you may feel as though you are in the Caribbean. It's painted pink, and there's an indoor pool, lots of plants, even a waterfall. You are still in Jacksonville, Florida, but you are also in for some fun. How many hotels have free air hockey and foosball games just waiting for players, or tennis courts (free racquets and balls available at the front desk), or both an indoor and a heated outdoor pool? Located just five minutes from the airport, this 489-room hotel also offers a fitness center, free airport shuttle service, and coffeemakers and irons/boards in every room. The concierge floor is popular with corporate travelers. Montego's Restaurant in the main lobby serves breakfast, lunch, and dinner.

BED-AND-BREAKFAST INNS

I f you're looking for a place to stay that's not a resort or a hotel/motel, Jacksonville has a handful of bed-and-breakfast inns that can accommodate you. No doubt, the city would have had more inns to offer but for the Great Fire of 1901 that left much of downtown in ashes. We recommend eight: one built new as a bed-and-breakfast inn, the other old homes now lovingly restored.

Jacksonville's bed-and-breakfast inns are located in three parts of town: Historic Springfield, a national historic district called Riverside, and Jacksonville Beach. The Springfield and Riverside inns are popular with business travelers because they're so close to downtown. The Riverside inns are also within walking distance of shops, restaurants, the St. Johns River, and the Cummer Museum of Art. The inns in Jacksonville Beach are all within a block of the ocean and close to downtown Jacksonville Beach, which offers lots of nightlife, restaurants, and shops. They're popular with anyone who wants to get some sand in his or her shoes. They're also close to the Mayo Clinic and to Naval Station Mayport. Either location—Riverside or Jacksonville Beach—provides a great opportunity to live vicariously as wealthy downtown residents inhabiting a big old house near the St. Johns River, or as wealthy beach residents waking up to an ocean view.

We've included one other bed-and-breakfast inn, a former estate on the river in Orange Park, a suburban city about 10 miles south of Jacksonville. We mention this inn because it's too beautiful to leave out. It's also convenient for anyone spending time on the Westside, near Naval Air Station Jacksonville.

All the inns accept credit cards. Several will accept small pets and children. We've noted which ones accept what and the ages allowed. All are nonsmoking, and all provide some sort of breakfast. Only two of the inns are wheelchair accessible. Rates at all but one of these inns stay the same year-round, but it's definitely worth asking about specials, especially if you're considering an extended visit.

PRICE CODE

The price code reflects average room cost per night based on double occupancy.

$	Less than $100
$$	$100 to $125
$$$	$126 to $150
$$$$	$151 to $175

RIVERSIDE

Dickert House $$–$$$
1804 Copeland Street
(904) 387–4762
www.dickert-house.com
Betty Dickert is proud of her huge 1914 home just off the St. Johns River. She wants her guests to enjoy it as much as possible, and often invites them to sip a cup of tea and chat in her warm, friendly kitchen. There are three suites for rent in the main house. All include a sitting room and private bath, a full hot breakfast in the dining room, and room amenities like cable TV, VCRs, and telephones. Guests can also rent the carriage house, which is wheelchair accessible. Dickert also owns an apartment building across the street, which she rents as four furnished two-bedroom suites with a sitting room and

full kitchen. These are often let for extended stays. This inn allows children of all ages as well as small pets.

The Inn at Oak Street $$-$$$
2114 Oak Street
(904) 379-5525
www.innatoakstreet.com

At 31, proprietor Tina Musico may well be the youngest innkeeper in Jacksonville. She says a little naivete worked to her advantage several years ago when she and her husband, Robert Eagle, bought their 1902 10,000-square-foot, wood-frame vernacular home in the heart of Riverside. When they first saw the three-story house, Tina says, it was stripped down to its studs inside, yet she and Robert fell in love with it. They liked the grand feel of the place and were eager to renovate. Little did they know it would take two years of their lives to put the house back together again. The inn has six bedrooms, each with a flat-screen television with a DVD player hidden away in an antique armoire, wine refrigerator, wireless Internet connection, hair dryer, telephone, and private bath. All the rooms are nonsmoking, and three of them on the second floor also have private balconies. The decor is stunning, more to minimalist than the clutter look, with fabulous antique furniture and rugs. Tina says she had great luck finding antiques on eBay and calls the 1854 French Art Deco armoire in one of the bedrooms her most fabulous find. It's 8 feet wide and over 6 feet tall and was bought from an antiques dealer in Illinois. Guests eat a full gourmet breakfast in the formal dining room, which can include homemade Sunrise Frittatas and sausage roll, homemade bread and granola, and some sort of fresh fruit compote. Tina also offers a wine hour daily at 6:00 P.M., complete with munchies and something sweet. The formal dining room also serves as a meeting room for corporate clients, which Tina says the inn is seeing more and more of lately. The Inn at Oak Street is 10 minutes from downtown Jacksonville and a stone's throw away from a popular new shopping center, Riverside Market Square,

which features several popular eateries. Tina's managed to utilize her entire house, including the basement, where there's a spa room featuring massage and nail services. There's also a gift shop that sells the inn's cozy monogrammed bathrobes, and private dinners are available on the premises cooked up by the innkeepers. And if you're interested in renovating old homes, be sure to ask Tina where the 24 8-foot doors came from. It's quite a tale! The Inn at Oak Street welcomes children ages 12 and older.

Local inns are popular spots for small weddings. Not only do guests stay at the inn, but the ceremony and reception—even the honeymoon—can be held there, too.

Plantation Manor Inn $$$$
1630 Copeland Street
(904) 384-4630
www.plantationmanor.com

Teddy Roosevelt was president in 1905 when the head of a Jacksonville bank built this Greek Revival home, complete with Doric columns. From its initial grandeur, the house fell into disrepair and eventually became a flophouse for transients. Enter Jerry and Kathy Ray, who bought the home in 1987, the year it was condemned by the city, and spent four long years renovating it. Today this nine-bedroom bed-and-breakfast inn enjoys a four-diamond rating by AAA. All the rooms have private baths, and some of the bathrooms have the original claw-foot bathtubs from 1905. The rooms are all furnished with antiques as well as modern conveniences like cable TV, telephones, hair dryers, irons, and even thick terry-cloth bathrobes. A full hot breakfast is served in the dining room every morning. Be sure to bring your bathing suit: There's a lovely pool out back in the ivy-laden garden. It's a perfect place to take a dip and sip a drink after a long day touring or working in Jacksonville.

Jacksonville's Ronald McDonald House is available for families with a child age 18 or younger who's being treated at a local medical facility. Families stay for free, but they must have a referral from a doctor, nurse, or hospital social service worker.

Riverdale Inn   **$$$-$$$$**
1521 Riverside Avenue
(866) 808-3400
www.riverdaleinn.com
This big blue mansion on Riverside Avenue enjoys a wonderful location on what used to be Jacksonville's Millionaire Row. It's a block off the St. Johns River, a block from The Cummer Museum of Art and Gardens, 2 blocks from Memorial Park on the river, and within walking distance of several of the city's hippest, in-town shopping and eating districts.

It took experienced innkeepers Carolyn Whitmire and Linda Walm (sisters who cut their teeth on an inn on Amelia Island) 22 months to renovate this three-story 1901 home. They added 12 bathrooms and spent lots of money refinishing the original hardwood floors. The house was built by William Kelly, a turpentine baron, and updated by architect Henry Klutho in 1921 after the Great Fire. (See our History chapter for details on the Great Fire.) There are eight rooms to rent, all filled with antiques and named after streets in this historic neighborhood. Two of the rooms have working gas fireplaces, including The Park Suite, which used to be the home's master bedroom. All the rooms have DSL, HBO, private baths, hair dryers, and robes. A full breakfast is served in the inn's two dining rooms and always includes fresh fruit and something hot like omelettes or French toast with apples. Finally, there are two rooms in a renovated garage in back that are fully wheelchair accessible. But what makes the Riverdale most unique is the pub and restaurant on the first floor. The Gum Bunch Pub serves beer, wine, and cocktails and The Row serves dinner seven days a week, brunch on Sundays. Both are open to the public.

St. Johns House   **$**
1718 Osceola Street
(904) 384-3724
www.stjohnshouse.com
There are three rooms for rent in this traditional bed-and-breakfast inn located in a 1914 private home 1 block from the St. Johns River in Riverside. Two of the rooms, each with a queen-size bed, are in the big house. The Blue Room has a view of the river and a private bath. The Green Room lacks a view and shares a bath with innkeeper Joan Moore and her husband. The third room, in the carriage house, offers a double bed and its own bathroom and feels something like a tree house because the predominant view out the window is trees. All rooms have cable TV, telephones, coffeemakers, and hair dryers. Children of all ages are allowed in this bed-and-breakfast inn, but not pets (although the innkeepers have a friendly golden retriever named Kingsley). A full hot breakfast is served every morning on the sunporch, where guests enjoy a view of the river along with their meal. The inn is closed in July and August, when the innkeepers escape the Florida heat and humidity for the blissfully cool temperatures of Maine.

SPRINGFIELD

The Heritage Bed & Breakfast   **$-$$$**
1217 Boulevard
(904) 301-1232
www.theheritagebb.com
This sprawling century-old pink Victorian is located in Springfield, which is currently a transitional neighborhood in downtown Jacksonville. (More on that in a moment.) The inn enjoys a lovely location facing an expansive green space called Klutho Park. Guests can be seen rocking on the front porch swing, sipping iced tea and eating homemade cookies while they watch

a lazy afternoon unfold in the park. Innkeepers Lena Castro and Paul Hout have put a lot of thought into the B&B, which features four guest rooms, each with a private bath. Each room is named after a family member, like Aunt Fannie's peach-colored room or the olive-colored Serafina and Ilario Room named in honor of Lena's Sicilian grandparents. All rooms feature cable TV, and the inn itself is fax and Internet accessible. Wake up to the smell of fresh coffee and homemade muffins, pancakes, and/or quiche, and enjoy a leisurely breakfast in the landscaped backyard, which features a therapeutic Jacuzzi disguised as a reflection pond. Business travelers who dislike staying in big chain hotels say they enjoy this B&B because it has the feel of home but is only five minutes from downtown Jacksonville. Now, the neighborhood. Historic Springfield was a premier downtown neighborhood around the turn of the 20th century. Sadly, much of the neighborhood fell into disrepair during the sixties, seventies, and eighties. In the past several years, however, Springfield has been enjoying a revival. The sound of hammers and electric saws has replaced the sound of police sirens; families are moving back to the neighborhood, and businesses are opening their doors. It's also becoming a mecca for a growing community of young artists, who are buying or renting huge spaces that can accommodate both their galleries and their residences. Springfield residents like to compare their neighborhood with downtown Savannah—another once-dilapidated historic neighborhood that was rejuvenated by intrepid urban pioneers.

JACKSONVILLE BEACH

Fig Tree Inn $$-$$$
185 Fourth Avenue South
Jacksonville Beach
(904) 246-8855, (877) 217-9830
www.figtreeinn.com
Visit this inn in June and pick ripe figs from an ancient, prolific tree in the back-

Some bed-and-breakfast inns have a resident dog or cat. Be sure to ask about pets if you're allergic.

yard. And that's not the only thing that makes this B&B unique. The owners/ innkeepers of the Fig Tree do not live on the premises. Instead, they decided to live nearby so they could rent the entire house should guests desire. And many do, for family reunions, weddings, and bridal and baby showers. There are six bedrooms for rent in this beach home built in 1915, including one suite that comes with a kitchenette, refrigerator, and microwave. Every room has a private bath, queen- or king-size bed, wireless Internet access, cable TV and VCR, iron/board, and hair dryer. There is also limited wheelchair access in the Grape Room downstairs, and the Garden Room has a canopied bed and Jacuzzi tub (which makes it a popular pick for newlyweds). On weekends the innkeepers cook up the Fig Tree Special, a cross between French toast and a waffle, in the inn's newly renovated kitchen, which features two ovens and a six-burner stove. The rest of the week a continental breakfast, often including fresh figs, is served in the breakfast room. Children ages 10 and older are welcome here, depending on occupancy. The Fig Tree is beautifully decorated and extremely clean, and the innkeepers say guests enjoy sitting on its front porch, once dubbed one of the most engaging front porches in the city by a local magazine.

The Fairbanks House, a B&B on Amelia Island, offers a "Girls Just Wanna Have Fun" getaway. It's a slumber party for "the girls," who stay in the same room and eat lots of complimentary goodies supplied by innkeepers. Prices vary depending on the size of your group and the length of your stay. Visit www.fairbankshouse.com for details.

So, You Want to Be an Innkeeper?

If you've always thought you'd like to give up the daily grind someday and open your own bed-and-breakfast inn in an idyllic spot, you may want to learn more about the business of innkeeping before you leap.

"Innkeeping is no longer a hobby or second investment opportunity," says David Caples, owner of Lodging Resources Workshops (www.lodging resources.com). "This is a hardball entre-preneurial business." For over a decade, Caples has run a school for aspiring innkeepers out of his oceanfront inn, the Elizabeth Pointe Lodge in Fernandina Beach, Florida, located on Amelia Island, a beautiful barrier island north of Jack-sonville. For 10 years before that, Caples took his seminars on the road and hosted educational programs for aspiring innkeepers all over the country.

These days, according to Caples, the minimum average investment in a bed-and-breakfast inn is a million dollars, so those seriously considering the business of inn-keeping had better do their home-work before they try to pass the test. Caples advises his students to buy an inn with their head (and calculator) and not their heart. His most popular workshop is a comprehensive one called "How to Acquire and Start Up a Bed & Breakfast." It runs for three consecutive days, usually over a weekend; Caples, who's a graduate of the master's program at Cornell Hotel School, is the program's creator, director, and main speaker.

Participants usually arrive early Friday at the Elizabeth Pointe Lodge, a big gray 25-room inn Caples owns with his wife, Susan. The lodge looks as though it's been plucked off the coast of Rhode Island and set down in Florida. Depend-ing on bookings at Elizabeth Pointe, stu-dents may stay either at the lodge or at another bed-and-breakfast inn nearby on Amelia Island. Upon arrival, each student is handed a heavy three-ring binder that's the textbook for the next three days.

Seminars begin at 2:00 sharp Friday afternoon with a look at the latest trends in the lodging industry. For instance, B&Bs have always been a favorite pick of travelers—at least partially because they offer a hearty homemade breakfast every morning included in the price of the stay. Hotel chains like Hampton Inn have caught on to that idea and now offer an extensive complimentary breakfast as one of their amenities. Consequently, with breakfast included it costs about the same (if not less) to stay at a Hampton Inn for the night as it does at many B&Bs. This is what Caples means when he says nowadays running a bed-and-breakfast inn is a hardball, entrepreneurial business.

Friday's agenda also includes an hon-est look at whether the business of innkeeping is right for you. Caples forces participants to ask themselves questions such as "Does innkeeping fit my lifestyle?" and "Will innkeeping meet my economic needs?" Caples says that a second income stream usually lies behind many a small inn's success story. In other words, "Don't quit your day job," he warns. "Some start-ups (especially when renovations are required) drain the new innkeepers' resources to the point that there are no operating funds to market the inn once it is open." He likes to describe innkeeping as a hands-on, roll-up-your-sleeves, physically demanding job that often doesn't provide minimum-wage pay for the owner.

If you've gotten cold feet at this point in the course, the group dinner on Friday night may help warm them up again. Participants eat dinner at the Elizabeth Pointe Lodge and are joined by area innkeepers who answer questions about the nuts and bolts of being an innkeeper. This dinner is filled with fresh voices, funny tales, and frank discussions about the business of operating an inn. It's also a good time for participants to get to know one another as well as other innkeepers.

Saturday is devoted to what Caples likes to call "The Feasibility Study." After breakfast at the lodge, he analyzes the advantages and disadvantages inherent in the three basic ways one acquires a bed-and-breakfast inn. Caples explains how to look at a property to see if it might become a viable B&B or how to purchase a property that's already a B&B and how to build a B&B from the ground up. There are also guest speakers, an accountant to talk about cash-flow formats, and a banker to talk about sources of financing.

On Sunday, Caples's wife, Susan, takes charge. She talks about purchasing everything from linens to computers and about staffing, from housekeepers to cooks. Students get checklists for starting up a B&B as well as a behind-the-scenes tour of the Elizabeth Pointe Lodge. "Remember, there's no personnel department, no marketing department, no purchasing agent or bookkeeper except you," says Caples.

The price tag for this three-day seminar includes lodging as well as dinner Friday night and a full breakfast and lunch on Saturday and Sunday.

If by the end of the seminar you still want to own a B&B, and many people do, Lodging Resources Workshops also offers a Bed-and-Breakfast Boot Camp for graduates of the seminar. Again, Caples draws upon the resources of the Elizabeth Pointe Lodge, which he calls "a working classroom." The boot camp provides students a special hands-on opportunity to learn what it's really like to run a B&B. Students, or Innkeeper Apprentices as Caples likes to call them, pay for the right to crack eggs in the kitchen, change bed linens in a guest room, and work the night audit shift learning lodging revenue reporting, posting, and operating report processes. Each apprentice goes home with a 200-plus-page resource book that includes operating forms and reports as a guide to setting up their own inn system. It's three days and two nights of long hard work—and that's exactly the point: An innkeeper's day is not an easy one, and if you're thinking about owning a B&B, that's a good thing to know ahead of time.

Pelican Path B&B by the Sea   **$$–$$$$**
11 North 19th Avenue
Jacksonville Beach
(904) 249-1177, (888) 749-1177
www.pelicanpath.com

Joan Hubbard, a marriage and family therapist, and her civil engineer husband, Tom, always wanted to own a bed-and-breakfast inn. So they sold their large home in downtown Jacksonville, bought a piece of oceanfront property in Jacksonville Beach, and built the inn of their dreams. They now live above the store, so to speak, on the third floor. The two floors below them are dedicated to the inn. The great room on the ground floor is the heart of this inn, which has a real European feel. The great room, which doubles as a breakfast room, has a beautiful expansive view of the ocean, the beach, sand dunes, and sea oats. There is also a kitchen with pass-through, where Joan chats away with the guests as she cooks them a full hot breakfast featuring eggs and fruit every morning. The inn has four rooms, all on the second floor. Two are oceanfront with private balconies; two have ocean views and access to the downstairs patio. All have king-size beds, private baths with oversized spa tubs, TVs with cable and VCRs, refrigerators, coffeemakers, hair dryers, and telephones. The rooms are named for various seabirds, which can be seen on the beach outside the inn. There are binoculars and birding books to help you identify local wildlife. Hop on a beach bike, provided free by the inn, at low tide and ride to nearby shops, restaurants, and bars.

ORANGE PARK

**The Club Continental
on the St. Johns**   **$–$$$**
2143 Astor Street, Orange Park
(904) 264-6070, (800) 877-6070
www.clubcontinental.com

Step back in time to Old Florida in the early 1920s, when wealthy Northerners built large Mediterranean-style estates under the live oak trees, full of Spanish tile, shady courtyards, and gentle fountains. Such is the look of the Club Continental on the St. Johns River, built in 1923 by Caleb Johnson, heir to the Palmolive Soap Company, better known today as the Colgate-Palmolive Company. He called his home Mira Rio, and judging by some old photographs hanging in the club's bar, it was quite the party house—complete with a special drink still served at the bar today, the formula for which is a well-kept secret. The property, with its beautiful gardens, has stayed in Johnson's family and today is owned and operated by his heirs. They've managed to retain the Old Florida feel while turning it into a successful business. The Club Continental is a private dining and tennis club with 600 members, plus a 22-room bed-and-breakfast inn. Seven of the rooms are in Mira Rio, the old house, and most of these have river views. The remaining 15 rooms were built in 1992 in a separate building. These rooms are by far more popular. All have balconies overlooking the St. Johns River, microwaves, and refrigerators. They're decorated in a cool green with dark wicker furniture. Several of the rooms have a Jacuzzi and a gas fireplace. A free continental breakfast is available in Mira Rio. Pets are allowed on request, and the inn is wheelchair accessible. There are seven tennis courts, and children will enjoy swimming in one of three pools. You can even arrive by yacht and dock at the club's marina. This may well be the only inn in Florida where turtles living in an elaborate courtyard fountain literally come when you call them. Be sure and have the turtle food ready!

RESORTS

Jacksonville is proud of its five world-class resorts, which are booming as popular destination points for many travelers. They're so popular that most have just completed major multimillion-dollar renovations.

Golf and tennis are the two common denominators at each resort. They've all got both in good measure, but you may have to give the edge to the Amelia Island Plantation for tennis because it's the locale for a women's tennis tournament, the Bausch and Lomb Championships, every year. Four of the resorts are oceanfront; two, at this writing, have major day spas; and one has a AAA five-diamond restaurant, one of only four restaurants in Florida with that designation.

One thing essential to a good resort is a room with a view, and all these resorts have rooms with spectacular ocean views or golf course views—or in some cases views of both. All have sizable banquet and meeting facilities, day programs for children, and health and fitness centers.

They're all great places to stay, and picking just one won't be easy. So come back year after year, and stay at them all!

PRICE CODE

Based on information available at the time of publication, we offer the following price code (average charge for double occupancy in peak season) as a general guide. Please note that fluctuations in price occur frequently.

$$	$99 to $150
$$$	$151 to $250
$$$$	$251 to $350
$$$$$	$351 to $450

Amelia Island Plantation $$–$$$$$
P.O. Box 3000
Amelia Island 32035-3000
(904) 261-6161, (888) 261-6161
www.aipfl.com

All Florida developers should be required to visit this resort before they're allowed to build anything in this state. They'll see a thick tree canopy that's been left largely intact despite large-scale resort development. Because the Plantation developers decided to leave the trees several decades ago, they now have a memorable world-class resort nestled beneath a forest of live oak, cypress, and palm trees. The Plantation is located on the southern half of Amelia Island about 25 minutes from Jacksonville and 25 minutes to downtown Fernandina Beach. It's a sprawling resort, but you'd never know it because the trees give it such a sense of place. This is the resort to come to if you want to rent a one-, two-, or three-bedroom villa (condo) for a week. There are 420 to choose from, many oceanfront, all owned by wealthy out-of-towners who allow the Plantation to rent their place. If you don't want a villa, the 249-room oceanfront Amelia Inn and Beach Club will cater to your every need. All the rooms at the inn are oceanfront with balconies, and if you stay on an upper floor, you have a second great view, west over the tree canopy to the marsh.

There are 54 holes of golf here and a golf school that's the envy of other resorts. There also are 23 tennis courts with all kinds of tennis clinics, so you'll likely go home a better tennis player than when you arrived. Another thing that really sets this resort apart is its Nature Center, located behind the reception center in the village shops. It's a small science museum where visitors of all ages can learn about the local environment. The Nature Center also offers a plethora of tours and activities, from birding to kayaking. If a ramble isn't your thing, head for The Spa at Amelia Island Plantation, which has been renovated and now features an unusual service called Watsu. It's basically an underwater massage in a special swimming pool with special sea minerals. Watsu followers say there's no better way to relax. The Plantation also has an award-winning year-round program for children called Kids Camp Amelia. A program for teenagers, Teen Explorers, includes golf clinics, sunset sailing, and kayak trips. The resort offers some half-dozen restaurants for guests. At some of them, kids eat free when ordering from the children's menu with an adult ordering an entree from the dinner menu.

The Lodge & Club $$$-$$$$$
607 Ponte Vedra Boulevard
Ponte Vedra Beach
(904) 273-9500, (800) 243-4304
www.pvresorts.com

With just 66 rooms, the Lodge is the smallest of Jacksonville's resorts. It's a boutique resort, and that's why guests love it. It's a mile and a half south of the Ponte Vedra Inn & Club, the Lodge's sister property, also located on Ponte Vedra Boulevard. Built in 1989, all the rooms here are oceanfront with either a terrace or balcony. In April 2003 the Lodge completed a $4.5 million renovation that gave each room a complete makeover. The larger rooms have fireplaces and even small kitchens with microwaves and refrigerators. All rooms have coffeemakers,

---

All of these resorts have great shopping opportunities, but two in particular stand out: the Gallery of Shops at the Ponte Vedra Inn & Club and the Spa and Shops at Amelia Island Plantation. Shopping at each of these places is a day trip in itself.

---

large bathrooms, irons/boards, in-room safes, fluffy bathrobes, triple sheets, and complimentary newspapers. You'll enjoy eating your meals in the circular ocean-front dining room, which is intimate, like the resort itself, and features a fireplace for cozy meals in cooler months. There are three swimming pools at the Lodge—one for adults, one for children, and a six-lane lap pool located across Ponte Vedra Boulevard at the resort's fitness center. The fitness center is a beehive of exercise. You can take an aquacize class, run on the treads, or hop in the sauna. Since the Lodge is owned by the same company that owns the Ponte Vedra Inn & Club, Lodge guests often "head north" to take advantage of such inn amenities as excellent golf and tennis instruction, a day spa, two championship golf courses, shops, and restaurants. A nice touch: The Lodge (and the Ponte Vedra Inn, for that matter) publishes a nightly news sheet that's brought to your room when the maid comes to turn down your bed. The news sheet lists all the activities for the day ahead, including tidal charts and sunrise and sunset times.

Ponte Vedra Inn & Club $$-$$$$$
200 Ponte Vedra Boulevard
Ponte Vedra Beach
(904) 285-1111, (800) 234-7842
www.pvresorts.com

This is it. The epicenter. The reason "Ponte Vedra" is synonymous with "wealthy." The Ponte Vedra Inn & Club started more than seven decades ago when the National Lead Company carved a small resort for wealthy vacationers out of a desolate tract of windswept oceanfront property. Since then an entire community of expensive homes and shops has sprung up around this 300-acre, 222-room campus-style resort. And the wealthy vacationers still come as they have, in some cases, for generations. Why do so many return so often? No doubt it's the miles of beautiful white Atlantic Ocean beach right outside their bedroom door—and the 36 holes of championship golf, the 15 Har-Tru tennis courts, and the four sparkling oceanfront pools. It's definitely the award-winning day spa, which pampers Mom (and Dad) from head to toe while the kids are well entertained in the Kids Club. No other local resort offers an oceanfront health and fitness center where you can work out while you look out on the Atlantic Ocean.

The award-winning accommodations are another big attraction. They feature a sitting room; a microwave, refrigerator, and coffeemaker; in-room safe; and not one but two television sets with HBO. Other amenities include a spacious marble bathroom, track lighting, oceanfront balcony or terrace, feather pillows, triple sheets, terrycloth bathrobes, and twice-daily maid service, which includes turndown service and a chocolate mint on your pillow every night. Most of all, the regulars return because they like the people who run this resort. The employees, some of whom have worked here for a quarter of a century, know the value of friendly, excellent service. Guests are treated with great respect by everyone from parking valets to the general manager. The Ponte Vedra Inn & Club earned AAA's highest honor, five diamonds, in 2002.

Be sure to ask about seasonal resort packages for the best deals. For instance, there's a bed-and-breakfast package that can really save you money on your room rate, especially if you choose to eat dinner off property at the myriad nearby Beaches restaurants. Oh, and the resort has a no-tipping policy. Instead, a nightly gratuity is charged to your account.

The Ritz-Carlton, Amelia Island $$$–$$$$$
4750 Amelia Island Parkway
Amelia Island
(904) 277–1100, (800) 241–3333
www.ritzcarlton.com

It's hard to figure out just why this resort has such a good aura. Maybe it's the complimentary chocolate chip and oatmeal-raisin cookies baked by the pastry chef that are waiting for guests when they check in. Or maybe it's the wood-paneled

If you didn't get a meal on your flight to Jacksonville, don't go hungry on your flight home. The Ritz-Carlton Amelia Island will fix you a box lunch to carry on board and keep you well fed from takeoff to touchdown.

lobby lounge overlooking the ocean, where guests naturally gravitate to chat, sip coffee, read the newspaper, or have a drink. Maybe it's just that the guests themselves are here on vacation and happy to be relaxing on a beautiful island at a beautiful resort. Whatever the reason, this 449-room property is a wonderful place. It's played host to presidents, vice presidents, and first ladies. It's where wealthy Jacksonville doctors like to escape for a weekend getaway.

The Ritz is located 28 minutes from Jacksonville International Airport and about 20 minutes from downtown Fernandina Beach, a quaint fishing village. All rooms have ocean or coastal views, meaning that your room faces the ocean directly or from an angle. (The coastal views are fine, and the rooms a bit less costly.) All rooms have private balconies and are decorated in muted tones of blue and gray with chintz curtains and bedspreads. The large bathrooms are done in gray marble; a fresh rose in a silver bud vase supplies a splash of color. Room amenities include twice-daily maid service, plush terry-cloth robes, in-room safes, and a comfy chaise lounge with the latest editions of *Gourmet* and *Condé Nast Traveler* at your bedside.

There's no shortage of things to keep you busy: golf and tennis, a beautiful heated outdoor pool and an indoor heated atrium pool, a complete health and fitness center and day spa, personal trainers, a children's pool and playground, nanny service, and the Ritz Kids day camp. The resort staff also has lots of fun putting together theme weekends and holiday activities. For instance, at Christmastime the pastry chef creates a huge

A Seat in the Kitchen

The other day we told a friend that we were going to eat dinner in the kitchen of the Ritz-Carlton's famous five-diamond resort restaurant, The Grill. Her reaction surprised us.

"Why would anyone want to eat dinner in the kitchen?" she said. "The dining room there is spectacular. It has a beautiful oceanfront view."

She had a point. But a seat in the kitchen and a seat in the dining room are two different experiences. One is cinema verité, culinary theater at its finest; the other is serene, romantic dining.

The Grill at The Ritz-Carlton Amelia Island is the only restaurant on the First Coast (and in the entire Ritz-Carlton chain) where you can actually eat a five- or ten-course dinner in the kitchen. It's the same food that's served in the dining room, complete with different wines for each course. Food lovers find it fascinating and fun.

To get to your kitchen table, you walk through The Grill's dining room, where the waiters talk sotto voce and the oceanfront view is a lovely dinner companion. But step through the doorway into this spotless kitchen and you're in another world.

"Where are my three lobster appetizers?" yells a waiter.

"You got them," replies the pantry chef.

"Someone else picked them up," barks the waiter, impatient.

"How fast do you want it?" asks the executive chef, stepping in.

"In about 30 seconds," replies the demanding waiter.

Both chefs get to work.

Kitchen guests are seated in a former storage room with a large picture window and a view, directly in front of them, of the seven chefs on the cooking line. The little half-moon table seats up to four, but the room itself gives diners a measure of privacy. John Travolta ate in the kitchen twice while he was in Jacksonville filming the movie *Basic*. Autograph seekers don't bother you in the kitchen; they don't even know you're there.

Sitting behind the glass wall also keeps diners safely out of the way as waiters run in to pick up their orders, as chefs run across the kitchen to retrieve something out of a refrigerator, and as dishwashers race by with a stack of freshly washed gold-trimmed plates.

The Ritz does not advertise its seat in the kitchen. There's no need—it's strictly an insider's word-of-mouth affair. The result: The kitchen table is usually booked every night of the month.

The famous Ritz-Carlton service does not suffer because you're eating in the kitchen. David, our waiter, started us off with champagne and our first appetizer: one Nantucket bay scallop in a hot-pepper salsa. It was good, but just *one* scallop? David subtly explained the importance of pacing yourself. "There's lots of food ahead, so if you need me to slow down, let me know." The same goes for the wines. Don't feel that you need to drain each glass and have another—you could become too inebriated to enjoy your entree, much less dessert.

The bread arrives, baked fresh daily on-site, followed by the second appetizer: three grades of Iranian caviars and, yep, more champagne. David pointed out two folded white Ritz-Carlton aprons sitting on our table. "Feel free to put those on and walk around the kitchen," he said. "Ask questions, talk to the chefs; we had one couple in here once who even did some cooking."

Cooking at a five-diamond restaurant? No way!

As we gathered up the courage to venture into the kitchen, a parade of chefs dropped by to say hello, common practice in the kitchen when orders are not coming in at too frenetic a pace. Their résumés read like a *Gourmet* magazine list of top culinary schools: The Culinary Institute of America in Hyde Park, New York; Johnson and Wales University in Providence, Rhode Island; Le Cordon Bleu Culinary Program in Pittsburgh. After culinary school, all chefs who join the Ritz-Carlton must still spend a year or so working in the kitchen of The Café, a less-expensive eatery at the resort, before (and if) they are allowed to move up to The Grill.

Cooking in a busy kitchen like this, where on average 100 dinners are served each night, is very tactical. The executive chef shouts orders to six other chefs in a brigade system like an army colonel shouting orders to his captains and sergeants. "You have to make sure you sound off well. Otherwise orders can get confused," said Matthew Medure, a con-sultant at The Grill. Medure worked as executive chef at The Grill for six years and earned the restaurant's first five-diamond award before striking out on his own to open two extremely popular Jacksonville-area restaurants.

"Ordering entrees: two lobsters, one halibut, one bison," shouted 32-year-old Richard Arnoldi, who's normally the executive sous chef at The Grill but moved into the executive chef position for the night. Arnoldi is a graduate of Johnson and Wales, where his father and grandfather were both professors.

After the fresh asparagus salad and the seared foie gras with Vidalia onions, and two different white wines, including a Sauterne, we don our aprons and head into the kitchen. Patrick, the pantry chef who's in charge of all the salads, doesn't seem too busy at the moment.

"We loved that little cookie thing with our asparagus salad," we say.

"Oh, the Parmesan tuille," he said. "They're really easy to make." He demonstrates how to lay some grated Parmesan cheese on a plate and microwave it for 45 seconds. It's cohesive and pliable after that, and you can shape it into a cone. Voila! A Parmesan tuille. Now that's something we can try at home.

We pause to talk to a sous chef who's been sautéing meat over a gas stove most of the night. He slides several "lollipops" of lamb onto a plate and slices off an extra chop. "Want to try it?" he asked. Of course, he didn't have to ask us twice. It's rare, tender, and melts in our mouths.

It's time to return to the table for an intermezzo, a palate-cleansing small glass of orange juice flavored with anise. But before we go, the salad chef, Patrick, holds out a raw oyster on the half shell topped with a dollop of salsa. "Bottoms up," he said.

Two more sous chefs bring our entrees, lean grilled bison with garlic mashed potatoes, and the sommelier brings a bottle of 1998 Calon-Segur, a perfect French red to complement the meat. It's all very delicious, and we're both getting very full—too full for dessert, if you can believe it.

We know this is a mistake, because the Hawaiian white chocolate soufflé with malted Belgian chocolate ice cream looks very tempting. But at this point it's just impossible. And we only had the five-course meal. A 10-course meal seems out of the question, but maybe you'll want to give it a try.

The price of a five-course "Seat in the Kitchen" dinner is $125 per person; wine with each course costs an additional $75. A 10-course dinner is $175, plus an additional $100 for wine. Reservations are required.

gingerbread house, big enough to walk into, for the hotel lobby, and the resort offers sleigh rides on Florida snow (the white sandy beach, where else?) complete with a bonfire and hot chocolate at the end of your sleigh ride. Don't miss dinner at The Grill, the hotel's AAA five-diamond oceanfront restaurant (see the Close-up in this chapter), or the Sunday brunch, which has been named "Best Brunch on the First Coast" by *Water's Edge* magazine.

Sawgrass Marriott
Resort & Beach Club $$-$$$$$
1000 PGA Tour Boulevard
Ponte Vedra Beach
(904) 285-7777, (800) 228-9290
www.marriotthotels.com/jaxsw
Walk in the front door of the Sawgrass Marriott and you'll know right away you're someplace special. You'll find yourself in a lush atrium lobby with a sweeping view of the 13th tee at the TPC Stadium Course, home every year to The Players Championship. Add to that view a large lagoon and a waterfall and you have one impressive man-made vista. This resort is located in Ponte Vedra, just a five-minute walk to the Sawgrass Shopping Center, with its impressive array of shops and restaurants. It's also a five-minute drive to The Cabana Club, the resort's oceanfront oasis, where guests can access the beach. The Marriott runs a free shuttle service to and from The Cabana Club and to area golf courses, so guests don't need a car. Golf opportunities abound here because the resort has a cooperative marketing agreement with five area golf courses, including the Stadium Course. The Marriott likes to boast that guests can play 99 holes of golf. There are also 17 tennis courts on four different surfaces; three outdoor pools, two heated; and two whirlpools, complimentary bicycles, and 24-hour access to a fitness center with saunas and a spa. (Don't be surprised when you get your bill, and a resort fee is tacked on to every room to pay for these amenities, including the shuttle service.)

The Sawgrass Marriott offers 508 rooms, including 24 suites and 80 two-bedroom villas. The guest rooms are decorated with a Florida feel and include fluffy robes, coffeemakers, and twice-daily maid service with nightly turndown. The

You don't have to be a resort guest to use the spa services. Just call the spas to make an appointment.

resort offers a year-round day camp for children called the Grasshopper Gang. Children ages 3 to 12 enjoy treasure hunts, beach and pool activities, arts and crafts, you name it, while Mom and Dad are off enjoying some free time. There are a variety of restaurants at this resort—don't miss the Sunday Jazz Brunch at the Cafe on the Green or dinner at The Augustine Grille (see Restaurants). There's also a popular outdoor grille called The 100th Hole—the only place to go after you've played 99 holes of golf.

The Sawgrass Marriott offers 56,000 square feet of meeting space and bills itself as the largest meeting resort between Atlanta and Orlando. A 20,000-square-foot spa, already named The Spa at Sawgrass, is under construction and should be fabulous when completed. It will incorporate North Florida architectural accents like clapboard wood siding along with a Zen garden and 19 treatment rooms.

RESTAURANTS

Jacksonville residents are spoiled when it comes to fresh seafood. This city, grown up next to an ocean and bisected by a major river, enjoys all kinds of fresh fish. From fried whiting to tuna sushi, boiled shrimp to broiled red snapper, Jacksonville is a seafood lover's delight. Seafood is a menu staple whether you're eating at Palm's Fish Camp in North Jacksonville or Restaurant Medure in Ponte Vedra.

The importance of seafood in Jacksonville is reflected in the city's many seafood festivals and special events. The Isle of Eight Flags Shrimp Festival is anything but shrimpy, attracting thousands to Fernandina Beach each spring. The annual Kingfish Tournament, dedicated to reeling in the largest kingfish anglers can find on a given weekend in July, is the largest of its kind in the country (see the Annual Events chapter).

If you decide you'd like to eat something from the turf instead of the surf, Jacksonville can accommodate you with first-class steak houses like Morton's and Ruth's Chris. Veal dishes are a specialty at many restaurants, including Giovanni's in Jacksonville Beach and Ocean 60 in Atlantic Beach. And don't forget that you're still in the South; local barbecue restaurants like Bono's, Fred Cotten's, and Sonny's serve up beef, pork, and chicken barbecue that's sure to satisfy all the meat-eaters in your family.

In short, visitors never leave Jacksonville hungry, and many are impressed with the high level of food that's served here.

This chapter offers some suggestions on where to eat. We've chosen not to mention national chain restaurants, figuring you've already eaten at those in your own hometown. The listings are organized by neighborhood because Jacksonville is a city of neighborhoods, which you will quickly learn as you travel around town. If you're interested in eating typical Jacksonville cuisine, see the Close-up later in this chapter and read what the experts say is the quintessential food of the River City. Some of their answers may surprise you.

Our advice on reservations is simple: Make them. A reservation will cut your wait at some of the more popular restaurants, where you could find yourself standing outside in the heat with a crowd of hapless tourists if you don't have them.

Best of all, dress is casual at almost every Jacksonville restaurant. By that we don't mean shorts, flip-flops, and bathing suits; we do mean that men forgo coats and ties and women wear sundresses or nice pants and sandals. We also recommend a summer sweater, especially for women, because some eateries are so cooled by air-conditioning they're downright chilly.

Unless otherwise noted, the restaurants listed in this chapter accept major credit cards. Most restaurants in Jacksonville are closed on Thanksgiving, Christmas, and New Year's Day, so if you want to dine out then, be sure to call ahead. Also keep in mind that some of the more popular eateries are closed early in the week for private parties. If you're trying to eat out on Monday, definitely call ahead first. Most of all, *buon appetito!*

PRICE CODE (PER ENTREE)

$	Less than $6
$$	$7 to $12
$$$	$13 to $18
$$$$	$19 and over

BAYMEADOWS

Daruma Japanese Steakhouse $$–$$$
8535-10 Baymeadows Road
(904) 739-3239

If you sit at the sushi bar, you get to pick up your food from a nifty miniature train that circles the bar. The sushi bar features different specials every day. Daruma's also features hibachi tables and a full menu of tempura, teriyaki, and sukiyaki dishes. There is a full-service bar, and takeout is available. Open for lunch Monday through Friday and dinner daily.

Enrico's Ristorante $$–$$$
10920 Baymeadows Road
(904) 538-9882

Owner/chef Enrico Petrilli serves up classic Italian dishes and romantic atmosphere. Seafood is a specialty, with dishes including frutti di mare, calamari fra diavolo, and pesce Portofino. Enrico's also serves a variety of veal and chicken dishes and, of course, favorites made with fresh pasta. There's an extensive wine list to complement the dishes.

The Front Page Grille & Catering $–$$
9150 Baymeadows Road
(in the Holiday Inn)
(904) 448-6900

Front Page Grille & Catering is decorated with front page headlines and has a nostalgic American atmosphere. The menu offers made-from-scratch items such as Carolina-style pork tenderloin, chicken potpie, baby back ribs, steaks, fresh catch, sandwiches, pastas, and salads. There is a full breakfast menu and daily specials. A daily happy hour at the full bar is served and offers half-price appetizers. Open daily for breakfast, lunch, and dinner.

Gubbio's $–$$
5111 Baymeadows Road
(904) 731-9900

Named after a small town in Italy, Gubbio's has a lunch menu of Italian favorites such as pizzas, calzones, pastas, and subs. For dinner there are daily specials, or try Gubbio's signature dish, Chicken Milano, served with a white cream sauce and topped with melted mozzarella. The seafood, veal, lasagna, fettuccine Alfredo, and shrimp primavera are popular, too.

Bread is made fresh daily. Finish your meal with a cup of cappuccino. Beer and wine are served. Open for lunch Monday through Friday and dinner daily.

The Jacksonville Junior League publishes one of the best local cookbooks, featuring popular regional recipes. The cookbooks are on sale at most Jacksonville bookstores.

India's Restaurant $–$$
9802-8 Baymeadows Road
(904) 620-0777

Vegetarians especially love this popular Indian restaurant located in a busy strip center at Baymeadows and Southside Boulevard. Start your lunch or dinner with samosa—crisp fried triangles of dough stuffed with delicately spiced potatoes, peas, and, if it's your pleasure, meat. The vegetable curry and chicken tandoori entrees are specialties of the house that will tantalize your taste buds. Be sure to order some naan—a light, flat Indian bread baked in a clay oven. A cold Indian beer, such as King Fishers, complements the meal. Health-conscious diners may want to order mango lassi, a mango-flavored yogurt drink. Kids eat for half price from the buffet, and a children's menu is available. Dinner specials are featured each evening. For dessert there is kulfi (Indian ice cream) and rice pudding. Beer and wine are served. Open for lunch Monday through Saturday and dinner daily.

Joseph's Pizza and Italian
Restaurant $$–$$$
9802 Baymeadows Road
(in Baymeadows Village)
(904) 642-3444

Family owned and operated and serving fine Italian cuisine for more than 30 years, Joseph's features hot pasta dishes, gourmet pizzas, sandwiches on homemade Italian bread, seafood, chicken, and fresh veal entrees. Slices of pizza and calzones make for a quick lunch. There are also daily lunch specials. Beer and wine are served. Catering and corporate lunch deliveries available. Open daily for lunch and dinner.

The farmers' market at 1780 West Beaver Street is a great place to buy fresh fruits and veggies. But you're not likely to find this market written up as a tourist attraction in Gourmet *magazine. Jacksonville's farmers' market is located in an industrial part of town, and it's a real working-person's market.*

Mediterrania Restaurant $$-$$$
3877 Baymeadows Road
(904) 731-2898
Old-world atmosphere and good service make this family-owned-and-operated Greek and Italian restaurant an area favorite. Fresh seafood, veal chops, and rack of lamb are the specialties. For dessert try one of the Greek specialties. Beer and wine, especially a large selection of Greek wines, are offered. Catering is available off-site or at the restaurant. A banquet room is also available. Open for lunch Monday through Friday and dinner Monday through Saturday.

Yoshi's Japanese Restaurant $$-$$$
9866-8 Baymeadows Road
(904) 642-3978
For a truly authentic Japanese experience, dine in Yoshi's tatami room and leave your shoes at the door. Sushi and tempura are the specialties, and the sukiyaki is a customer favorite. For something different, Yoshi often prepares a special dish for the evening. Finish the meal with a scoop of Japanese ice cream. Beer and wine are served, and takeout is available. Open for lunch and dinner Monday through Friday, dinner only on Saturday.

DOWNTOWN

Bravo! Ristorante $$$-$$$$
225 Coastline Drive
(in the Adams Mark Hotel)
(904) 633-9095
www.adamsmark.com/jacksonville
At Bravo! Ristorante the entertainment is as good as the food. Delicious Northern Italian cuisine and wood-fired pizzas are served by professional singers performing Broadway tunes and light opera. The restaurant is located in the lobby of the Adams Mark Hotel on the north bank of the St Johns River. Private dining is available for small groups. Dinner is served Monday through Saturday.

Cafe Nola $$
33 North Laura Street
(904) 366-6911, ext.221
Cafe Nola, located in the lobby of the Jacksonville Museum of Modern Art, serves homemade soups, salads, and sandwiches. It's the ideal place to take a break and get a bite after viewing modern art all morning. Open until 6:00 P.M. Monday through Friday.

De Real Ting Cafe $$
128 West Adams Street
(904) 633-9738
This Caribbean restaurant features dinner and dancing Friday and Saturday and a weekday lunch. During Sunday's dinner, there is a live jazz performance at the cafe. Specialties are jerk or curried chicken, jerk shrimp, conch fritters, Jamaican patties, steamed red snapper, and roasted fish. For something different, try the curried goat or the oxtail. There's also a daily lunch special and several vegetarian dishes. Beer and wine are served, and happy hour is Friday afternoon. Lunch is served Tuesday through Friday. Dinner is served Friday, Saturday, and Sunday.

Fred Cotten's Barbeque $$
2623 North Main Street
(904) 356-8274

For some of the best barbecue in Jacksonville, Fred Cotten's is worth the trip. Located in a small, smoky storefront on Main Street, just north of the city's downtown business district, Fred Cotten's has been serving many of the city's movers and shakers and workers alike for more than 30 years. It's not unusual to see a mayor or former mayor munching on a pork rib sandwich, while a crew of utility workers sits one table away.

Juliette's $$$
245 Water Street
(904) 355-7118

Located in the Omni Hotel, across from the Times-Union Center for the Performing Arts, Juliette's is a great place to go for dinner or for dessert after a show. Dine on the terrace overlooking the atrium. The lunch menu has create-your-own pasta dishes, soups, salads, and light fare such as the popular black bean soup and the shrimp or salmon Caesar salad. Along with the chef's nightly specials, the dinner menu features cuisine de la marche (cuisine of the market) and changes seasonally. In the morning there is a full breakfast buffet. Juliette's lounge carries beers of the world, and the full-service bar has a weekday happy hour. Open for breakfast, lunch, and dinner daily.

La Cena $$$-$$$$
212 North Laura Street
(904) 633-9255
www.lacena.com

Longtime Jacksonville restaurateur Jerry Moran (owner and operator of La Pasta Fresca in Orange Park) has returned after a hiatus with La Cena in a downtown storefront. Opened in late 2002, La Cena is a fine-dining Italian restaurant that attracts some of the city's heavy hitters. Moran, a native of Long Island, New York, who worked in a number of New York City restaurants before heading south, specializes in homemade egg pasta. The shellfish used to make such dishes as linguine alla vongale is shipped in from the northern United States. The wine list is limited but includes a fair assortment of excellent Italian wines. Dinner is served Tuesday through Saturday. There's seating for about 80 diners, and reservations are a must. Most of the tables turn over just once each night. "We take solid reservations," Moran says. "A table will be waiting for you when you arrive, and it's yours for the night."

Laura Street Cafe $$
50 North Laura Street
(inside Bank of America Tower)
(904) 356-5568

This jazzy cafe celebrates the annual Jacksonville Jazz Festival with numerous photographs and posters on display. Order at the counter from a menu offering low-fat, low-cholesterol dishes such as chicken primavera and baked breast of chicken sandwich, or the hummus or tabbouleh vegetarian sandwiches. A frequent order for breakfast is the egg-and-cheese pita pocket with your choice of ham, bacon, or sausage. The cafe has an in-house bakery, and catering and delivery are available. Open weekdays for breakfast and lunch.

The Mudville Grill downtown on Adams Street is a popular lunch spot around noon and a popular sports bar the rest of the time. Kids eat free at all Mudville Grills on Tuesday nights. For more info on the downtown location, call (904) 353-0052.

The London Bridge
English Pub and Eatery $$
100 East Adams Street
(904) 359-0001

The London Bridge is another recent addition to the downtown dining and drinking scene. Opened in 2002 in the heart of Jacksonville's business district, the London Bridge pub is one of the favorite after-work haunts for the city's young professionals. The restaurant serves classic British pub food such as bangers and mash, fish-and-chips, cottage pie, and Scottish eggs. The beer list includes 50 brands. Lunch and dinner are served daily, and there's live music every Monday, Friday, and Saturday. Wednesday nights are reserved for sporting events on the telly, and Thursday nights feature trivia contests.

Southend Brewery & Smokehouse $$$
2 Independent Drive (Jacksonville Landing)
(904) 665-0000

Southend serves classic regional and American cuisine. The meats are smoked, the grilled items are cooked over hickory wood, and the pizzas are baked in a wood-burning oven. Along with lunch and dinner specials, the menu includes pasta, seafood, salads, burgers, sandwiches, ribs, and chicken. A kid's menu is available. Dine indoors or outdoors on the covered pavilion or balcony. A full bar is served, and cigar smoking is permitted. Six types of beer on tap from the in-house brewery range from light ale to stout. The upstairs banquet facility is also used for late-night dancing Friday and Saturday; a DJ spins the tunes. Open daily for lunch and dinner.

Southern Paradise $$
229 West Forsyth Street
(904) 358-1082

Southern Paradise blends home style and gourmet. A full breakfast menu offers hotcakes and French toast from the griddle, omelettes, breakfast burritos, homemade muffins, bagels, and biscuit sandwiches. Breakfast specials include coffee and juice. An express lunch (served in 15 minutes or less) has hot and cold sandwiches, burgers, wraps, soups, salads, and more. From the home-style menu, choose from seafood, steaks, pastas, sandwich melts, fried baskets, and dishes such as meat loaf, country fried steak, and chops, along with a large selection of fresh veggies. Children have their own selections. Ask for the monthly flier listing lunch specials. Open weekdays 7:00 A.M. to 3:00 P.M.

Uptown at LaVilla $$-$$$
820 North Davis Street
(904) 355-2300
www.uptownlavilla.com

What better place to listen to live jazz while you eat than in the Jacksonville neighborhood where Duke Ellington used to perform whenever he came to town. (You can read more about LaVilla, a historic downtown neighborhood, in our chapter on African American tourism.) The Uptown at LaVilla is located directly across the street from the Ritz Theatre, which makes it a great choice either before or after a show there. It's also just a hop, skip, and jump from other downtown venues like the Times-Union Center for the Performing Arts. The restaurant is small and intimate; it seats about 100. The cuisine is American with Southern influences. Jazz is performed by local and regional musicians during dinner Friday and Saturday. There's no cover charge for the shows, but there is a $3.00 entertainment fee added to your bill to pay the musicians. The Uptown at LaVilla also serves lunch.

Worman's Bakery & Deli $
204 Broad Street
(904) 354-5702

Open for breakfast and lunch, Worman's is a Jacksonville tradition since 1923. Worman's is known for its Reuben sandwiches, matzo ball soup, and corned beef and pastrami sandwiches. In the morning order a blintz, corned beef omelette, or bagel with lox and cream cheese. A kosher menu is available. There is a large selection of imported beer and wine and gift baskets filled with gourmet items. Catering is available, both private and corporate. Worman's makes pastries, wedding cakes, executive box lunches, and, for morning meetings, continental breakfast items served with coffee and juice. Open for breakfast and lunch Monday through Saturday, with free delivery in a limited area (with a minimum order).

SAN MARCO/SOUTHBANK

bb's $$$
1019 Hendricks Avenue
(904) 306-0100
Named a "Top 20 New Restaurant in Florida" by *Florida Trend*, bb's offers chic dining and exceptional food. The menu includes numerous appetizers, pizzas, and sandwiches, along with daily dinner specials. Try the almond-dusted calamari, tuna tartare, or the wild mushroom pizza, and finish with one of the delectable desserts made in-house. Beer and 50 wines are available by the glass. The bar is a popular spot for socializing as well as eating, since bb's is smoke-free. A separate counter handles take-out orders. Open for lunch and dinner Monday through Saturday.

Bistro Aix $$$
1440 San Marco Boulevard
(904) 398-1949
Modeled after a French bistro, Bistro Aix is dark and cozy—a very romantic setting. The food? Exceptional. The menu has mostly Provençal and Mediterranean dishes like artisan breads, hummus, grilled pizzas, risottos, and roasted chicken with garlic. Try the roasted tomato soup and the lamb with ratatouille, or the seared tuna over root vegetable puree with roasted red peppers and verjus. Bistro Aix's wood-fired oven produces tasty, inventive pizzas.

Bistro Aix also has a martini bar and an international wine list with a focus on California wines, tap beers, and bottled microbrews. The smoke-free dining room features original 1940s brickwork, a curved marble-and-copper "chef's bar," and an exhibition kitchen. Outdoors, it's garden patio dining. The Aixpress Market offers desserts and specialty drinks, and there are adjacent private dining and conference facilities. Parking is behind the restaurant on Philips Street. The dining room is open Monday through Friday, serving lunch and an afternoon menu. Dinner is served nightly.

Cafe Carmon $$$
1986 San Marco Boulevard
(904) 399-4488
Cafe Carmon has a contemporary and elegant atmosphere that showcases the innovative American cuisine created by executive chef Roderick Tizol. With blends of Asian, Latin American, French, and Italian influences, Tizol achieves a new American style of cuisine. Dine indoors or outdoors on the patio. Beer and more than 100 wines are served, 25 wines by the glass. Open for lunch and dinner Monday through Saturday.

Chart House $$$
1501 River Place Boulevard
(904) 398-3353
Located on the south bank of the St. Johns River since 1982, Chart House serves fresh fish, seafood, steaks, and prime rib. It also has a 65-item salad bar with homemade dressings, hand-tossed Caesar salads, pasta, fruits, and caviar. Start the meal with coconut crunchy shrimp or the seared ahi. Entree selections include tenderloin medallions, seafood linguine, Australian lobster tail, and a vegetarian bowl, along with daily fish specials. Save room for chocolate lava cake with vanilla ice cream and warm chocolate sauce. A full bar is served. Reservations are suggested but not required. Open for dinner daily. The Chart House will also open for lunch for parties of 30 or more.

Havana-Jax $$
2578 Atlantic Boulevard
(904) 399-0609
If you find yourself hankering for a Cuban sandwich or arroz con pollo, this festive restaurant at the intersection of Beach and Atlantic Boulevards is worth a try. Owner Silvia Pulido serves up authentic Cuban dishes such as the signature paella. The menu also includes chicken, steak, roast pork, and seafood dishes. Dinners come with rice, black beans, and plantains. A large dessert selection features Cuban pastries. Beer, wine, and wine-based drinks are served along with Café

Cubano and tropical milkshakes. Lunch orders can be phoned or faxed in. Fine cigars are available for purchase, to be enjoyed after you leave the restaurant. Open for lunch and dinner Monday through Saturday.

Smokey Bones Barbecue near Regency Square Mall is Jacksonville's upscale barbecue joint. The restaurant resembles a mountain lodge in Denver. Ribs are cooked in a smoker. Call (904) 724-7120 for more info.

La Nopalera Mexican Restaurant $$
1629 Hendricks Avenue
(904) 399-1768

The food and service are consistently good at this family-owned-and-operated Mexican restaurant. The waitstaff constantly replenishes the chips and salsa. La Nopalera serves traditional Mexican dishes such as tamales, fajitas, and pork tacos. There are daily specials as well. For dessert there is flan and sopapillas. Beer, wine, and margaritas are served. Open for lunch and dinner Monday through Saturday.

The Loop Pizza Grill $$
2014 San Marco Boulevard
(904) 399-5667

Located on the San Marco Square since 1981, the Loop Pizza Grill combines the convenience of a fast-food restaurant with the individual attention and quality of a restaurant with table service. There's no hassle, and no tipping is required. The Loop remains consistent in serving quality food at reasonable prices. Try the char-broiled Loop burger, the original Chicago-style pizza, or the thin-crust pizza with one of the Loop's soups or salads. Leave room for a hand-dipped milk shake or brownie sundae. Beer and wine are served. Open for lunch and dinner daily.

Matthew's $$$$
2107 Hendricks Avenue
(904) 396-9922

This is Jacksonville's only four-diamond, four-star restaurant. Chef/owner Matthew Medure continues to collect accolades, and his restaurant keeps garnering top votes from publications like *Florida Trend* and *Folio Weekly.*

Ask about the chef's tasting menu, which pairs each course with an appropriate wine. Matthew's has an extensive wine list with more than 400 selections, receiving an Award of Excellence from *Wine Spectator.* Dine indoors or outdoors in the courtyard. Dress is business-casual, jackets optional. Open for dinner Monday through Saturday. Reservations are recommended.

Morton's of Chicago Steakhouse $$$$
1510 Riverplace Boulevard
(904) 399-3933

Morton's is a great choice for such well-cooked classics as filet mignon, rib lamb chops, and whole baked Maine lobster. Vegetables are wholesome and fresh. Portions are generous here, so come hungry. The wine list is extensive and complements the beef and seafood dishes that make Morton's famous. For dessert, don't miss the Godiva Hot Chocolate Cake—chocolate cake topped with fresh raspberries and vanilla ice cream. Chocolate lovers rave about the cake's warm, gooey center.

New York Italian Deli $$
3333 Beach Boulevard
(904) 398-1089

Family owned and operated, this Italian deli serves New York–style pizza, hot and cold Philly-style sandwiches, calzones, and stromboli. Customers particularly enjoy the pizzas, available by the pie and by the slice, along with the lunch and dinner specials. The full-service bar, The Red Zone, has a daily happy hour and nine TVs for watching your favorite sports. There's karaoke on Friday and live entertainment on Saturday. Dine in, take out, or call for dinner delivery. Open for lunch and dinner Monday through Saturday.

Pom's Thai Bistro $$$-$$$$
1974 San Marco Boulevard
(904) 338-0269

Pom's is an upscale white-tablecloth restaurant. The food served here includes such traditional Thai fare as spring rolls and pad thai, but it also features creative dishes such as seared tuna and Chilean sea bass prepared with a Thai touch. All the entrees come with delicious jasmine rice and as much hot pepper as you can stand. Be sure to try the Bangkok ice cream for dessert—coconut ice cream with banana fried pastries, topped with honey. Yum. Lunch is served Monday through Friday, dinner Monday through Saturday.

River City Brewing Co. $$$
835 Museum Circle
(904) 398-2299

Chef Larry Grosshans serves regional Florida cuisine featuring seafood, steaks, chicken, and pasta, along with daily specials. Select one of the new additions to the menu. The house specialty is the seafood jambalaya. The restaurant/microbrewery offers great views of the St. Johns River and downtown Jacksonville. Handcrafted British ales include the popular Jag Light. Dine inside or out on the deck. There's a weekday happy hour, and live entertainment is featured on weekends. Banquet space is available for groups up to 350. Open for lunch and dinner Monday through Saturday, with brunch on Sunday.

Ruth's Chris Steak House $$$$
1201 Riverplace Boulevard
(inside the Jacksonville Hilton)
(904) 396-6200

The perfect place for a romantic dinner or to treat out-of-town guests, Ruth's Chris is the "home of serious steaks." A Best of Jax winner for Best Restaurant and Best Steaks in Jacksonville, Ruth's Chris serves Midwestern custom-aged U.S. prime beef,

cooked in 1,800-degree ovens specifically designed and built for Ruth's Chris. In addition to steak, the menu includes some fresh seafood, live Maine lobster from the tank, and several choices of a la carte side dishes. A full bar is served with an extensive selection of wines. Open daily for dinner. Reservations suggested.

AVONDALE/RIVERSIDE

Biscotti's $$$
3556 St. Johns Avenue
(904) 387-2060

Enjoy a gourmet meal or just coffee and dessert. A coffeehouse/restaurant, Biscotti's is located in Avondale's shopping district. Chef Carlos's pasta, beef, and fish specials are popular dishes (part of their appeal are the fresh spices and generous portions), along with gourmet salads, pizzas, and sandwiches. You'll also find a good selection of coffee drinks and dozens of desserts made fresh by the pastry chef. Coffee can be purchased by the pound. Beer and wine are served, with more than 40 wines available by the glass or bottle. Friday and Saturday, a full menu is served until midnight. Takeout is available from the menu. Off-site catering is also available, and the restaurant can accommodate large parties. Open daily for breakfast and lunch, dinner Tuesday through Saturday, and an innovative brunch on Sunday.

Bistro 17 $$
1171 South Edgewood Avenue
(at Highway 17)
(904) 387-6609

This colorful, artsy bistro is a fun, energetic, and affordable place to get a bite to eat. Blackboard menus list both food and wine. Menu items include salads, pastas, fresh fish, pizzas, Atsugi beef, salmon steaks, mussels Provençal, and escargot. All entrees, including the burgers and sandwiches, are served with salad or soup. Children have their own selections. Save room for one of the many decadent

CLOSE-UP

Official Food

Key West has its Key lime pie. Boston has its Boston baked beans. Even tiny Brunswick, Georgia, about an hour north of Jacksonville, has its Brunswick stew. So what's the official food of Jacksonville?

The short answer to this question is that there's no consensus. We asked three impartial food experts and got three different answers.

Dan Macdonald, longtime food editor for the *Florida Times–Union,* has given much thought to the idea of Jacksonville's official food. He believes *the* quintessential food, distinctive only to Jacksonville, is the "Lubi"—a fast-food sandwich that's sold only four places worldwide, and all four places are right here in Jacksonville. "It's a steaming sandwich of ground sirloin, mustard, mayonnaise, sour cream, pepper sauce, and cheese that's so gooey you have to eat it with a knife and fork," said Macdonald.

Lubies are sold at the four family-owned Lubi's Restaurants (the one at 500 North Third Street in Jacksonville Beach is especially popular), and some Jacksonville residents just can't live without them. "Sometimes I just get this craving for one," said Linda Stout, an Atlantic Beach resident and Lubi lover who always orders her Lubi with one of the store's popular cherry-limeade drinks.

The fresh-ground sirloin, which is never frozen (a key to a successful Lubi) is packed inside a bread boat carved from a loaf of soft bread. It's topped with all the condiments, including a homemade pepper sauce. A Lubi comes in several varieties: the Original Famous Lubi, the Mozzarella Lubi, the Chili Lubi, the Stroganoff Lubi, the Mean Machine, and the Fiesta Lubi, which have kept Lubi lovers returning for more than 20 years.

Ron Wolf, program manager for the Culinary Institute of the South, a cooking school at Florida Community College at Jacksonville, has a different idea of Jacksonville's official food. He gives the nod to swamp cabbage, an indigenous food that rural folks have been eating in North Florida for hundreds of years.

Swamp cabbage comes from the cabbage palm, a tree that grows plentifully in Jacksonville, which is good because this is not exactly an environmentally sensitive food. You have to "86" the tree in order to get to the swamp cabbage. Typically, the exterior of a cabbage palm tree is chopped away and the interior, or center, is boiled in salted water. "It tastes exactly

desserts. Beer and more than 150 wine selections are available at retail prices. You pay only a $5.00 corkage fee and can take home what you can't finish. Private banquet facilities are available. Open Monday through Saturday for dinner.

Casbah Cafe   **$$**
3628 St. Johns Avenue
(904) 981–9966
Casbah Cafe serves Middle Eastern and Mediterranean cuisine. Customers enjoy the falafel, the lamb kabobs, and the Cas-

like hearts of palm," said Wolf, who concedes that swamp cabbage is not often found on a restaurant's menu. But if you happen to see it, don't be afraid to order it, Wolf advised. "It's delicious."

Also delicious, and much more plentiful, is fried shrimp, the official food pick of Catherine Enns Grigas, dining editor for *Water's Edge* magazine, a big glossy published in Jacksonville that reflects life in the coastal south. "Jacksonville has the best shrimp around," said Grigas. That's because local shrimpers working out of Mayport, a tiny fishing village near the mouth of the St. Johns River, ply the waters off Northeast Florida every day in shrimping season to haul in the fattest and finest shrimp they can find. That shrimp is bought not only by local restaurants but also by restaurants around the state. A typical Jacksonville fried shrimp dinner includes lightly fried shrimp; hush puppies; coleslaw; french fries, baked potato, or cheese grits; and a vegetable like corn, lima beans, or collard greens. Restaurants serve shrimp many ways, from boiled to breaded in coconut, but it's fried shrimp that Grigas said is the real taste of North Florida. Palm's Fish Camp on Heckscher Drive makes some of the best lightly battered fried shrimp in the area, and so does O'Steens Seafood Restaurant in St. Augustine.

"The other food that I would say is indigenous to Jacksonville is the soft-shell crab," said Grigas, but she admits that it's difficult to call this Jacksonville's official food because it's so seasonal. "You almost have to get lucky and catch a special at a restaurant," said Grigas. Travel along Heckscher Drive on the Northside and you'll likely see fishermen in tiny boats hauling in crab traps from the St. Johns River and its tributaries. You can always buy soft-shell crabs directly from the fishermen and cook them yourself. "Just make sure they're still alive," said Grigas. "That's how you know they're fresh."

Interestingly, none of our food experts picked barbecue as the official food of Jacksonville. Barbecue is often "the people's choice" when it comes to eating out, and there is a plethora of barbecue restaurant chains in town, such as Woody's, Sonny's, and Bono's, to satisfy such culinary cravings. But as food editor Dan Macdonald put it, Jacksonville is not known for any distinctive style of barbecue, although it is known for its tangy mustard barbecue sauce. "But that's not a food," he said, "that's a condiment."

bah pizzas, not to mention the selection of desserts and pastries. Children's choices are available. Dine indoors or outdoors on the garden patio. In the hookah lounge you can sit on the floor and eat at low tables. The cafe serves African coffees and has a global beer and wine selection. Artwork is for sale. Belly dancers perform Thursday through Saturday nights. For something different, try the hookah pipes—3-foot ornate Middle Eastern water pipes for smoking flavored tobacco. Open daily for lunch and dinner.

European Street Restaurant $$$
2753 Park Street
(904) 384-9999

1704 San Marco Boulevard
(904) 398-9500

5500 Beach Boulevard
(904) 398-1717

Happy hour at European Street features beer, beer, and more beer. This Northeast Florida institution is known for its massive selection of brews on tap and in bottles—20 drafts and more than 130 bottles, to be exact. European Street's flagship Riverside location features a daily happy hour from 2:00 to 9:00 P.M. with two-for-one specials on all beer and wine. The term "happy hour" fits well, because when the place is packed and the beer is flowing, it's hard to spot a frown in the house. The Listening Room in the San Marco location features small bands, local and regional, every Thursday. Open daily 10:00 A.M. to 10:00 P.M.

Heartworks Gallery & Cafe $$
820 Lomax Street
(904) 355-6210

Lots of fresh herbs and unusual vegetables are used in creative preparations. Favorites include the made-from-scratch hummus in a pita, carrot dog, black bean burrito, vegetable pizza, soup du jour, and the daily specials. Owner Elaine Wheeler makes the pastries. Coffee drinks include latte mochas, cappuccino, and espresso, specially blended for Heartworks. Dinner features vegetarian gourmet with several selections of entrees, changing weekly. Reservations are requested for large dinner parties. Sunday brunch boasts such treats as fresh fruit pancakes and spinach omelette pies. Open for lunch Monday through Saturday, dinner Thursday and Friday, and Sunday brunch. Located inside the Heartworks Art Gallery.

Moss Fire Grill $$
1537 Margaret Street
(904) 355-4434

The Moss fire Grill serves made-to-order Southwestern cuisine in a friendly, casual atmosphere. Hearty selections from the munchies list include spinach con queso, chicken tortilla soup, and a fresh veggie quesadilla. Also on the menu are several large burritos, tacos, sandwiches, and salads. Dinner entrees include tuna and other fresh fish, grilled salmon, pork loin, homemade crab cakes, and other nightly specials. For dessert try the chocolate peanut butter pie, Key lime pie, or another homemade dessert. A children's menu is available. Beer and wine are served, and there's a daily happy hour. Open for lunch and dinner Monday through Saturday.

Sterling's Cafe $$$$
3551 St. Johns Avenue
(904) 387-0700

Elegant yet comfortable—that best describes this longtime Jacksonville favorite that serves American and European cuisine. Try the portobello mushroom Napoleon: a marinated and grilled mushroom cap layered with spinach, goat cheese, roasted red peppers, and thin slices of zucchini and squash, all drizzled with balsamic vinaigrette and truffle oil. Open for lunch and dinner Monday through Saturday and brunch on Sunday. Reservations are suggested.

THE BEACHES

Al's Pizza $
303 Atlantic Boulevard, Atlantic Beach
(904) 249-0002
www.alspizza.com

Who would have thought you could turn a coin-operated car wash into a popular restaurant? But that's just what happened at Al's Pizza in Atlantic Beach. The modern decor, outdoor seating, and, of course, tasty pizzas, calzones, and salads have made Al's one of the top spots in the Beaches for a casual evening out.

The restaurant, which has expanded since it opened in 1995, is popular with neighborhood families as well as young couples. Owner Al Mansur introduced the infamous white (or sauceless) pizza to

Jacksonville. Al's also offers a wide variety of traditional and nontraditional toppings, including eggplant, artichoke, sun-dried tomato, feta cheese, and salami, as well as the BLT pizza with bacon, lettuce, and tomato. Al's has a second location on Highway A1A in Ponte Vedra and is open for lunch and dinner seven days a week. Parking is limited.

Aqua Grill $$$
950 Sawgrass Village Drive
Ponte Vedra Beach
(904) 285-3017

If it's variety you crave, try Aqua Grill. The upscale eatery offers 14 different specials every night—everything from fresh seafood to Black Angus steaks—in an atmosphere that is best described as casual elegance. During the 16 years that Cary Hart and his family have owned and operated the restaurant, Aqua Grill has earned a strong following from the locals in Ponte Vedra Beach. It's particularly popular among golfers looking for a good meal after hitting the links.

The restaurant has 150 seats inside and 60 outside. And if it's not too hot, Aqua Grill's outdoor seating—among an herb garden and fountain—is a pleasant experience. There's also a lounge with full-service bar. Lunch and dinner are served every day except Sunday, when only dinner is served.

The Augustine Grille $$$$
1000 PGA Tour Boulevard
Ponte Vedra Beach
(904) 285-7777

Located in the Sawgrass Marriott Resort & Beach Club, the Augustine Grille offers some of the best fine dining at the Beaches. The golfing decor befits the famous Tournament Players Championship golf course located nearby. Try executive chef Telford Willis's specialty: Chilean sea bass. Dinner only is served Monday through Saturday. Reservations are suggested.

Want something good to eat but not feeling too hungry? Try the appetizers at Simon's Wine Bar in San Marco at 1004 Hendricks Avenue. The portions are big enough to fill you up, not out. For more information call Simon's at (904) 396-8088.

Barbara Jean's
at Old Ward's Landing $$
15 South Roscoe Boulevard, Palm Valley
(904) 280-7522

Casual Southern dining doesn't get much better than Barbara Jean's, overlooking the Intracoastal Waterway in Palm Valley, just west of Pont Vedra Beach. This is excellent food served on paper plates. Diners are as varied as the 15 fresh vegetables served every day. On any given visit you're just as likely to see women dripping in diamonds as you are patrons wearing flip-flops.

Specialties include Maryland-style crabcakes, pot roast, meat loaf, and chicken-fried steak smothered in gravy. Finish off dinner with a slice of the fresh fruit cobbler. Barbara Jean's serves lunch and dinner seven days a week.

Beach Hut Cafe $
1281 Third Street South
Jacksonville Beach
(904) 249-3516

Opened in 1988 by Richard Downing and his wife, Desiree, Beach Hut is the place to go for breakfast in Jacksonville Beach. The portions are generous, and the service is friendly. This is a favorite among locals and visitors alike; don't be surprised if you find yourself sitting next to members of the rock band Limp Bizkit, who are Jacksonville natives.

While Beach Hut serves both breakfast and lunch, the restaurant is best known for its breakfast. The place serves about 1,000 eggs a day. There are 31 picnic tables and six chairs at the counter. The restaurant is open seven days a week from 6:00 A.M. to 2:00 P.M. Seating is first-come, first-served, so allow plenty of time, especially on the weekends.

Bonefish Grill   **$$$**
2400 South Third Street
Jacksonville Beach
(904) 247-4234
www.bonefishgrill.com
Since opening in January 2003, the Bone-fish Grill in south Jacksonville Beach has fast become one of the most popular restaurants and nightspots at the Beaches. Bonefish Grill is part of the Out-back restaurant empire, but each restaurant is owned and operated separately. The spacious bar is the place to meet and greet on Friday and Saturday nights. The restaurant serves a wide variety of fresh seafood dishes, and there are lots of creative daily specials. One of our favorites is the Atlantic Salmon Newirth: grilled swordfish topped with sautéed spinach, feta cheese, artichoke hearts, and lemon-basil butter. Bonefish also offers a very tasty prosciutto-wrapped monkfish that's topped with a mushroom marsala sauce. After dinner, which is served daily, retire to the full bar to chat and listen to recorded jazz music. The Bonefish offers preferred seating. Each night 20 percent of the 200 seats are held for those with reservations, with the balance of the seating going to walk-in diners.

Bukkets Oceanfront Grille   **$$**
222 North Oceanfront Drive
Jacksonville Beach
(904) 246-7701
Located just off Jacksonville Beach's boardwalk, Bukkets specializes in oysters, wings, seafood, salads, and sandwiches. With a full bar and entertainment, it's frequented by a mostly younger crowd. Lunch and dinner are served daily; happy hour every day from 3:00 to 6:00 P.M.

China Coral   **$$**
830-12 Highway A1A North
Ponte Vedra Beach
(904) 273-8776
If you're in the mood for seafood but want it a little spicier, China Coral is a good option. China Coral serves Shanghai, Mandarin, and Szechwan dishes. In addition to the regular menu, there are daily lunch combination dishes and dinner specials. Favorites include fresh fish and seafood entrees, crispy fish and crispy duck, and a stir-fried string bean dish. Beer and wine are served. Open daily for lunch and dinner.

Chizu Japanese Steak and
Seafood House   **$$$**
1227 Third Street South
Jacksonville Beach
(904) 241-8455
Ask a local chef where he or she likes to go for an evening out at the Beaches, and chances are the answer will be Chizu. Opened by Bobby Nakajima in 1984, Chizu has become one of the most popular restaurants at the Beaches. Consequently, the 225-seat restaurant is usually packed on weekend nights. It's worth the wait.

At Chizu, which means "1,000 cranes" in Japanese, you can watch real pros at work at the sushi bar or teppanyaki grills. At the grill you can get teriyaki flavoring on your choice of steak, chicken, or shrimp, combined with a side order of the traditional fried rice. Chizu, which has an extensive sushi menu, is open seven days a week for dinner only. Reservations are not accepted.

Cruisers Grill   **$-$$**
319 23rd Street South
Jacksonville Beach
(904) 270-0356
Some people will go anywhere for a good hamburger, and if you're one of those people, you need go no further than Cruisers. Many say this unassuming little restaurant, across the parking lot from the

Pablo 9 Theaters, is the best place in town for a juicy, flavorful burger. Throw in a side of fries (cheese fries, if you're really throwing caution to the wind) and you'll fill your belly for under $10. Not in the mood for a burger? Try a quesadilla or a catfish sandwich. Both are good here. And if you think you can also manage an appetizer, Insiders recommend a basket of Cruisers' fried mushrooms.

Dolphin Depot $$$
704 North First Street
Jacksonville Beach
(904) 270-1424
Consistently voted one of the 25 best restaurants in the Jacksonville area, the Dolphin Depot's menu is anchored, as its name suggests, by fresh seafood dishes. But the Depot's chef, Jason Kurtzo, also serves up a good assortment of meat specialties, including rack of lamb, stuffed quail, cherrywood-smoked baby back ribs, and pork osso buco. The setting is cozy and intimate, with seating for just 55. The longtime waitstaff entertains diners with a thorough review of that night's offerings. The restaurant serves beer and a wide selection of wines by the glass. Dinner is served daily, with seatings from 5:30 to 9:00 P.M. Reservations are accepted.

Dwight's Bistro $$$$
1527 Penman Road, Jacksonville Beach
(904) 241-4496
After two hurricanes, two restaurants, and two kids in St. Thomas, Virgin Islands, wisecracking chef Dwight Delude said "too much" and moved to Jacksonville Beach. Local diners are indeed grateful.

Don't be fooled by the rough exterior. Opened in 1996, Dwight's Bistro is a cozy 40-seat place that has quickly gained a strong following among area connoisseurs looking for consistently great meals and an extensive wine list. The Mediterranean-style bistro serves fresh ravioli and pasta, crab cakes, grilled quail, veal, and lamb. Dinner is served Tuesday through Satur-

day; beer and wine only. With only eight tables, reservations are a must.

Ellen's Kitchen $
1824 South Third Street (in Pablo Plaza)
Jacksonville Beach
(904) 246-1572
Ellen's has been serving breakfast and lunch at the Beaches for more than 40 years. A full breakfast menu is served all day. Known for homemade sausage gravy and hash browns, Ellen's is also famous for Pat's special (two eggs on top of hash browns with melted cheese) and its crab cake Benedict. There are early-bird specials before 9:00 A.M. For lunch the menu is sandwiches, burgers, pork barbecue, BLTs, patty melts, and sandwich salads, as well as daily specials.

First Street Grille $$$
807 North First Street, Jacksonville Beach
(904) 246-6555
First Street Grille offers ocean views from the indoor multilevel dining room and the outdoor deck, covered patio, and tiki bar. Seafood is the specialty, including Chilean sea bass, tuna, and grouper prepared differently each night. The restaurant is also known for its prime rib and rack of lamb. The lunch menu includes homemade shrimp and chicken salad, New Orleans–style muffuletta sandwiches, and a variety of daily chef's specials. A favorite is the bayou shrimp.

The full-service bar features a weekday happy hour and offers an extensive wine list. Live entertainment, including light jazz and oldies, is played Wednesday through Sunday. Open for lunch and dinner daily; complimentary valet service.

Freebird Cafe $$
200 North First Street, Jacksonville Beach
(904) 246-BIRD
This rock 'n' roll–themed restaurant is owned and operated by Judy and Melody VanZant—the wife and daughter of late Lynyrd Skynyrd frontman Ronnie VanZant.

Looking for beachfront dining? The readers of Folio Weekly *picked First Street Grille in Jacksonville Beach as their top waterfront choice.*

The restaurant features New Southern cuisine, with such specialties as cornmeal-crusted trout, blackened catch Alfredo, crab-stuffed mushrooms, and spicy fried green tomatoes. There are also a number of Skynyrd food favorites, including a family recipe of Ronnie VanZant's mother—Sister Skynyrd's famous chili.

The full bar offers a weekday happy hour. Big-name acts perform throughout the week (see the Nightlife chapter). You can dine indoors or outdoors on the balcony. Open Saturday and Sunday for lunch and Tuesday through Sunday for dinner and late-night food. Reservations accepted.

Gene's Seafood Restaurant $$
1249 Penman Road, Jacksonville Beach
(904) 241-9333

Gene's serves some of the best seafood in Jacksonville at affordable prices. For an appetizer try the gator tail, lobster bites, or calamari fritti. Shrimp dinners, fresh fish specials, and seafood combinations are standards. The Italian seafood casserole is a signature dish, along with the Dream Boat—a combination of sautéed crab, shrimp, and mushrooms. Gene's also serves steak and chicken entrees. There's a full bar. Open for lunch and dinner daily.

Giovanni's $$$$
1161 Beach Boulevard, Jacksonville Beach
(904) 249-7787

A Beaches tradition for more than 30 years, Giovanni's offers fine dining in an elegant setting, featuring seafood dishes and innovative continental cuisine with an Italian flair. A full bar is served. The upstairs piano bar offers up tunes Tuesday through Saturday. Open for dinner Monday through Saturday.

Hala Cafe $$
1451 Atlantic Boulevard, Neptune Beach
(904) 249-2212

Located in a strip center on Atlantic Boulevard, Hala Cafe makes up for its lack of a great view with fresh Middle Eastern cuisine. You can get freshly baked pita bread and such specialties as hummus, falafel, and tabbouleh. Wine and beer only. Hala, which means "welcome" in Arabic, is open 11:00 A.M. to 9:00 P.M. Monday through Saturday. No reservations.

Harry's Seafood Bar and Grille $$$
1018 North Third Street, Jacksonville Beach
(904) 247-8855

This New Orleans–style eatery features fresh seafood, steaks, and authentic Cajun cooking. Signature items are the jambalaya and the étouffée along with the popular shrimp embrocettes and grilled lobster pasta. Harry's also serves wings, pasta dishes, salads, and sandwiches. Try one of the daily specials or the soup of the day. There is a full-service bar with a daily happy hour. Open for lunch and dinner daily.

Hell's Kitchen
(at Fly's Tie Irish Pub) $$–$$$
177 East Sailfish Drive, Atlantic Beach
(904) 246-4293
www.flystieirishpub.com

After training at Ballymaloe Cookery School under renowned Irish chef Darina Allen and working at a number of restaurants, from Sligo to Cork, Ralph Tiernan returned to Northeast Florida and his family's Fly's Tie Irish Pub to cook Irish staples with a creative twist. There's live music most evenings and some of the best poured Guinness in Northeast Florida.

Homestead Restaurant $$
1712 Beach Boulevard, Jacksonville Beach
(904) 249-9660

It's family-style dining in a cozy log cabin at Homestead Restaurant, serving home-cooked meals since 1947. The Homestead is famous for its fried chicken but also serves seafood and steaks, pot roast, meat loaf, and chicken potpie, along with heaping bowls of vegetables and fresh biscuits. For dessert try a slice of cheesecake, strawberry shortcake, apple pie, or Key lime pie. A full bar is served. Open for dinner daily. Brunch on Sunday features gospel singers.

Ichiban $$$
675 North Third Street, Jacksonville Beach
(904) 247-8228
Ichiban features three dining choices: the teppan or hibachi tables where you can watch the chef prepare your food, the sushi bar, or Western-style seating with a menu of tempura and teriyaki dishes. Take advantage of the early-bird specials each evening. For dessert there is fried ice cream and fried cheesecake. Ichiban has a full-service bar with selected fine wines. Open for dinner daily and a weekday lunch (call for lunch hours).

Jason's Deli $$
2330 Third Street, Jacksonville Beach
(904) 246-7585
Jason's Deli offers heart-healthy dishes, soups, and salads and traditional deli sandwiches and super spuds. This is an ideal place for a quick lunch. The signature sandwich is the New Orleans–style muffuletta. Jason's Deli also has a salad bar with 33 choices and free ice cream. Kids eat for $1.99. Beer and wine are served. Delivery is available as are catering and box lunches. Open for lunch and dinner daily.

JJ's Bistro at JJ's Cuisine and Wine $$$
330 Highway A1A North (Shoppes at Ponte Vedra), Ponte Vedra Beach
(904) 273-7980
Dine on the French Riviera at an umbrella-topped table with French music in the background—without ever leaving Northeast Florida. The Bistro has nearly 40 menu items for lunch and dinner as well as daily specials. You'll find French/Mediterranean entrees of chicken, seafood, and pasta as well as salads, sandwiches, soups, and pastries. Beer and wine are served. The wine bar and wine cellar provide more than 250 selections available by the bottle and 20 available by the glass. Dine indoors or outdoors. JJ's gourmet store carries pastries and lunch and dinner entrees to go. Off-site catering is available for large or small functions. Open for lunch and dinner Tuesday through Saturday.

Kevin's Grille $$$
2429 South Third Street (Costa Verde Plaza), Jacksonville Beach
(904) 242-0004
One of the newer restaurants at the Beaches, Kevin's Grille specializes in pasta, steaks, seafood, and California-style pizzas, which come with a variety of inventive toppings such as seafood and blackened tuna.

For starters try the seared tuna, a sushi-grade tuna sliced and served with pickled ginger, wasabi, and chopsticks. For your main course try the grouper in a peppery brandy-tomato cream sauce served over angel hair pasta or the Sheer Bliss—jumbo shrimp over a puree of artichoke hearts, yellow peppers, red onions, diced tomatoes, mozzarella, and scallions. Garlic rolls are homemade.

Dine indoors or outdoors at the fountain courtyard. The full bar has a daily happy hour from 5:00 to 7:00 P.M. Entertainment is featured in the courtyard Friday through Sunday. Open for lunch and dinner Monday through Saturday and brunch and dinner on Sunday.

Lighthouse Grille $$$
2600 Beach Boulevard
Jacksonville Beach
(904) 242-8899
Lighthouse Grille is located on the Intracoastal Waterway and Beach Boulevard as you enter Jacksonville Beach. The restaurant offers beautiful views of the waterway and the surrounding marshes. You can eat and watch the large pleasure boats make their way up and down the Intracoastal Waterway or catch breathtaking sunsets.

The restaurant serves a menu for all appetites: seafood, steaks, ribs, chicken, sandwiches, burgers, and entree salads. For starters try the Louisiana seafood gumbo or fresh-baked croissants with honey butter. Entree selections include seafood platters, fresh fish of the day, prime rib, killer hot dogs, and seafood po'boy sandwiches. Children's selections are available, and a full bar is served. Dine in or take out. The outdoor patio has its own bar. Limited reservations accepted, along with phone-ahead seating. Open for lunch and dinner daily. The Lighthouse Grille now features live music on the outside deck Thursday and Friday evenings.

LuLu's Waterfront Grille $$
301 North Roscoe Boulevard, Palm Valley
(904) 285-0139
Located on the Intracoastal Waterway in Palm Valley, LuLu's can be reached by car or by boat. The menu offers seafood, steaks, chicken, pasta, and salads. A full bar is served, and there's a weekday happy hour. Dine indoors or outdoors on the screened waterfront deck. Open daily 11:30 A.M. to 10:00 P.M., with a Sunday brunch.

Lynch's Irish Pub $$
514 North First Street, Jacksonville Beach
(904) 249-5181
Sure, the Guinness is tasty, but Lynch's, an authentic Northern Irish pub, also serves Irish stew, corned beef and cabbage, shepherd's pie, bangers and mash, fish-and-chips, steaks, and pasta. There is also a full range of appetizers, sandwiches, and daily specials. The full-service bar has 25 imported beers on tap. Live entertainment is featured almost every evening (see the

Looking for a neat place close to downtown to drink and dine? We suggest the Havana-Jax Cafe at 2578 Atlantic Boulevard in St. Nicholas (904-399-0609). The cantina area is quite lively, while the restaurant's black beans and rice is simply scrumptious.

Nightlife chapter). Open for lunch Saturday and Sunday and dinner daily.

Magellan's Oceanfront Dining $$-$$$
333 North First Street, Jacksonville Beach
(904) 247-2644
www.magellans.com
Located in the same building as the Atlantic nightclub, Magellan's dining room overlooks the ocean. The casual setting is an ideal spot for a full night on the town. After dinner wander into the Atlantic for live music. The restaurant features mainstays such as rack of lamb and filet mignon as well as specialties such as a seared black peppercorn–encrusted ahi tuna served over pan-fried sushi rice cakes and topped with a ginger and soy infusion. There's a full bar and over 200 different wines. Lunch and dinner are served daily. Magellan's also offers complimentary stretch limo service for up to eight people in the Beaches area. Check with the restaurant for details.

Manuel's Deli and Fine Wines $$
880 Highway A1A, Suite 5
Ponte Vedra Beach
(904) 273-4785
Manuel's offers more than 400 labels of wines, 10 different imported cheeses, chocolates, jellies, baked breads, and desserts. Sandwiches are made with Boar's Head meats and cheeses. Try the Cuban sandwich and the black beans and rice. In addition to indoor seating, there are tables outside under the awning. An extensive selection of gourmet items can be packaged in made-to-order gift baskets. Friday evening features wine tasting, and there are periodic wine dinners. Open for lunch and late-lunch Monday through Saturday.

Mario's at the Beach $$
1830 South Third Street
Jacksonville Beach
(904) 246-0005
Mario's is a casual, family-friendly restaurant that serves New York–style pizzas, Long Island rolls, stromboli, hot pasta dishes, and more. Along with the home-

made sauces and vegetarian dishes, Mario's is known for its chicken, veal, and shrimp entrees. Lunch and dinner specials are also offered. Dine indoors or outdoors on the patio. Delivery is available. Open for lunch and dinner Monday through Saturday.

Matsu Japanese Steakhouse $$$
1515 North Third Street, Jacksonville Beach
(904) 249-4290
Matsu Japanese Steakhouse has a large sushi and sashimi bar, a teppanyaki table, and a traditional menu of seafood, steaks, tempura, sukiyaki, yakitori, and teriyaki dishes. They even serve tempura (deep-fried) cheesecake for dessert. A full bar is served. Open for dinner daily.

Max's International Restaurant and Grand Ballroom $$$
1312 Beach Boulevard (Beach Plaza)
Jacksonville Beach
(904) 247-6820
Enjoy upscale European ambience and moderate prices. Max's menu features chicken and fish dishes with a Northern Italian flair, as well as a variety of eclectic European cuisine. You can sit at fountain-side tables in the dining room overlooking the gallery or outdoors in the ivy-covered courtyard. Beer and wine are served. Open Tuesday through Saturday for lunch and dinner and Sunday for brunch.

Mezza Luna Deli Pizzeria Ristorante $$$
110 North First Street, Neptune Beach
(904) 249-5573
Located in the heart of Neptune and Atlantic Beaches' restaurant row, Mezza Luna offers a casual, relaxed atmosphere. Owner Gianni Recupito is an old hand at running popular restaurants in the Jacksonville area. The chicken and veal specialties are popular choices, as are the seafood specials and wood-burning oven pizzas. The dessert favorite? Why, tiramisu, of course. There's a full-service bar with a weekday happy hour and an extensive wine list. Open Tuesday through Sunday for dinner.

The Moon Grille & Oyster Bar $$
1396 Beach Boulevard, Jacksonville Beach
(904) 241-1894
The Moon Grille & Oyster Bar is a boisterous, fun place with sports on the televisions, live music, and lots of food. Specialties include fresh oysters, crawfish, and peel-and-eat shrimp. The full lunch and dinner menu also has a seafood emphasis. The game room includes four pool tables. A full bar is served, and there is a daily happy hour. Trivia is featured Tuesday and Thursday nights. A magician performs on Wednesday night. Open for lunch and dinner daily.

Ocean 60 $$$$
60 Ocean Boulevard, Atlantic Beach
(904) 247-0060
This place has got it all: great food, great wine list, and great art. It's an intimate 50-seat restaurant with a large, inventive menu cooked up by chef Daniel Groshell, a graduate of the Culinary Institute of America in Hyde Park. His wife, Rachel, is the general manager and has made certain that the attentive servers can answer all your menu questions. The Groshells like to say their food is served "rustic," as opposed to artful—meaning that it hasn't been over-worked or overtouched in the kitchen.

This is fine dining with a Mediterranean or New World cuisine that includes lots of fresh seafood. Take the Tuna Escabeche appetizer. Groshell sears the tuna, then marinates and serves it with a chilled salsa fresca. It's his own twist on ceviche, the seafood standby so popular in Latino lands. For soups, the French onion with cheese rusks—a bread-cheese combo floating on top—gets raves from most diners. A house salad and vegetable come with every entree, but if you want an additional salad, try the grilled shrimp salad with candied garlic and feta. You just can't go wrong ordering fresh shrimp this close to the shrimp boats in Mayport.

Things really get interesting when it comes to choosing an entree. There's chicken in white wine sauce, Italian carbonara with scallops, and rack of lamb with a special demiglaze sauce. The more adventurous fish lovers may want to try the two-pound snapper, imported from Costa Rica, which Groshell fries whole, complete with head, tail, and eyes. It arrives stretched across your plate and scored so that you can easily eat one side, then flip the fish and eat the other. If you're really hungry, consider a $35 bowl of soup. It's a bouillabaisse chock-full of as much fresh fish as Groshell can get his hands on, then topped with a three- to five-ounce lobster tail that's been buttered, breaded, and baked. The desserts are also inventive, including a chocolate brownie lightly flavored with Mexican chilies.

Ocean 60 is one of the only restaurants in town where you can order a $2.00 two-ounce "taster" of wine from the extensive wine list to see if you like the selection enough to order a glass or even a bottle. It makes for some fun sampling. Ocean 60 is open for dinner Monday through Saturday and can also be booked for private parties.

Parson's Seafood Restaurant $$
904 Sixth Avenue, Jacksonville Beach
(904) 249-0608

The Parson family is well known for its seafood restaurants, which originated in Mayport. The family-style restaurant has a separate bar and an extensive menu of seafood as well as steaks and chicken. Try a shrimp sandwich for lunch or the popular super combo seafood platter for dinner. Children have their own menu selections. There are three separate dining rooms and an outdoor patio. The private dining room seats 50. The full bar offers daily happy hour specials. Open for lunch and dinner daily.

Plantains $$$
One Ocean Boulevard (at the Sea
Turtle Inn), Atlantic Beach
(904) 249-7402
www.seaturtleinn.com

Plantains serves Floribbean cuisine: a mixture of local Florida ingredients with Caribbean spices. Rated a "Top 25 Restau-

rant in Jacksonville," the menu changes based on seafood availability but always includes steaks and pastas. Specialties include the crab-crusted grouper and the oven-roasted salmon. You'll have an ocean view whether dining indoors or on the boardwalk patio. Wednesday's lunch features a buffet. Live entertainment is featured Thursday, Friday, and Saturday evenings and during Plantains' award-winning Sunday brunch. A full bar is served. Dinner reservations are suggested, especially on weekends. Look for chef's cooking classes, wine dinners, and table menu samplings throughout the year. Open daily for breakfast, lunch, and dinner and Sunday brunch.

Player's Cafe $$
262 Solana Road, Ponte Vedra Beach
(904) 273-5595

Player's Cafe sports a golf theme and a "wall of fame" of some golfing giants. The menu has something for everyone, and everything is homemade. Try a fresh grouper sub, Cuban sandwich, Philly cheesesteak, cordon bleu sandwich, or some homemade soup. The full breakfast menu, which includes eggs Benedict, draws a huge crowd, and there are early-bird specials until 9:00 A.M. Catering and weekday delivery service for breakfast or lunch is available. Open daily for breakfast (all day) and lunch.

Ragtime Tavern and
Seafood Grille $$$
207 Atlantic Boulevard, Atlantic Beach
(904) 241-7877

Long considered one of the Jacksonville area's top restaurants, Ragtime specializes in fresh seafood and several daily specials to choose from, along with several pasta dishes. Ragtime doesn't take reservations, but the food is worth any wait. Popular menu items include the bayou bouillabaisse, the sesame tuna, and the Ragtime shrimp. The customer favorite from the taproom brewery is Red Brick Ale. There is a full-service bar with happy hour Monday through Friday and live entertainment

Thursday through Sunday. Open for lunch and dinner daily and Sunday brunch.

Restaurant Medure $$$$
818 North Highway A1A (The Veranda)
Ponte Vedra Beach
(904) 543-3797

Jacksonville restaurateur Matthew Medure (Matthew's in San Marco) has done it again with this classy and chic restaurant. Selected by *Florida Trend* magazine as one of the state's top new restaurants, Restaurant Medure offers a sophisticated dining experience and private dining rooms. The menu is haute cuisine with an emphasis on a wide variety of local and imported fish and seafood, cooked with Southern, Mediterranean, Asian, and Middle Eastern influences. The lounge offers a full bar. Entertainment is featured periodically. Open Monday through Saturday 5:30 to 10:00 P.M. Reservations suggested. Read about Matthew's cooking classes in the Shopping chapter.

Ritespot $$
1534 North Third Street
Jacksonville Beach
(904) 247-0699

If it's home-style cooking you want at reasonable prices, this is the spot. A casual, smoke-free eatery located in the North Beach Plaza, Ritespot's daily specials and menu feature fresh seafood, Mayport shrimp, fresh fish, chicken-fried steak, pork chops, and pot roast, to name a few dishes. Fresh vegetable choices include mashed potatoes and gravy, shucked corn, collard greens, and black-eyed peas. Corn muffins and biscuits are served with the meal. Save room for a homemade milk shake. A full bar is served. Dine in or take out. Open for dinner daily.

Sawgrass Grille and The Tavern $$-$$$
43 PGA Tour Boulevard
Ponte Vedra Beach
(904) 285-3133
www.tavernatsawgrass.com

Eddie and Linda Limon have been serving up American cuisine with an Asian influence in their cozy New York–style pub for the past decade. Try the ginger-soy salmon or bourbon rib eye steak. Other favorites include prime rib, herb-crusted rack of lamb, and veal saltimbocca. The full-service bar has a good wine selection and a daily happy hour. Karaoke is featured every Wednesday and Friday. Open for lunch and dinner daily, the Sawgrass Grille also offers catering services.

Semolina International Pastas $$
330 Highway A1A North (Shoppes at Ponte Vedra), Ponte Vedra Beach
(904) 273-9080

If you're a pasta lover who's ever thought it would be a great idea to marry pasta with other ethnic dishes, this eclectic restaurant is for you. Give the enchilada pasta a try. It's a Southwestern dish with Mexican flavors served over penne pasta. There's also chicken parmigiana and chicken marsala served over linguine. Beer and wine only. Lunch and dinner served daily.

Sergio's $$$
1021 Atlantic Boulevard, Atlantic Beach
(904) 249-0101

Owner Sergio Zucchelli serves classic Northern Italian and continental cuisine. Located in the Atlantic Village shopping center, Sergio's menu offers a variety of fresh Northern Italian pasta dishes, veal dishes, Black Angus steaks, fish, and chicken entrees. A full-service bar is also offered. Sergio's is available for banquets and private parties. Open for dinner Tuesday through Sunday. Reservations suggested.

Shelby's Coffee Shoppe $$
200 First Street, Neptune Beach
(904) 249-2922

Shelby's is popular among locals, who walk or ride their bikes on weekend mornings for coffees from around the world, lattes, mochas, espresso, and cappuccino. The breakfast and dessert menus include muffins, bagels, Danish, cakes, ice cream, and fresh fruit. The lunch menu offers specials of the day, soups, salads, and sandwiches. Hot or cold chai tea is also available. Dine indoors or outdoors with patio and courtyard seating. Saturday and Sunday mornings feature a piano bar, and some evenings you'll hear acoustic guitar. Open daily at 7:00 A.M.

Singleton's Seafood Shack $$
4728 Ocean Street, Mayport
(904) 246-4442
Located 1 block before the ferry, this restaurant has been serving seafood since the 1960s. Favorites include the fried shrimp dinner and the blackened or grilled fish. There are daily lunch and dinner specials as well as fresh catch of the day. Dine inside or on the enclosed porch overlooking the St. Johns River. A full bar is served. Adjacent to the dining room, Captain Ray's Model Boat Museum features more than 200 models. Open for lunch and dinner daily.

Six Burner $$$
967 Atlantic Boulevard, Atlantic Beach
(904) 249-9910
Named after the six-burner stove in the display kitchen, this restaurant offers cooking sessions every other Tuesday, demonstrating different cooking methods and preparations (call for themes). Owners Craig and Julie Dion and chef Mike Ramsey have created a menu of classic cuisine, offering old and new favorites of steak, seafood, pasta, chicken, veal, and lamb dishes. You'll find steak Diane, veal Oscar, and shrimp scampi among the choices, along with a variety of nightly specials. Beer and more than 50 wines (20 by the glass) are served. Open nightly for dinner. Reservations accepted.

Sliders Oyster Bar and
Seafood Grille $$-$$$
218 First Street, Neptune Beach
(904) 246-0881
Insiders love the casual, friendly atmosphere of this restaurant located 1 block from the ocean. Sliders is known for its good homemade food at affordable prices. Specialties range from simple

grilled fish tacos to more elaborate entrees like Butter Nut Grouper. For lunch we like the mahi Casino sandwich, a combination of grilled mahi, cheddar cheese, bacon, and scallions. The menu also features plenty of nonseafood choices like pastas, salads, and chicken-cheese-spinach quesadillas. By the way, if you want a great local souvenir, buy a Sliders T-shirt, which features the restaurant's pink flamingo logo. Eat inside or out on the patio at this kid-friendly restaurant. (See our Kidstuff chapter.)

Solana Garden Deli/Restaurant $$
302 Solana Road, Ponte Vedra Beach
(904) 285-7474
The menu at this beach restaurant includes hot and cold sandwiches made with Thumann's meats, burgers, hot dogs, pastas, salads, and hot plate specials. Try a Reuben sandwich, the patty or tuna melt, or the open-face roast beef. A full breakfast is served every morning. Desserts, made fresh daily, include chocolate and carrot cakes, a variety of cookies, and New York crumb cake. Beer and wine are available. Dine in, take out, or have your order delivered (in a limited area). Catering service is available. Bring them a recipe—or let them choose—and they'll make your cakes and pies. Open daily for breakfast and lunch.

Sticky Fingers $$
363 Atlantic Boulevard, Atlantic Beach
(904) 241-7427
www.stickyfingers.com
This Memphis-style rib house features ribs, chicken, and barbecue that is slow-smoked for hours with aged hickory wood. Rib connoisseurs will enjoy the Memphis dry ribs, prepared with the traditional dry spice rub and no sauce. Sticky Fingers has three rib flavors: Memphis Wet, slathered in Sticky Fingers' Memphis original sauce; spicy hot; and Carolina sweet. Try the hickory-smoked chicken and turkey wings. The menu also includes rotisserie-smoked chicken, burgers, dinner salads, and tempting desserts.

Dine indoors or outdoors on the screened patio. There is a happy hour every weekday. Open daily for lunch and dinner.

Sun Dog Diner $$$
207 Atlantic Boulevard, Neptune Beach
(904) 241-8221
This Art Deco restaurant has cozy booths separated by glass and chrome and '50s-style counter stools. The emphasis is on steak, seafood, and pasta dishes. Entrees include seared sesame tuna with ginger sauce, Caesar salad, grilled tuna salad, blackened New York strip, and bacon pork tenderloin with Kentucky bourbon sauce. The grill features seven styles of half-pound hamburgers.

For dessert there's upside-down apple pie and Oreo cheesecake. The weekend brunch offers steak and eggs, plus oatmeal pancakes and grilled vegetable omelettes. There's live music nightly. Visit the diner's Cobalt Room, an after-dinner cigar room offering an extensive list of premium cigars, fine cognacs, and single-malt scotches. Open for lunch and dinner daily with brunch on Saturday and Sunday.

Sunny Caribbee $$-$$$
100 First Street, Neptune Beach
(904) 270-8940
www.sunnycaribbee.com
Catch a little of the island flavor at Sunny Caribbee. Lunch and dinner are served every day. The upstairs bar is open until 2:00 A.M. daily, and a late-night menu is available until 1:00 A.M. The specialties include jerk chicken with mango salsa; oversize salads, including the seafood Cobb salad with shrimp and crabmeat; and seafood platters galore. For dessert try the Key lime pie. Friday and Saturday nights feature live music and dancing upstairs. Call ahead for reservations.

Tama's Sushi Restaurant $$$
106 First Street, Neptune Beach
(904) 241-0099
This small, casual beach restaurant has quickly become a favorite among Beaches' sushi lovers. Tama's features a full sushi bar and tempura, teriyaki, and katsu dishes in a smoke-free atmosphere. The seafood combinations are customer favorites. Beer, wine, and sake are served. Sushi and menu takeout are available. Open for dinner Tuesday through Sunday.

The Tavern & Grille Room at Sawgrass Village $$$
500 Sawgrass Village, Ponte Vedra Beach
(904) 285-3133
The Tavern is reminiscent of an old New York City tavern, and you'll immediately feel welcomed. The menu includes several types of cuisine, from American and Caribbean to Mediterranean and Asian. For starters try the lumpia rolls or the fresh hand-rolled sushi. Favorite dinner selections include the ginger-soy salmon, herb-crusted rack of lamb, bourbon rib-eye steak, and veal saltimbocca. The full-service bar has a good wine list and a daily happy hour. The Tavern also provides on- and off-site catering. Open for lunch Monday through Friday and dinner daily.

Thai Room $$$
1286 South Third Street
Jacksonville Beach
(904) 249-8444
Thai Room is spacious yet cozy and smoke-free. Dine at a table near the fountain or in one of four large booths complete with Thai pillows. Chef Thong Thine's specialties are crispy duck, snapper Lad Na, noodles of the drunk, and green curry. A large menu selection includes several vegetarian and spicy dishes, along with satay (chicken or beef), a customer favorite. For dessert there is purple sweet rice topped with coconut and served warm. The restaurant serves beer and has a large wine selection. Dine in or take out. Open for lunch Monday through Friday and dinner daily.

The 3rd Street Diner $$
223 Ninth Avenue South
Jacksonville Beach
(904) 270-0080
If you find yourself at the Beaches and have a hankering for breakfast—no matter

what time of day or night—fear not. The 3rd Street Diner is the ticket. "We serve breakfast 24/7," says owner and operator Nick Koutroumanos. Well, almost. The diner, opened in 2003, serves food from 6:00 A.M. to 2:00 A.M. seven days a week. Breakfast items are always available. Lunch and dinner dishes are also served. Specialties include fresh seafood and pasta dishes and Greek standards such as stuffed grape leaves, seafood mousaka, Greek salads, and gyros. There's a full bar. All of the baked goods are made at the restaurant. For dessert we recommend the New York–style cheesecake. Like any good diner worth its salt, 3rd Street Diner sports a granite counter and a fully stocked jukebox.

Tra Vini Italian Ristorante $$$$
216 Ponte Vedra Park Drive
Ponte Vedra Beach
(904) 273-2442

Gianni Recupito, owner of Mezza Luna in Neptune Beach, built a masterpiece with Tra Vini, which means "on the vine." Italian marble and tile, hand-painted murals, and high ceilings give Tra Vini an elegant dining atmosphere. Rich Italian pasta and seafood dishes are served along with such favorites as Angus steaks, tenderloin of buffalo, and veal chops. Ask for the snapper livornaise and osso buco; neither is on the menu, but they are frequently requested. Dine indoors or outdoors. A full bar is served. Private parties can be held in the wine cellar. Open nightly for dinner. Reservations accepted.

The Tree Steak House $$-$$$
725 Atlantic Boulevard, Atlantic Beach
(904) 241-5600

Man and woman can't live by seafood alone . . . even if you are at the beach. The Tree Steak House, in a strip center in Atlantic Beach, is the ideal alternative, especially if you don't want to have to take out a second mortgage to pay for dinner. The house specialty is rib-eye steak that your waiter will cut at your table, if you so desire. The rib eye costs $1.75 an ounce. OK, maybe you do want

seafood: Try the cashew grouper. Dinners are served with a baked potato and salad. Tree Steak House also features a full bar and lounge. Dinner is served daily.

Uli's European Restaurant $$$
216 11th Avenue South, Jacksonville Beach
(904) 241-4969

This charming old-world restaurant serves haute German cuisine: wiener, jaeger, Holstein, and veal schnitzels; sauerbraten; potato pancakes; and daily fresh seafood. Try one of Uli's signature steaks or filets or one of the house specials. Ice creams and desserts are homemade. Uli's offers German draft beers and more than 60 wines. Full service catering is available. Open for lunch and dinner Tuesday through Sunday.

FORT GEORGE

Palms Fish Camp $-$$
6359 Heckscher Drive, Fort George
(904) 251-3004

If you were to drive along Heckscher Drive and see Palms Fish Camp, chances are good you'd keep driving right past the shabby-looking place. What a mistake. Insiders know that if you want country-style seafood—and plenty of it—in Jacksonville, the place to go is Palms Fish Camp.

It's best to arrive early for the seafood buffet dinner. Grab yourself a table and wait for chef Art Jennette to ring his dinner bell, signaling the start of the buffet. And what a buffet. There are mounds of lightly breaded fried shrimp, whiting filets, pans of homemade stuffed blue crabs, delicious cheese grits, collard greens, and scalloped potatoes with pieces of seafood. The seafood buffet is $16.95 per person. If you plan to go on a weekend, you'd best make reservations. The restaurant is small and fills up quickly.

On Thursday night Chef Art puts on an all-you-can-eat fish fry, featuring fried shrimp and whiting. The price is a bargain at $7.95. There's also a lunch buffet Monday through Friday from 11:00 A.M. to 1:30 P.M.

The restaurant overlooks the salt marshes off the St. Johns River. Be sure to check out the sunsets over the marsh.

TINSELTOWN/SOUTHSIDE

China Gourmet $
9734-11 Deer Lake Court
(904) 998-2121
In the mood for wonton soup, egg rolls, and chicken fried rice? How about some sushi, like a California roll? Then head to China Gourmet, where there's a full sushi bar and Chinese buffet all day long. This modern restaurant is located off Southside Boulevard, right next door to the Tinseltown movie theaters. The "all u can eat" buffet is the big attraction and includes both the Japanese sushi bar and the Chinese buffet. Current prices are $6.99 for lunch and $8.99 for the buffet dinner. Fresh items are rotated periodically throughout the lunch rush (and it's a big one) and evening. Dinner also includes fresh seafood on the all-you-can-eat buffet tables, such as snow crab legs, mussels, and shrimp. Also on the dinner buffet line are roast beef, salmon—just about anything your heart desires. China Gourmet specializes in large parties and has a private room that can hold up to 250 people. Open Monday through Sunday, this is just the type of restaurant Jacksonville loves: a plentiful all-you-can-eat buffet at an affordable price.

Gallery Eclectic Bistro $$$$
9753 Deer Lake Court
(904) 997-8320
The food is the real art in this modern-style restaurant, which features a decor almost as artful as the food presentations. Gallery Eclectic is a popular lunch spot for workers at nearby Southside office parks, when the afternoon menu includes a variety of wraps, homemade soups, salads, and sandwiches. Be sure to try the blue crab cake appetizer, served on a bed of citrus-cucumber relish with a remoulade sauce. The restaurant's eclectic surf and turf is a popular entree and includes lobster ravioli in a light sauce with a six-ounce filet that's been wrapped in bacon and stuffed with Gorgonzola cheese. Yum-yum. If you have room for dessert, share a hot chocolate soufflé. It's enough to feed a party of four, and it's delicious. The wine list is extensive, and expensive, but then, if you're eating here, that probably won't matter.

All the art displayed in the restaurant is for sale, with well over half of the proceeds going directly to Wolfson's Children's Hospital right here in downtown Jacksonville. If you're looking to have a glass of wine with a friend after work, the Gallery is a great choice. Drinks are two-for-one Monday through Friday from 3:00 to 7:00 P.M. Dinner is served daily.

Jacksonville Ale House $$
9711 Deer Lake Court
(904) 565-2882
www.alehouseinc.com
When all the other restaurants have closed in Tinseltown, this one is still open (until 2:00 A.M.), serving drinks and a full menu. Value is the buzzword at this sports-themed, family-friendly restaurant. The decor is nautical, and the space is large, wood paneled, dark, and cool—a welcome relief from the hot Florida sun. TVs set high on the walls surrounding the 30-seat bar are tuned to sports and news channels There are 32 beers on tap, from domestic to imports to microbrews, and happy hour starts early, at 11:00 A.M., most days of the week.

The menu is about what you'd expect from a sports-themed restaurant. There's everything from chicken wings and nachos to fillets and ribs. There's also a raw bar with oysters, clams, and shrimp. Lunch is extremely popular here, so arrive either on the early or late side if you don't want to wait for a table. Lunch specials, for $4.95, change daily. Most entrees are under $10, and the menu includes a full selection of pasta dishes, burgers, salads, and sandwiches. There are 30 Ale House restaurants in this Florida-only chain, and children get a free scoop of ice cream for dessert in every one of them.

Kan-Ki Japanese Steakhouse & Sushi Bar $$$
4483 Southside Boulevard
(904) 642-2626

The serene Japanese rock gardens outside the front door belie the bustle of activity you find when you step inside Kan-Ki Steakhouse. This is a busy place on Saturday night, when 14 Japanese chefs are furiously slicing and stir-frying dinner for guests at 14 different tables. If you don't like to watch a chef put on a show, you can also sit at a quiet four-top or even the sushi bar, but there, again, the showier aspects of Japanese cooking return.

Guests come to this restaurant for two reasons: the fresh sushi crafted right before your eyes at the sushi bar and the tender Black Angus beef used in stir-frys. The shrimp should also not be overlooked. They're imported fresh from the Gulf of Mexico and are sweet and delicious in sushi creations or in the tempura. Be sure to start your lunch or dinner with an order of edamame, which are boiled and salted soybeans. Appetizers just don't come any more healthful. After that, sip a bowl of miso soup and you're ready for your entree. Good Japanese food is simple but high in quality, and Kan-Ki, located in Tinseltown and convenient to Southpoint hotels, does not disappoint. It's open Monday through Friday for lunch from 11:00 A.M. to 2:00 P.M. and for dinner from 4:00 P.M. till closing.

Madrid $-$$
11233 Beach Boulevard
(904) 642-3741

If you love Latino food, Madrid is an excellent choice for either lunch or dinner. Located in an unassuming strip center on the Southside, this gaily decorated restaurant bursts with personality when you step inside. It's open daily from 11:00 A.M. to 9:00 P.M. except Sunday.

The Venezuelan owners serve up popular dishes from a variety of Latino countries. Their Cuban sandwich of ham and roast pork is popular with the lunch crowd, as is their delicious version of the Cuban shredded beef specialty *ropa vieja*. *Sopas,* or soups, are considered a specialty of the house and come with an entree if you wish. They make just three: black bean, chile verde, and caldo gallego—white bean soup with Spanish sausage and potatoes. We liked the chile verde best. This sopa of roasted, peeled, and diced green chilies, slow cooked with a light chicken broth, goes down smooth but, depending on your level of peppery comfort, can pack quite a punch. The owners also make a popular Venezuelan dish that melts in your mouth called arepas, corn cakes filled with ropa vieja, picadillo, roast pork, and cheese. Finish it all off with a Nicaraguan dessert called Tres Leches—pound cake dipped in a mix of three different types of milk—and you've gone "Latino" without ever having to leave the states. It costs about $10 per person to eat here if you drink water and don't order beer or wine.

Moe's Southwest Grill $
9700-3 Deer Lake Court
(904) 620-8436

If you're looking for a hearty meal that won't break your bank account, come here. There is no decor at this small restaurant located in a Tinseltown strip mall, but the food is great. It's made from fresh ingredients, and there's plenty of it. The most popular menu item is a big burrito called the Homewrecker for $5.69, which is chock-full of rice, beans, your choice of meat, cheese, salsa, guacamole, sour cream, and lettuce. There are three main-ingredient choices: chicken, steak, or tofu, which is the soy/vegetarian option. The names of most of the menu items will confound you; for instance, what's a "Joey Bag of Donuts"? It's a burrito of rice, beans, choice of meat, cheese, and salsa for $4.99, of course. Kids meals cost just $2.99 and include a hard or soft taco or a burrito, plus a soft drink and a cookie. The original Moe's is a popular eatery on Peachtree Street in Atlanta. This is a new franchise, and the owner is already looking to expand to other Jacksonville neighborhoods like San Marco and the Beaches.

Pattaya Thai Restaurant $$
10916 Atlantic Boulevard
(904) 646-9506

Pattaya Thai is among Jacksonville's first Thai restaurants, and it's still a favorite. Located in a strip mall near Craig Airport, Pattaya Thai is a quiet oasis of good food. In fact, the readers of *Folio Weekly,* a free local magazine, voted Pattaya Thai the best Thai restaurant in Jacksonville for seven years in a row. The portions are large, the food is fresh, and the chefs do not use MSG. Be sure to order the spring rolls—they're delicious, as is the pad thai. All the soups are homemade (the coconut soup is especially good). All dishes can be ordered from mild to way, way, way hot.

Tony Roma's $$$
4521 Southside Boulevard
(904) 996-6990

If you've never eaten at a Tony Roma's, you're in for a treat. Tony Roma's, as the restaurant likes to say, is famous for ribs. Indeed, if you're not a rib lover, you may want to rethink your restaurant selection. Baby back ribs begin at $12.49 for half a slab and go up to $17.99 for full slabs. The ribs come with one of Tony's four famous sauces, or you can get a sampler platter with a variety of sauces. The sauces range from sweet, like Carolina Honey, to Tony Roma's Red Hot. There's also a smoky sauce called Blue Ridge Smokies and the granddaddy of them all, Tony Roma's Original, a tomato-based sweet sauce. For an appetizer, the onion loaf is extremely popular. It's lightly breaded whole onions, formed into a loaf and deep-fried.

Those who don't eat ribs can order from the rest of the extensive menu, which includes soups, salads, burgers, and grilled chicken. But the ribs in this contemporary, exposed-brick Texan restaurant are the thing, and you often see customers leaving with a four-pack of Tony's sauces to enjoy at home. Located in its own stand-alone restaurant on the edge of Tinseltown, Tony's is open daily from 11:00 A.M. until closing.

MANDARIN

Clark's Fish Camp Seafood
Restaurant $$-$$$
12903 Hood Landing Road
(904) 268-3474

Tucked away on Julington Creek at the foot of Hood Landing Road, this former fish camp turned seafood restaurant has been serving up watery wonders for decades. In the early days it was a ramshackle wooden shanty that sold bait and tackle next to a boat ramp. Nowadays it's a ramshackle wooden shanty that sells seafood and prime rib next to a boat ramp. These days, though, the screened porch has been glassed in and air-conditioned, but you can still eat outside on the deck overlooking scenic Julington Creek. Just bring some bug juice and make sure there's a breeze, or the mosquitoes will eat *you* for dinner.

This is a favorite restaurant for boaters, who often pull up in their boat, tie up to the deck, and eat inside. If you're adventurous, try the Florida gator tail (yep, tastes like chicken) or the fried catfish. The fried shrimp dinner is as delicious as you'd expect here, and it comes with fried hush puppies and two sides, like coleslaw and a baked potato or french fries. Landlubbers can order chicken or red meat, including prime rib.

Clark's has a large, loyal following, so try to get here as early as possible. There's a good chance you'll have a wait on the weekends, and the restaurant only accepts reservations for parties of eight or more. Clark's also serves lunch on Saturday and Sunday starting at 11:30 A.M. Monday through Friday it opens at 4:30 P.M. and closes by 10:00 P.M. The old fish camp style of this restaurant, plus its location on the creek, makes it a great choice for anyone who'd enjoy seeing what rustic Florida was once all about.

NIGHTLIFE

"Clubbing" in Jacksonville can be a challenge since many of the most popular nightclubs are far apart. This means that your designated driver could do some major driving if you're bar-hopping from one side of town to the other. But new clubs are opening all the time, especially at the Beaches, so bar-hop within a certain neighborhood to minimize travel—or taxi fares—and still have a good time.

Patrons must be 21 to buy alcohol in Florida, though 18-to-21-year-olds are permitted inside most clubs; they just can't buy an alcoholic drink. All bars and clubs must close by 2:00 A.M.

Many of Jacksonville's best nightspots are also popular restaurants, so count on parking problems and crowded venues. We've noted cover charges when they apply and also the general type of crowd each club attracts.

Count on very casual dress at most Beaches bars—we're talking flip-flops and jeans. In fact, some Beaches residents operate under this motto: "No shoes, no shirt, no problem." On the Southside and downtown, however, club attire is dressier, along the lines of business professional.

Finally, Jacksonville's casino ships are popular entertainment. The only casino gambling for landlubbers in Florida is on Native American reservations, which are located mostly in Southern Florida. But the slot machines and blackjack tables come to life once cruise ships are a mile offshore in international waters. There are two casino ships in Jacksonville, both based in Mayport for easy access to the Atlantic.

i
Information about many Jacksonville nightclubs can be found on the Internet at www.jaxclubs.com.

THE BEACHES

AJ's Food, Fun & Sports
1728 North Third Street
Jacksonville Beach
(904) 246-8099
AJ's is a great place to watch sports, although don't dare call it a sports bar. It's a restaurant with nine television sets tuned to football games or other sporting events. It's a place where you can eat prime rib or New York strip as you watch the Seminoles and Gators. The restaurant also offers a full complement of fried, sports bar–type food, such as chicken wings. In fact, on Wild Wednesday, it's all the chicken wings you can eat for $6.95 from 4:00 P.M. till close. Just don't call it a sports bar.

The Atlantic
333 North First Street, Jacksonville Beach
(904) 249-3338
Mature 20s-and-older patrons frequent The Atlantic, which is decorated like a New Orleans bordello with huge gilded mirrors, red velvet curtains, and comfy couches. The inside club area is somewhat small and spills into Magellan's Oceanfront Restaurant, but there's room enough for live music and dancing, especially on the weekend. The outside oceanfront bar starts its happy hour at 3:00 P.M. The Atlantic is located in the same complex as the Ocean Club, and finding a parking place around here can take awhile.

Bo's Coral Reef
201 Fifth Avenue North
Jacksonville Beach
(904) 246-9874
www.bosclub.com
Open since 1964, Bo's Coral Reef is the only gay and lesbian nightclub at the Beaches. Bo's offers nightclub yin and yang: a totally rocking dance floor in the

main bar and a quiet outdoor patio bar in the garden. This place is big, too, 6,000 square feet, and comes complete with a 16-foot video screen for football games, live parties, or concerts. Bo's is located just 1 block off the ocean. Be sure and try one of Bo's Famous Frozen Margaritas, just $3.00 on Tuesday nights.

Bukkets Baha Beach Club
222 North Oceanfront, Jacksonville Beach
(904) 246-7701
Young navy enlisted men in their 20s hang out at this bar on the boardwalk in Jacksonville Beach. The outside beachfront area is popular year-round; it's a great place to sit with friends and enjoy beer, wings, and the Atlantic Ocean. This is a busy corner of Jacksonville Beach, and the people-watching around here is great. If that doesn't amuse you, shoot a round of pool inside on one of Bukkets many pool tables.

Champs Lounge
1000 PGA Tour Boulevard
Ponte Vedra Beach
(904) 285-7777
Champs is located downstairs in the Sawgrass Marriott Hotel, which itself is a treat to see. The crowd here is usually older, often hotel guests, but also locals who are looking to kick off their shoes and have some fun. This is a good place to meet men who've come to the resort to golf. There's live music Wednesday through Saturday starting at 8:30 P.M., and when you need a break, check out Cascades, the bar right outside Champs in the Marriott's atrium lobby. Cascades serves late-night meals for revelers who've worked up an appetite.

Freebird Cafe
200 North First Street, Jacksonville Beach
(904) 246-2473
www.freebirdcafe.com
Ronnie VanZant's famous lyric "If I leave here tomorrow, will you still remember me?" is immortalized in this cafe started by his widow, Judy, and daughter, Melody. Authentic Skynyrd memorabilia, as well as gold and platinum records, is encased on the walls of this eatery reminiscent of a Hard Rock Cafe. (See the Close-up in this chapter for more on Jacksonville's own Lynyrd Skynyrd band.) Freebird Cafe may be a bar and a restaurant, but at heart it's a music club where bands new—and not so new— perform. Blues guitarists from all over the country often play here. There's usually a cover charge in the evening depending on who's performing. Freebird is located in the heart of Jacksonville Beach, directly across the street from Bukkets and just a few blocks away from Ocean Club, the Atlantic, Lynch's, and the Ritz.

The Fly's Tie
177 Sailfish Drive, Atlantic Beach
(904) 246-4293
www.flystieirishpub.com
If you've ever been to Ireland, you'll quickly realize that The Fly's Tie is pretty close to the real thing, right down to the lace curtains on the windows. Guinness is often the beer of choice in this small, smoky pub, where people actually play darts and corned beef and cabbage is served on special nights. Celtic Soul, a popular Irish band with a strong regional following, often plays concerts here. Tuesday night is open-mike night, and Guinness is a dollar cheaper than usual all night long. Weekends usually bring live Irish folk music and a loyal crowd of Irish pub lovers.

The Lemon Bar
120 Atlantic Boulevard, Neptune Beach
(behind the Sea Horse Oceanfront Inn)
(904) 246-2175
This is as Insiders as it gets. The Lemon Bar is a popular hangout for Neptune Beach and Atlantic Beach residents who love to ride their bikes to the bar for an evening cocktail. It's sort of hard to find, located behind the Sea Horse Oceanfront Inn and on the ocean. The motel folks operate the bar, though it doesn't feel like

Lynyrd Skynyrd

If you grew up on Jacksonville's Westside in the late sixties and early seventies, chances are you have a Lynyrd Skynyrd story to tell. For the uninitiated, Lynyrd Skynyrd, a popular Southern rock band, was named after Leonard Skinner, a gym teacher at Robert E. Lee High School in Jacksonville who suspended two of the band members for repeated dress code violations, including hair that touched their ears. Ronnie VanZant, the band's undisputed leader, organized the group in 1964. It initially played under many names before arriving at Lynyrd Skynyrd, a "disguised dis" to the old coach. (Leonard Skinner, by the way, is actively involved in helping keep the band's memory alive. He often attends Skynyrd events and signs autographs.) Perhaps the group's most famous song is "Freebird," which, according to BMI, has been played on the radio more than two million times. The opening lyrics seem to foreshadow Ronnie Van-Zant's fate: "If I leave here tomorrow, will you still remember me?" By October 20, 1977, the band was riding high, en route to a gig in Baton Rouge, Louisiana, when its chartered plane literally ran out of gas over a Mississippi swamp. The resulting crash killed three of the seven band members, including Ronnie VanZant. These days, Lynyrd Skynyrd still exists with three original band members and Ronnie's younger brother Johnny singing vocals.

a hotel bar—it feels much more separate than that. Patrons like to sip frozen concoctions while listening to the waves crash on the beach. The bar is weather dependent, however, and has closed in the past during winter months and rainy periods. Best to call first.

Lynch's Irish Pub
514 North First Street, Jacksonville Beach
(904) 249–5181

On Monday this Irish pub isn't so Irish. It's eighties night, and the 20-to-30-year-olds who pack the place for a retro evening wouldn't have it any other way. Lynch's is known for its good music, good pub food, good drinks, and good Guinness. If you want the Irish pub thing, go early, around 5:00 P.M. That's when you can order a plate of fish-and-chips and talk with the bartenders, who hail from Northern Ireland. Lynch's was voted the best pub in Jacksonville in 2000 by the readers of *Folio Weekly* magazine. It serves a full menu until 1:30 A.M.

Monkey's Uncle
1850 South Third Street
Jacksonville Beach
(904) 246–1070

When you just have to karaoke, come here. The karaoke machine is located right by the front door, so if you're really embarrassed about your performance, you can make a quick getaway. The drinks are cheap and strong here, and the crowd skews older. Monkey's Uncle has been a watering hole at the beach for years. It's located in a strip center near a popular movie house and includes a pool room and an indoor patio bar. On Friday there's usually a live band starting at 9:30 P.M.

Moon Grille and Oyster Bar
1396 Beach Boulevard, Jacksonville Beach
(904) 241-1894

It's hard to put a label on the Moon Grille. Families often come here on Friday and Saturday nights during baseball season because the bar is located in a strip center right next to a large Little League complex. Moon Grille has the feel of a sports bar with its numerous TVs, but there's also live music, which makes it popular with 20-somethings out on the town. And then there are the oysters, which draw a crowd all their own. These oysters are brought in fresh from Appalachicola, a town on the Gulf coast of Florida, south of Tallahassee; oyster lovers swear by them.

Ocean Club
401 North First Street, Jacksonville Beach
(904) 242-8884

The Ocean Club is a current favorite on the Beaches club scene. It's located in a renovated lounge right on the ocean. There's a huge room for dancing, a pool room, an outside oceanfront deck, and a big bar to sit around, order drinks, and meet people. *NOTE:* There is a dress code here, unusual for Beaches nightspots, which means no flip-flops, sneakers, shorts, or jeans. Lots of would-be patrons get angry over this, but the club has no problem filling up; in fact, there's usually a long line to get in, despite a cover charge of about $3.00 on Friday and Saturday nights. The Ocean Club is popular with just about everyone ages 25 to 45.

Pete's Bar
117 First Street, Neptune Beach
(904) 249-9158

Author John Grisham turned Pete's Bar into a national icon when he made it a featured locale in his book *The Brethren.* Pete's was the first bar to open in Duval County after Prohibition, and it no doubt has some regulars who've been coming ever since. The crowd here is very mixed: neighborhood residents who play pool and drink longnecks and tourists who've read that no bar-hopping excursion to the Beaches is complete without a stop at Pete's. This place can get mighty crowded, which makes it difficult to find a seat. Oh, and if you value your life, try not to bump into a pool player while he or she is taking a shot. They're not very gracious about it.

Ragtime Tavern and Seafood Grille
207 Atlantic Boulevard, Atlantic Beach
(904) 241-7877

Ragtime is a very popular brewpub, bar, and tapas bar (and that means three full bars here) a block from the ocean. It's also a popular restaurant (see the Restaurants chapter). The crowd here is more mature, late 20s and up, and an entire core of regulars who live within walking distance hardly let a night go by without a visit. Be sure to try a glass of Dolphin's Breath, a popular beer brewed on the premises and named by a local contest winner. Ragtime is a good place to meet a Jaguar, a Jaguar cheerleader, or a naval officer. Expect large crowds here on the weekend and live music in the brewpub that reverberates throughout the restaurant and tavern.

The Ritz Cocktail Lounge and Package Store
185 North Third Avenue
Jacksonville Beach
(904) 246-2255

Friendly. That's the best way to describe the Ritz, which is one of the most popular nightspots at the Beaches. The drinks are cheap, and the waitstaff and bartenders are accommodating. There's also a big bar with lots of seats, which makes this a good place to meet new people. The Ritz also has live music, a small dance floor, and plenty of pool tables—though when things get pumping, it can get so crowded that it's difficult to dance or play pool.

Giovanni's Restaurant on Beach Boulevard in Jacksonville Beach has a cozy piano bar that's a romantic place to share a nightcap with someone special.

Roxy
14185-1 Beach Boulevard
(904) 223-3622
Roxy's is a favorite nightspot with 18-to-25-year-olds. It's located west of the Intracoastal Waterway in a strip center not far from the University of North Florida. That's why Monday night is College Night at the Roxy, and the place is often packed. Roxy's has a big dance floor, which fills up quickly on another popular night, Saturday, which is Latin Night. Tuesday, drinks are $2.00 and DJs spin into the wee hours. Friday is Ladies Night, which means drinks are a dollar, plus cover.

Shelby's Coffee Shoppe
200 First Street, Neptune Beach
(904) 249-2922
A bustling coffee shop by day, Shelby's turns into a popular coffee bar at night, complete with live music, beer, wine, and, of course, coffee. For 22 years Shelby Hicks has been serving up smiles and a warm cup of coffee for Beaches residents. At some point just about everyone who lives in Atlantic and Neptune Beaches has walked or pedaled to her shop, which is located a block from the ocean. Families come here at night to sit at an outside table, chat with friends, sip a glass of wine, enjoy the music, and let the kids run around the large patio area well within the watchful eyes of their parents. During day-

The Florida Highway Patrol often sets up late-night roadblocks on Beach and Atlantic Boulevards, the two main highways leading to the Beaches, to check for drunk drivers or anyone driving with a revoked or suspended license.

time it's not uncommon to see locals sipping coffee or tea at one of Shelby's tables as they hold a planning meeting for a local festival or volunteer project. Local photographers and artists display their work in the shop, which otherwise is simply decorated with wooden tables and painted concrete floors. Shelby's is especially popular on Friday nights when local bands offer up free music. It's open Sunday through Thursday from 7:30 A.M. to 10:00 P.M., Friday and Saturday from 7:00 A.M. to 11:00 P.M.

Sneakers
111 North First Street, Jacksonville Beach
(904) 482-1000
www.sneakerssportsgrill.com
You'll have to go a long way to find a sports bar with as many television sets as this one: 85 small screens; 6 huge, high-resolution ones; and 5 flat, high-definition sets around the inside bar. On Monday nights during football season, the bar is also the set for a live television show broadcast by a local station about the Jacksonville Jaguars. Sneakers is located right across the street from the ocean (and the historic Red Cross Life Saving Station), which means there's a lovely covered patio with, yep, outdoor TV sets. It's also within walking distance of a half dozen popular Jacksonville Beach nightclubs. At night you can't miss the place: The entire building is trimmed in light blue neon and looks as though it's about to take off. Sneakers is popular with just about everyone, especially during football season.

Sun Dog Diner
207 Atlantic Boulevard, Neptune Beach
(904) 241-8221
As the name suggests, this is largely an eatery (see the Restaurants chapter), but after 9:30 P.M. it's also a club with a full bar, dance floor, and live music. Sun Dog is located a block from the ocean, across the street from the Ragtime Tavern and Seafood Grille. Locals come to hear friends play music—everything from acoustic guitar to modern jazz. The decor

is great; it's a new diner built to look like an old one.

DOWNTOWN

The Bud Zone
Alltel Stadium, 1 Stadium Place
(904) 854-0614

There are two hotspots in Alltel Stadium: the football field and The Bud Zone, Jacksonville's ultimate 15,000-square-foot sports bar. The Bud Zone is open to the public for every Jaguars away game, and it's open for Monday-night football and college football, too. Ticket holders can also hang out in The Bud Zone during every Jaguars home game, where fans watch the action live from the Zone's balcony or on one of its 55 plasma televisions. To get to The Bud Zone, park your car in Lot D at Alltel Stadium, then enter the stadium through Gate 4 and take the escalators to the Bud Zone Level. The food is standard sports bar stuff: chicken wings, sandwiches, jumbo hot dogs, and away-game specials like two-for-one drinks. In addition, there's a set here for live broadcasts of the *Coach Del Rio Show,* which incorporates the stadium and Bud Zone patrons in some of its shots.

Casbah
5628 St. Johns Avenue
(904) 981-9966
www.thecasbahcafe.com

Looking for something fun, new, and different? Check out the Casbah, a popular Middle Eastern–style cafe. For $8.00 you can smoke flavored tobacco (apple, banana, grape, etc.) in a hookah, a large pipe with several hoses. Hookah fans say they're hooked on this smooth way to enjoy tobacco. Belly dancers will keep you entertained Thursday through Saturday as you sample delectable vegetarian dishes. The Casbah also offers a large selection of global beers like a Kingfisher from India or a Zambesi from Zimbabwe. There's usually a nice crowd here in the evenings, mostly young professionals.

Eclate
331 East Bay Street
(904) 354-8833
www.eclateclub.com

Step inside this modern downtown jazz club and you'll feel a bit like Dorothy in *The Wizard of Oz.* That's because Eclate doesn't feel like your typical Jacksonville club; it feels like someplace in Chicago or Atlanta. Located downtown, a short walk from the Adams Mark and Omni hotels, Eclate is a pioneer. It's one of the first new businesses to stake a claim in an area that for decades was the sole domain of bail bondsmen and bums. Now this sleek, smoke-free club is attracting large crowds to hear a variety of local, regional, and national upcoming jazz musicians. There's a small cover at the door, and you should definitely call ahead for reservations so you can get a private leather booth near the music. If you don't you'll find yourself standing in the club's bar area, which actually is not a bad thing because there's plenty of room to grab a stool and listen to music while striking up a conversation with other jazz aficionados. Eclate serves only beer and wine and heavy appetizers in the evening, and it's become a popular lunch hangout and after-work spot for attorneys and state prosecutors who work nearby.

Endo Exo
1224 Kings Avenue
(904) 396-7733
www.clubendoexo.com

This is as hip as it gets in good old Jacksonville. In fact, Endo Exo describes itself as "more South Beach than San Marco," referring in part to the downtown Jacksonville neighborhood where it's located. There are three basic areas to this club: the main bar, where most people hang out; the outside patio, where smokers gather; and a dance floor that has big couches and a bed. There's live music on Friday and Saturday nights, which means a $5.00 cover charge for clubgoers. There's also a dress code because Endo likes to think of itself as a place for the 21-to-55 crowd, not for teeny-boppers. The code calls for stylish dress, which the owner says means no hats, no T-shirts, and no flip-flops. Be sure to check out Endo's Web site; the club's owner works as a computer consultant by day.

Jack Rabbits
1528 Hendricks Avenue
(904) 398-7496

Located in a transitional area of San Marco, Jack Rabbits is hard to miss. It's painted bright red outside and looks something like a hole in the wall. Inside, the decor is, well, grungy, but the people who come here don't really care. They come to hear good live music, which Jack Rabbits delivers, from local groups to national touring acts like Dick Dale, the king of the surf guitar. Call the club for show schedules and ticket information.

Metro
2929 Plum Street
(904) 388-7192

There's always something at Metro, which calls itself Jacksonville's leading gay and lesbian nightclub. It's located in Riverside, a near-downtown neighborhood close to the intersection of College Street and Wil-lowbranch Road. Often-outrageous female impersonators are popular here most every night of the week. On Thursday Sondra Todd (a female impersonator) hosts Sondra Todd's Star Search, which is popular with emerging talent of all per-suasions. Metro opens at 4:00 P.M. Monday through Friday, 6:00 P.M. on Saturday, and noon on Sunday.

River City Brewing Company
835 Museum Circle
(904) 398-2299
www.rivercitybrew.com

Voted the "Best Singles Bar in Jack-sonville" in 2001 by the readers of *Folio*

Weekly magazine, River City enjoys a beautiful location on the south bank of the St. Johns River. It's a popular after-work spot for downtown professionals as well as a favorite watering hole for tourists. There's a large outside deck where bands play every Friday. There's also a large indoor bar that makes it easy to strike up a conversation with someone while you're waiting for your drink. On Thursday a local improvisational group presents a free interactive comedy show.

Square One
1974 San Marco Boulevard
(904) 306-9004

Home of the Martini Monday, Square One is a hip club located in the heart of San Marco. It's popular with young professionals, who often come after work for happy hour from 4:00 to 7:00 P.M., when beer, wine, and mixed drinks are all half price. Square One is also a good place to go later in the evening after a movie or dinner in San Marco. There's always something happening, from live music to DJs, and there's often a cover after 10:00 P.M., when the bands begin playing. If you get hungry, check out the Pom Thai restaurant upstairs.

SOUTHSIDE AND MANDARIN

Bourbon Street Station
1770 St. Johns Bluff Road
(904) 641-8777
www.bourbonstreetstation.com

If you like to go club hopping but don't like to drive all over the place, come here. Bourbon Street Station offers five clubs all under one roof, each with a totally differ-ent atmosphere, in a very large space that used to be a home improvement store. You pay a single $10.00 cover charge that gets you into everything, starting with Bourbon Street, a replica of the famous New Orleans hot spot. This Bourbon Street comes complete with sidewalks, street lamps, fire hydrants, a sax player, a

i *Restaurant Medure on Highway A1A North in Ponte Vedra has a great jazz bar that rocks on Friday and Saturday nights.*

psychic—even girls on balconies throwing beads. You might be tempted to spend the entire night on Bourbon Street, but you probably won't because there's so much to do here. There's Mardi Gras, a Top 40 and hip-hop dance club; Crazy Horse Saloon, a country bar; The Varsity Club, which features live bands and a karaoke bar; The Blue Room, a piano bar; and Studebaker's, featuring music from the seventies and eighties. It's a great concept: one building, one cover, and five totally different clubs. Jacksonville has embraced it, and chances are you will, too.

The Comedy Zone
I-295 and San Jose Boulevard, Mandarin
(904) 292-HAHA (4242)
www.comedyzone.com
Located inside the Ramada Inn Mandarin, the Comedy Zone is the place to go in Jacksonville for anyone who believes laughter is the best medicine. Brett Butler has performed here, so has Carrot Top, even Mickey Rooney. The club doesn't get as many celebrity acts as it would like, but lesser known comedians can be very entertaining. The Ramada Inn also offers special package deals that include a room, dinner, and tickets to the show. Otherwise, show tickets range from $6.00 to $9.00, depending on the night.

Seven Bridges Grille & Brewery
9735 North Gate Parkway
(904) 997-1999
This is a good place to come for drinks or dinner before or after taking in a movie at Cinemark Tinseltown, a 20-screen movie complex on the other side of the parking lot. Seven Bridges is also a popular after-work place for Southside employees. Be sure to try one of the brewery's six different microbrews. The Sweet Magnolia Brown Ale is especially popular.

South Street Tavern and Grille
9720 Deer Lake Court
(904) 996-8882
Located in an entertainment area called Tinseltown, South Street claims to have the largest dance floor in Jacksonville. The dance floor is put to good use, especially on Tuesday when free tango lessons are offered to all comers. On Monday the karaoke crowd takes over. Someone once described the clientele here as divorced men and women 28 to 45 back on the circuit and looking for a good time. Expect a cover charge.

GAMBLING VENUES

La Cruise Casino
4738 Ocean Street, Mayport
(904) 241-7200, (800) 752-1778
www.lacruise.com
Jacksonville's casino ships are popular with gamblers and nongamblers alike. The gamblers like to climb aboard for obvious reasons; the nongamblers enjoy the opportunity to get out on the water for as little as five bucks a ticket. La Cruise offers two decks of entertainment, including food, bars, live music, big-screen TVs, and, of course, blackjack, slot machines, and bingo. Cruises are generally twice a day from 11:00 A.M. to 4:00 P.M. and 7:00 P.M. to midnight.

Orange Park Kennel Club
455 Park Avenue, Orange Park
(904) 646-0001
www.jaxkennel.com
There are a handful of greyhound tracks in Northeast Florida, all owned by the same company. We think the track in Orange Park is the best; certainly it's the most popular. You can cheer your dog to the finish line from a variety of vantage points here, including railside, the grandstands, the Paddock Club clubhouse, or the Favorites Eatery and Lounge, a grill. The Orange Park Kennel Club is easy to find—just south of the intersection of I-295 and Park Avenue. It's open Monday through Saturday (except Tuesday) at 7:45 P.M. There are matinees on Wednesday and Saturday at 12:30 P.M. and Sunday at 1:00 P.M. Entry fees are minimal, 50 cents to $2.00, and sometimes you can even get in free—say, if you're a senior citizen attending a matinee.

> *For the very latest on what bands are playing where, pick up a copy of* Folio Weekly, *Jacksonville's free alternative magazine.*

The Poker Room
6322 Racetrack Road
(904) 646-0002
www.jaxkennel.com

Located on the second floor of the St. Johns Greyhound Park, The Poker Room is operated by the Jacksonville Kennel Club. The dogs no longer run here, but you can watch them run (and see other sporting events) on television as you play Texas hold 'em, 7-card stud, Omaha, 7-card stud 8 or better, Omaha 8 or better, and crazy pineapple. Expect to buy at least $40 worth of poker chips if you want to get into a game. Once you do you can hold 'em and fold 'em at one of 40 tables in this smoke-free room. The busiest time of the week is Saturday afternoon, when the owners say the place fills up with their two major types of customers: college students and retirees. The minimum age to play here is 18; even the youngest participants quickly learn that they are playing not against the dealer, but against other players. The pots reach over $50 quite often, and it's customary to tip the dealer a buck or two if you win a hand. The Poker Room offers a full bar and a snack bar with deli sandwiches, hot dogs, and other foods.

SunCruz Casino
4378 Ocean Street, Mayport
(904) 249-9300, (800) 474-DICE
www.suncruzcasino.com

SunCruz and La Cruise are located within a quarter mile of each other in the historic fishing village of Mayport and consequently are very competitive. They both offer the same basic amenities: twice-daily cruises, food, drink, big-screen TVs, and ocean gambling once the ship gets a mile off the Florida coast and into international waters. SunCruz has the advantage of being the first cruise ship you see when you drive into Mayport, though La Cruise has been in town longer. SunCruz operates a smaller ship (up to 600 passengers) than La Cruise and is owned by the largest casino cruise company in Florida.

SHOPPING ⊛

orty-five percent of all travelers go shopping. So says the U.S. Commerce Department, which identified shopping as the second most popular, spontaneously planned activity for travelers after sightseeing.

What follows should give shoppers, spontaneous or otherwise, a starting point. We've focused on several popular shopping areas where tourists are likely to travel, including the Beaches, Riverside Avondale, San Marco, and the malls. Downtown Jacksonville isn't a shopping mecca because, like a lot of cities, most of the stores headed for the suburbs in the sixties and seventies. But Jacksonville Landing and a few scattered specialty stores are still downtown draws.

By and large, the Jacksonville shopping experience is about bargains, and the malls are the best place to get good deals. Many specialty stores, however, are latching onto this bargain spirit and have started a new type of sale: Stores mail out cards advertising a big one-day sale that begins early, often at 8:00 A.M., with 40 percent off all sale merchandise. By 9:00 A.M. the discount has been reduced to 30 percent, and by 10:00 A.M. the sale stuff is 20 percent off. In the final 11:00 A.M. hour of the sale, merchandise is discounted just 10 percent. At noon the sale is over.

In this chapter we describe Jacksonville's main shopping areas, followed by a listing of our favorite specialty shops. We couldn't possibly list all the fine stores in Jacksonville, that would be a book unto itself, but we've tried to provide a representative sample. We've also included a description of the closest outlet malls, which are about 40 minutes south of Jacksonville in St. Augustine.

Jacksonville is a great place to find items with a beach theme—fish, flamingoes, surfers, that sort of thing. The city is also a big football town, so if you're looking for logos, especially University of Florida Gators, Florida State Seminoles, or Jacksonville Jaguars, we can accommodate. In the end, there's no shortage of places to spend your money in Jacksonville. May you find plenty of bargains to spend it on!

MALLS AND SHOPPING CENTERS

Avenues Shopping Mall
10300 Southside Boulevard
(904) 363-3060
The Avenues is located in that amorphous area of Jacksonville called the Southside, more specifically at I-95, exit 98 at Philips Highway. There are more than 160 stores, kiosks, and eateries here, including anchor stores Dillard's, Parisian, Belk, JCPenney, and Sears. You'll also find such well-known shops as Williams-Sonoma, Jos. A Bank Clothier, Talbot's, Banana Republic, Abercrombie & Fitch, Eddie Bauer, The Pottery Barn, and more. MAC Cosmetics has a stand-alone store, which is a favorite place to buy hip, high-quality makeup at affordable prices. Rack Room Shoes is another popular store chock-full of good-quality shoes at lower prices. Gretchen's Hallmark is a great place to go just after a holiday for sale items. Arrive early, however; there's usually a line of people doing the same thing. Football Fanatics sells myriad items with your favorite team logo on it, and NASCAR Thunder is one of the most

---

A new mall is under construction at J. Turner Butler Boulevard and St. Johns Bluff Road. St. Johns Town Center, with over a million square feet of stores and restaurants, is set to open in March 2005.

i

---

popular stores at the mall, selling everything to do with NASCAR. The mall has a busy food court as well as free covered parking decks and large uncovered parking lots.

Gateway Shopping Center
5184 Norwood Avenue
(904) 764-7745

Located on the city's Northside, Gateway caters to an African-American clientele. There are more than 60 shops and businesses in a combination indoor shopping mall and large outdoor strip center. You'll find stores like Footlocker, Payless Shoes, Radio Shack, and Rent-a-Center. There are also several music stores that sell the very latest in hip-hop and rap music. Gateway is enjoying a rebirth after years of neglect, and the new owners are working hard to attract new businesses, but many of the stores are not yet filled. The mall is a big transfer hub for city buses, and there is a large and constant police presence because of a satellite police station located in the strip center outside the mall.

Jacksonville Landing
2 East Independent Drive
(904) 353-1188

This is a great place to enjoy a view of the St. Johns River while you shop or eat. This riverfront marketplace in the heart of downtown Jacksonville has more than 35 specialty shops and a good mix of eateries. The Nine West Shoe Outlet is a favorite store. So are Starbucks Cafe, Foot Locker, The Toy Factory, and a big fresh-fruit market called Apple a Day. You can browse and browse and browse at B. Dalton Bookseller. The marketing department here likes to say that the Landing is where the action is, and that's often true. The Landing hosts everything from pep rallies on big football weekends to the city's annual Christmas tree lighting ceremony. The city runs a reasonably priced parking lot next door to the Landing. You can also arrive here by boat and dock for free on the St. Johns River just steps away from the shops and eateries.

Orange Park Mall
1910 Wells Road, Orange Park
(904) 269-2422

Located in the Jacksonville suburb of Orange Park, this mall features anchors Belk, Dillard's, JCPenney, and Sears. The mall also has a large Books-A-Million, an Old Navy, and a state-of-the-art AMC 24-screen theater that's a popular hangout for area high school students. In between shopping, grab a quick bite to eat at the food court, or let the kids ride the indoor carousel. The mall has 120 stores and kiosks brimming with goods. The only drawback is that the traffic around this mall can be ferocious, so plan accordingly.

Regency Square Mall
9501 Arlington Expressway
(904) 725-1220

Regency, Jacksonville's first big shopping mall when it opened in the 1960s, is the closest large mall to downtown hotels and to the Beaches. There are more than 170 specialty stores, plus anchors Dillard's, Belk, Sears, and JCPenney. You'll also find Victoria's Secret, The Disney Store, Gap, The Limited, Petite Sophisticate, The Bombay Company, The Children's Place, and much more. The Chick-Fil-A in the large, newly renovated food court has earned its place in musical history as the place where Fred Durst, of Limp Bizkit fame, first met some of his bandmates. Old Navy is one of the most popular stores in the mall and attracts lots of customers. There are six movie theaters inside the mall and a 24-screen movie megaplex outside the mall in a separate, stand-alone theater complex. The Jacksonville Sheriff's Office operates a large satellite police station from the mall, which has increased police presence not only in the mall parking lots but also in the entire neighborhood.

Sawgrass Village
Highway A1A, south of J. Turner Butler Boulevard, Ponte Vedra

Sawgrass Village is located directly across TPC Boulevard from the Sawgrass

Marriott Resort. In fact, resort guests are some of the Village's best customers. There are some 40 specialty shops and eateries here. The Green Bean is a popular coffee shop and an inevitable Saturday morning stop for many Ponte Vedra residents. Sea Saw Children's Shop has a lovely selection of children's clothes for special occasions at prices most of us can afford. Lemon Twist is a local favorite carrying a lot of Lily Pulitzer clothes, and Wickets is a great clothing store for the entire family, especially men. Sawgrass Village also boasts a liquor store, ABC Fine Wine and Spirits; a Publix grocery store; and an Eckerd Drugs.

Shops of Historic Riverside Avondale
On St. Johns Avenue between Talbot and Engleside Avenues

This is one of the prettiest places to shop in all of Jacksonville. St. Johns Avenue is located in Riverside and Avondale, two historic neighborhoods with majestic oak trees and elegant old homes, some dating back to the early 1900s. Stroll along St. Johns Avenue, or detour down a shady side street toward the river to take in more beautifully renovated homes. There are some 60 boutiques, restaurants, art galleries, and spas on St. Johns Avenue and nearby Herschel Street. White's Books Cards & Gifts is a good place to check out popular titles, magazines, and a large selection of home accessories. Biscotti's is a popular neighborhood eatery (see the Restaurants chapter). Casablanca is one of the best day spas in the city, as well as a great place to get your hair done. Just make sure you have an appointment or it's virtually impossible to get in.

Shops of San Marco
Downtown on San Marco Boulevard by Atlantic Boulevard and Hendricks Avenue

San Marco Square is one of the more charming of Jacksonville's shopping areas. Some 30 shops, eateries, and art galleries make up the Square, which is located on three streets: San Marco and Atlantic

Boulevards and Hendricks Avenue. The Grotto is a popular wine store that hosts wine tastings every Thursday for $5.00. (You get a portion of that back if you buy the featured wine.) The Write Touch is a small stationery store with a big selection of fine stationery and desk accessories. A cooking store called In the Kitchen sells all kinds of cooking accessories and hosts cooking classes with popular local chefs. Edward's is a much loved tobacco shop, which also sells good "guy" gifts such as walking canes, picture frames, and chess sets. Stellers Gallery is well worth a stop even if you aren't looking to buy artwork. Breeze through and you'll feel like you've been to a contemporary art museum. Theatre Jacksonville is one of the best places in the city to see a community theater production, and check out Bistro Aix if you're ready for lunch or dinner (see the Restaurants chapter).

St. Augustine Outlet Center and Belz Factory Outlet World
I-95, exit 95 at SR 16
(904) 825-1555, (904) 826-1311

Talk about outlet heaven. Two huge outlet malls blanket the east and west sides of I-95 at exit 95. The St. Augustine Outlet Center is located on the west side of the interstate, with 95 name-brand factory stores like Bass, Bose, Coach, Donna Karan, Gap, J. Crew, Nine West, Reebok, Rockport, and more. On the east side of the interstate is the Belz Factory Outlet World, with 75 factory outlet stores, including Samsonite, Easy Spirit, Nike, Banana Republic, Polo Ralph Lauren, Tommy Hilfiger, Lenox, and Royal Doulton. Both outlet malls have food courts, huge parking lots, and bargains galore. The outlet malls are a good 45-minute drive south of Jacksonville on I-95.

Town Center
Where Atlantic Boulevard meets the Ocean in Atlantic and Neptune Beaches

Located across the street from the ocean, this charming shopping area is only about 3 blocks long and 2 blocks wide and is

For unique candy, visit Three Sisters Chocolate on San Jose Boulevard in Mandarin. The candy is made in the store, and if you don't see what you want, candymakers will create it for you. Special-order chocolate-covered strawberries, totally enrobed in chocolate, are a real taste treat.

surrounded by beautiful beach homes. To understand the geography, it helps to realize that the north side of Atlantic Boulevard is Atlantic Beach and the south side is Neptune Beach. Town Center encompasses both communities. The Book Mark is consistently voted the best independent bookstore in the city by readers of Folio Weekly, the city's free alternative magazine. If you're lucky, you'll catch your favorite author here for a reading and book signing. Shelby's is a popular coffee shop and general gathering place for Beaches residents. Lots of business seems to get done here by Beaches residents, who like the informal, laid-back setting at both the indoor and outdoor tables. Be sure to get a free sample of the homemade fudge sold in the back. Patina is a wonderful gift shop owned by two Atlantic Beach ladies who travel to France every year to bring back unusual but affordable gifts. Much of their merchandise is priced at about $25. Ukulele is a fun clothing and gift store with a Hawaiian flair. Cobalt Moon is a great place for travelers to take a yoga or Tai Chi class on a walk-in basis. Town Center also boasts two of the most popular nightspots in the city: Pete's Bar and Ragtime (see the Nightlife chapter).

ANTIQUES

Avonlea Antique Mall
11260 Beach Boulevard
(904) 645-0806
This place calls itself the largest antiques mall in North Florida, and though that's

hard to prove, walk inside Avonlea and you realize it might be true. You can spend an entire day here just walking around browsing different dealers' displays. There's furniture, art glass, antique toys, tons of jewelry, old leaded glass windows, clothes, books—the list goes on and on. Avonlea is located in a busy strip center off Beach Boulevard, near the University of North Florida. It's open seven days a week and until 8:00 P.M. on Thursday and Friday. There's also a yummy cafe snuggled inside a corner of the mall that's a nice place to eat lunch or sip a cup of hot tea and enjoy something sweet.

The Pine Cottage
4000 St. Johns Avenue
(904) 381-9148
www.thepinecottage.com
This is the place to go in Jacksonville for pine furniture, either painted or with a wax finish. Located in Riverside Avondale, The Pine Cottage will build you a custom-reproduction piece of furniture out of old wood in their warehouse or sell you an antique off the floor. From beds to benches, armoires to armchairs, this store has it all.

BEAUTY AND NAIL SALONS

Acu Nails
975 Atlantic Boulevard, Atlantic Beach
(904) 247-9511
The Vietnamese owners of this shop, located in a Publix shopping center in Atlantic Beach, couldn't be more attentive. They offer total nail care for men and women and discounts for high school students. It's best to call for an appointment, but fear not, Mrs. Kim will always squeeze you in.

Adonai at San Marco Beauty Salon
1030 Hendricks Avenue
(904) 396-5000
Located in San Marco, this salon is a good choice for guests staying at downtown hotels, especially on the Southbank.

Adonai caters to women of color, specializing in weaves and relaxers as well as cuts and occasional colors. No nails or facials here, though, and don't forget to make an appointment or you won't get seen.

Alpha Beauty Clinic
4131 Southside Boulevard
(904) 998-9977

The specialists at Alpha will do things to your body you may have never heard of before, such as a Japanese oxygen facial or a Lomi-Lomi massage. You can also get less exotic body treatments here such as waxing and manicures/pedicures. This salon is convenient to guests staying at hotels in the Southpoint area.

Anthony and Sandra Day Spa
1936 San Marco Boulevard
(904) 398-9777
www.anthonysandraspa.com

This San Marco day spa enjoys a convenient location for tourists staying in hotels on the Northbank or Southbank. Anthony and Sandra (who are husband and wife) have assembled a team of beauty specialists who do it all, from hair care to nail care, facials, and massages. The friendly staff will do their best to get you an appointment as soon as you need one.

Calvin Cole Salon and Day Spa
675 Atlantic Boulevard, Atlantic Beach
(904) 246-6622

Calvin Cole enjoys a great location in Atlantic Beach, within walking distance of the shops and hotels of Town Center. It's a good solid place to get your hair cut and colored and to get your nails done. You can enjoy a massage here, too. Call first and they'll usually squeeze you in.

Casablanca Beauty Center & Day Spa
3609 St. Johns Avenue
(904) 389-5533

It's best to call ahead if you want an appointment. But once you're on the appointment track, you'll be treated like a king or queen whenever you're here. Casablanca is known around the city for its

makeovers; in fact, this is where the Jaguar cheerleaders come every fall before taking to the field. Experts will do your makeup, hair color, haircut, waxing, massage, nails—you name it. In fact, ask about the Day of Beauty. You'll leave a better you.

Daryl Powers Salon & Spa
115 Professional Drive, Suite 106
Ponte Vedra
(904) 285-7776

400 East Bay Street
(904) 353-5300
www.darylpowers.com

Daryl Powers salons like to think of themselves as leaders in the field of beauty for both women and men. There are two locations to choose from: Ponte Vedra or downtown along the river in the Berkman Plaza. Services include hair design and color, nail care, skin care, and massage therapy. Appointments can be tough to come by, though, in the Ponte Vedra location.

Dirty Blonde Salon
2409 South Third Street
Jacksonville Beach
(904) 241-4247

This is a very cool little place. Count on getting a good haircut and good color here. It's also a popular stop for waxing and facials. Best of all, you won't have to wait months for an appointment. And you don't have to be a blonde either.

Hair Cuttery
Avenues Shopping Mall
(904) 363-1156

You know the score. No appointments necessary. Hair care for the budget conscious. This salon is located inside the mall, and it's convenient to anyone staying in the Southpoint area.

The Spa at the Ponte Vedra Inn and Club
200 Ponte Vedra Boulevard, Ponte Vedra
(904) 285-1111

You don't have to be a guest at the Ponte Vedra Inn and Club to enjoy The Spa. Anyone with an appointment and some extra bucks in his or her pocket can come here and live like the rich, if only for a few hours. This popular day spa does it all, from haircuts to facials, nail care, body scrubs, and massages. Most customers get more than one beauty treatment. In between, say, the facial and the massage, relax in a quiet garden with a pool, whirlpool, and fountain, and sip complimentary mimosas or sparkling water. You'll leave relaxed and feeling like a million bucks.

BOOKSTORES

B. Dalton Bookseller
Jacksonville Landing
(904) 353-3377
Located on the first floor of the Landing, this bookstore is a blessing for downtown workers as well as travelers frequenting downtown hotels. It's one of the more popular and enduring shops at the Landing, and the staff never seems to mind how long you browse.

Barnes & Noble Booksellers
9282 Atlantic Boulevard
(904) 721-2446

11112 San Jose Boulevard
(904) 886-9904
www.bn.com
Barnes & Noble has two locations in Jacksonville, but travelers are more likely

to frequent the store on Atlantic Boulevard because it's closest to downtown, the Beaches, and the Southpoint area. Both stores are good places to sip a latte and thumb through some books. Both locations also host occasional author book signings; call for the latest happenings.

Book Mark
299 Atlantic Boulevard, Atlantic Beach
(904) 241-9026
Consistently voted the best independent bookstore in the city, the Book Mark is a great place to go if you want a good read but need some help finding it. Owner Rona Brinlee has many connections with agents and publishers and brings in popular authors several times a month for readings and book signings. If she doesn't have the book you want, she'll order it and have it to you in a matter of days. The Book Mark is 1 block from the ocean, which makes it a great stop for beachgoers who need a beach read. Free gift wrapping is also a plus.

The Book Nook
1620 University Boulevard West
(904) 733-4586
If you're looking for a bookstore in the San Marco area, drive a little farther south on San Jose Boulevard to The Book Nook in Lakewood and you'll find yourself in the middle of book heaven. The Book Nook is located in a big shopping center anchored by a Winn-Dixie grocery store. In the front of this large store you'll find the mass-market books mixed in with lots of gifts. Step inside further and you'll find a big selection of science fiction paperbacks and romance novels. Better yet, there's a huge selection (no exaggeration) of magazines along one side of the store. The owner says he services a diverse clientele, so he must carry a diverse selection of books and magazines. If you can't find it here, the store will order it for you, and chances are if you need a gift that's not a book, you'll find the perfect something here, too.

Books-A-Million
Marsh Landing Shopping Center
Jacksonville Beach
(904) 805-0004
www.booksamillion.com

Missing your hometown newspaper? There's a good chance you can pick up a copy at Books-A-Million. As the name suggests, there are probably a million books here, many of them discounted. There is also a large selection of newspapers and magazines. But there is one drawback: It can be hard to find what you want here, even harder to get a busy staff person to help you. The store sports a fun children's area, where kids can make themselves at home, and a coffee shop.

Borders Books & Music
8801 Southside Boulevard
(904) 519-6500
www.borders.com

Located in the Timberlin Parc shopping center near the Avenues Mall, Borders offers many popular free children's programs, which are described in detail in the Kidstuff chapter. It's convenient to travelers staying in the Southpoint area: Hop on J. Turner Butler Boulevard heading east, exit on Southside Boulevard heading south, and stay on Southside Boulevard until you see the store on your left. Not only does Borders have a good coffee shop, but it also hosts author readings and free musical events. Call the store for dates and times, or pick up a free copy of the in-store newsletter next time you're there.

Chamblin Book Mine
4551 Roosevelt Boulevard
(904) 384-1685
www.chamblinbookmine.com

Ron Chamblin has collected more "new, used, and nonexistent" books here than some public libraries. He also sells magazines, comic books, records, CDs, books on tape, and videos. There are more than a million items in the store and lots more in storage. This store is a maze of stuff, but if there's a book you want, Ron Chamblin can usually put his hands on it. Come

---

Need a beach read? Saboteurs: The Nazi Raid on America *details how a group of bumbling Germans landed on Ponte Vedra Beach in 1942 with orders to blow up key U.S. industrial sites. Written by Michael Dobbs, a reporter at the* Washington Post, *the nonfiction book is a big seller at the Book Mark in Atlantic Beach.*

---

here when you have time to browse. You won't be disappointed.

CHILDREN'S CLOTHING AND TOYS

Amy's Turn
1415 North Third Street, Jacksonville Beach
(904) 241-5437

Budget-conscious shoppers will enjoy browsing through the clothing and toys at Amy's Turn. Some things are more used than others, so make sure you have time to search for the great bargains that are here. Your pocketbook will be happy with the results. Amy's Turn also sells consignment clothes for teenagers and very hip adults, but it's the baby stuff that fills the rooms. Some of it is brand-new!

The Hobbie Horse
3550 St. Johns Avenue
(904) 389-7992

This is the type of store that would appeal to your wealthy godmother. There's a large selection of traditional children's clothing, as well as fancy toys like Madame Alexander dolls and porcelain tea sets. There's also a good selection of mother/daughter outfits.

Lollipop Lane
241 Atlantic Boulevard, Neptune Beach
(904) 246-0001

From clothes to toys, there are bargains galore in this tiny consignment store. The owner, Beth, is very child-friendly and doesn't mind if your kids pull out a few toys to play with while you shop. Some items are brand-new; others are gently used. Definitely worth a stop.

Old Navy
Regency Square Mall
(904) 722-3977
www.oldnavy.com
Old Navy at Regency is one of the busiest stores in the entire mall. It's a great place to come for sturdy, hip clothing for kids of all ages. And if you happen to catch a sale, the store's already affordable clothes turn into real bargains. If you're closer to Orange Park, there's also an Old Navy at the Orange Park Mall.

See Saw Children's Shop
Sawgrass Village Shopping Center
Ponte Vedra
(904) 285-3218
If you're looking for a special outfit for a special occasion, this is a good store to visit. The clothes are traditional here, which means that your two-year-old daughter won't end up looking like a miniature pop star. The prices here won't break the bank either. This is a popular store for grandmothers who are buying a sweet dress for their granddaughter, as well as Ponte Vedra residents who don't feel like traveling miles to the nearest mall.

The Toy Factory
Jacksonville Landing
(904) 353-4874
www.thetoyfactory.com
Business travelers who've promised to bring home a surprise to their son or daughter will appreciate the convenience of this store located in Jacksonville Landing, in the heart of downtown. The Toy Factory is packed with classic toys, from Brio train sets to yo-yos. There's also cool new toys, books, and a good selection of inexpensive toys your child can buy with his or her allowance money.

Wynken, Blynken and Nod
522 North Third Street
Jacksonville Beach
(904) 249-3838
This is a good store to check out if you're creating a nursery or redoing a child's room. There is lots of furniture, some of it fanciful, in this old house turned shop. You can also buy room accessories such as bedding, lamps, and art rugs.

GIFT SHOPS

The Bath and Linen Shoppe
2058 San Marco Boulevard
(904) 398-7147
Slip between sheets so soft that you feel enveloped in luxury, or step into fluffy terry-cloth slippers that feel like small pillows on your feet. Such are the delights of The Bath and Linen Shoppe, a San Marco tradition for more than three decades. You can outfit your entire bed or bath here with the finest Italian linens, French soaps, and Asian silk kimonos. Owners Edward and Kelly George, who are brother and sister, may sell luxury, but they know it's service that keeps them in business. This is also a good place to shop (so is their Ponte Vedra store) if you need a gift for that person who has everything. They'll make handy suggestions to help you find it.

Cobalt Moon Gift Shop
217 First Street
(904) 246-2131
www.cobaltmooncenter.com
Step into this store and you'll instantly feel transported to Northern California, where the clothes are diaphanous, music means drumming and chanting, and the incense

---

i *A great souvenir, especially for winter travelers, awaits you at the grocery store. Pick up a bag of Florida oranges and a bag of Florida pink grapefruit. The grapefruit couldn't be sweeter, and the oranges make great juice. Friends back home will love you for it.*

---

is always burning. The gift shop, located inside a much larger healing center (a great place, by the way, for travelers to take a yoga or Tai Chi class), offers a good collection of CDs and books as well as candles, incense, and clothing.

Cowford Traders
3563 St. Johns Avenue
(904) 387-9288
The name of this gift shop harkens back to the early, early days of Jacksonville, when the city was called Cowford and was not much more than a pit stop on the river along the Kings Road. This shop is a lot more sophisticated than its name implies. There's everything from furniture to kitchen items to writing paper here. Even if you're "just browsing," there's a good chance you won't leave Cowford Traders empty-handed.

Edward's
2016 San Marco Boulevard
(904) 396-7990
Edward's, which likes to call itself "more than just a tobacco shoppe," enjoys two locations, one in San Marco, the other in Ponte Vedra at the Sawgrass Village Shopping Center. Both shops carry a large selection of fine cigars, pipes, and tobacco. You'll also find good "men gifts" such as fountain pens, walking canes, and chess sets. And guess what: You can smoke in the store!

Hibernia
108 First Street, Neptune Beach
(904) 249-7321
www.hiberniahandmade.com
As Irish stores go, this one is not what you might expect. Forget about the traditional Waterford crystal or Belleek porcelain. Instead, Hibernia carries handmade crafts by current Irish artists from both Ireland and Northern Ireland. There's beautiful wood furniture, lots of pottery, clothing made from handwoven Irish linen, unique silver and gold jewelry, and artsy knick-knacks for your home.

In the Kitchen
1950 San Marco Boulevard
(904) 346-4222
If you love to cook, you'll love this store. All the nuts-and-bolts cooking items you could possibly need are sold here, from paella pans to pastry dough cloths. Then there are the fun things that make your kitchen (and home) special, such as copper pans, Italian ceramic serving dishes, and handmade spice racks. Oh, and did we mention the cookbooks! There are two additional shops in Atlantic Beach and Ponte Vedra. The latter store joins the San Marco store in offering frequent cooking classes and cooking demonstrations by popular local chefs (see the first Close-up in this chapter).

Patina
40 Ocean Boulevard, Atlantic Beach
(904) 242-4990
If you like French Country antiques, you'll enjoy shopping here. There are some lovely pieces of French and British antique furniture for sale, as well as a much wider selection of affordably priced merchandise such as antique wineglasses, kitchen linens, and sugar and creamer sets. But what's most fun is the unexpected, affordable antique treasures bought by the owners on one of their annual buying trips to France or England; most of these items sell for less than $25.

The Pineapple Post
2403 South Third Street
Jacksonville Beach
(904) 249-7477
www.pineapplepostgifts.com
Wealthy Ponte Vedra matrons have been shopping at this store for years. They know it's one of the best places at the beach to come for an elegant wedding gift, a present for their grandchild, or just something beautiful for their home. There's also a good selection of outdoor items, a whole wall of specialty soaps and beauty cremes, lots of Florida beachy items such as serving dishes in the shape of a fish, and much

Cooking Classes "In the Kitchen"

Normally, In the Kitchen, a cookware and cooking accessory store in Ponte Vedra Beach, is a pretty sedate place. But on Wednesday afternoon at 1:00, when Matthew Medure is cooking, the place is buzzing with excitement. Matthew, as his fans call him, is the handsome chef and owner of two of Jacksonville's most popular eateries—Matthew's Restaurant in San Marco and Restaurant Medure in Ponte Vedra. He's the current king of Jacksonville cuisine.

On this day, 16 students take a seat at the counter, eager to watch the personable chef make whatever specialty he's decided to create. They've each paid $40 for this sold-out demonstration and lunch. Many bring their own notepads and pens to record the recipes. "I came off the golf course just to be here this afternoon," says one Ponte Vedra matron, who considers herself a gourmet cook but still comes to all of Matthew's Wednesday-afternoon cooking classes because she learns so much from just watching him.

Matthew is cooking veal rib eye with a sherry-rosemary oyster mushroom sauce and pan-roasted sliced potatoes with lemon and onion. "Veal rib eye is a boneless veal chop," explains Matthew. "It's equivalent to the Delmonico." Students take notes as he generously sprinkles the five-to-six-pound roast with olive oil, kosher salt, and pepper, then sears it on top of the stove and pops it

into a 350-degree oven.

Next up, the potatoes. "You know this red potato is fresh because you can scrape your fingernail along it and come away with some skin," he says, scratching the potato with his thumbnail. Matthew asks for a volunteer to assist in making the potato dish. Surprisingly, only one person steps forward. Perhaps the students are a bit intimidated—more likely they want to watch, not work.

Matthew cuts the potatoes quickly, like a machine, and the student artfully arranges the thin slices in a frying pan that's been generously dosed with olive oil. Then he thinly slices one white onion, which the student volunteer places on top of the potatoes. Matthew sprinkles the dish with more olive oil, kosher salt, and pepper. "I love the flavor of olive oil, salt, and pepper," he says. "I don't think you need anything else. That works with everything." Before this dish goes into the oven, Matthew squeezes one fresh lemon over the potatoes. This, too, is accomplished quickly and skillfully. He squeezes the lemon with one hand and cups his other hand underneath. The lemon juice slips through his cupped fingers, but the lemon seeds do not. The potatoes head into the oven to cook at 350 degrees for 30 minutes.

Now, the sauce, which when complete looks more like exotic mushroom soup than a topping for the veal. Matthew begins by showing the students how to cut an oyster mushroom by slicing off the small ears. "Throw away the stalk," he says. "It's too woody to bother with."

"To flavor the mushrooms, we're going to do garlic," he says. This prompts questions from the students. "Do you like elephant garlic?" one asks. "How do you know if garlic is fresh?" asks another. Matthew answers the questions as he cleans the cloves. "Elephant garlic doesn't have much flavor," he says. "And when garlic is really fresh, it's hard to get the skin off." Next Matthew shows the students how to cut a leek, then invert it like a deck of cards to check for dirt. "Sometimes the innermost part of a leek can be tough, so I pull it out," he says. The mushrooms and leeks simmer on the stove in olive oil, kosher salt, and pepper. A series of ingredients follow: the garlic, some chopped fresh rosemary, a quarter cup of dry sherry, a cup and a half of chicken stock, some sliced prosciutto, some half-and-half, some fresh Parmesan, and a tablespoon of butter. The students are in awe and also, by now, quite hungry.

Matthew pulls the veal out of the oven. "That should be medium rare," he says, poking the meat with his finger. "How do you know?" a student asks. "I just know," he says. But to be sure, he grabs a sharp knife, sticks it in the center of the meat, and then touches the blade to his upper lip. If the steel blade feels cold, the meat is still raw. If it's warm, the meat is just right. If it's hot, the meat is well done. "Just right," Matthew announces.

The food is ready to eat, but Matthew makes everyone wait another 10 minutes so that the veal can rest. "It's important to let veal rest as long as you can," he says, spooning the pan juice over the meat. "It tastes better." He entertains the students with stories about growing up in the food-service business in New Castle, Pennsylvania, and making 50,000 to 60,000 meatballs a week at his father's shop. Matthew, by the way, studied at the Culinary Institute, then worked as executive chef at The Ritz Carlton on Amelia Island before opening the two Jacksonville restaurants with his brother, David.

He sets up the plates on the counter and serves the potatoes and veal with generous spoonfuls of sauce. The crowd goes wild. This is one meal they all say they'll be making again, and somehow you expect they really will.

Matthew Medure holds his cooking classes twice a month at both the Ponte Vedra and San Marco In the Kitchen stores. Register early; the classes fill up well in advance. In the Kitchen also offers Saturday-morning hands-on cooking classes, which are very technique oriented, as well as themed demonstration classes on Thursday and Friday nights. Themes include Tuscan cooking, Florida seafood, and how to make sushi. All classes are $40 per person. Call (904) 280-1140 in Ponte Vedra and (904) 346-4222 in San Marco for reservations. In the Kitchen will also arrange special cooking classes for private groups and corporations.

more. The attentive staff will steer you in the right direction if you need help. They'll also wrap your gift for free and send it anywhere it needs to go. (The shipping costs money, but you won't have to pay the Florida sales tax if it's sent out of state.)

Sea Shells and Coral
230 Boardwalk, Jacksonville Beach
(904) 241-9031
Located on the boardwalk in front of the Atlantic Ocean, this is a good place to supplement the shell collection you've gathered on the beach. There are baskets and baskets of shells here, including conch shells, olive shells, starfish, and shark teeth. And the prices are great.

Shorelines
109 First Street, Neptune Beach
(904) 246-9133
If you want a fun Florida souvenir with a flamingo or a palm tree on it, come here. If you're looking for a funny card to send someone, come here. If your child wants to spend his or her allowance on neat "stuff," come here. You'll understand why this is one of the most popular stores at the beach once you enter and see the selection of affordable and unusual merchandise.

Square
1027 Park Street
(904) 354-2880
www.square-ware.com
Convenient to downtown, this shop in Five Points sells hip wares for your home or office—things that the 20-something crowd would enjoy buying or owning. Check out the unusual collection of lamps and desk accessories. One very popular item: handmade vegetable glycerin soap from California, which the shopkeepers slice and sell by weight.

III Lions
1950 San Marco Boulevard
(904) 396-9519
You'll find lots of goodies in this popular shop located on the square in the heart of San Marco. III Lions is named for the lion

sculpture in the square out front. It's also evidence of the artful sensibilities of the owners. Inside, you'll find handmade jewelry by local and regional artists, hand-painted dishware by popular Mississippi artist Gail Pitman, neat garden accents, and bath-and-body products. The store also has antique collectibles and furniture on consignment, which further adds to the eclectic but interesting atmosphere.

The Write Touch
1967 San Marco Boulevard
(904) 398-2009
www.thewritetouch.com
If you've never known the pleasure of a fine pen gliding across fine stationery, stop in at The Write Touch and give it a try. The store calls itself a "San Marco tradition," and it is. When a local mother needs a birth announcement, she comes here. When a bride needs a wedding invitation, she comes here. When a busy executive needs personalized stationery, he or she comes here. The stationery is fine, the service is friendly, and you'll enjoy the shopping experience.

GOLF

Edwin Watts Golf
4082 South Third Street
Jacksonville Beach
(904) 246-7893

3507 Southside Boulevard
(904) 641-5334

1540 Wells Road, Orange Park
(904) 264-9801
www.edwinwatts.com
There are many golf stores to choose from in Jacksonville, but Edwin Watts Golf stands out, if only for its sheer size: The three locations combined have the largest golf inventory in Northeast Florida. A friend once bought a golf bag at the Jax Beach store for $10. Granted, it was basically a tube covered in vinyl, but the price was great. From clothing to clubs, you're bound to find something you want at one

of these golf superstores. The store on Southside Boulevard is the largest of the three and convenient to travelers staying in the Southpoint area.

Lauden Golf of Ponte Vedra
330 Highway A1A
(904) 543-1433
www.laudengolf.com
Serious golfers may already know about Lauden Golf, a national golf products manufacturer headquartered in Jacksonville. Owner Jim Laudenslager is often behind the counter of his Ponte Vedra store, an unassuming place where all the local PGA Tour players come to get their clubs repaired. Laudenslager owns the patent on 108 golf-related products, including a club he calls the No. 1 golf club in Florida—the Trifecta, made from 100 percent maraged fairway woods. The Ponte Vedra shop is bustling in the spring at TPC time. You can also get video golf instruction here: Lauden videotapes your swing then analyzes it for about $100.

North Florida Golf Ball Co.
815 Beach Boulevard, #4
Jacksonville Beach
(904) 247-5377
www.northfloridagolfball.com
If you hit a $5.00 golf ball into a water hazard, chances are it will end up here. The owner periodically dons scuba equipment and cleans out the ponds at various golf courses. He then resells the balls, either wholesale or retail, at his Jacksonville Beach shop. Prices, depending on the quality of the ball when it's fished out of the lagoon, range anywhere from 50 to 80 percent less than if you buy it new.

Paradies PGA Tour Shop
Jacksonville Airport
(904) 741-8500
If you missed your chance to get golf accessories while you were in Jacksonville, fear not: This airport store sells a good range of PGA Tour merchandise. You can't miss the store; it's in the airport's atrium shopping area. Just don't try to take your new golf club on the plane—airport security will not be pleased.

PGA Tour Stop
World Golf Village, St. Augustine
(904) 940-0418
www.tourstop.com
This large two-story golf superstore befits a golf mecca like World Golf Village. Everything known to man and woman that has to do with golf is sold here, from furniture with a golf theme to all kinds of golf clothing to special bracelets said to help cure a golfer's aches and pains. There are also four large hitting areas where you can try out the myriad clubs for sale.

Tournament Players Club
110 TPC Boulevard, Ponte Vedra
(904) 273-3235
Although this is a semiprivate club, the golf shop is open to the public. It has a great selection of golf shirts, many with a little logo that says TPC, which also stands for The Player's Championship, the big annual golf tournament played on the Sawgrass Stadium Course. It's a great gift for the golfer in your life! Tell the security guard at the west gate to the Sawgrass Country Club that you want to go to the golf shop, and he or she will let you through.

JEWELRY STORES

Jacobs Jewelers
204 Laura Street
(904) 356-1655
Travelers staying at downtown hotels will appreciate Jacobs Jewelers' convenient location just off Hemming Plaza. Jacobs has been serving Jacksonville since 1890 and is well-known for its diamonds and fine china—as well as for the 15-foot cast-iron clock located just outside its front door.

Miriam's
1958 San Marco Boulevard
(904) 398-7393
This very popular store is located in San Marco. Miriam's specializes in hip, unusual

jewelry often seen on the streets of New York City. The store also has a large selection of silver jewelry as well as gold and gemstones. And if you need to consign that diamond engagement or wedding ring your ex gave you, Miriam's is a good place to do it.

Underwood Jewelers
3617 St. Johns Avenue
(904) 388-5406

330 Highway A1A North, Ponte Vedra
(904) 280-1202

2044 San Marco Boulevard
(904) 398-9741
www.underwoodjewelers.com

This is Jacksonville's most popular jewelry store. Underwood Jewelers first opened in 1928 in Palatka, selling watches and diamonds, before expanding to Jacksonville in the 1940s. Today Underwood carries a large selection of jewelry by such name-brand jewelers as Hildalgo, Cartier, and David Yurman. There's also a large selection of fine china, silver, and gifts.

MEN'S CLOTHING

Abercrombie & Fitch
Avenues Shopping Mall
(904) 519-8989

With cool clothes for the young man in your life, Abercrombie's is college casual and definitely hip. It's a good place to find a sweater at Christmas or a T-shirt and shorts in the summer.

Jos. A. Bank Clothiers
Avenues Shopping Mall
(904) 519-8800
www.josbank.com

Jos. A. Bank Clothiers is a good place to shop if you need a new suit or a pair of business-casual pants. The store offers a wide selection of good quality, classically styled clothing as well as formal wear, shoes, and golf wear. There is also a second location on Marsh Landing Parkway in South Jax Beach.

Karl's Clothier
240-3 Highway A1A North, Ponte Vedra
(904) 280-1345

This is where the Jaguars shop for custom clothing—suits made from Italian wool or shirts from Sea Island cotton. It takes about two and a half weeks to receive your custom clothing once you've been fitted, but there are also off-the-rack suits and sportswear in fashion-forward and American classic designs. Leather goods such as shoes and belts are also sold at this location and in Karl's second store, on St. Johns Avenue in Riverside Avondale.

Rosenblum's
5500 San Jose Boulevard
(904) 733-8633

Open for more than 100 years, Rosenblum's sells men's apparel from casual to dress, including a good selection of shoes. The best word to describe this store is quality. Service would be a good word after that. Rosenblum's has a second location in Jacksonville Beach.

MUSIC STORES

CD Warehouse
217 Third Street, Neptune Beach
(904) 249-8822

This is a good place to get rid of the CDs you don't listen to anymore. Sell them to the store, and use the proceeds to buy some new music. CD Warehouse has a fine selection of both new and used CDs, and the store will order anything you need that's not in stock.

Coconuts Music & Video
9450 Arlington Expressway
(904) 724-4444

Located across the street from Regency Square Mall, this store is a good place to buy concert tickets through Ticketmaster. Don't wait in line at the Coliseum for those tickets, come here where the lines are shorter and the ambience more pleasant. Plus you can pick up a new CD in the process.

Musicland
Jacksonville Landing
(904) 350-0005
www.samgoode.com
This busy downtown music store has a good inventory of all the latest titles. The friendly staff will take the time to help you find what you need. The store is located on the first floor of the Jacksonville Landing, convenient to all the downtown hotels.

Smash Music
1034 Park Street
(904) 633-9161
Located in Five Points, this is perhaps Jacksonville's hippest music store. It sells all kinds of the latest music, from heavy metal to hip-hop, electronica to down tempo. You can also bring in your used CDs for trades and money off new music. Smash Music also has a store at the beach in the back of a place called Caribbean Connection, a neat little shop that sells everything from incense to Dr. Martens to clothes your teenager would die for.

SURF SHOPS

Aqua East Surf Shop
696 Atlantic Boulevard, Neptune Beach
(904) 246-2550
www.aquaeast.com
Aqua East is the Big Kahuna of local surf shops. It feels like a chain clothing store when you first walk inside, with its large collection of really cool bikinis and baggies, sandals and T-shirts. But walk upstairs, where the new and used surfboards are sold, and the talk is all surf. Aqua East also offers lessons on how to get up on that board.

Secret Surf Shop
115 First Street, Neptune Beach
(904) 270-0526
www.secretsurfshop.com
This place is located 100 yards from the ocean, and it's not unheard of to see an OUT SURFING sign on the door. The owner of this tiny shop (it's only about

400 square feet) lives upstairs, yet he's managed to pack it full of cool merchandise, including bikinis, baggies, T-shirts, and new and used surfboards. You can also rent a board here, pick up some good tips on where to surf, and stock up on sun-care items for your skin.

Need organic fruits and veggies? Head to Native Sun Natural Foods at 10000 San Jose Boulevard in Mandarin. It's the largest health food store in Florida and includes a deli, a dairy, a bulk foods section—even healthy foods for your pet.

Sunrise Surf Shop
834 Beach Boulevard, Jacksonville Beach
(904) 241-0822
www.sunrisesurfshop.com
This is where local surfers like to shop. Sunrise has a great collection of wet suits and new and used surfboards, as well as boards to rent for an afternoon. Teenagers love the cool T-shirts and the store's frequent two-for-one specials.

WOMEN'S CLOTHING

Blair Woolverton
3624 St. Johns Avenue
(904) 387-0312
Located in Riverside Avondale, this store carries an eclectic collection of clothes, most of them casual, all of them artsy. Give yourself plenty of time to look through the packed racks; you'll be happy with the results. Blair Woolverton is a local fashion designer, and many of the clothes in the store are her designs.

Burlington Coat Factory
9824 Atlantic Boulevard
(904) 724-4543
When Jacksonville shoppers want a bargain, this is where they go. Don't be put off by the name; Burlington Coat Factory sells far more than coats. It's a huge ware-

CLOSE-UP

Hot Sauces

Shopping for a quintessential Jacksonville souvenir? Head to a specialty food or grocery store and buy a bottle of locally concocted pepper sauce. Northeast Florida is a hotbed for the fiery stuff, which sells for about $3.00 a bottle. Several popular brands are manufactured in the Jacksonville area and sold round the nation. Others are manufactured abroad by local companies and sold round the world.

The area's condiment commerce started in the early eighties when Chris Way, owner of Barnacle Bills, a St. Augustine restaurant, wanted to create a fish sauce. He grabbed some Datil peppers, tomatoes, and honey and started mixing. Food historians believe that Datil peppers are unique to St. Augustine. They think that the peppers crossed the ocean from Cuba to La Florida in the early 1800s (perhaps aboard a slave ship) then found their way into New World gardens surrounding the Spanish stronghold of St. Augustine.

Way's concoction was an instant hit, and demand quickly grew. A customer who worked at the Winn-Dixie grocery store chain promised Way that he'd get the sauce on his store's shelves if Way would start bottling it. By 1985 Way realized that he had a hot commodity on his hands and started bottling the sauce.

He formed a company—Dat'l Do-it, Inc.—planted 1,500 Datil pepper plants on the Dat'l Do-it corporate farm, and developed new products like Hellish Relish, Hot Vinegar, and Datil Pepper Jelly. He even opened a Dat'l Do-it Hot Shop on historic St. George Street in St. Augustine. By 1993 bottles of Dat'l Do-it hot sauce graced the tables of homes

house of a place with racks and racks of clothing, from work clothes to play clothes. The Atlantic Boulevard location is near Regency Square Mall, a not-too-far drive from downtown, the Beaches, and Southpoint.

Edge City
1017 Park Street
(904) 353-9423
www.gunnel.com
Hip teenagers will want to buy everything in this store, which is located downtown in Five Points. There are dresses, tops, shoes, and pants by Betsey Johnson, Vivienne Tam, and French Connection. The prices are good, too.

Emily Benham
3635 St. Johns Avenue
(904) 387-2121
If you dress in hip New York–style clothing, you have to wear hip New York–style shoes. This is the best place to go in Jacksonville for the latest shoes and purses. Catch a sale at this Avondale shop and you'll really leave a happy camper.

and restaurants across the nation, and sales reached nearly half a million dollars.

These days Way and his partners have cut back on some types of marketing, but say that sales are still increasing. For instance, they closed the store on St. George Street because the sauce was sold all over town anyway and a corporate store wasn't necessary. They stopped growing their own peppers because it was too time-consuming. Area farmers could grow them just as well, and they were happy for the work. But Way and his team have continued to get their pepper sauce and other products on more and more shelves in stores like Wal-Mart, Target, and Kmart. And, as they say, Dat'l Do-it.

The success of Dat'l Do-it fired up other hot sauce aficionados like Tom Nuijens, who owns Half Moon Bay Trading Company in Atlantic Beach. Half Moon's biggest seller is a line of Iguana-brand pepper sauces, which he manufactures in a factory in the hills outside San Jose, Costa Rica. Nuijens, an avid surfer, then imports the sauces and sells them round the world, from Australia to Sweden.

Nuijens used to be the creative director at a large Jacksonville advertising agency, and it shows. All the pepper sauces are artfully labeled with an iguana on the bottle and come with names like Iguana Mean Green, Iguana Island Pepper, Iguana Triple X, Iguana Bold Gold, and Iguana Radioactive. (Can you guess which one's the hottest?)

Nuijens says his pepper sauce is so popular that restaurant owners complain to him that people steal the bottles from the tables. Still, there must be lots of people who buy it, because the company enjoyed three-quarters of a million dollars in sales in 2001. Iguana pepper sauces are sold in specialty food stores at the Beaches as well as through the company's warehouse at 210 Mayport Road in Atlantic Beach. The warehouse is open Monday through Friday from 9:30 A.M. to 4:30 P.M., except when, as Nuijens puts it, "there's surf."

j. Ashley
3588 St. Johns Avenue
(904) 388-2118
This Avondale store sells cool casual clothing and awesome evening wear in the latest New York City styles. You'll be ahead of the Jacksonville fashion curve when you wear clothing from here, and for many, that's a good thing.

Krista Eberle
2020 San Marco Boulevard
(904) 396-2711
If you like fashion-forward clothing that echoes what's hot in New York City right now, make it a point to shop here. Krista Eberle stocks designer clothing by Nicole Miller, BCBG, Michael Stars, and more. The clothes are hip, and so is the store.

Lemon Twist
Sawgrass Village Shopping Center
Ponte Vedra
(904) 280-5955
Newcomers to Florida who aren't familiar with Lily Pulitzer clothing need to check out Lemon Twist, virtually the Jacksonville headquarters for these Palm Beach designer fashions. The shop carries a lot of Lilys, including mother/daughter outfits,

Hot Pans in Tinseltown is a kitchen store, a gourmet shop, and a restaurant all rolled into one. We like to watch the Food Network on the plasma-screen TV while shopping for a springform pan and pausing to eat grilled shrimp over field greens with mango sauce. Call (904) 394-7421 for more info.

sweaters, skirts, dresses, and pants for both women and girls. Pulitzer is the Palm Beach socialite who began designing cotton sundresses in the sixties. Her clothes caught on when Jackie Kennedy started wearing them. A classic Lily is a sleeveless cotton sundress in a bright, Key West–floral design. Lemon Twist has sales twice a year, when the Lilys are marked down and a bit more affordable.

Sharon Batten
**2405 South Third Street
Jacksonville Beach
(904) 246-9436**
Need a Chanel suit? This is your store. Sharon Batten's carries the real deal, designer clothes at designer prices, from Michael Kors to Luca-Luca. Unless you're a millionaire, the best time to shop here is during the store's semiannual sales, when merchandise is marked down as much as 75 percent.

Venus Swimwear Outlet Store
**11744 Beach Boulevard
(904) 265-8487
www.venusswimwear.com**
Looking for a very Florida bathing suit? Head to the Venus Swimwear Outlet Store located near the swimwear factory in an office park off Beach Boulevard. Tops and bottoms are sold separately, so its mix and match here. The prices are high—$26 to $45 for each part, a top and a bottom—but the swimsuits are killer, especially if you have the figure to wear one. The outlet store also has lots of sales and clearance prices on beachy dresses and cover-ups as well as last year's swimsuit designs. If you look really good in a Venus swimsuit, try entering the annual Venus Swimwear Model Search; you can find out more at the company's Web site. The outlet store is open Monday through Saturday 10:00 A.M. to 6:00 P.M. and Sunday noon to 5:00 P.M.

ATTRACTIONS

Jacksonville is an outdoor town. Even visitors find that they're more active here than they normally are at home. In the summer, once the day begins to cool off, neighborhoods, parks, and the beaches come alive. Chances are very good you'll find yourself doing something here that you don't usually do at home, say riding bikes or walking on the beach, fishing from a kayak, or horseback riding in the surf.

The diversity of attractions here, coupled with Jacksonville's natural beauty, keeps visitors coming back year after year. According to Jacksonville and the Beaches Convention and Visitors Bureau, 5.14 million tourists visited Jacksonville in 2003. Repeat visitors come back to play tennis, golf, fish, or just lie on the beach.

We definitely recommend you experience something historic on your visit(s) here. Number one on our to-do list is Kingsley Plantation, an indigo and cotton plantation of the early 1800s that is now a national park. There's a "big house" where owner Zephaniah Kingsley used to live and the remnants of many small tabby huts where his slaves lived. It's a very special place.

We also recommend at least one tour, be it a ghost tour of downtown, an art tour at the Cummer Museum, or a self-guided tour of Jacksonville's history at the Museum of Science and History. After all, who doesn't like to go home a little smarter having learned something on vacation?

In addition to the listings in this chapter, please see the Arts, Parks, and Kidstuff chapters for more ideas on things to do in Jacksonville. We've done our best to include up-to-the-minute information about hours and admission fees, but if you're on a tight budget or tight schedule, please call ahead to check if anything has changed since this book has been published.

PRICE CODE

$	Less than $5
$$	$6 to $10
$$$	$11 to $15
$$$$	$16 and over

Adventure Landing $$$$
1944 Beach Boulevard
Jacksonville Beach
(904) 246-4386
www.adventurelanding.com
There are two Adventure Landings in Jacksonville, but the one in Jax Beach is better. There's an extensive video arcade, bumper cars, laser tag, miniature golf, a virtual roller coaster, and a robotics performance of singing and dancing bears for toddlers. The whole family will enjoy the water park, with its huge slides and large swimming pool. (There's been at least one wedding at the top of the largest water slide, but as they say, it's all downhill after that.) There are separate prices for the water park, which is only open in summer, and for the attractions such as bumper cars and laser tag. Each added attraction costs $5.99, but special value packages are available at different times of the year. Adventure Landing is open weekdays until 10:00 P.M., midnight on the weekends.

American Red Cross Volunteer
Life Saving Corps
2 North Ocean Front, Jacksonville Beach
(904) 249-9141
www.redcrosslifeguard.org
Built in 1947, this is one of the oldest buildings in Jacksonville Beach. Better yet,

Florida's hurricane season runs from June to November. **i**

Saving Lives

Quietly tucked away on the ocean in Jacksonville Beach, sandwiched between a multimillion-dollar hotel and a multimillion-dollar restaurant, lives one of Jacksonville's oldest traditions. It's the American Red Cross Volunteer Life Saving Corps, which started in 1912 as a way to teach young men how to save lives in ocean rescues.

Today there are women in the ranks, the beaches are crowded like never before, and rip currents kill more swimmers than sharks and lightning combined. The Volunteer Life Saving Corps weathers every storm, changing with the times and remaining the only all-volunteer lifeguard agency left in the country.

To join the Corps you have to be at least 16 years old and a strong swimmer. Would-be lifeguards must also pass a four-month training program, which includes endurance tests such as a 550-meter swim (22 laps) in 10 minutes or less and a mile run on the beach in 8 minutes or less. There is also a written test based on textbook studies and performance tests, where students perform standard surf rescues both with and without a buoy.

About 70 lifeguards are needed to work the 18 lifeguard towers in Jacksonville Beach. Monday through Saturday, members of the Corps wear red swimsuits and are paid by the City of Jacksonville Beach. But every Sunday and holiday during summer, these same lifeguards don a navy blue swimsuit and volunteer as members of the Volunteer Life Saving Corps, thereby maintaining a tradition that began long before they were born.

A tradition in itself, the Volunteer Life Saving Corps is also a tradition within some families. Fathers have worked here, and so have their sons or daughters.

The ranks of the Corps include more than 5,000 alumni, some who were lifeguards as far back as the thirties and forties. These days their stomachs may sag and their hair may be gray, but those who can still pass the endurance tests are still allowed to "sit the towers" as volunteer lifeguards on Sunday and holidays—and many of them do.

The men and women of the Volunteer Life Saving Corps continue to sit the tower Monday through Sunday from 7:00 A.M. to 7:30 P.M. in Jacksonville Beach, constantly scanning the water for swimmers in trouble. It's been this way for more than 90 years, and if the volunteer lifeguards have their way, it will be this way for at least 90 years to come.

the Volunteer Life Saving Corps, which started in 1912, is the oldest life saving corps in the United States. Over the years, lifeguards have rescued literally thousands of drowning people. If the guards are not too busy dealing with beach emergencies, they'll take you on a free tour of their building, which includes dorm rooms and a tower with a killer view up and down the coast. (See the Close-up on this page for more on the long tradition of the Volunteer Life Saving Corps.) Free.

Annabelle Lee and
The Lady St. Johns   **$$$$**
Wharfside Way
(904) 306-2200
www.rivercruise.com
Some say the St. Johns River, which runs
through the heart of Jacksonville, is the
soul of the city. The best way to see the
beauty of this 310-mile-long waterway is
from the water, and the *Annabelle Lee* and
The Lady St. Johns make it easy to do just
that. Authentic paddleboats will take you
up and down the St. Johns while you
enjoy lunch or dinner, dancing, and the
great sights. You can also book the boats
for weddings, company picnics, even an
outing to St. Augustine. Both the
Annabelle Lee and *The Lady St. Johns*
have been in operation for years. Prices
vary, but generally a dinner and dancing
cruise will cost about $45 per person and
a luncheon cruise about $30 per person.
Reservations are required.

ATP Headquarters   **$$$$**
201 ATP Tour Boulevard, Ponte Vedra
(904) 285-6400
www.atptennis.com
The Association of Tennis Professionals is
the governing body for men's professional
tennis. At tour headquarters in Ponte
Vedra, there are 17 tennis courts of grass,
clay, and cushioned hard surface. Tennis
fans of all ages can take lessons or clinics
from former tour players. There's also a
nice little pro shop that sells tennis togs.
Call in advance for class and clinic schedules or court reservations.

Cummer Museum of Art
and Gardens   **$-$$**
829 Riverside Avenue
(904) 356-6857
www.cummer.org
Don't miss the city's premier art museum.
Upon her death in 1961, Ninah Mae Holden
Cummer bequeathed her home, gardens,
and collections for the Cummer Museum.
This is a soothing place, full of quiet
beauty and old-world charm. The collection of Meissen porcelain is one of the

three finest in the world. There are strong
collections of European and American art
as well as a significant collection of
Japanese woodblocks. Perhaps best of all
are the two acres of English and Italian
gardens along the St. Johns River, which
Mrs. Cummer created out of Florida's
sandy soil. The Cummer also has an
award-winning children's wing, called Art
Connections, which is somewhat bitter-
sweet because Mrs. Cummer was unable
to have children. (See the Kidstuff chapter
for more on Art Connections.)

The Cummer is closed on Monday and
major holidays and is open Tuesday and
Thursday from 10:00 A.M. to 9:00 P.M. On
Wednesday, Friday, and Saturday the
museum is open from 10:00 A.M. to 5:00
P.M. A good time to visit the Cummer is
Tuesday after 4:00 P.M., when museum
admission is free.

*For an up-to-the-minute calendar of
cultural events in Jacksonville, visit
www.culturalcouncil.org.*

Fort Caroline National Memorial
12713 Fort Caroline Road
(904) 641-7155
www.nps.gov/foca
Few people realize that the first European
settlers to come to America settled in
what is now Jacksonville, Florida. They
were French Huguenots, Protestants who
settled somewhere near the mouth of the
St. Johns River in 1564 and built Fort de la
Caroline in honor of King Charles of
France. The Spanish were outraged
because they had already claimed "La
Florida" as their own after Ponce de Leon
"discovered" it in 1513. The Spanish sent in
troops, who killed the French settlers,
destroyed their fort, and reestablished La
Florida as a Spanish territory. Nothing
remains of the original Fort de la Caroline;
in fact, archaeologists are still trying to
find it. But those early French settlers are
remembered at this memorial, where visi-

tors can walk through an "interpretive rendering" of their fort. The Huguenots likely befriended the Timucuans, the Native Americans they met when they landed, and the Timucuans are also remembered here. Don't miss the Timucuan hut and the ancient Native American log canoe at the visitor center. Wear your walking shoes, because you will likely do some walking. The fort lies at the bottom of a long, steep hill, but there are other gentle trails through marshland and forest that you may enjoy.

Everything here is free, and the park is open daily except Christmas from 9:00 A.M. to 5:00 P.M. (See the Tours chapter to find out how you can get to Fort Caroline by boat.)

Jacksonville-Baldwin Rail Trail
849 North Center Street
www.coj.net
This city park was created from 14.5 miles of unused railroad track (formerly the Seaboard Railroad Line) that's now a paved path for bikers, hikers, and in-line skaters. It's a great place to exercise for miles without having to worry about cars. There are three trailheads: East Head, a third of a mile north of Commonwealth Avenue on Imeson Road; Western on Brandy Branch Road, a quarter of a mile north of Beaver Street; and Baldwin, in the city of Baldwin, just off Center Street. There is a visitor center here. Many think that the Baldwin trailhead is the best of the three because there are restaurants

and convenience stores nearby. (There are also convenience stores at some of the seven crossroads that intersect the rail-trail.) There are no bicycle rental stores near the rail-trail. Three near the hotel/tourist centers are American Bicycle Company, Jacksonville Beach (904-246-4433); Bicycles Etc., near Southpoint hotels (904-733-9030); and Open Road Bicycles, near downtown (904-388-9066). Free.

Jacksonville Equestrian Center $-$$$$
13611 Normandy Boulevard
(904) 573-3150
www.jaxevents.com

Anyone with an interest in horseback riding will appreciate this new facility. Located on Jacksonville's Westside near the Cecil Commerce Center, the equestrian center includes a 123,000-square-foot indoor arena that seats 4,000 spectators around a show ring. There are also two outdoor rings and an outdoor practice ring, as well as barns where owners can board their horses. This venue was built for horse shows and competitions, but it also gives horse lovers a place to ride. The center is located on 832 acres and shares some of that land with the Cecil Recreation Complex. That complex includes a large community center and a four-field fast-pitch softball complex for girls. There's also an indoor Olympic-size pool that's open to all Jacksonville residents. Admission to the pool is free.

Jacksonville Fire Museum
1408 Gator Bowl Boulevard
(904) 630-0618

This free museum of fire history is a true portal to the past. It's housed, appropriately, in an old fire station—the Catherine Street Station—which for decades was manned solely by black firefighters. The building itself was destroyed in the Great Fire of 1901 and rebuilt a year later. It was moved from Catherine Street to its present location in 1993. There's an extensive display on the Great Fire, which historians believe was the biggest fire ever in the South (see the sidebar later in this chapter). Visitors can also learn what life was like in a fire station at the turn of the 20th century, when horses pulled fire wagons and firemen slid down brass poles. (See the Kidstuff chapter for more on how the museum uses history to teach fire safety.) Museum hours are limited, so call before you go to make sure it's open. Free.

Picnicking is allowed on Jacksonville's beaches, but open fires or grills are verboten.

Jacksonville Historical Center
1015 Museum Circle
(904) 398-4301

This little museum is hard to find but definitely worth the extra effort it will take to get inside its doors. Even those who don't love history will appreciate the center; Jacksonville's history has been boiled down to some of its most interesting moments, such as the Great Fire and the city's early role in the silent-film industry. There are wall displays full of pictures and easy-to-read explanations about big moments in the history of Jacksonville. Now, how to find this self-guided center: Driving south across the Main Street Bridge, you can see the Jacksonville Historical Center just to the left. The Maritime Museum is just to the right of the bridge. Park near the Museum of Science and History and walk past the Maritime Museum, under the Main Street Bridge via the Southbank Riverwalk to the Jacksonville Historical Center. Admission is free. We recommend a quick call ahead to make sure the center is open on the day you wish to visit. Free.

Jacksonville Maritime Museum
1015 Museum Circle
(904) 398-9011
www.jaxmarmus.com

The Maritime Museum is dedicated to preserving the maritime history of Jacksonville, and if you like ship models, this is the place for you. There are some 30 models here, the centerpiece of which is a 14-foot model of the USS *Saratoga,* an aircraft carrier once based at Naval Station Mayport. It's now mothballed in Rhode Island while the Saratoga Museum Foundation raises funds to open it to the public. Admission is free, but donations are greatly appreciated. The museum is open Monday through Thursday 10:30 A.M. to 3:00 P.M., Friday and Saturday 10:30 A.M. to 5:00 P.M., and Sunday 1:00 to 5:00 P.M. Free.

**Jacksonville Museum of
Modern Art**   **$–$$**
333 North Laura Street
(904) 366-6911
www.jmoma.org
JMOMA occupies a renovated space in a 1931 Art Deco building that used to house the Western Union Telegraph Company. The city's new downtown library wraps around the museum, which gives JMOMA an added luster of vitality. The collection here includes more than 700 works of art and is strongest in regional art, photography, and prints. Alexander Calder, Robert Rauschenberg, Frank Stella, and Helen Frankenthaler are also represented here. Be sure and bring the children to the top floor, where there's an interactive family learning center called ArtExplorium. It teaches kids all about line and design, photography, and folk art. And on your way out, don't miss Cafe Nola (short for North Laura). It's a great place to eat lunch or sip a pot of tea and enjoy something sweet. The museum is closed Monday and opens every other day of the week at 11:00 A.M. Closing hours vary. On Wednesday the museum is open until 9:00 P.M., and admission is free from 5:00 to 9:00 P.M.

Lunch

i *One of the best movie theaters around is at the Jacksonville Museum of Modern Art, where you can see documentaries and foreign films you won't see anywhere else in town.*

Jacksonville Zoo and Gardens $$–$$$
8605 Zoo Parkway
(904) 757-4462
www.jaxzoo.org
The Jacksonville Zoo feels a lot like Disney's Wild Kingdom theme park in Orlando. There's an African village with lush vistas, a South American village with tropical landscaping, the ruins of a 1,000-year-old Mayan temple, and even a large plain filled with exotic animals. The zoo holds more than 900 species of critters from apes to zebras. Don't miss the rare black bears in the Wild Florida exhibit, the elephants (one was donated to the zoo by Michael Jackson), or the flock of pink flamingos. We see so many of the plastic flamingo variety in Florida, it's a kick to see the real thing. Kids will enjoy feeding nectar to the Australian lorikeets, petting goats at the petting zoo, and most of all riding the Okavango Railroad, a 1.3-mile trip around a portion of the zoo's 60-plus acres. The zoo is located on the water near the confluence of the Trout and St. Johns Rivers. This means you can also take a "zoo cruise," a 30- to 40-minute ecotour of both rivers. You may even see a manatee. Tickets for the railroad or for the zoo cruise cost extra. The zoo is open from 9:00 A.M. to 6:00 P.M. in summer and 9:00 A.M. to 5:00 P.M. in winter.

Karpeles Manuscript Library Museum
101 West First Street
(904) 356-2992
One of seven manuscript libraries in the national Karpeles Museum network, this free museum is a quiet jewel in Jacksonville. Altogether, the seven Karpeles Libraries form the world's largest private collection of important original manuscripts and documents. The originals circulate among the seven libraries, which means that at any given time, there are 40 original documents on display in Jacksonville in exhibitions such as Great Moments in Medical History or World War II, Beginning to End in the Pacific. Visitors can also see the original draft of the Bill of Rights, or the original score of "The Wed-

ding March," or Einstein's description of his theory of relativity. The museum also hosts exhibitions by local artists throughout the year in its beautiful old building, formerly The First Church of Christ Scientist, built in 1921. The Karpeles is open Tuesday through Saturday from 10:00 A.M. to 3:00 P.M. Free.

Kingsley Plantation
11676 Palmetto Avenue
(904) 251-3537
www.nps.gov/timu
This is the former home of Zephaniah Kingsley, once one of the biggest slave traders in America. He married a young African princess, Anna Jai Kingsley, who was sold into slavery by an opposing Seneglaese tribe when she was just 13. Anna Jai bore Zephaniah four children and helped him run his plantations. These days Kingsley Plantation is operated by the National Park Service. The plantation house, the oldest remaining plantation house in Florida, has had many owners since Zephaniah and likely doesn't look a whole lot like it did in his day. A number of haunting tabby slave quarters stand as eerie reminders of a painful era in American history. Park rangers give excellent daily tours, explaining in great detail what life was like at Kingsley Plantation in the early 1800s. Kingsley is open every day except Christmas from 9:00 A.M. to 5:00 P.M. Admission is free. (See the Tours chapter to learn how to arrive at Kingsley Plantation by water.)

LaVilla Museum and
Ritz Theatre Complex $-$$
829 North Davis Street
(904) 632-5555
LaVilla was once a thriving African-American neighborhood in downtown Jacksonville, and this museum attempts to bring it back to life. Different rooms echo different aspects of African-American life at the turn of the 20th century. There's a schoolroom, a church, a living room, and a barbershop. The museum also explores the history of African-Americans in Northeast Florida, well before "La Florida"

You may want to consider becoming a member of the Jacksonville Zoo. The price of membership is actually less than it costs a family of four to visit the zoo twice in one year.

became a state in 1845. There is also an animatronic exhibit remembering two of LaVilla's most famous citizens, James Weldon Johnson and his brother, John Rosamond Johnson, who wrote the words and music to what became known as the Negro national anthem, "Lift Every Voice and Sing." In addition to the LaVilla Museum, there's an art gallery here that displays the work of African-American artists. (See the African-American Tourism chapter for more on this complex.) The museum is open Tuesday through Friday 10:00 A.M. to 6:00 P.M., Saturday 10:00 A.M. to 2:00 P.M., and Sunday 2:00 to 5:00 P.M.

Mandarin Store and Post Office
12471 Mandarin Road
(904) 260-9983
Around the turn of the 20th century, Mandarin was a quiet farming community. Walter Jones ran a general store, and the post office was located inside that store from 1911 to 1964. Today the general store remains much as it was, with items still for sale on the shelves. This is a great place to bring the kids to show them what shopping used to be like before the days of Super Wal-Mart. Also, don't miss the small room in the back of the store where artifacts from the *Maple Leaf* are on display. That was a Union transport ship that sank

Looking for a neat venue for a big party? You can rent the entire Range of the Jaguar setting at the Jacksonville Zoo and Gardens. Guests dine against the backdrop of a Mayan temple, complete with real jaguars. Proceeds help support animal care and educational programs at the zoo.

The Great Fire

Friday, May 3, 1901, started innocently enough with spring temperatures on the rise and a westerly wind keeping the air from feeling too still. But the day quickly turned devastating. At 12:30 P.M. a cinder from a chimney landed on fibers drying in the sun at the Cleaveland Fiber Factory at Union and Davis Streets. In short order, the fibers caught fire, and so did the wooden factory building. Eighteen-mile-an-hour westerly winds fanned the flames, which quickly consumed more wooden buildings.

The Jacksonville Fire Department scrambled to put out the flames. Every one of the city's 40 firefighters was called to duty, as were five horse-drawn carts, a pumper, a hook and ladder, a truck, and the fire chief. Still the fire spread, spurred by high winds carrying burning embers. Eventually 2,368 buildings encompassing 146 city blocks burned to the ground. At the height of the inferno, Savannah residents more than 100 miles to the north saw a bright glow on the horizon. In North Carolina, it's said, residents saw the smoke.

After seven hours of chaos, firefighters finally got a break. The wind died down, and an hour later the fire was brought under control. Remarkably, only seven people died in what has come to be called the biggest blaze ever in the South, yet 10,000 Jacksonville residents were left homeless. The nation rallied to help. Within days nearly $230,000 in cash and $200,000 in goods came from all over the country as Jacksonville began to rebuild.

off Mandarin Point in 1864. Much of the history of this area is wrapped around Harriet Beecher Stowe, author of *Uncle Tom's Cabin*. She used to live on a small farm right down the street from the store. During her 15 winters in Mandarin, Stowe grew oranges and helped open a school for children of freed slaves. She also raised money to rebuild the school when it burned to the ground in mysterious fire. Papers regarding her life in Mandarin, including a modern-day portrait of Stowe by a highly regarded local artist, are on display at a community center next door to the Mandarin Store. The Mandarin Store and Post Office is open the first and third Sunday of every month from 1:00 to 3:00 P.M. or by appointment. Free.

**Museum of Science and History and
The Alexander Brest Planetarium $$
1025 Museum Circle
(904) 396-6674
www.themosh.org**
There are really two museums here—a science museum and a local history museum— so, as you might imagine, this is a busy place. On the history side, an exhibition called Currents of Time gives visitors the history of Northeast Florida from the days of the Timucuans to the present. There are also artifacts from the *Maple Leaf*, the Union transport ship sunk in the St. Johns River during the Civil War. Science-wise, visitors can get up close and personal with a life-size replica of a right whale, one of the rarest whale species in

the world, which calve off the coast of Jacksonville every winter. Visitors can also meet the museum's mascot, Tonka, an ancient alligator snapping turtle. Tonka, or another critter of local interest, is often brought out to greet the public on weekdays at 2:00 P.M., when a museum naturalist hosts a show-and-tell called Featured Creature. The planetarium offers a variety of programs, including Cosmic Concerts, which are free with your museum admission. Kidspace is a popular permanent exhibit for children five and under. (Find out more in the Kidstuff chapter.) MOSH is open Monday through Friday 10:00 A.M. to 5:00 P.M., Saturday 10:00 A.M. to 6:00 P.M., and Sunday 1:00 to 6:00 P.M.

Museum of Southern History
4304 Herschel Street
(904) 388-3574

The Confederacy is remembered at this museum, which is primarily dedicated to

Local kids love the weeklong science camps at the Museum of Science and History, featuring themes like "I Can Be a Scientist" or "Dino Darlings."

Southern heritage. Civil War artifacts such as uniforms and weapons are on display here, but most people visit this museum to use its extensive library to look up ancestors who fought in the war. The library comprises some 2,500 volumes to help make your search a successful one, as well as army and navy records from the 1860s. Of course, it's best if you're looking for a Confederate relative, since that's what most of the books are about, but there is also a smaller collection of Union directories. The museum is open 10:00 A.M. to 5:00 P.M. Tuesday through Saturday. Admission is free, but a donation is much appreciated.

KIDSTUFF 👫

In the early 1990s Jacksonville found itself on *Money* magazine's list of 50 Fabulous Places to Raise a Family. The magazine reported what local residents (especially navy families) had known for a long time: The combination of community, cost of living, weather, and especially the Atlantic Ocean made Jacksonville a good place to put down roots.

There's a lot for children to do in Jacksonville, thanks in large part to its weather (year-round warm temperatures and sunny skies) and its geography. The city grew up on the banks of the St. Johns River then expanded east to the Atlantic Ocean to include the beach. Think of Jacksonville's beaches as one giant public park. Here children can teach themselves, year-round, how to surf by practicing over and over on relatively small waves, or they can attend summer surf camp to learn the basics of balancing on a board from experienced surfers. And, if you think surfing is just for boys, you need to head to the beach and see who's out there. Girls are learning to surf in record numbers in the United States, and by and large, the boys don't mind sharing the waves with them.

The beach is also a great place to do many other year-round family-oriented activities such as picnic, ride bicycles, fish, fly a kite, take a long walk (added bonus: shell gathering), kayak, swim, camp at Hanna Park, or simply relax.

Ditto the St. Johns River and its tributaries, which offer countless places for children to fish. If you want your children to stay on land, just head to the closest riverbank and cast a line. But better yet, call one of several guide companies and head out in a kayak to fish. Bonus: Children will get a firsthand lesson in environmental science as they experience an estuary system and see the critters that live in it. Children under 16 do not need a fishing license in Florida, but they will need a hat and some sunscreen, so plan accordingly. Be sure to read our Parks chapter for more ideas on things to do outdoors.

And there are other highlights: a museum of science and history designed just for kids, an art museum with an award-winning children's education wing, more parks to explore, and swimming pools, water parks, and water slides to enjoy.

If you want to hit the road, there are easy day trips that offer children some fabulous history lessons. Check out our Day Trips chapter for some fun ideas. And if you're really feeling energetic, you can always drive to Orlando for the day and take in a theme park; it's only about two hours away.

For up-to-the-minute information on things to do, check out the weekend section of the *Florida Times-Union*. It's included in the newspaper every Friday and will give you a great lineup of the current events.

As we write this introduction, this chapter is *au courant,* but it will never hurt to use the phone numbers provided to call ahead to be certain nothing has changed. Happy trails, and may your children enjoy Jacksonville as much as ours do!

PRICE CODE

$	Less than $6
$$	$6 to $10
$$$	$11 to $15
$$$$	$16 and over

THE INSIDERS' TOP 10 LIST OF MOMS' FAVORITES

1. The beach. Buy some cheap sand toys and head to the ocean. It will keep kids of all ages occupied for hours. Parking can be hard to find, so here's a real insider's tip: Drive to Atlantic Beach, and park in designated parking places near the accesses on Beach Avenue. These places fill up fast, so go early.

2. Museum programs. Local museums know that children are some of their best patrons and cater to them. The Moms' Network speaks highly of the Art in the Afternoon classes at the Cummer Museum of Art and Gardens. It's a weekly hour-long art class for kids ages 4 to 10. The cost is $7.00 per child. But arrive early—classes fill up fast.

3. Neighborhood parks. From small pockets of green to the granddaddy of them all, Kids Kampus, parks are an important part of Jacksonville. Don't miss the large community park in Jacksonville Beach called Sunshine Park. It was the brainchild of two volunteer moms, who spent two years planning it, soliciting donations, and organizing volunteers to build it.

4. Storytimes. This is a great way to introduce your children to new books. The big chains have the space to really go all out and include snacks and crafts in their storytimes.

5. Animal adventures. The Moms' Network is big on the Jacksonville Zoo. The Alligator Farm in St. Augustine is also a big winner; so is BEAKS, a nonprofit sanctuary on Big Talbot Island for injured birds. And if you're looking for a fun day trip, try Marineland, south of St. Augustine.

6. St Johns River Ferry. For $2.75 you can put your car on a ferry and cross the St. Johns River between the fishing village of Mayport and Fort George Island. It's a short trip, but kids of all ages enjoy getting on a boat, especially with the car. Departures are basically every 30 minutes, but call (904) 241–9969 for a more detailed schedule.

7. Camping and fishing. There are some beautiful and convenient camping spots within the city limits. And bring a rod and reel, because you can wet a line at most campgrounds.

8. Football. Jacksonville residents are passionate about football. From the Florida Gators to the Florida State Seminoles to the Jacksonville Jaguars, it's easy to take in a game if you visit at the right time of year. Tailgating, as you may expect, is equally big around here.

9. Public libraries. Jacksonville has beefed up its public library system, and it shows. Most branches offer free family programs, faithfully attended by many moms and kids of all ages.

10. *First Coast Parent.* A monthly newspaper with up-to-the-minute listings of events and programs for children. It's free, and you can pick it up, where else, at the library!

MUSEUMS

Art Connections at the Cummer Museum of Art and Gardens $-$$
829 Riverside Avenue
(904) 356-6857
www.cummer.org
Art museums don't get much better than this. Your child will enjoy learning about art, science, and imagination on the computers at Art Connections, which is an entire award-winning wing of the Cummer Museum of Art and Gardens built just for kids. Children use the computer to learn such principles of art as shape, color, line, and texture. Or they can roll up their sleeves and do a rubbing or a collage. They can also learn about Florida history through paintings in the Cummer's collection or watch a movie about Picasso. (See the Arts chapter for more on this Jacksonville jewel.) Admission to Art Connections is the same as general museum admission. Best of all, admission is free every Tuesday evening from 4:00 to 9:00 P.M. Check out the Cummer's Web site to find out about art classes and special events.

Jacksonville Fire Museum
1408 Gator Bowl Boulevard
(904) 630-0618
Firefighting has come a long way since the 1800s when Jacksonville residents

used to throw glass balls filled with water at a fire. Some of these early "fire extinguishers" are on display at the Jacksonville Fire Museum; so is a big exhibit on the Great Fire of 1901, which wiped out most of Jacksonville. The museum's most prized possession is a steam pumper from 1898. It had to be pulled by horses, which lived in the fire station under the same roof as the firemen. The museum itself is housed in the old Catherine Street Fire Station, which was destroyed in the Great Fire and rebuilt soon after. The entire complex is adjacent to Kids Kampus, Jacksonville's children's park. Admission is free, but at this writing the museum is only open on Wednesday from 9:00 A.M. to 4:00 P.M., so plan ahead if you want to visit. (See the Attractions chapter for more about this museum.)

Most locals stay out of the sun between 11:30 A.M. and 4:30 P.M. in summer. They also lather on the sunscreen whenever they go to the beach.

**Kidspace at the Museum of
Science and History** $$
**1025 Museum Circle
(904) 396-6674
www.themosh.org**
Museum curators call Kidspace a hands-on area that encourages kids to learn to love science. Children just call it fun. Your climbing toddler will find herself hanging from the limbs of a huge indoor tree house. And once you pull her away from that, she'll love the water area, which is basically a low trough with water running through it and lots of water toys inside to play with. (Plastic smocks are hanging nearby to help your child stay dry. Right!) There's also a large wooden train set within easy reach for would-be conductors. Kidspace is located on the main-floor lobby, but children will be interested in the rest of the museum as well, including the Alexander Brest Plane-

tarium—it's a great place to track Santa's progress in December as he leaves the North Pole and heads to Jacksonville. (See the Attractions chapter for more on this museum.) Ask at the front desk about animal programs. The museum keeps lots of critters (snakes, turtles, etc.), which specialists bring out for feeding and petting at various times of the day.

Sprinkles Children's Museum $
**101 West First Street
(904) 632-2FUN**
It's hard to find a place that both toddlers and teens enjoy, but this is it. The Sprinkles museum is housed in a large, lovely space on the ground floor of the Karpeles Manuscript Library. Here kids can pretend to be a doctor, an actor, an athlete, a musician, even Sprinkles the Clown, the museum's namesake. Exhibits are designed to get kids to think about career choices; for instance, the Doctor Exhibit has a motorized hospital bed and X-ray and blood pressure machines and is sponsored by a local hospital. The Athlete Exhibit has lots of exercise equipment and is sponsored by the Jacksonville Jaguars. There's also a library full of children's books and puzzles, a tearoom where kids can sit at tiny tables and have a tea party, a grocery store brimming with plastic fruits and vegetables, and a closet full of dress-up clothes and a stage to wear them on. Adults can take the elevator upstairs for some quiet time in the Karpeles Manuscript Library. Be sure to call ahead because the hours vary.

Sprinkles Playroom, Mandarin $
**Mandarin Landing Shopping Center
10601-1 San Jose Boulevard, Suite 1
(904) 880-2202**
A chip off the old block, the Mandarin Sprinkles Playroom is a lot like its older cousin, Sprinkles Children's Museum. The Mandarin version still has a grocery room, a tea party room, a doctor's room, and a place for dress-ups. But this museum, which is located right next door to a Publix grocery store, also has an outdoor area

where kids love to ride tricycles and play in sandboxes and little houses. The Mandarin museum also has different events than the downtown museum, so call ahead for schedules.

ANIMAL ATTRACTIONS

BEAKS
12084 Houston Avenue
(904) 251-BIRD
Located on Big Talbot Island en route to Fernandina Beach, this nonprofit bird sanctuary is well worth the effort to find and visit. When you pull into the parking lot, the welcome committee—a pair of peacocks—will usually stroll over to greet you. Children love walking the trails in this pristine North Florida setting and stopping at various bird cages housing injured birds being nursed back to health. About 2,000 injured birds are brought to the sanctuary every year. Some, like a bald eagle, became permanent residents. Someone shot him in the wing, and he can never live in the wild again. Admission is free, but donations are very welcome. The sanctuary is open for visits Tuesday through Sunday noon to 4:00 P.M. All other hours are by appointment. Free.

Jacksonville Zoo and Gardens $$-$$$
8605 Zoo Parkway
(904) 757-4462
www.jaxzoo.org
Kids will enjoy throwing peanuts to the elephants, roaring at the lions, and riding the 1.3-mile Okavango Railroad through the Plains of East Africa. Be sure to stop at the Okavango Petting Zoo, where goats will nibble at your buttons, and walk through the giant aviary where 50 different species of birds fly over your head. Definitely bring a stroller, and if you visit in the summer, arrive early when the temperature is cooler (or else you really will think you're in Africa). This is a great place to bring a picnic. (See more about the Jacksonville Zoo in the Attractions chapter.)

Make sure your child wears sneakers or some other type of sturdy shoes to the Jacksonville Zoo. Most kids run around the zoo from the moment they arrive to the moment they leave, and sandals will just increase the chances of tripping and falling.

Marineland $$-$$$
9600 Ocean Shore Boulevard
(904) 460-1275
www.marineland.net
Why drive all the way to SeaWorld when your child can stand on an elevated trainer's platform, hold a fish in his or her hand, and have a dolphin jump up and eat it right here in Jacksonville? Marineland was the first oceanarium built in Florida, in 1938, and thanks to a dedicated few, it's still open today. There may not be a killer whale here, but there are plenty of dolphins, sea lions, penguins, and flamingos. There's also a 450,000-gallon reef oceanarium where your son or daughter can snorkel or scuba dive. Oh, and don't forget a change of clothes. Those dolphins make a big splash when they jump for their fish. (See more about this attraction in the Day Trips chapter.) Marineland is open every day except Tuesday.

St. Augustine Alligator Farm $$-$$$
Highway A1A South
(904) 824-3337
www.alligatorfarm.com
This could well be the single best place to take your children in all of Northeast Florida. Kids are fascinated by alligators, a true Florida attraction, and this place is wall-to-wall alligators—more than a thousand of them. Guests walk on a wooden boardwalk and peer down at the gators lying in pools below. For an added attraction, visit at feeding time; then you'll see these creatures, which appear so sedentary, move faster than most people ever realized they could. Kids will also enjoy the large collection of rare birds and

Turtle Watch

You could say that Mort Hanson has hundreds of grandchildren. But his grandchildren are all four-legged reptiles and live in the ocean. Hanson, founder and director of the Beaches Sea Turtle Patrol, Inc., hops in his special dune buggy every morning from May 1 to October 31 to patrol Jacksonville's beaches for sea turtles. That's because solitary female loggerhead turtles (and sometimes leatherbacks) faithfully crawl ashore on these beaches, the same beaches where they were born, to lay their eggs. They dig a hole in the sand, push out about 100 golfball-size eggs, cover the nest with sand, then return to the sea. Even Mort has a tough time catching this happening, but he regularly patrols the beaches during nesting season for signs that a female has crawled ashore (turtle flippers leave a distinctive pattern in the sand). Once Hanson locates a nest, he dates it and stakes it off to protect the eggs while they develop. Children are usually curious about these little havens and fascinated to learn that there are sea turtles growing inside them.

It takes about two months for the eggs to develop, and the sand temperature, interestingly enough, helps determine the sex of the hatchlings. Scientists have found that cooler sand tends to produce more males, while warmer sand produces more females. Nature has programmed the hatchlings to dig their way out of their nests by the light of a full moon, which guides them to the ocean. It's important that no artificial light from, say, a street lamp or a restaurant confuses the hatchlings or they will lose their way and end up smashed on the road.

Jacksonville families, with Mort hovering like an expectant grandfather, have been known to sit by these nests nightly, waiting for them to hatch so that they can see the hatchlings scurry to the water and begin their life in the sea. Hanson operates a 24-hour sea turtle hotline (904-242-8111) so beachgoers can report problems or get nest updates.

snakes. Naturalists offer hourly programs, which could include a chance to hold a snake or pet a baby alligator.

SPORTS AND LEISURE

Adventure Landing $$$$
1944 Beach Boulevard
(904) 246-4386
www.adventurelanding.com
This is Jacksonville's answer to Disney World, and it will cost you almost as much for a family visit. It's an amusement park with two locations, one in Orange Park and the other in Jacksonville Beach. The Jax Beach location is nicer, so we've listed that address. Kids can ride go-carts, play laser tag and miniature golf, hang out in the video arcade, hit balls in a batting cage, and ride a simulated roller coaster. Best of all, there's a huge water park with some very big water slides that older children especially will enjoy. Each added attraction costs $5.99, but there are deal packs if you want to enjoy multiple attractions.

Antique Carousel in St. Augustine $
Intersection of Highway A1A and San Marco
No phone

More than 2,000 carousels were built in the United States between the 1880s and 1930s, but only some 165 are still in service. The wooden carousel in St. Augustine, built in 1927, still has the magic. Kids of all ages love to climb aboard a white charger with a wooden mane and race round and round to the finish. The carousel is open every day until midnight.

The First Tee $$-$$$
1157 Golfair Boulevard
(904) 924-0401

Sponsored by the World Golf Foundation, this nine-hole course was built to teach golf to economically disadvantaged kids, but anyone can play here. It's located on the Northside on a beautiful old golf course. The First Tee is geared to kids, and the pros are very accessible if you have a question about your stroke.

Sawgrass Stables $$$$
4185 Corbin Road
(904) 940-0200

This is the stuff that memories are made of. If you want to take your child horseback riding on the beach, June McDonald at Sawgrass Stables is a good person to call. She'll meet you at a designated beach access in Ponte Vedra with her horses, and away you'll go. Don't expect to canter through the breakers, however. Most rides are just walks with a touch of trotting. She also offers trail rides in Guana State Park. Making memories doesn't come cheap, though. A one-hour beach ride costs $65. A 90-minute beach ride is $80.

The University of North Florida Aquatic Center $
4567 St. Johns Road South
(904) 620-2854

Sometimes you just feel like swimming in a pool instead of the ocean, and when that time comes, the sparkling 50-meter Olympic-size pool at UNF fits the bill. It's covered for year-round swimming, but in summer the sides are open for sunshine and sunbathers. Children will also enjoy watching the divers at the deep end perform stunts off the high and low boards. Swim for the day, or take swim lessons, diving lessons, or synchronized swimming classes.

Rent beach cruisers and ride on the beach at low tide. It's the best park in town! FYI: Florida law requires that all cyclists under age 16 wear a bicycle helmet. Violators can be fined.

PARKS, WATER PARKS, AND PLAYGROUNDS

Kids Kampus
1410 Gator Bowl Boulevard

This is the city's premier park for children. It's 10 wonderful acres of playground equipment and amusement located downtown in Metropolitan Park on the St. Johns River. At an area called Safe City children can borrow tricycles and helmets and ride on 4 miniature blocks of Jacksonville's downtown, stopping at red lights and schools and stores made from Little Tykes houses. Best of all, there's a wonderful water park here with squirt guns, sprinklers, jungle gyms —even a small water slide. It's only open in summer, when it's a great place to cool off. Lifeguards make sure nothing gets too wild. Admission is free. (For more on this and most of the parks in this section, see the Parks chapter.)

Sunshine Park
Corner of South Beach Parkway and Osceola Street, Jacksonville Beach

This is truly a community park. It's the brainchild of two Beaches moms, who worked for two years raising the money, designing the park, and organizing the hundreds of volunteers who built it in just five days. There are all kinds of play structures for children to climb on, crawl through, and swing on; and there are neat things built into the structures themselves, such as musical instruments and artistic tiles created by local kids. Admission is free.

Tree Hill Nature Center $
7152 Lone Star Road
(904) 724-4646
www.treehill.org
Tree Hill is a city park and wildlife preserve located right in the middle of a Jacksonville suburb called Arlington. It's more than 70 acres of gentle walks in the woods, swamp areas, wildflowers, and wildlife-viewing areas. There's also an indoor nature center, where kids can learn about the environment and the critters that live in it. Bottom line: This is a good place to teach your children about nature.

Don't miss the World of Nations Festival held each spring in Metropolitan Park. It's arguably the best family festival Jacksonville offers its residents.

Walter Jones Historic Park
11964 Mandarin Road
(904) 260-9983
Want to know what life was like on a farm by the river in the 1870s in Jacksonville? Then come here. There's a restored farmhouse that dates back to 1875 and a cedar-sided barn of the same period. There's also a beautiful boardwalk along the riverfront, a nature trail, and shaded picnic facilities. Guides in period dress will show you around the park and tell you what the farmstead was like in the 1800s and how it has changed through the years. There's also an exhibit of items recovered from the *Maple Leaf*, a Union ship that sank off nearby Mandarin Point in 1864 during the Civil War. Free.

The Water Playground at
Kathryn Abby Hanna Park $
500 Wonderwood Drive
(904) 249-4700
This water park, located in the heart of Hanna Park, is open only from the middle of April through September. Children ages nine and under are welcome here, and they will love splashing around in the sprinklers and climbing on the plastic playground equipment. Lifeguards keep vigil. Admission to the water park is covered by your admission to Hanna Park itself.

CAMPING

Huguenot Memorial Park $
10980 Heckscher Drive
(904) 251-3335
Anglers love Huguenot Park, which is located on a small spit of sand and silt bordered by the Atlantic Ocean on one side and the St. Johns River on the other. It's the only beach left in Duval County where you can drive your car onto the sand, which means the beach is crowded with day trippers who bring cars, grills, umbrellas, and big coolers. There are just 72 campsites at Huguenot for tents or RVs, and most of these sites have spectacular views across the St. Johns River to the ships at Mayport Naval Station. But be careful swimming here. The park is located near where the St. Johns empties into the Atlantic Ocean, and there are tremendously swift tidal changes and, unfortunately, too many drownings.

Kathryn Abby Hanna Park $-$$$$
500 Wonderwood Drive
(904) 249-4700
It's hard to imagine a camping spot that feels so away from it all but actually is well within the Jacksonville city limits—25 minutes from downtown. There are 450 acres of pristine North Florida woodland for kids to run wild in, a mile and a half of secluded beach, trails for hiking and biking, and 60 acres of stocked freshwater fishing. The

300 campsites fill up fast (many are occupied by RV campers who stay for a while), so call ahead for a reservation. Hanna officials have also built four one-room cabins that are air-conditioned and a great place for families to rent. There's a two-night minimum on the cabins, which rent for about $34 a night. Whether you come for the day or spend the night, it seems everyone leaves a happy camper.

ON STAGE

Jacksonville Symphony Orchestra $$$
300 West Water Street
(904) 354-5547
www.jaxsymphony.org
The Jacksonville Symphony offers a Family Series every season that's a great way to introduce children to the world of Beethoven and Bach. The series includes a Halloween concert called Symphonic Spooktacular (even the conductor dresses up) and a Holiday Pops Concert in December. The symphony plays outdoors in Metropolitan Park during spring and summer, and carloads of families come to sit on the grass and enjoy the music. Tickets can be purchased at the box office or online.

River City Playhouse $$-$$$
1026 South Edgewood Avenue
(904) 388-8830
This theater is dedicated to performances for children—from classic fairy tales to original educational productions. Some plays feature young actors from the theater's acting classes and workshops; others feature professionals from the theater's paid staff. Either way, the productions are always high quality and the theater, which seats 150, is usually full.

Theatreworks, Inc. $$-$$$
1 East Independent Drive
(904) 353-3500
www.theatreworksjax.com
Theatreworks is not a theater or even a theater company. It's a nonprofit organization that brings live professional children's touring productions to Jacksonville. There's also a Super Sunday series for families at Florida Theatre, which includes musicians, smaller dramatic productions, and ethnic dance troupes. Most performances are sellouts, so be sure to get reservations. Check out the Web site for a schedule of upcoming events.

KIDS NIGHT OUT

Al's Pizza $$-$$$$
303 Atlantic Boulevard, Atlantic Beach
(904) 249-0002
www.alspizza.com
We've never met a kid yet who didn't like Al's Pizza. Buy it by the slice, or buy it by the pie. We recommend the White Pizza, made with ricotta and fresh tomato, or the Spicy Caribbean Pizza that tastes like jerk chicken. There's also lots of other things to eat here, like calzones, salads, BLTs, and subs and pastas. Al's has three other locations, including one downtown in Riverside. All of them are very kid friendly.

Your child will love creating a "beary good friend" at the Build-A-Bear Workshop at the Avenues Mall. It's also a great place for birthday parties. Call (904) 538-0760 for more info.

Chick-Fil-A $
Five locations around town
Monday or Tuesday night is kids night at Chick-Fil-A (depending on the restaurant), and that means kids will eat for less and be entertained in the process. Some nights there's a magician; other nights it's a clown who'll paint your face. Either way, there's usually free ice-cream cones with lots of toppings, provided you buy a kid's meal. Children love the chicken nuggets here. By the way, all Chick-Fil-As are closed on Sunday so that employees can spend time with their families. The restaurants also have indoor playgrounds.

Throw a bottle of meat tenderizer into your beach bag. It's the best thing to sprinkle on a jellyfish sting.

Golden Corral $
Five locations around town
Without sounding like a commercial, let us just say that Jacksonville loves the Golden Corral, where you can eat and eat and eat at a very reasonable price. Even the most finicky child will find something to enjoy here, from macaroni and cheese to steak to pizza. Children age three and under eat free.

The Loop $$
Eight locations around town
www.looppizzagrill.com
Kids will gobble up the chicken fingers, hamburgers, hot dogs, pizza, and fries. There are also salads and soups. Check out the menu online.

Sliders Oyster Bar and
Seafood Grille $$-$$$
218 First Street, Neptune Beach
(904) 246-0881
Try Dawson's Fish Dinner, named after the owner's daughter. It includes a nice piece of white fish, some fresh broccoli, and great mashed potatoes that even the pickiest eater will enjoy. Or order your child a burrito filled with black beans, chicken, or beef. Parents will especially enjoy it here because they can still feel as though they're eating someplace cool, even with the kids along. Dine inside or out at this popular Beaches eatery, where the food is fresh and families are welcome.

SWEETS

The Edgewood Bakery $
1022 South Edgewood Avenue
(904) 389-8054
If you go to the River City Playhouse for a children's theater performance, stop in at the Edgewood Bakery a few doors down

and pick up some gingerbread cookies. Children have been enjoying them for decades. They're legendary!

Peterbrooke Chocolate Factory $-$$$
1470 San Marco Avenue
(904) 398-2489
Watch chocolate made into all sorts of delectables, including chocolate-covered pretzels, chocolate-covered strawberries, and chocolate-covered Oreos and graham crackers. The free samples alone are worth the trip. Peterbrooke is a local chocolatier with a production center (listed above) and five area retail stores. If you can't make it to the factory, don't miss the chocolate.

Rita's Italian Ice $
393 North Third Street
(904) 246-1762
There's nothing sweeter after a day in the hot sun at the beach than to head to Rita's in Jacksonville Beach for an Italian ice. You can't miss the place; it's on the main drag near the Jacksonville Beach City Hall. Rita's has many flavors of Italian ice, including such exotic ones as mango and passion fruit. Try mixing the ice with some soft ice cream for a gelati.

STORYTIMES

Barnes & Noble Booksellers
11112 San Jose Boulevard
(904) 886-9904
www.bn.com
Moms in the know don't miss this storytime every Monday at 10:30 A.M. There's also a musical program called Clap and Sing on the fourth Friday of every month at 10:30 A.M. All programs are free, and there are often special events, so call the store.

Borders Books & Music
8801 Southside Boulevard
(904) 519-6500
www.borders.com
Every Friday at 10:30 A.M. employees read a story to the assembled throngs, who also

enjoy snacks and often a craft with the program. There are additional programs during any given month, including new stories read by a local children's book reviewer. Call the store to find out the latest. Free.

Shrink and Slide Family Play and Resource Center
14444 Beach Boulevard
(904) 223-0072
This is an interesting place. The owners, who are both clinical psychologists, sell large wooden play structures, the kind you put in your backyard. The play structures are on display all over this large store, turning it into an indoor playground. The owners also operate a small bookstore

The best ice-cream store in town is Brusters on Atlantic Boulevard near the intersection of Kernan Road. Be sure and try the seasonal specials, including blackberry and apple-caramel ice creams. Call (904) 221–1441 for more info.

here, selling all kinds of family-issue books, from potty training to explaining death to your little one. Storytime is held at the top of one of the play structures every Monday from 10:00 to 10:45 A.M. It's a great place to visit if it's raining or if it's so hot outside that you can't bear the thought of going to a park. Free storytime.

ANNUAL EVENTS

For a medium-size city, there are many interesting and entertaining things to do in Jacksonville. For instance, on New Year's Eve Jacksonville residents pack the Jacksonville Landing for a midnight fireworks display just like New Yorkers pack into Times Square.

Many of our big events center around sports—football classics like the Toyota Gator Bowl and the Florida-Georgia game or golf classics like The Players Championship. April and May have become festival season with a different festival either downtown or at the beach almost every weekend before the weather gets too hot.

The city of Jacksonville provides a great online event planner at www.coj.net/events that gives the exact dates (they often vary from year to year), times, and phone numbers for many events around Jacksonville. Enjoy!

JANUARY

Toyota Gator Bowl Classic
Alltel Stadium, 1 Stadium Place
(904) 798-1700
For over 50 years the Gator Bowl Association has been leading the charge when it comes to New Year's Eve and New Year's Day celebrations in Jacksonville. At the heart of the celebrations is the Toyota Gator Bowl Classic, a New Year's Day college football game featuring such big-name teams as Florida State or Notre Dame. The festivities begin on New Year's Eve when the Gator Bowl Association sponsors a festive downtown parade starring the marching bands from the two universities playing in the Gator Bowl. Afterwards, parade watchers usually get a bite to eat then head downtown to the Landing or Metropolitan Park for an evening of free music and midnight fireworks sponsored by the city.

Dr. Martin Luther King Jr. Parade
Downtown
(904) 775-0540
Marching bands from all over Northeast Florida practice for weeks in preparation for the annual downtown Jacksonville parade honoring Dr. Martin Luther King Jr. Church youth groups build floats, high school ROTC members shine their shoes, and homecoming queens have their hair done. This parade, which takes about two hours from start to finish, honors Dr. King's dream that one day man would not be known for the color of his skin.

Dr. Martin Luther King Jr. was no stranger to Northeast Florida. On June 11, 1964, he was jailed for trying to eat at an all-white restaurant at the Monson Motor Lodge in St. Augustine. A day or two later, members of King's nonviolent contingent went swimming in the Monson's all-white swimming pool to protest King's arrest. The manager became so enraged when King's followers refused to get out of the pool that he dumped muriatic acid into the water near where the protestors were swimming. It was an act heard round the world. There are many celebrations to honor the memory of Dr. Martin Luther King Jr. on his birthday, from church services to this parade in downtown Jacksonville.

FEBRUARY

Battle of Olustee Reenactment
US 90, 2 miles east of Olustee
(386) 758-0400, (877) 635-3655
Every February hundreds of Civil War reenactors gather at the Olustee Battlefield State Historic Site about 90 miles west of Jacksonville to commemorate the largest Civil War battle ever fought in Florida.

Confederate troops knew a force of some 5,500 Union soldiers was marching west to try to take Florida. They chose to make their stand in a forest east of Olustee because the area had certain strategic advantages: There's a lake called Ocean Pond on one side of the forest, a nearly impassable swamp on the other, and only a narrow passage between them. Veteran troops from Savannah arrived to reinforce Confederate troops already in Florida. By the time the two sides met in battle on February 20, 1864, each force had about the same number of troops. The men fought in the open forest until dark and then Union troops began a hasty retreat. The Union lost 1,861 soldiers that day, the Confederates 946. Many of the Union casualties were black troops—former slaves—who were unarmed. Reenactors strive for accuracy when they bring the battle back to life every year, and this is one history lesson you won't want to miss. The reenactment always happens over a weekend so the dates change every year. Call ahead for dates and times.

Black History Month
Various locations

From the Jacksonville Zoo to the Ritz Theatre, there are a number of citywide celebrations in honor of Black History Month. For starters, there are open houses at African-American historical sights such as the Clara White Mission, dance and music performances at the Ritz Theatre, and a Black History Day Tribute at the Museum of Science and History. See our African-American Tourism chapter for more on black history in Northeast Florida and local African-American sites. And check out www.coj.net/events for details on these dynamic events.

Much Ado About Books
Prime Osborn Convention Center
100 West Water Street
www.muchadoaboutbooks.com

Sponsored by the Library Guild, this fundraiser has generated hundreds of thousands of dollars for the Jacksonville Public Library—money used to buy books and computers and to sponsor after-school programs. The one-day event brings nationally known authors to Jacksonville for writing seminars, readings, and signings. The celebration is also marked by a dinner gala at the home of a prominent Jacksonville resident, giving guests a chance to mingle with the authors and enjoy good food and fellowship.

You don't have to be a professional cyclist to participate in the MS-150 Bike Tour to raise money to fight multiple sclerosis. The 150-mile ride starts at the World Golf Village and heads south to Daytona Beach then back again in just two days. Call (904) 332-6810 for more information.

MARCH

Concours d'Elegance
The Ritz-Carlton Hotel, 4750 Amelia Island Parkway, Amelia Island
(904) 636-0027

Even if you don't especially like car shows, you'll enjoy this one. Guaranteed. The Concours d'Elegance, which is French for "parade of elegance," is a vintage car show with over 1,000 of the sweetest classic cars you've ever seen. It's a trip through time with Bugattis, Packards, even ultra-rare Pierce Arrows. The event is held at the Golf Club of Amelia Island, in the shadow of the Ritz-Carlton resort. Stroll around this beautiful course and peruse the cars, or park yourself on a green and watch the cars parade by. The show is a huge draw for the area resorts and hotels, which fill up early with car enthusiasts. A relatively short time after this event began, classic car owners and top auto magazines rated it as one of the top three Concours in the country behind the Pebble Beach Concours in California and the Meadow Brook Concours in Michigan.

CLOSE-UP

Annual Whale Sightings

Like swallows returning to Capistrano, northern right whales return from New England every winter to the warm waters off Northeast Florida to bear their young.

Two longtime scientists at Marineland of Florida, David Caldwell and Melba Caldwell, first noticed this phenomenon in the early 1960s. They'd stand atop an oceanarium at the seaside theme park, gaze at the Atlantic, and watch the whales bask in the warm, shallow waters off the Florida coast. It wasn't long before they realized one whale became two on a very consistent basis and that the waters off Jacksonville, Ponte Vedra, and St. Augustine were the whale's natural calving grounds.

The northern right whale is the most endangered whale species in the world. Scientists now believe only 300 northern right whales are left in the Atlantic Ocean. There are southern right whales in the waters off Australia, but they don't travel into this hemisphere.

The Caldwells shared their observations on northern right whale reproduc-tion with scientists at the New England Aquarium, who were already so alarmed at the severely low numbers of this once plentiful species that they came to witness the Caldwells' theory in the flesh.

In short order Marineland became the headquarters for the Marineland Right Whale Survey project, which continues to this day. Volunteers from as far north as Cumberland Island, Georgia, to as far south as Flagler Beach, Florida, can call Marineland whenever a right whale is sighted offshore, especially a right whale with a calf. Sightings are most frequent in December, January, and February but have been known to continue into March and April. Marineland tries to document a sighting with photographs. At the end of calving season, it sends its collective data to the New England Aquarium. Scientists there keep a photo ID catalogue of the whales and assign each one a number to help keep track of the population.

Sadly, right whale sightings off the Northeast Florida coast are few and far between. These days the biggest danger

Gate River Run
Downtown Jacksonville
www.gate-riverrun.com
For over 25 years, the Gate River Run has been drawing world-class runners to Jacksonville for the nation's second-largest 15K race. This run showcases the city and the St. Johns River. Competitors must run through downtown and over two of the city's five main bridges, including the rather steep Hart Bridge at the end of the race. And with more than $50,000 in prize money, as well as travel expenses for top runners, the USA Track and Field Association calls the Gate River Run its national championship event. In

to these slow-moving creatures (they move, on average, about 1 mile an hour) is getting run over by a ship. Hence the U.S. Navy, the Coast Guard, and commercial ships are working together to try to prevent this. When a right whale is sighted during calving season, ships radio the Coast Guard, which broadcasts the sightings to all ships in the area, warning them to slow down and be on the lookout for the whales.

Marineland is becoming proactive in trying to find right whales and document them with photographs. Marineland scientists have applied for and received grant money to lease slow-flying planes called Air Cams, which were designed for National Geographic photographers to use in wildlife studies in Africa. The planes make great platforms for Marineland scientists with telephoto lenses to get good photographs of right whales. Pilots fly in a box pattern, a typical search-and-rescue strategy, in areas predetermined by previous sightings. The planes are also relatively quiet, so they don't scare away the whales if any are found.

Photographs are an important way of identifying right whales, which form callosities, or callouslike growths, on top of their heads at a very young age. The cal-

losities are made from tissue similar to fingernails; because they are light in color, they stand out clearly. To scientists, a whale's callosities are just like a fingerprint, making each whale identifiable as an individual.

In 2002 Marineland scientists experienced unbelievable whale-sighting luck. In one week they photographed three pairs of right whales from a blimp on loan from Fuji Film. Two pairs were mothers with their calves; the other pair was two adults.

Scientists believe 15 calves were born off the South Georgia and Northeast Florida coast in 2002. In a normal year 11 calves are born, so that makes 2002 an above-average birth year. "When you only have 300 individuals, you have to question how many are actually available to get pregnant in any given year," said Joy Hampp, current coordinator of the Marineland Right Whale Survey project.

Hampp says it's an absolute thrill to see a right whale. "It's really a privilege," said Hampp. "They are so rare we don't know how long we'll be able to see them off our coast. Plus, they are 45 feet long and weigh 60 tons. To see them in the water frolicking with their babies is just an experience of a lifetime for many people. It's something you never forget."

1995 Todd Williams became one of the fastest runners to finish the race at 42:22. And if you're not in shape to compete in the 15K, there are other runs the entire family can enjoy. At 8:00 A.M., an hour before the 15K, there's a noncompetitive 5K run and walk for charity. After the 15K there's a 1-mile fun run for children 13 and

under and the 25- to 40-yard Diaper Dash for babies.

Blessing of the Fleet
Downtown Riverfront
(904) 630–3690
This ritual happens every spring at the start of boating season. Whether you own

a yacht, a sailboat, or even a dinghy, a prominent city spiritual leader will sprinkle holy water on (or near) your vessel during a large public ceremony. It's a tradition that dates back to the early days of Christianity when fishermen and their boats were blessed in the name of safe seas and successful catches.

Pack a picnic dinner and head to Jacksonville Beach for a free pops concert performed by the Jacksonville Symphony Orchestra. For schedule information go to www.jacksonvillebeach.org or call (904) 247-6100, ext. 6.

The Players Championship
TPC at Sawgrass, Ponte Vedra
(904) 273-3383
www.playerschampionship.com

Watch the best professional golfers vie for the winner's cup on the Stadium Course at the Tournament Players Club at Sawgrass. Early in TPC week, the galleries are small and fans can walk next to their favorite golfer. By the weekend, though, the course is packed and you have to hustle to stay close to Tiger Woods. Many people try a different approach and just park themselves by a favorite hole and watch the golfers come by. This premier event comes with just one warning: The weather is sometimes as big a story as the golf, with torrential downpours, biting wind, or, if you're lucky, spring temperatures and sunny skies. See the Golf chapter for more on this popular event.

APRIL

The Bausch & Lomb Championships
Amelia Island Plantation
(800) 486-8366
www.ameliaislandplantation.com

Start with nine straight days of world-class women's tennis, stir in a beautiful resort dripping with picturesque Spanish moss, and you have the recipe for a sports lover's delight. There is one slight drawback, however. The field of players at the Bausch & Lomb is never set until the last minute. Consequently, if you buy your tickets early, as most people do, and Monica Seles pulls out two days before the start of the tournament, you may be disappointed. Such are the vagaries of all professional women's tennis tournaments, however, and if this happens to you, you'll probably attend anyway (you can't get a refund) and have a great time watching other big-name and not-so-big-name tennis stars work hard for their money.

World of Nations Celebration
Metropolitan Park
(904) 630-3690

There is a growing diversity in Jacksonville, and nowhere is it more evident than at the World of Nations Celebration. Local immigrants representing their native lands, from Vietnam to Mexico, the Philippines to Russia, set up booths selling goods from their homelands. There is also musical entertainment such as Thai dancing or African drumming as well as delicious international cuisine. This is a great family event.

Riverside Avondale Spring Tour of Homes
(904) 389-2449
www.riverside-avondale.com

This is the city's premier home tour, on which participants have the chance to see inside about a dozen historic homes, churches, schoolhouses, and even gardens. At each stop, guides share anecdotes about the building and the community of Riverside Avondale. The homes are especially interesting because they've usually undergone extensive renovations and redecorating. Tour officials will give you a map of the sites when you buy your tickets and you can walk or drive between them. (We advise driving because the area is spread out.) In the end you'll leave Riverside Avondale with a new knowledge of the neighborhood, which is listed on the National Register of Historic Places as one of the largest historic districts in the Southeast.

Jacksonville Jazz Festival
Metropolitan Park
(904) 630-3690

The Jacksonville Jazz Festival is a great opportunity to hear world-class jazz right here in the River City in the riverside venue of Metropolitan Park. Jazz greats like Grover Washington Jr., Al Jarreau, Spyro Gyra, and the Manhattan Transfer have all played in this four-day festival. The Great American Jazz Piano Competition at Florida Theatre traditionally kicks off the festival. Some call the competition the best event of the entire festival—as four or five jazz pianists compete for top honors live on stage in an intimate setting. In 1983 Harry Connick Jr. competed in the Great American Jazz Piano Competition and lost—in fact, he didn't even place. He was just 16 at the time.

Springing the Blues Festival
SeaWalk Pavilion, 6 North Oceanfront
Jacksonville Beach
(904) 249-3972
www.springingtheblues.com

There's fun for the entire family at this popular event, which includes a crafts market, children's games, plenty of local seafood, and even a 5K run. But what everyone really enjoys is the music—blues tunes from the Mississippi Delta to Chicago. Some of the acts are well-known while others are just getting started, but they all play the blues like they mean it. The music will not disappoint and neither will the setting, which is right next to the ocean in Jacksonville Beach.

Opening of the Beaches Festival
Downtown Jacksonville Beach
(904) 247-3972

Every spring the Beaches officially open for the season. This is something of a misnomer, of course, because the beaches never close, but it's a good excuse to have a festival, and this one starts with a big parade that typically includes more Shriners zooming around in electrified minicars than you can shake a stick at. Local and regional bands play in the evening at the outdoor band shell in Jacksonville Beach. Surrounding the band shell are all the makings of a festival, including kids' rides and food booths.

MAY

Wavemaster's Surf Contest
Jacksonville Beach
(904) 241-0600

He's 50. He's been surfing all his life. Sure, he's not as quick as the youngsters who rule the waves nowadays, but he still thinks of himself as a surfer and always will. He decides to enter the Wavemaster's Surf Contest, the largest open amateur surfing contest in Florida, run by a bunch of guys just like himself (the Wavemasters). He arrives at sunrise on the big day, ready for his first heat. The waves are small, lousy really, but he manages to shine. The surfer in him really comes through and he wins his age group. The prize is not a trip to Maui, but winning is what it's about, and it makes him feel good all year long.

Spring Music Festival
Metropolitan Park
(904) 630-3690

Every spring Jacksonville sponsors a free music festival at Metropolitan Park, a beautiful riverside venue in downtown Jacksonville. This one-day festival usually coincides with Memorial Day and features

---

Fancy yourself an author? The Florida First Coast Writers Festival is held here every May. Attend workshops, meet agents, and recharge your creative juices. Go to www.opencampus.fccj.org/WF for more information.

The Jacksonville Film Festival is held every May and includes a screenwriting competition. Go to www.jacksonville filmfestival.com for details.

an evening of music by well-known bands. There is no admission, but you may have to pay $5.00 to park your car. And don't bother with that picnic basket—the guards won't let you bring it in. Instead, you must buy food and drink from a plethora of vendors who pay the city for the right to operate in the park.

Crawfish Festival
Location varies
(904) 378-0708
Either you love 'em or you hate 'em, those ugly little crawdaddys, closely associated with all things Cajun, including zydeco music. If you love 'em, by all means, enter yourself in one of the hourly crawfish-eating contests and see how many you can stuff into your mouth without throwing up. If you hate 'em, you can still enjoy the zydeco music at this weekend-long festival where 25,000 pounds of crawfish are boiled or fried for the eating pleasure of festivalgoers. The location of this festival changes, so call for latest info.

Isle of Eight Flags Shrimp Festival
Fernandina Beach
(904) 261-3248
www.shrimpfestival.com
This festival is anything but shrimpy. It's a four-day salute to the area's most famous crustacean, beginning with a Shrimp Festival Parade and ending with the Blessing of the Shrimp Fleet. Shrimping evolved into a modern commercial industry in Fernandina Beach in the early 1900s when fishermen started using motorized shrimping boats instead of rowboats to haul in their catch. This allowed them to go farther into the ocean to find shrimp and use bigger and better nets to catch them with. Needless to say, you can get shrimp cooked all kinds of ways at this festival. After you eat, stroll

along the docks and appreciate the shrimp boats that brought this North Florida delicacy to you.

The Kuumba Festival
Location varies
(904) 630-3690
Kuumba, which means "creativity" in Swahili, is the perfect name for this family festival, which celebrates African-American pride, culture, and creativity. The festival usually starts with a parade of participants dressed in colorful costumes of African royalty. There's African music, dancing and cuisine, and honors for the achievements of local African Americans.

Scout Blast
Location varies
(904) 388-0591
Jacksonville's Scout Blast is one of the 10 largest scout shows in the United States. Thousands of scouts from all over North Florida and South Georgia attend for a unique weekend of scouting and special events. Scout Blast also gives the public a chance to see what scouts are doing as each pack, troop, and post demonstrates skills, programs, hobbies, and activities they've learned in scouting. Scouts sell tickets to the event, which also helps them earn money for their troops. In 2004 Scout Blast was held at the Northeast Florida Equestrian Center, but locations have also included Naval Air Station Jacksonville.

The Mug Race
Rudder Club of Jacksonville
8533 Malaga Avenue, Orange Park
(904) 264-4094
This annual race is billed as the longest river sailboat race in the country. It's held on the first Saturday in May and is sponsored by the Rudder Club of Jacksonville, a local group of sailing aficionados. Over 200 sailboats enter the 38-mile race every year from Palatka to Jacksonville. The winner gets bragging rights for a year and "The Mug." For more on the race, see the Boating and Water Sports chapter.

JUNE

Florida Sports Awards
Times-Union Center for the Performing Arts
300 West Water Street
(904) 731-7100
This official sports awards show for the state of Florida is broadcast live on television throughout the state from Jacksonville's Times-Union Center for the Performing Arts. The awards, called Jaspers, honor top professional players, coaches, and teams statewide in football, soccer, baseball, and more. But that's not all. Perhaps most importantly, the Florida Sports Awards also celebrates local high school athletes for their performances throughout the year. It's a big honor for the kids and their schools.

Fiesta Playera
Jacksonville Beach
(904) 249-3972
www.fiestaplayera.com
Move over Miami—for a few hours at least Jacksonville feels as Caribbean as you. People from all over the state are drawn to this festival honoring Hispanic culture in Northeast Florida. Puerto Rico is especially well represented here with its bold flag hanging aloft and on sale at nearby booths. The music will have you dancing in no time, and the chicken and rice will leave you feeling satisfied. Whatever you do, stick around till midnight. That's when festival participants walk backwards into the Atlantic Ocean. It's a Puerto Rican tradition performed annually on June 23 in honor of St. John the Baptist as a way of cleansing one's soul.

Sail Jacksonville
North and Southbank Riverwalks
(904) 630-3690
Spectacular. That's a good word to describe this festival of tall ships. Sail Jacksonville has it all, including a pirate battle with cannons firing on the St. Johns River and the Norway Viking Ship Race. Ship tours and seamanship demonstrations are available when the ships are dockside.

Best photo opportunity: the Parade of Sail, when the ships arrive en masse in downtown Jacksonville. The *Schooner Freedom,* a 72-foot topsail based at the marina in downtown St. Augustine, usually participates in the Parade of Sail. So does the *Schooner Voyager,* a 100-foot gaff-rigged 1840s schooner replica that's based at the foot of Centre Street in Fernandina Beach. Children will enjoy their own special festival area on Hogan Street by the Jacksonville Landing that includes music, arts, crafts, and even special guests from the Jacksonville Zoo.

JULY

Freedom, Fanfare & Fireworks
Fourth of July Celebration
Downtown Riverfront
(904) 630-3690
The city of Jacksonville celebrates the Fourth in a big way with a two-day festival downtown along the Riverfront and in Metropolitan Park. The festivities begin the day before with a downtown parade and a free concert. Then on the Fourth, there's another, bigger concert in Metropolitan Park, usually with a popular country music star like Wynonna Judd. The evening ends with a fireworks display over the St. Johns River. Best of all, this event is free, except for the $5.00 you pay to park and the money you spend buying food and drink inside Metropolitan Park (the city won't let you bring your own).

Liberty Fest–Independence Day Celebration
SeaWalk Pavilion, 6 North Oceanfront
Jacksonville Beach
(904) 249-3868
If you'd rather celebrate the Fourth of July at the beach, Jacksonville Beach also does things up in a grand way. And there are big crowds (150,000 one year) to prove it. Liberty Fest begins early in the day with bands, a burger cookoff, and Frisbee dog

demonstrations. All this happens at Sea-Walk Pavilion in Jacksonville Beach, right next to the ocean. By 9:30 P.M. everyone is ready for the large, booming fireworks display, which can be seen for miles up and down the beach.

Vendors cook up fresh delights, from funnel cakes powdered with sugar to hot dogs smothered in mustard, catsup, relish, and onions. More ambitious revelers may decide to pack their own food and set up on the beach for a day full of swimming and eating.

The Bellsouth Greater Jacksonville Kingfish Tournament
Sisters Creek Marina
8203 Hecksher Drive
(904) 251-3011
www.kingfishtournament.com
Only 1,000 boats are allowed to enter this weeklong fishing tournament, each one paying $350 to fish for the biggest king-fish in Northeast Florida. Fisherfolk return year after year to enter this tournament even though it's usually hotter than Hades all week long. Participants don't seem to mind, though, in part because the prize structure is so enticing—more than $700,000 in boats, cash, and other prizes. Early in the week there's a Junior Angler Tournament, a chance for young ones to try their hand at catching an elusive kingfish. If you're a landlubber, it's fun to sit in the stands and watch as anglers bring in their catch for weighing. There's also music in the evenings and a carnival for kids.

AUGUST

Jaguars Preseason Games
Alltel Stadium, 1 Stadium Place
(904) 633-2000, (800) 618-8005
www.jaguars.com
Football fans start to glow this month. They smile more often, and friends notice a spring in their step. After seven months of waiting, fans can see the Jaguars play at Alltel Stadium again. College football

gets underway in earnest this month, too. Need we say more? Check out the Jaguars's Web site for a game schedule.

SEPTEMBER

Riverside Arts Festival
Historic Riverside Park
Corner of Post and Park Streets
(904) 389-2449
It's not often you get to compare an art festival to the Energizer Bunny. But the comparison works here, because after 30 years this festival still keeps going and going and going. About 130 artisans and craftspeople from all over the state set up booths along the sidewalk of this pretty park near the river to sell their wares. And thousands of people come to buy them. This two-day art festival is also kid-friendly. Artwork by local schoolchildren is show-cased at the event, and there's a Children's Fun Zone run by the Cummer Museum of Art where kids can enjoy crafts such as spin painting and architectural rubbings.

American Heart Walk
Downtown
(904) 739-0197
Annually 3,000 to 8,000 people participate in this walk, raising about $700,000 for the American Heart Association. The walk usually begins at 9:00 A.M. and covers a 3-mile course from Friendship Fountain Park, over the Acosta Bridge, through downtown, and back over the Main Street Bridge. Participants often collect donations ahead of time, and walkers who raise $100 or more receive a Heart Walk T-shirt. There's also a health fair and activities for children.

OCTOBER

The Florida-Georgia Game
Alltel Stadium, 1 Stadium Place
(904) 630-3690
This annual match-up between college football rivals is played on a Saturday, but University of Florida and University of

Georgia fans begin arriving the Wednesday before. They come in 40-foot RVs for five days of tailgating, showcasing elaborate feasts and even more elaborate decorations. If you attend the game, take a few minutes to walk through RV City, where there's lots of friendly rivalry and partying between Gator and Bulldog fans. After all, there was a reason this game earned the nickname "World's Largest Cocktail Party."

The Greater Jacksonville Agricultural Fair
Jacksonville Fairgrounds, Downtown
(904) 353-0535
Like all good agricultural fairs, this one offers a lot. For 4-H participants it's a livestock show, for cooks it's a chance to win a blue ribbon, and for country music fans it's a chance to hear a different musical act every evening. And children of all ages can scare themselves silly on death-defying rides. The fair usually lasts 11 days, with the best music and largest crowds on the weekends.

NOVEMBER

Jacksonville Sea and Sky Spectacular
The Beaches or NAS Jacksonville
(904) 542-3152
The Sea and Sky Spectacular is a fancy name for an air show. But there are many who believe this air show deserves the moniker because it's just so awesome. Feel the ground shake as the Blue Angels fly low overhead, imagine the stamina of aerobatic pilots who repeatedly loop the loop and battle g-forces with every bank and roll, and cheer as U.S. Marine amphibious assault units "take" Jacksonville Beach. Organizers plan to rotate the show yearly between the Beaches and Naval Air Station Jacksonville on the Westside for optimum viewing pleasure.

Veterans Day Parade
Downtown
(904) 630-3690
Veterans Day is an important day in Jacksonville, where the United States

Tailgating is an annual activity every fall in Jacksonville. According to the Touchdown Tailgate Guide, the No. 1 thing football fans need for a successful tailgating party is jumper cables.

Navy is one of the largest employers. Patriotism rules at this downtown event, which features military members of all ages from junior ROTC cadets to retired veterans. The governor of Florida often leads the parade along with the mayor, as thousands of parade watchers line the streets to cheer for high school marching bands, veterans posts, military commands, and the Jacksonville Fire and Rescue Department.

Jacksonville Light Parade
St. Johns River, Downtown
(904) 630-3690
Jacksonville prides itself on being a great family town, and events such as this justify the claim. Bring the grandparents, bring the kids, and head to the Riverfront on the weekend following Thanksgiving for a boat parade. Local captains decorate their boats in creative Christmas themes with thousands of lights and then parade their boats in front of judges at the Jacksonville Landing. It's a great way to get into the holiday spirit. And that's not all—the evening ends with a large fireworks display. It's no wonder the Southeast Tourism Society named the Jacksonville Light Parade one of the top 20 events in the Southeast.

DECEMBER

Wolfson's Art & Antiques Show
Prime Osborn Convention Center
(904) 202-2886
For more than 25 years, this art and antiques show has been raising money for Wolfson's Childrens Hospital. Dealers from all over the world participate. Guest lecturers are also invited. Recent speakers

include HRH Princess of Kent, who spoke on Louis XIV and the arts of 17th-century France, and Carolyne Roehm, interior and garden/floral designer, who discussed home design. There are also new exhibitions each year, ranging from heirloom silver to table settings designed by area hostesses. Lunch is prepared daily by a local restaurant, and tea and pastries are served in the afternoon.

New Year's Eve Celebration
Downtown
(904) 630–3690
Ring in the New Year in downtown Jacksonville with fireworks along the St. Johns River at midnight. The Gator Bowl Association adds to the festivities with a 5K Gator Bowl run in the morning and a parade in the afternoon. There are also pep rallies at the Landing for each of the teams playing in the Gator Bowl. There are usually New Year's Eve concerts around town, too, so be sure and check www.coj.net/events for the performance schedule. Best of all, these citywide festivities are free.

THE ARTS

There are those who say there's an arts deficit in Northeast Florida, and if you compare Jacksonville with, say, New York or San Francisco, we come out on the bottom. In its own way, however, Jacksonville has much to offer. We have our own symphony, our own pops orchestra, and the oldest continually operated community theater in the country. The city is a prime stop for traveling ballet productions and for traveling Broadway musicals, and we have one of the busiest dinner theaters in the Southeast. It draws busloads of guests from all over the region.

Jacksonville is also becoming a hub for visual artists. It's known as a great place for collectors to start an art collection because of the many "undiscovered" local artists whose work is still affordable. All you need is a good "eye" and a modest purse to get started. We've listed several excellent galleries to help you find what's out there.

This chapter is organized three ways: by venue, by production company, and by gallery. With just a phone call, you can find out "who's doing what where" all over town

THE VENUES

Alhambra Dinner Theatre
12000 Beach Boulevard
(904) 641-1212
www.alhambradinnertheatre.com
The Alhambra has been a little moneymaker since it opened in 1967. Dinner is all-you-can-eat buffet style, followed by one of Broadway's best musicals or comedies. Lead actors are paid equity, which means there's a consistent level of high-quality performances. Be sure to make reservations—large groups love this place, and the 406-seat theater fills quickly. Once you get those reservations, arrive early to avoid long buffet lines. And get dessert when you get your meal, or you may return to find the dessert table more or less empty!

Florida Theatre Performing Arts Center
128 East Forsyth Street
(904) 355-2787
www.floridatheatre.com
Florida Theatre opened in 1927 as a deluxe movie house. The interior of this 1,900-seat theater looks something like a Moorish palace, with touches of Art Deco thrown in for good measure. Sadly, there are only four theaters like this left in the state. Florida Theatre hosts hundreds of performances every year, from the Hong Kong Ballet to Judy Collins. They say that this is where Elvis Presley played his first indoor concert. Florida Theatre is a short walk from downtown hotels.

Friday Musicale Auditorium
645 Oak Street
(904) 355-7584
The Friday Musicale is a true Jacksonville tradition. It started in 1890 as a club for local women who enjoyed music and playing instruments like the piano. Today the club meets in a beautiful downtown building with its own modern 250-seat auditorium. Members host free concerts every Friday evening from October through May. The auditorium is also a popular place for music teachers to hold recitals. Located downtown in Riverside, the auditorium is available for rent. Call ahead for a concert schedule.

Bring a blanket or bring the lawn chairs. The City of Jacksonville Beach sponsors many free concerts in its outdoor band shell at SeaWalk Pavilion. Call the events hotline for the latest schedule: (904) 247-6100, press 6.

THE ARTS

Arbus, a free local arts magazine, is a must for the latest on the arts. You can usually find a copy at a coffee shop or bookstore.

Jacksonville Veterans Memorial Arena
300 A. Philip Randolph Boulevard
(904) 630-3900
There's not a bad seat in the house in this 16,000-capacity arena, which plays host to the likes of Aerosmith and Britney Spears. It's also a popular site for high school graduations, ice-hockey games, professional bull riding, and family shows like the circus. The arena opened in 2003 and features an outdoor sculptural display by Spanish artist Jaume Plena called *Talking Continents.* The artwork is composed of seven figures (for the seven continents) sitting atop flagpoles. The artists says these figures, which light up at night, are holding a silent conversation with each other, celebrating the arena's function as a meeting place for people. Fun arena fact: It took 2,000 tons of structural steel to build it, enough to build 1,500 cars.

Metropolitan Park
1410 Gator Bowl Boulevard
(904) 630-0837
From rap concerts to the symphony's outdoor family concert series, Starry Nights, a lot happens at Metro Park. Located on the St. Johns River, this beautiful outdoor venue can hold up to 20,000 persons. Seating in large concert situations basically means a blanket or chair on the grass, but there is also a canopy area to the back of the stage that holds 860 per-

sons and is a good place to be if it rains. The Jacksonville Jazz Festival is held here every year. Sadly, the city usually does not allow picnic baskets inside the park for concerts. It wants you to buy from the vendors who line the park and pay the city for the right to sell food and drink at Metro Park events.

Nathan H. Wilson Center for the Arts
11901 Beach Boulevard
(904) 646-2222
www.fccj.org
Located on the South Campus of Florida Community College at Jacksonville (FCCJ), the college calls the Wilson Center a state-of-the-art learning facility for students. We say it's also a sweet little theater enjoyed by the entire community. The main stage seats 530, and because it's so intimate, there's not a bad seat in the house. An art gallery near the theater entrance, called The South Gallery, displays work by both students and professionals. The South Gallery is open 30 minutes prior to every performance so that you can take in the exhibition as well as the show. The FCCJ Artist Series offers theatrical presentations here, such as Jackie Mason and the Glenn Miller Orchestra. Call the Wilson Center for an event schedule, or visit its Web site.

Times-Union Center for the Performing Arts
300 West Water Street
(904) 630-3900
Located downtown across the street from the Jacksonville Landing and several large hotels, this is the city's premier performing arts facility. There's a symphony hall (home to the Jacksonville Symphony Orchestra) as well as two theaters—one very large, the other very small. Traveling productions of big-name Broadway shows, part of the FCCJ Artist Series, are performed here. The Times-Union Center was renovated in the mid-nineties and now has state-of-the-art sound systems and theater production facilities.

The Cultural Council of Greater Jacksonville is the city's clearinghouse for the arts. The council compiles a great monthly arts calendar available on their Web site at www.culturalcouncil.org.

THE PLAYERS

Jacksonville Children's Chorus
(904) 514-4468

Some 30 voices strong, the Jacksonville Children's Chorus is the official children's chorus for the Jacksonville Symphony Orchestra. It's divided into a girl choir, a boy choir, and a concert and chamber choir. Under the direction of Twila Miller, the chorus has performed with the Jacksonville Symphony Orchestra at the Times-Union Center for the Performing Arts and at many civic events, as well as area schools, churches, and senior centers. Each singer in this diverse group must audition to be a part of the chorus. Singers, and families, must be dedicated to singing: Chorus members log many hours practicing for concerts and traveling all over town to perform.

Jacksonville Symphony Orchestra
300 West Water Street at the Times-Union Center for the Performing Arts
(904) 354-5547
www.jaxsymphony.com

Under the solid artistic leadership of Brazilian conductor Fabio Machetti, the Jacksonville Symphony Orchestra provides consistently top-caliber performances, often with guest appearances by top-name artists. The symphony, now well into its second half century, begins playing in mid-September and continues for 38 weeks through early June. The cornerstone of the season is the Masterworks series, which features selected works of top-name composers, but you can also enjoy a pops concert, a Friday-matinee coffee concert, or a family concert under the stars in Metro Park.

Players by the Sea
106 North Sixth Street, Jacksonville Beach
(904) 249-2022

A former in-line skating rink has been transformed, believe it or not, into a cozy community theater in Jacksonville Beach. The productions here are pretty typical of community theater everywhere and can make for an enjoyable evening out. Players also has a busy children's program called Acting Up, which includes special theatrical performances by the kids as well as a popular summer camp.

Fogle Fine Arts, a gallery and framing business on Philips Highway, is a must-stop if you're looking to buy art. Check out the computerized database at www.foglefineart.com.

River City Band
(904) 355-4700
www.rivercityband.com

Jacksonville's official brass band of 22 musicians plays America's music, including jazz and swing. This is the band the mayor calls when he needs music for an official function. The band also sports several ensembles for hire, which play everything from Dixieland to easy rock and roll. The River City Band plays free concerts all over town. Go to their Web site or call for a schedule.

River City Playhouse
1026 South Edgewood Avenue
(904) 388-8830

For over 25 years the River City Playhouse has provided Jacksonville with quality children's theater productions. The playhouse seats 150 and is frequently sold out with happy children enjoying performances. The paid staff produces fairy tales, educational productions, and classical children's theater. You don't have to be a kid to enjoy the show. Call the playhouse for schedules and ticket information.

Theatre Jacksonville
2032 San Marco Boulevard
(904) 396-4425
www.theatrejax.com

Since its opening in 1919, Theatre Jacksonville has continued to produce community theater, making it one of the longest

Jacksonville's Own

If you can't find C. Ford Riley painting up in his Mandarin studio on the St. Johns River, you'll find him hunting in the North Florida woods, paddling in an Amelia Island marsh, or fishing in a swamp off Black Creek. He never leaves on one of these excursions without a sketchpad, which is why the paintings that result from his getabouts are so good. They're lifelike but still artistic, a peaceful sigh in an ever-changing world. It's not an over-statement to call Riley Jacksonville's

Jamie Wyeth. Certainly, the CEOs and football coaches who pay thousands for his paintings seem to think so. Riley also paints birds and other Florida wildlife, reminiscent of John James Audubon, and he paints abstracts, which haven't quite caught on yet like the rest of his work. Less-well-heeled art collectors can still own his work: Riley also produces signed limited-edition prints, which are sold at Stellers Gallery.

running community theatres in the Southeast. And you don't keep 'em coming by producing schlock. This is the grande dame, if you will, of the city's community theaters. It's located in San Marco, which makes for a delightful evening out: dinner at a San Marco restaurant before the show, then coffee or drinks at a San Marco club afterward—all within walking distance.

Theatreworks, Inc.
1 East Independent Drive
(904) 353–3500
www.theatreworksjax.com
Theatreworks is a nonprofit organization dedicated to bringing live professional children's theater to Jacksonville. Organizers say that every performance uses the arts to help educate children in math, science, history, language arts, or creative writing. Performances are often productions of such famous children's books as *The Boxcar Children* or *Ferdinand the Bull*. Shows are usually held at Florida Theatre or The Wilson Center for the Performing Arts. Weekday performances are packed with excited children on field trips, many

of whom are enjoying a theatrical production for the first time. Theatreworks also presents a Super Sunday series of performances for families at Florida Theatre.

ART GALLERIES

Alford Studio and Gallery
1563 Alford Place
(904) 398–5788
Located in a small out-of-the-way strip center in San Marco, this gallery is well worth the extra effort it will take you to find it. Owner Sandra Alford is a clothing designer with a loyal following of wealthy, hip Jacksonville ladies. Artist John Bunker, one of Jacksonville's renowned local artists—and a former director of the Cummer Museum of Art—paints in this gallery every Friday when he's in town. Alford also represents several Italian artists, including sculptor Enzo Tocoletti and still-life painter Marco Gizzi. There's also a unique collection of giftware, including signed art glass, and affordable jewelry made by artists.

Cultural Center at Ponte Vedra Beach
50 Executive Way, Ponte Vedra Beach
(904) 280-0614
www.culturalcenterpvb.org

Every neighborhood should have a cultural center like this. It's a place for artists and budding artists of all ages to take art classes and show their work. Every spring the center hosts an art extravaganza, which includes an exhibit honoring professional artists from Ponte Vedra and beyond. The center is also a great place to catch free or inexpensive concerts and music classes. Call or visit the Web site for the latest schedule of events.

Fairfax Gallery
4216 Herschel Street
(904) 384-7724
www.fairfaxgalleries.com

Fairfax Gallery is a local favorite for colorful impressionistic paintings by contemporary artists. There are two locations, the one listed above in Avondale and another in Ponte Vedra Beach. Fairfax Gallery represents state, national, and international artists who paint pictures that look like they're straight out of the south of France.

First Street Gallery
216 First Street, Neptune Beach
(904) 241-6928

If you're looking for affordable art by local artists, this friendly gallery is a must-see. All the artists who display their work in the store must also work at the gallery. There's beautiful jewelry, unusual wood pieces, eclectic pottery, and lots of landscapes done in paint or photography. Some of the artwork sells for thousands of dollars, but most of it won't break your budget and will make for a pleasing addition to your home, office—even wardrobe.

J. Johnson Gallery
177 Fourth Avenue North
Jacksonville Beach
(904) 435-3200
www.jjohnsongallery.com

You can't miss this gallery. It's a huge, 15,000-square-foot, canary-yellow

---

If you're a young professional, you may want to join the Up and Cummers. Members support the Cummer Museum of Art and Gardens and enjoy lots of art-oriented social events, too. The top event is the monthly Art After Work: Cocktails and Culture at the Cummer. Go to www.cummer.org for more information.

Mediterranean-style building constructed in 2001 across the street from the ocean in Jacksonville Beach. Jennifer Johnson made a bold decision when she chose to spend millions building this state-of-the-art facility in Jax Beach, which has long had a somewhat seedy reputation. But she (and many others) believes that reputation is changing, hence her multimillion-dollar investment. Johnson, a Johnson & Johnson Company heiress, is herself an excellent photographer, and there's a lot of photography for sale here by nationally and internationally known photographers. There're also paintings and sculpture, much of it modern, by artists of the same caliber. The gallery hosts several major exhibits of fine art each year. It's open Monday through Friday 10:00 A.M. to 5:00 P.M. and Saturday 1:00 to 4:00 P.M.

Mussallem Oriental Rugs and Fine Art
5801 Philips Highway
(904) 739-1551

One of the most enduring and astonishing art galleries in all of Jacksonville is located inside a rug store. But don't be misled. This gallery carries some serious art dating back to the 16th century. There's also a great collection of glass, including works by Tiffany and Stuben. It takes several hours to wander around this huge space, which also encompasses the rug collection. And you can rent the elegant gallery space for private functions—Mussallem's will even cater it for you.

Learn about downtown art galleries firsthand on the first Wednesday of every month. That's when Downtown Vision sponsors the First Wednesday Art Walk. The event, which is free, runs from 5:00 to 8:00 P.M. Get your map stamped at each stop along the way and win a free gift! For more information go to www.downtownjacksonville.org or call (904) 634-0303.

R. Roberts Gallery
3606 St. Johns Avenue
(904) 388-1188
www.rrobertsgallery.com

Art lovers on a budget will find something affordable here; this gallery carries a wide variety of media, from original paintings to limited-edition serigraphs to blown glass. The gallery represents many artists, but one in particular stands out: Mackenzie Thorpe of England. If you don't know his work, you'll love it as soon as you see it—colorful, whimsical paintings, prints, and sculpture perfect for a child's room.

Stellers Gallery
1409 Atlantic Boulevard
(904) 396-9492
www.stellersgallery.com

Stellers Gallery has two locations: the larger, listed above, in San Marco and a second, rapidly expanding gallery in a strip center in Ponte Vedra. All art galleries should be this busy. Stellers's success comes in part because it's the exclusive gallery for Jacksonville's most famous painter, C. Ford Riley (see the sidebar earlier in this chapter). In fact, Riley's brother, Scott, operates the galleries. Plenty of other artists are represented here, too. In the end, though, if you want a marsh landscape to decorate your walls, this is the place to get it.

TOURS AND CRUISES

In Jacksonville, when you say the word "tour," most people think you're talking about the PGA Tour, headquartered in Ponte Vedra. That's because Jacksonville is not a place where you can hop on a Grey Line bus and have someone show you the sights. That said, there are motorcoach tours, but reservations need to be made in advance, and in some cases you need a large group. A good way to see Jacksonville is by neighborhood, and we've listed some tours to help you do that. You can also get a great feel for the city from the water, and we've got tour operators to help you do that, too.

HISTORY TOURS

Alpha Kappa Alpha's Tour of Historical Black Sites in Metro Jacksonville
(904) 356-0110
There are 30 stops on the entire tour, but guides with Alpha Kappa Alpha (the country's first black sorority) will tailor their program to fit your interests. Some of the sites include the Clara White Mission, a soup kitchen started in 1904 by a former slave and still in operation, and Bethel Baptist Institutional Church, which began in 1838 as an integrated church with six charter members back when slavery was still the law of the land. (For more about African-American sites, see the chapter on African-American tourism.) Reservations for the AKA Tour of Historical Black Sites must be made in advance.

Destinations Unlimited Tours
9951 Atlantic Boulevard
(904) 722-8100
www.destinationsunlimitedtours.com
If your group is looking to book a history tour of Jacksonville or St. Augustine, Destinations Unlimited is a good bet. The owners have been in the tour bus business

since 1985 and operate a fleet of buses ranging from 25-passenger minibuses to 56-passenger luxury coaches. Destinations also offers day tours to Savannah or Ocala/Silver Springs for, say, a husband or wife who's tagging along with a spouse attending a convention. The company also hosts travel clubs for senior citizens in Jacksonville, Northeast Florida, and Southeast Georgia. Tour organizers plan luncheons and early get-togethers for seniors to learn about upcoming trips. The company operates a 24-hour travel hotline, (904) 399-2770, which lists upcoming tours from Orlando to New York City, as well as more information on the senior citizen travel clubs. Destinations will also arrange airport transfers for your group.

Jacksonville Haunted History Specialty Tours
(904) 276-2098
www.ghosttracker.com
These guided tours are offered by reservation only. Tour guides dressed in period clothes mix stories about Jacksonville's history with stories about Jacksonville's hauntings. Tours start at the Andrew Jackson Memorial in front of the Jacksonville Landing (Jackson, guides say, never stepped foot in Jacksonville even though the city is named for him.) Guides take you up Bay Street to show you where the first city blocks were laid out. You'll also hear how the Great Fire of 1901 got started and how it left certain buildings haunted. Then you'll head over to the Florida Theatre and the original Barnett Bank building for more tales of history and hauntings. Jeff Reynolds, who runs

Stay off the sand dunes, and don't pick the sea oats. State law protects both, and disrupting them may result in fines.

131

Jacksonville Haunted History Specialty Tours, also owns Northeast Paranormal Research. His company has been featured on the Discovery Channel, and he's been studying ghostly happenings all over the Southeast for about 15 years now. Haunted History tours cost $10.00 for adults and $5.00 for children. Discounts are available for groups.

Jacksonville Historical Society
317 A. Philip Randolph Boulevard
(904) 665-0064

The Historical Society runs "heart of the city" walking tours that include City Hall, one of only two excellent Prairie School city halls in the country. Guides will also tell you all about the Great Fire of 1901, which destroyed most of downtown and changed the face of Jacksonville forever. Tours must be booked in advance.

Tales of Our City
(904) 733-8352

9-5
M-F

Every October, just in time for Halloween, a service organization called The Port of Jacksonville Pilot Club hosts guided walking tours of city cemeteries. Tour guides are full of tales from the crypt about some of the city's more "permanent residents," like Captain Zebulon Willey, buried at the Old City Cemetery downtown. He brought the shipping industry to Jacksonville but wasn't a big favorite with his neighbors. Old Zeb apparently liked to blow his ship's whistle all night long whenever he returned to port. The Old City Cemetery and Historic Evergreen Cemetery have some of the prettiest trees in the city, huge old oaks decorated with olive green Spanish moss. History buffs will feel right at home here. Proceeds from the tours, which are held only in the fall near Hal-

loween, go to the club's community service projects.

Tour Time
(904) 282-8500

Jim Uccio is a private tour operator who provides van and motorcoach tours of area sights. Generally lasting about six hours, the tours include downtown Jacksonville, St. Augustine, and Amelia Island. Van tours operate seven days a week from most of the downtown Jacksonville hotels.

Walking Tour of Riverside Avondale
2623 Herschel Street
(904) 389-2449

Riverside Avondale Preservation Inc., (RAP) publishes several brochures about walking (or driving) tours of what it calls "A Great American Neighborhood." The brochures take you past some of the more noteworthy homes in both Riverside and Avondale, two neighborhoods rich in architectural heritage. See the "Marble House," completed in 1928; Riverside Baptist Church, designed by renowned Palm Beach architect Addison Mizner; and the Lane Residence, a riverfront Tudor mansion that's the largest house on the largest lot in the neighborhood. The brochures have maps, which make the tours easy to follow. You can pick up the brochures at the RAP offices. RAP can also arrange a small group walking tour for $5.00 per person. The tour takes about an hour and ends with tea at a nearby bed-and-breakfast.

Walter Jones Historical Park
11964 Mandarin Road, Mandarin
(904) 260-9983

Mandarin is now a sprawling suburb of Jacksonville, but back in the late 1800s it was a quiet farming community along the St. Johns River. Tour guides will explain what life was like on a typical Mandarin farmstead after 1865, when farmers grew citrus, vegetables, and rice and shipped their produce down the St. Johns to Jacksonville. There's a farmhouse here once owned by Major William Webb, a retired Union major who fought in the Civil War.

 Portuguese men-of-war are dangerous creatures. They look like a turquoise balloon with tentacles floating in the water, and their painful stings can cause temporary paralysis, even shock.

His restored barn dating back to 1865 is also on display at this 10-acre city park. There's also a lovely boardwalk right along the river, which provides a great way to get up close and personal with the St. Johns. Entrance to the park is free, as are the guided tours. Just make sure you set up your tour in advance. There is also a covered pavilion and picnic tables for post-tour relaxation.

HOME TOURS

Riverside Avondale Spring Tour of Homes
(904) 389-2449

If you love to walk through old homes that have been renovated, this is the tour for you. Every year Riverside Avondale Preservation Inc. hosts a tour of 10 locations—many of them are houses, but churches, condos, and gardens are also included. Walk from location to location and get a great idea of what it would be like to live in Riverside Avondale, a beautiful downtown suburb of Jacksonville where many of the homes were built in the early 1900s after the Great Fire of 1901. The home tour is usually held in April.

Springfield Tour of Homes
(904) 353-7727

Springfield is the oldest suburb in Jacksonville. It started in 1863, before the Civil War ended, and quickly grew so that by 1893 there were some 300 Victorian mansions here. Sadly, like many other downtown neighborhoods, Springfield fell into disrepair by the 1960s and 1970s, and many of those beautiful old Victorians became crack houses. Today the neighborhood is enjoying a comeback, as urban pioneers buy what's left of these old homes and totally renovate them. The makeovers are remarkable, and you can see how homeowners do it on the Springfield Tour of Homes in May. There is also a Christmas Home Tour in December, when Springfield mansions are decked out in holiday finery. Call Springfield Preservation

Tour Jacksonville from the air aboard a hot-air balloon. Cost for a one-hour morning ride for two: $425. That includes a champagne brunch. For more info call (904) 725-0119.

and Restoration, Inc., for exact tour dates, which vary every year.

MUSEUM TOUR

CALL
=
AOK

Cummer Museum of Art and Gardens
829 Riverside Avenue
(904) 356-6857
www.cummer.org

Most women would love to get their hands on just one of the pieces of Meissen porcelain in the Cummer's vast collection. There's also a wonderful painting by Thomas Moran of Ponce de Leon in Florida back around 1513, during his search for the Fountain of Youth. These and other objets d'art can be seen on a highlight tour of the museum's collection, held twice a week on Tuesday at 7:00 P.M. and Sunday at 3:00 P.M. Tours are free with museum admission—a real deal on Tuesday when admission is free from 4:00 to 9:00 P.M. (For more on the Cummer Museum, see the Attractions chapter.)

SUN

NATURE TOURS

Birds, Botany, and Breakfast
Guana River State Park
Ponte Vedra Beach
(904) 825-5071

Park rangers will take you on a two-hour walking tour, during which you might see (depending on your luck and the season) little blue herons, great blue herons, bald eagles, and barn owls. Park rangers will also tell you about everything from edible plants to Indian burial mounds. After the walk, there's coffee, orange juice, and doughnuts for breakfast. The tour is held

CLOSE-UP

The Great Florida Birding Trail

According to a 2001 survey by the USDA Forest Service, birding is the fastest-growing outdoor recreational activity in the country, especially in the South. So it's no wonder that the Great Florida Birding Trail has attracted thousands of tourists to Northeast Florida since it began in 2000.

Modeled after a similar birding trail in Texas, the Great Florida Birding Trail incorporates a tourist guide and highway signage to lead birders to the best birding sites in Florida. The trail started with 135 sites in 18 East Florida counties and a similar number of sites in both West and South Florida. Bird lovers themselves nominate the sites based on their first-hand experience of fabulous places to see birds, from colorful songbirds to rare shorebirds. The free guide includes maps to help tourists find and follow the sites.

"The whole point is to promote wildland conservation," says Julie Brashears,

statewide coordinator of the Great Florida Birding Trail, who adds that birding is an economic boon for local communities. Conserving wildlands attracts birds, said Brashears, and birds attract birders, who spend tourist dollars in hotels, restaurants, gift shops, and gas stations. "This is a way to demonstrate to communities that their wildlands have value."

Indeed, the Florida Fish and Wildlife Conservation Commission, which sponsors the Great Florida Birding Trail, helps push this notion of birding to promote wildland conservation by calling on traveling birders to leave behind a "birding calling card" wherever they spend their tourist dollars. For instance, a birder who eats at a Jacksonville restaurant is asked to leave a calling card on the table with the tip. The calling cards are available on the trail's extensive Web site: www.florida birdingtrail.com. The cards explain the

one Saturday every month. Call the Ranger Station for exact dates and times. (For more information on the park, see the Parks chapter.)

Tree Hill Nature Center
7152 Lone Star Road
(904) 724–4646
www.treehill.org
Did you know that mockingbirds, the state bird of Florida, are excellent mimics? And did you know that Spanish moss lives off

the air and doesn't harm the live oak trees it drapes itself upon? You'll learn all sorts of details about the Northeast Florida woods on guided nature tours the first Saturday of every month from 10:00 A.M. to noon. This is a nice outing for the entire family, including elderly relatives, because the trails are very gentle. Tree Hill is a 40-acre preserve owned by the city of Jacksonville and located in the heart of suburbia. There are two guided nature walks: a short one that's about a mile and

notion of birding as big business—a business that's possible only when there's enough natural habitat left in a community to attract birds.

Thankfully, Jacksonville still has some of that habitat left in the form of city, state, and federal parks. Nine Jacksonville parks and preserves are listed on the Great Florida Birding Trail, mostly clustered around the mouth of the St. Johns River. Many of the sites are good for year-round birding; others are more seasonal because they get very "buggy" in the summer, when only the most dedicated birder would venture forth.

"A lot of these sites are really good places to see shorebirds," said Brashears. For example, Huguenot Park is a good place to see least terns, a small seabird listed as a threatened species. "Least terns look a lot like gulls, only smaller. They feed by plunging into the water for fish and can be seen from the beach."

The Jacksonville area is also a good place to see such songbirds as painted buntings, which Brashears calls a technicolor jewel of the forest that looks more suited to the jungles of Costa Rica than the maritime hammocks of Northeast Florida. Painted buntings are indigo, crimson, and lime green and are plentiful in Northeast Florida during their breeding season, mid-April to mid-September.

There's another plus for birders who want to follow the Great Florida Birding Trail in and around Jacksonville. Fort Clinch State Park on Amelia Island has been designated one of the gateway locations for the trail. Birders can go to Fort Clinch and actually talk to a human being about the Great Florida Birding Trail. They can also pick up a trail guide and walk through a museum of sorts, with exhibitions about the trail and area birds. They can even borrow high-powered binoculars from park rangers free of charge to help them spot birds. Fort Clinch State Park, by the way, is said to be an excellent place to catch a glimpse of the rarely seen purple sandpiper. Birders flock to Fort Clinch from all over to get a look at these little creatures from November to January.

If you would like to tour Northeast Florida via the Great Florida Birding Trail, call for your free guide at (850) 488-8755 or visit www.floridabirdingtrail.com.

a longer one that's about a mile and a half. Admission is $2.00 for adults and $1.00 for children. (See also the Parks chapter.)

WATER TOURS

Gecko Latitudes Kayaking
(904) 824-7979, (866) 411-8011
www.geckolatitudes.com
Listen to the names of the kayak tours offered by Gecko Latitudes: Ancient City Sunset EcoTours, Silent Paddle EcoTours, Full Moon Dune EcoTours, Women Friendly EcoTours, Senior EcoTours—you get the idea. Gecko Latitudes operates out of St. Augustine, which means you can combine your kayak tour with a bit of sightseeing. And if you volunteer back home for a nonprofit environmental group like a wildlife rescue or The Nature Conservancy, mention that when you sign up. You'll get a discount on your kayak trip.

Kayak Adventures
(904) 249-6200, (888) 333-2480
www.kayakadventuresllc.com

You can't get more Northeast Florida than this: Kayak for two hours in the evening along the estuaries of Guana State Park, then come ashore for a Low Country boil—a one-pot wonder of shrimp, sausage, corn, and potatoes. Owner Walter Bunso will show you a Florida you've never seen before. He'll take you out for a moonlight paddle or to fly fish from a kayak. He's also certified to take disabled paddlers, from the blind to paraplegics, out on the water. Full-day and half-day excursions are available, and Bunso says that most trips are beginner-friendly.

Kayak Amelia
(904) 251-0016, (888) 30-KAYAK
www.kayakamelia.com

Learn the history of native Timucuans as you paddle your kayak on inland marshes and creeks. Ray and Jody Hetchka are certified Eco-Heritage Tourism providers, which means they know a heck of a lot about kayaking and the history and ecology of Amelia Island, a Northeast Florida barrier island. They're also really good about pointing out such local critters as herons and egrets; if you're really lucky, you may find yourself paddling next to a dolphin. Trip times depend on the tides and currents, but whenever you go, don't forget the sunscreen and the bug spray.

CALL

Kingsley Plantation/Ft. Caroline Boat Tour
(904) 641-7155

At this writing, this boat tour is not yet in operation, but the National Park Service hopes to have it up and running soon. Tourists will park at Sisters Creek Marina on Heckscher Drive, then take a boat to

Taking a cruise? You can park your car at the Jaxport Cruise Terminal while away. But hold on to your wallet. Parking costs $10 a day.

Fort Caroline National Memorial, the first European settlement in America. After visiting Fort Caroline, the boat will take you on to Kingsley Plantation, a former indigo and cotton plantation. The boat ride between Fort Caroline and Kingsley Plantation will take you on a beautiful stretch of North Florida waterway, through part of the 43,000-acre Timucuan Preserve. A guide aboard the boat will provide a great narration of the history of the area, as well as answer your questions. Call ahead, though, to make sure the tour is running.

BEER TOUR

Anheuser-Busch Brewery
111 Busch Drive
(904) 751-8117
www.budshop.com

If you like beer, this is one of the best deals in town. Take a free guided tour of the brewery and learn how beer is made, bottled, packaged, chilled, and stored. Or take a self-guided tour at your own pace and learn the same things. Either way, after your tour enjoy two free samples of any kind of beer made by Busch. Bud, Bud Lite, Natural, Natural Lite, Michelob, and Michelob Lite are made at the Jacksonville plant. The guided tours are held every hour on the hour from 10:00 A.M. to 3:00 P.M. The self-guided tours can be taken from 10:00 A.M. to 4:00 P.M. Tours are available Monday through Saturday; none on Sunday. The brewery also operates a great gift shop, where Bud lovers can buy all kinds of "stuff" with their favorite logos.

CRUISES

Two passenger cruise lines now have homeport ships in Jacksonville: Carnival Cruise Lines and Celebrity Cruise Lines. Both sail from the Jaxport Cruise Terminal located in North Jacksonville off Heckscher Drive. The ships serve passengers from all over the country, especially those from the Southeast who drive here to climb aboard.

The rule of thumb for cruising out of Jacksonville is this: Carnival offers shorter cruises with bigger ships, while Celebrity offers longer cruises with smaller ships. Either way, Jacksonville's cruise service will fit your budget and vacation schedule, and passengers report that leaving from the Port of Jacksonville is a hassle-free experience.

Carnival Cruise Lines
(800) CARNIVAL
www.carnival.com

Talk about convenient: You can leave Jacksonville on a Carnival ship at 4:00 P.M. Friday afternoon and return Monday morning at 8:00 A.M. Destination: Freeport, Bahamas. Price: about $300 per person. Lots of folks are taking advantage of this long weekend at sea, filled with food, entertainment, and plenty of relaxation. Carnival also offers four-, five-, and six-day cruises out of Jacksonville to the Bahamas, Key West, and Cozumel.

Tight fit: When big Carnival cruise ships pass under the Dames Point Bridge, it looks like the ships will hit the bridge. Fear not. There's about 6 feet of clearance.

Celebrity Cruise Lines
(800) 722-5941
www.celebrity.com

Celebrity offers 11- to 14-day cruises out of Jacksonville, and depending on the cruise, you can find yourself heading to the U.S. Virgin Islands, Barbados, Costa Rica, and lots more exotic locales. Celebrity currently sails the *Zenith,* a 1,375-guest ship, out of Jacksonville. Returning passengers report Celebrity cruises are a great way to really relax and get away from it all.

AFRICAN-AMERICAN TOURISM 🏛

Much has been lost, but much is being saved. That best sums up the state of African-American historical sites in and around Jacksonville. Local residents are working hard to preserve what's left of important buildings in once-thriving African-American neighborhoods like downtown's LaVilla. Two new museums have opened in recent years: the LaVilla Museum and the Durkeeville Historical Center. The city helped pay for renovations of the Ritz, an old movie house in LaVilla that's now a beautiful theater.

Despite all that has been lost, Jacksonville is still rich in African-American history. It's home to the oldest black college in Florida, Edward Waters College, which was started in 1866 by two leaders in the African Methodist Episcopal Church. Several of the campus buildings are on local historical registers.

No guidebook on African-American history in this area would be complete without including American Beach in Nassau County—the first black beach in Northeast Florida, dating from 1939. The area is threatened every day by golf course and hotel developers who'd love to get their hands on the property. If you go, be sure to look up MaVynee Betch, aka The Beach Lady, the heart and soul of American Beach (see the Close-up on the next page).

Some of the oldest African-American history in the nation lies south of Jacksonville in St. Augustine at Fort Mose (pronounced *moh*-SAY). In 1738, when Florida was still a Spanish territory, Fort Mose became a fortress and farming community for escaped slaves from Georgia and South Carolina. It exists today as an active archaeological site and a National Historic Landmark.

Finally, thanks to the efforts of local members of Alpha Kappa Alpha, the oldest black sorority in the United States, you can learn about Jacksonville's historic black sites on a guided tour, which sorority members will fashion to meet the needs of your group, large or small. Just book in advance. (See the Tours chapter for more on AKA's Tour of Historical Black Sites in Jacksonville.)

MUSEUMS

Durkeeville Historical Center
1260-1 West Seventh Street
(904) 598-0102

Durkeeville, the city's first housing project, started as an affordable, safe place for disadvantaged families. But by 1990 it was the worst neighborhood in the city with 7 murders and 275 violent crimes that year. In the late nineties the old Durkeeville was razed and a new public housing community was built in its place, one that includes playgrounds, a day care center, a retail strip, and 28 single-family homes. Over the years many noteworthy people have lived in Durkeeville, and their photographs and mementos are on display at the historical center, a grassroots museum.

Willie Gary, a successful plaintiffs' attorney, sponsors a football game every fall at Alltel Stadium called the Willie Gary Classic. It pits his alma mater, Shaw University, against Jacksonville's Edward Waters College and in the process raises money for both schools.

CLOSE-UP

The Beach Lady

Most people are a bit surprised the first time they meet MaVynee Betch, aka The Beach Lady. Perhaps it's her gray hair, in dreadlocks up to 15 feet long, which she carries folded over her arm—or maybe the animal skins and shells she wears for clothes or the fingernails that are so long they curl around themselves several times over. She looks like a nut (which she's not) or perhaps an artist (which she is). Few people would guess that MaVynee Betch has a proud lineage. Her great-grandfather, Abrams L. Lewis, started the Afro-American Insurance Company in Jacksonville in the early 1900s and shaped it into a multimillion-dollar corporation. He also branched into real estate and founded American Beach in 1935, the first beach community for African Americans in Florida. MaVynee and her sister went to the finest schools a black woman could attend in the fifties and sixties. (Her sister is the former president of Spelman College in Atlanta.) MaVynee became an

opera singer and achieved a career of some renown in Germany before deciding to return home.

MaVynee may be a character, but she has, single-handedly at times, fought to keep American Beach out of the hands of developers. The community is squeezed by resort expansion to its north and to its south, and developers are constantly making lucrative offers to property owners. MaVynee reminds these property owners of the cultural significance of American Beach, which she's also trying to get listed on the National Register of Historic Places. In addition to being the community's passionate defender, she's also its unofficial historian, with boxes of yellowed, dog-eared photographs and other mementos squirreled away in a trailer. She wants to open a museum chronicling the history and the heyday of this community but needs a benefactor with deep pockets to help her secure a museum building.

Ritz Theatre and LaVilla Museum Complex
829 North Davis Street
(904) 632-5555

The Ritz Theatre is located in LaVilla, a once-thriving downtown African-American neighborhood that blossomed after the Civil War, when freed blacks opened restaurants, shops, and laundries. There was also a movie house called the Ritz, which today has been totally rebuilt into a theater and museum complex. Such jazz greats as Duke Ellington and Cab Calloway once performed in LaVilla, and today the Ritz hosts all sorts of perform-

ances, from comedy and drama to jazz and dance. The LaVilla Museum, meanwhile, re-creates African-American life in the early 1900s in LaVilla. There's a room full of school artifacts, representing a LaVilla school; another filled with old medical equipment, representing a doctor's office; and another filled with old stained-glass windows and a piano, representing a church. The museum also pays tribute to James Weldon Johnson, author of "Lift Every Voice and Sing," and his brother, John Rosamond Johnson, who wrote the music for his brother's lyrics.

CLOSE-UP

The World's Fastest Human

Old-timers still talk about Bob Hayes and the first time he stepped onto a track at then Matthew Gilbert High School. "He was about 16," said Jimmie Johnson, a former administrator and coach at the school. "He started running, and we knew even before we put the clock on him, this kid was special, really special."

So began the sports career of Jacksonville native "Bullet" Bob Hayes, who sportswriters nicknamed the world's fastest human. His fleet feet carried him to the 1964 Summer Olympics in Tokyo, where he won a gold medal in the 100 meters, and on to Dallas where he played wide receiver with the Dallas Cowboys and helped the team earn a Super Bowl title in 1972. Experts say his speed on the gridiron changed the way pass coverage was played in the NFL by forcing coaches to implement zone defenses.

Still, despite a career full of records, NFL Hall of Fame voters did not vote Hayes into the hall in 2004. His disappointed fans say the voters refused to remember Hayes for his on-the-field glories (he still holds the Dallas Cowboys record for number of touchdown catches) but instead chose to remember him for his off-the-field problems with drugs.

Hayes died in Jacksonville in 2002 at age 59. A bronze statue called *Passing the Torch* anchors the A. Philip Randolph Heritage Park in East Jacksonville, the neighborhood where Hayes grew up. The statue shows Hayes running on his toes because artist Kristen Visbal says all the photos she studied of Hayes made it seem as if his feet never hit the ground.

In addition, thousands of middle school and high school students gather at Raines High School every year for the Bob Hayes Invitational Track and Field Meet, featuring more than 100 schools from five states. Hayes used to attend the meet every year, shaking hands and inspiring runners. Even without him, the event remains what Hayes envisioned it would be: a chance for aspiring athletes to showcase their talents.

The brothers were born in Jacksonville and are brought to life with animatronic figures that play the piano and sing.

HISTORIC SITES

Bethel Baptist Institutional Church
215 Bethel Baptist Street
(904) 354-1464
www.bethelite.org
This is the city's premier black church. It's also the oldest Baptist congregation in Florida, starting well before the Civil War in 1838. Bethel Baptist began as an integrated church with just six members, but by the time the Civil War ended, black members outnumbered white members, and the courts ruled that the black parishioners were the rightful owners. The church itself, built in 1904, has a stunning spire and is listed on the National Historic Register.

Clara White Mission
613 West Ashley Street
(904) 354-4162
In 1904 former slave Clara White used to feed hungry people who knocked at her door. Thus began the Clara White Mission, which really took shape when Clara's

daughter, Eartha, started a soup kitchen and named it after her mother. Eartha used to live above the store, so to speak, and today her former home is an extensive museum dedicated to local African-American history. Eartha White also started the first orphanage for black children in Florida. She was much admired by wealthy white dowagers, who often endowed her efforts to help poor blacks from the 1930s through the 1950s.

Edward Waters College
1658 Kings Road
(904) 355-3030
www.ewc.edu

Founded in 1866, this is the oldest institution of higher learning for blacks in Florida. Early teachers from New England gathered freed slaves in churches, box cars—anywhere they could—to teach them. In 1904 the school moved to its present site on Kings Road. Edward Waters College was started by two leaders in the African Methodist Episcopal Church, and a campus building, Centennial Hall (1750 Kings Road), was built in 1916 to commemorate the church's centennial. Today EWC has a football team, a basketball team, and some 700 students pursuing college degrees.

Historic Mt. Zion AME Church
201 East Beaver Street
(904) 355-9475

The Historic Mt. Zion AME Church has deep roots in Jacksonville. It was started in 1866 just after the Civil War by a group of Freedmen. The stained-glass windows alone are worth a stop at this church, which is listed on the National Register of Historic Places. The first church building burned to the ground in the Great Fire of 1901, and the church was rebuilt in 1902.

Kingsley Plantation
11676 Palmetto Avenue
(904) 251-3537
www.nps.gov/timu

This is the former home of Zephaniah Kingsley, a white slave trader and his wife,

Anna Jai Kingsley, a former slave from Senegal whom he bought when she was only 13. Kingsley raised indigo and sea island cotton here, but mostly he traded in slaves, which he bought in Cuba. At one point Kingsley had some 200 slaves at his plantation; they lived in cabins made from tabby, a substance as strong as concrete that's fashioned from oyster shells, lime, sand, and water. Those cabins still exist today, not far from the original plantation house, both grim reminders of America's past. Every year the National Park Service hosts the Kingsley Heritage Celebration, which features talks by visiting historians and authors, storytelling, and musical performances. Reenactors also show visitors how tabby was made, how cotton was spun, and how indigo was used to dye clothes. For more on this fascinating place, see the Attractions and Tours chapters.

Try and catch a performance of The Ritz Voices, a local youth chorus that's won awards for its dynamic singing.

Masonic Temple Building
410 Broad Street
(904) 354-2368

Built in 1912 and recently restored, this six-story redbrick building is the headquarters of the Masons of the State of Florida Grand East. It's also the starting point for many commercial and social activities in Jacksonville's black community. The Anderson Bank, the first black bank in Jacksonville, once occupied the basement of the building.

Old Brewster Hospital
1640 Jefferson Street

In 1901 the Old Brewster Hospital was a medical center for blacks and a nurse training school where young women learned everything from changing dressings to recognizing smallpox symptoms. Today the Old Brewster Hospital is a sagging, rundown redbrick building—but a

CLOSE-UP

Photograph ! Marker ,

Ax Handle Saturday

On August 27, 1960, Jacksonville was rocked by a bloody race riot that's come to be called Ax Handle Saturday.

It was one of the most violent days in the city's history, although it started peacefully enough with two passive demonstrations at the downtown lunch counters in W. T. Grant's Department Store and Woolworth's 5&10 Cent Store, both on Hemming Plaza. That's where 40 members of the NAACP Youth Council sat down at the "whites only" lunch counters and refused to get up until they were served.

They had done the same thing two weeks earlier, but this time, after the managers shut down the counters, the protesters were greeted with hate in Hemming Plaza. A crowd of about 150 white men, some carrying ax handles, was waiting for them.

The white men, including some members of the Ku Klux Klan, wanted to teach these "uppity" antisegregation protesters a lesson they'd never forget. They swung their ax handles and bats and chased the young black protesters through the streets. A few police officers who were

nearby at the time reportedly "turned their heads the other way" during the beatings.

By the time it was over, about 50 persons, both black and white, were hurt; no one was killed, and about 60 persons, both black and white, were arrested. But more than that, this quiet Southern town was shaken to its core. Whites realized that the civil rights movement wasn't going to be swept under the carpet, as the city's African-American community demanded justice—and progress.

In 2000, on the 40th anniversary of Ax Handle Saturday, the Jacksonville Historical Society placed a marker in Hemming Plaza in front of Jacksonville's city hall to commemorate the event. The city's first official marker honoring an important local event in the civil rights movement reads: "Although not the beginning of the Jacksonville civil rights movement, this conflict was a turning point. It awakened many to the seriousness of the African-American community's demand for human dignity and respect and inspired further resolve in supporters to accomplish these goals."

shadow of its former self. Nevertheless, a dedicated group of local history lovers is trying to raise the money to renovate the hospital and turn it into a museum.

Old Stanton School
Ashley and Laura Streets, LaVilla
Started in 1868, this was the first public school for black children in Jacksonville.

The school's namesake, Edwin Stanton, was secretary of war for Abraham Lincoln and a staunch abolitionist. By 1917 Stanton had become the only high school for blacks in Duval county. Poet James Weldon Johnson graduated from here and in 1894 became the school's principal. Johnson, by the way, was the first black man to pass the Florida bar exam.

The Rhoda Martin Museum of African-American Culture and Heritage
Corner of Fourth Street and Fourth Avenue South, Jacksonville Beach
In 1939 Mother Rhoda Martin, a former slave, started a four-room schoolhouse called the Jacksonville Beach School for the Colored. For decades that schoolhouse was the only school for "colored" children at the Beaches. The 2,184-square-foot brick building eventually became a wing of Jacksonville Beach Elementary School and was almost destroyed in 2000 when the elementary school was remodeled. It was saved from demolition in the final hour and moved to its current site. At this writing, there are plans to house a genealogical center in the museum as well as an exhibit of successful graduates of the school.

HISTORIC COMMUNITIES AND SITES

American Beach
On Amelia Island, 8 miles south of Fernandina Beach on Highway A1A
This community was founded in 1935 by the leaders of the Afro-American Insurance Company. Vacation cottages were used by company executives and employees who won sales contests. But word of the beach community spread quickly, and soon American Beach was more than a company town. It was the place to go in the Southeast for African Americans who wanted a beach holiday during segregation. Black-owned hotels sprang up, as did restaurants and a dance hall. Soon it was a thriving little community on the edge of what was once a very racist part of North Florida. To get to their oceanfront vacation homes, wealthy African Americans often drove nervously on remote country roads, worrying about what would happen if their car broke down or ran out of gas. Today some of the original families who bought back in the 1940s still own homes in American Beach. (Retired Florida supreme court justice Leander Shaw owns a home here.)

Homeowners are constantly pressured by developers who'd like to gobble up the community and turn it into a resort. (See the first Close-up in this chapter.)

Fort Mose
Off US 1, St. Augustine
(904) 461-2035
www.oldcity.com/mose
In 1738, when Florida was still a Spanish territory, Fort Mose (moh-SAY) became a haven for runaway slaves from Georgia and South Carolina. It was a fortress and farming community with about 100 members who were allowed to live freely under Spanish rule but in exchange had to defend St. Augustine against its enemies. The remains of the fort and its farming community, Gracia Real de Santa Teresa de Mose, are buried in the marsh on an island north of St. Augustine. Fort Mose was abandoned in 1763, according to detailed records kept by the Spanish. Those records also make it the first recorded free-black settlement in the history of the United States. Archaeologists and historians are hard at work trying to uncover this past. There are plans to build a museum out here, but the reality of that is still far away. On the last Saturday of February, the St. Augustine Archaeological Association and the Anastasia Island Park System host a living history event here called Flight to Freedom. Reenactors play the roles of runaway slaves, slave catchers, Native Americans, and Catholic priests. Visitors walk on ancient trails and encounter the reenactors and hear their stories. There's also an all-black militia in period dress awaiting visitors at the site of Fort Mose.

Lincolnville
Located near the heart of historic St. Augustine
Located in the heart of old St. Augustine, Lincolnville began as a settlement for freed slaves in 1865. Over the years it developed into a thriving black neighborhood with its own schools, shops, and dance halls. Dr. Martin Luther King Jr.

Former world heavyweight boxing champ Joe Louis's son, Joe Louis Barrow Jr., is the executive director of First Tee headquartered in St. Augustine. First Tee is an initiative by the World Golf Foundation and the PGA that uses golf to teach children life skills like discipline and goal setting.

stayed in several houses on Bridge Street in Lincolnville during a tumultuous visit in the 1960s, when he and many protesters were arrested after a civil rights march. The people who sheltered him still live in their homes. There's a high concentration of Victorian houses with gingerbread details in this neighborhood, which was placed on the National Register of Historic Places in 1991.

Olustee Battlefield State Historic Site
2 miles east of Olustee on US 90
Baker County
(904) 758-0400
The biggest battle of the Civil War fought in Florida was waged here in Olustee on February 20, 1864. Six white and three all-black Union infantry regiments battled with Confederate troops for five hours as the North tried to cut off supply routes from Florida that sent cattle to feed the Confederacy. Some of the all-black infantry were from the 54th Massachusetts, the black unit featured in the 1989 film *Glory*. But the South won this battle, which stymied efforts to separate Florida from the Confederacy. Civil War reenactors re-create the battle every February, right down to the "sutlers," the merchants who sold goods to the soldiers before battle. (For more on this historic site, see the Annual Events chapter.)

TOURS

Tour of Historical Black Sites
in Metro Jacksonville
(904) 356-0110
Whether your group is 5 or 50, members of the Alpha Kappa Alpha sorority will show you Jacksonville's black historical sites. AKA provides the tales; you provide the transportation. (See the Tours chapter for more information on AKA's Tour of Historical Black Sites.)

PARKS 🌳

When Harriet Beecher Stowe, author of *Uncle Tom's Cabin*, wrote the first travel book for Jacksonville in 1873, she waxed poetic about the area's outdoor charms. She wrote extensively in *Palmetto Leaves* about the St. Johns River, "the great blue sheet of water [that] shimmers and glitters like so much liquid lapis lazuli." She loved the number of wildflowers that grow here and thought you could find more only in Italy. Most of all, Stowe loved the climate and the opportunity to spend much of the winter outdoors.

These days some of the best places to enjoy the St. Johns River, the native flowers, and the weather are in Jacksonville's parks. We are rich in them. Jacksonville has about 350 city parks, and if you include all our state and federal parks, the city claims that Jacksonville has the largest urban park system in the country. City officials like to boast that Jacksonville has 96 acres of parks per 1,000 residents. The next two closest cities to us with that much parkland are El Paso and Oklahoma City—a mere 47 and 44 acres, respectively. Still, most Jacksonville residents will tell you that it's not enough; they want even more parks in the years ahead.

What follows is a list of some of the favorite parks in this park-crazy town, especially parks in areas where tourists are likely to (or should) ramble. For even more information on Jacksonville's park system, check on the Internet at www.jaxparks.com.

Bethesda Park
10790 Key Haven Boulevard
(904) 764-5531
Bethesda Park is well off the beaten path for the average tourist, but its particular charms make it well worth a mention. Like Hanna Park, this is a good place for a reunion or a company picnic. But here your event doesn't need to be subject to the vagaries of weather or charcoal grills. The Bethesda Park Lodge offers a full kitchen and restrooms for groups up to 216. There are also fully equipped cabins for overnight stays, each with four bunk beds, a restroom, and kitchenette. The big attraction here is a 20-acre stocked lake, where guests fish and canoe. A 1,400-foot boardwalk over a boggy area near the lake is an easy hike for almost everyone.

Guana River State Park
2690 South Ponte Vedra Boulevard
Ponte Vedra Beach
(904) 825-5071
When we think of Guana we think of kayaking, fishing from a kayak, and hiking past centuries-old Native American burial mounds. You can enjoy doing all this on your own, or you can take advantage of several tour opportunities, including kayak tours (outlined in the Tours chapter). Jacksonville businessman Herb Peyton sold these 2,400 acres to the state in the late eighties, saving this portion of Highway A1A from becoming a South Florida concrete jungle.

The park is located halfway between Jacksonville and St. Augustine and offers beach access, great fishing, and significant opportunities to learn about this country's earliest history. There are 17 historic and cultural sites within the park, including the remains of an early Spanish mission from the 1600s—Nativity of our Lady of Tolomato—and a water well built in the early 1800s by Minorcans that's listed on the National Register of Historic Places. There is no camping at Guana, but the Guana

---

Reservations are accepted at all state parks in Florida up to 11 months in advance. Call (800) I-CAMP-FL or (800) 326-3521.

ℹ️

CLOSE-UP

The Ribault Club

The first time we ever saw the Ribault Club it was but a shadow of its former self. The once-venerable 1928 building used to be a hangout for millionaires wintering in South Georgia and North Florida, but five years ago the building was rotten with termites, and state park employees were desperately seeking funds to save it before the clubhouse was eaten to its core.

Not any more. These days the termites are gone, and the park service has completed a $4 million four-year facelift. Thanks to a mix of state, private, and federal funding, the Ribault Club is back in the business of entertaining guests.

The Ribault Club enjoys one of the best locations in all of Northeast Florida. The big white plantation-style house with Georgian columns sits on the Fort George River in the Fort George Island Cultural State Park overlooking Little Talbot Island. Kingsley Plantation is just a short walk away. In the seventies and eighties, the building was headquarters for a country club, and many Jacksonville residents have fond memories of eating dinner there—the men, of course, in coat and tie, the women in smart dresses.

The state purchased the country club in 1989 and closed the golf course forever. Nature quickly took back most of the 18 holes, but you can still make out a bit of the old course underneath spreading palmetto bushes. Covered picnic tables have been added along the river under majestic live oak trees, where you can eat a snack and watch the world go by.

Lake area is such a popular fishing spot—especially for redfish—that the Park Service keeps it open 24 hours a day.

Huguenot Memorial Park
10980 Heckscher Drive
(904) 251-3335

Much of this city park's 450 acres is prime riverfront and beachfront property. The geography out here is exciting because the park is basically just a spit of land bordering the St. Johns River that then curves around into the Atlantic Ocean. On the inside of this horseshoe is Fort George Inlet. Park guests come here to camp in primitive riverfront campsites and to swim and fish. Campers also appreciate the bathhouse and the park's 24-hour security. This is also the only park in Duval County where you can still drive your car on the beach. Consequently, on sunny weekends the beach and inlet areas are packed with cars and guests setting up grills for picnics. But all this beauty comes with words of caution: The inlet area is subject to swift tidal changes, and there have been numerous drownings here.

Kathryn Abby Hanna Park
500 Wonderwood Drive, Atlantic Beach
(904) 249-4700

Hanna Park is a great place to get away from it all without having to get away from the city. Located at the beach, Hanna Park is 450 acres of natural Florida, the kind Harriet Beecher Stowe

Part of the old clubhouse is now a museum dedicated to the history of Fort George Island. There are videos to learn about manatees and bobcats, and an especially interesting display about the island's Native American shell mounds, which are many years older than Florida itself.

The rest of the club is for hire for weddings, family reunions, or corporate parties. But don't let that stop you from driving out to Fort George with a picnic basket in your backseat. Just follow the signs for Kingsley Plantation. Once you get to Fort George Road, don't turn left for Kingsley. Go along the river and wind your way toward the Ribault Clubhouse. It was and still is a relaxing place to visit, walk around, and step back in time to a more natural Florida.

More information on the Ribault Club can be found at www.theribaultclub.com.

The Ribault Club on Fort George Island is a charming place for weddings or private parties. COURTESY OF THE RIBAULT CLUB

probably enjoyed: thick forests, open beachfront, and plenty of salt- and fresh water fishing. With 293 campsites, this is often the park parents pick to introduce their young children to camping. If the campout turns into a disaster in the middle of the night, it's easy enough to pack up and go home without a long drive. The campsites have water and sewer hookups and electricity, and there's also a small store, bathhouse, and public laundry facility in the park.

Hanna Park offers a playground and summer water park for children, as well as biking and hiking trails. Dogs are allowed here as long as they're kept on a leash. Besides surf casting in the ocean, there are several freshwater lakes and ponds at Hanna. You need a valid Florida fishing license to wet a line here, and the freshwater areas are well stocked with largemouth bass, bluegill, sunshine bass, and catfish. If tent or RV camping isn't your thing, try one of four new rustic cabins. They rent for $34 a night and sleep four. (Bathrooms are still a walk away in the bathhouse.) Best of all, each cabin fea-

---

i

Jacksonville loves its two oceanfront parks: Kathryn Abby Hanna Park and Huguenot Memorial Park. Huguenot is one of the few parks in Northeast Florida where you can still drive your car on the beach.

---

tures a cute little screened-in porch, so you can eat outside without fear of bugs.

There is also a new oceanfront building here called Dolphin Plaza that's a perfect place for a wedding, Eagle Scout ceremony, or small corporate meeting. Dolphin Plaza is air-conditioned, has a refrigerator and outdoor grill, and has ocean views to die for. It seats 125 people banquet style, or 96 people classroom style, and rents for about $425 a day. Just be sure to book early—Dolphin Plaza is very popular.

Kids Kampus
1410 Gator Bowl Boulevard
Metropolitan Park

Kids Kampus is not a natural beauty (although it's beautifully located on the north bank of the St. Johns River) but a man-made wonder your children will adore. The best feature of Kids Kampus is the large free water park that's a great place for families to cool off in the summer. The water park has two areas: one for toddlers and one for bigger children, plus there are benches within the water park where parents can keep an eye on their kids and still get sprinkled. A small water slide, jungle gym, and squirt guns are found in the bigger kids' water park area.

This 10-acre park also offers an area called Safe City, where children don bicycle helmets and ride tricycles to learn how to bicycle safely on city streets. Safe City has a working traffic light, a railroad crossing, and small plastic versions of some Jacksonville buildings. This route is built on 2 inches of asphalt-looking rubber, so if anyone takes a spill, injuries will be minimal. Kids Kampus also offers a history of Jacksonville through innovative signage, ball fields, jogging trails, a 50-seat

amphitheater, and covered pavilions for picnics or birthday parties.

Little Talbot and Big Talbot Island State Parks
Heckscher Drive
(904) 251-2320
www.dep.state.fl.us/parks

These two state parks go together like bread and butter. Simply put, they are beautiful, and you won't be disappointed in the parks or the drive out to reach them. The Talbots are located about 20 miles east of Jacksonville and bear the names of the barrier islands on which they're located. Little Talbot is about 5 miles south of Big Talbot and is actually the bigger facility. There is no camping at Big Talbot Island State Park; Little Talbot offers 40 campsites (no cabins) on Myrtle Creek on the west side of the island. The beach is about a third of a mile away, and you have to cross Highway A1A to get there. Both parks have boat ramps, and you can rent bicycles and canoes at the ranger station on Little Talbot. The closest convenience store is 5 miles south of Little Talbot.

The big attraction at both of these parks is the beach, where you can swim and fish. Both offer picnic facilities and hiking trails. Just bring along plenty of bug repellant if you hike, or you won't last long on the trails. The Sarabay Center on the south end of Big Talbot Island is a scenic place for your next family reunion or company meeting. It can accommodate up to 55 indoors and 200 outdoors. Some huge beached tree stumps on Big Talbot offer great photo possibilities. Whole trees fell victim to erosion and ended up on the beach; others were put there to stop erosion. The trees have been worn smooth by time and tides and are much photographed by Insiders.

Northbank and Southbank Riverwalks and Friendship Fountain
Downtown

If you visit no other city parks, try to see these. The Northbank and Southbank Riverwalks and Friendship Fountain form

---

Hanna Park is a great place to plan a group cookout or company picnic. The large open-air shelters on the ocean are perfect for these events. Reserve by calling (904) 249-4700.

---

the heart of downtown Jacksonville. The riverwalks, which are basically boardwalks on the north and south banks of the St. Johns River, are great places for uninterrupted walks or runs anytime of the year. The Southbank Riverwalk, in particular, is a favorite exercise spot for Southbank workers who like to get up from their desks and "get the blood moving" during lunch. The Southbank Riverwalk ends (or begins) at Friendship Fountain, a large fountain that's especially picturesque when lit up at night. The Museum of Science and History and the Maritime Museum are located just off the Southbank Riverwalk near Friendship Fountain. There are shops and restaurants along both riverwalks, though the Northbank Riverwalk has more to offer in this regard because it includes Jacksonville Landing. City officials are expanding the Northbank Riverwalk from Riverside Park to Metropolitan Park, making a total distance of 3 miles.

Sunshine Park
Corner of South Beach Parkway and Osceola Street, Jacksonville Beach
Located about a quarter mile from the Atlantic Ocean, this is one of the most kid-friendly parks in Jacksonville. It's a great place for families to go after a weekend swim in the ocean. Mothers' groups from all over the city meet here during the week, making it a great place to strike up new friendships. Sunshine Park is the brainchild of two Beaches moms, who set out to build a community park in 1999. (See the Close-up on the next page.) It's full of play equipment, such as a castle maze to climb through, catwalks on which to practice balance, tire swings big enough to fit your child and his/her friends on, and cozy tunnels for making secret plans.

Timucuan Ecological and Historic Preserve
13165 Mt. Pleasant Road
(904) 221-5568
Not many cities can boast a 46,000-acre park within city limits. But thanks to the Timucuan Ecological and Historic Preserve, Jacksonville can do just that.

Pets are allowed in state campgrounds if you have proof of current vaccinations and pay a $2.00 fee.

Seventy-five percent of the preserve is water and marshland, but included within its boundaries are Kingsley Plantation, Fort Caroline National Memorial, the Theodore Roosevelt Area, and the Cedar Point Area. The preserve is named for the Native Americans who lived here for 4,000 years before the French and then the Spanish arrived. Learn more about the Timucuans and the arrival of the Europeans at the Fort Caroline National Memorial (see the Attractions chapter).

Since the park is largely water, the best way to get a feel for what it's really like is in a kayak, and tour companies are set up to help you do just that. (See the Tours chapter for information on Kayak Amelia.) The preserve is a great place to get up close and personal with alligators, wood storks, great blue herons, and manatees. There are hiking and shore fishing opportunities at the Theodore Roosevelt and Cedar Point Areas (don't forget your fishing license) and camping opportunities on elevated platforms at Cedar Point, but you'll need a boat or kayak to get to them.

Treaty Oak Park
Southbank Riverwalk
Jacksonville's Treaty Oak is the city's most famous tree. Some say it's 800 years old; others say it's merely 200. Some say Seminole Chief Osceola and General Andrew Jackson signed a peace treaty beneath its branches. Others say that's hogwash, that

From stargazing to counting bald eagle chicks in their nest, the City of Jacksonville hosts a variety of nature programs called NatureScope. For a calendar of events, go to www.coj.net and click on Department of Parks and Recreation.

CLOSE-UP

Building a Park

Sheri Nicholson and Julie Geissmann could write a book about what it takes to build a community park. The first chapter would be titled "Securing the Land," which these two moms accomplished early on when the city of Jacksonville Beach donated an acre of land for what would become Sunshine Park. Then Nicholson and Geissmann began the long task of raising more than $100,000 to build their dream. They wanted to include the community in the fundraising, so they planned events that would do just that. For instance, families paid $12 per child to design a tile at a local pottery studio. The colorful tiles were then fired and used to decorate the park. Nicholson and Geissmann also had children design the playground equipment and name the park. Finally, they organized hundreds of volunteers to build the park in just five days, much like an old-fashioned barn raising. The event involved enough materials and tools for all the volunteers, a child care area, and enough food to feed the builders breakfast, lunch, and dinner each day. The entire process took two years, but Nicholson and Geissmann say the key to success was never losing sight of their goal: a community park for Beaches families to enjoy.

the tree bears no historical significance other than it was saved from destruction in the early sixties by wealthy matron Jessie Ball duPont. Whatever you believe, this is a majestic tree and a perfect place for stressed-out travelers to unwind. It's located close to such Southbank hotels as the Hilton and Hampton Inn, and it's a lovely spot for reading or picnicking. If you visit, take home an acorn to plant in your backyard and perpetuate this wonderful tree.

 You can swim for free in any of the 34 pools the City of Jacksonville opens to the public from May through September. Call (904) 745-9630 for the pool nearest you.

Tree Hill Nature Center
7152 Lone Star Road
(904) 724-4646
www.treehill.org

Tree Hill is located about 15 minutes from downtown Jacksonville hotels. This is a great place to see what the North Florida woodlands look like. Take a guided or self-guided hike on one of the center's four trails, which cover a total of 50 acres. Enjoy exhibits on Florida black bears and the increasingly rare Florida gopher tortoise. Stand still as a statue in the butterfly house and see if a butterfly will land on your head. Learn how to plant a butterfly garden or an organic vegetable garden or how to build a pond. On Saturday Tree Hill offers FUN programs, which stands for Families Understanding Nature, but space is limited, so sign up early.

Visit if wheels

GOLF

The Northeast Florida climate is well suited for year-round play, and over the past three decades, the Jacksonville area has transformed itself into a golfing mecca. The area is home to 50—and counting—courses, many of which are renowned for their beauty and layout. Perhaps the most famed is the TPC at Sawgrass Stadium Course, the annual site of The Players Championship, one of the PGA Tour's most prestigious tournaments. Each spring the world's best professional golfers gather in Ponte Vedra Beach to compete for more than $1 million in prize money. The World Golf Village in northern St. Johns County, home of the World Golf Hall of Fame, further enhances the region's golfing status. The Jacksonville area is also home to several of the top touring pros, including Jacksonville native David Duval, Vijay Singh, and Rocco Mediate.

There's an abundance of course choices, ranging from plush oceanside resorts to popular public courses. In all, the area's 1,400 holes of golf offer challenges for players of all skill levels. Visitors can choose from dozens of quality public and semiprivate courses, with price ranges to fit every golfer's budget.

Sure, it gets hot in the summer, making afternoon play brutal, but the relatively mild winters compensate by allowing year-round play. Jacksonville's courses are mostly flat terrain. Another characteristic of Jacksonville courses: lots of water and marsh hazards. The abundance of marshes, especially at courses nearer the

ocean, provides habitat for all kinds of wildlife, including osprey, egrets, and even the occasional alligator.

All the courses listed below are open year-round unless otherwise noted. All distances are from the men's white tees.

Amelia Island Plantation Links Course
4700 Amelia Island Parkway
Fernandina Beach
(904) 261-6161
www.aipfl.com
Recognized by *Golf Magazine* as one of the best golf resorts in America, Amelia Island Plantation's 45 holes of championship golf capture the natural elements of the island's terrain while preserving the near-pristine habitat. Placed beneath a canopy of moss-covered oaks, the greens and fairways of two courses, featuring 27 holes designed by Pete Dye and 18 by Tom Fazio, border the ocean and coastal marshes.

Baymeadows Golf Club
7981 Baymeadows Circle West
(904) 731-5701
www.baymeadowsgolf.com
Designed by Desmond Muirhead and Gene Sarazen, Baymeadows Golf Club opened in 1969. It's conveniently located to downtown Jacksonville, just off I-95, about 3 miles south of the city.

The challenging par-72, 6,211-yard course features tight fairways, especially off the tees. With pine trees lining many of the fairways, there's little room for error. If you can break 80 at this course, you've earned some bragging rights, say the course pros.

Baymeadows boasts two signature holes, both island greens. The most difficult is the 18th—a long par 4 (400 yards from the white tees) that doglegs to the left before the approach to the green, which is surrounded by water.

There are two ways to get discounts at area courses: Become a member of Avid Golfers, www.avidgolfers.com, or purchase a discount pass from Paradise Golf at (904) 260-4653.

For help planning your golf outing or golf vacation, try Florida's First Coast of Golf (FFCG), a not-for-profit corporation that markets its Northeast Florida member hotels and golf courses throughout the world. You can choose from 21 hotels and 30 prestigious golf courses. For more information call (888) 859-8334 or visit www.florida-golf.org.

Greens fees, including cart, are $39 Friday through Sunday and $29 during the week. Carts are required; however, juniors, 16 and under, can walk. Baymeadows offers a fully stocked pro shop, PGA teaching pros, and a snack bar that serves sandwiches, beer, wine, and mixed drinks.

Blue Cypress Golf Club
University Boulevard North
(904) 762-1971

Blue Cypress is Jacksonville's newest golf course. Opened in November 2003, the nine-hole, par-36 course bills itself as the closest golf course to downtown Jacksonville. Situated on part of the former University Country Club course on property now owned by the City of Jacksonville, Blue Cypress is just a 15-minute drive from the city's business district. The course has a driving range and a snack bar that serves sandwiches, beer, wine, and mixed drinks. Green fees are an affordable $15 Monday through Thursday and $18 Friday through Sunday. Ask about the discounts for seniors, active military, firefighters, and police officers. The hole of interest: No. 5. It's a par 5, 475 yards. However, the green is 60 yards long and

Looking to play some low-key golf in Ponte Vedra? Try the Palm Valley Golf Club and Practice Range, where you can play nine holes for $9.00 plus tax. No carts, though—you gotta walk. Call (904) 285-2878 for more information.

slopes away. The distance from tee to hole isn't tough, but the putting is a bear.

The Champions Club at Julington Creek
1111 Durbin Creek Boulevard
(904) 287-4653
www.championsclubgolf.com

The Champions Club is located at the Julington Creek Plantation community in northwest St. Johns County, about 12 miles south of downtown Jacksonville. The par-72, 6,401-yard course was originally opened in 1988 as a nine-hole course. In 1991 new owners expanded it to a full 18-hole facility with clubhouse, restaurant, and practice driving range.

The semiprivate course was designed by former PGA Tour player and current ABC Sports golf commentator Steve Melnyk. The United States Golf Association used this links-style course in the summer of 2002 for a junior amateur qualifying tournament.

You can reserve a tee time two weeks in advance. Greens fees, including cart, are $45 Monday through Friday and $55 on the weekend. Special group rates are available. Walking the course is not permitted, and required attire includes collared shirts, soft spikes, and no denim. Champions Club has a full bar in the lounge and also offers an annual summer Kids' Clinic.

Cimmarone Country Club
2800 Cimmarone Boulevard (Route 210)
(904) 287-2000
www.cimmaronegolf.com

If you're looking for one of the toughest final holes in Jacksonville, as voted by local golfers, Cimmarone's your course. The 18th hole is 380 yards from the white tees, with the final 80 yards leading up to the green over water. Truth be told, the entire course is tough. Water and marsh come into play on 16 of the 18 holes. *Golf Digest* magazine gives Cimmarone four stars.

Designed by David Postelwaite and opened in 1988, the course is par 72 and

6,200 yards. The facility has a full-service restaurant, pro shop, driving range, and putting and chipping practice greens. Greens fees in summer are $45. The cost to play 18 holes peaks in March and April at $75. You can book a tee time seven days in advance.

The Course at Westland
**7502 Plantation Bay Drive
(904) 778-4653**

Unlike most of Jacksonville's other golf courses, which are located south or east of the city, Westland (as its name suggests) is located on the city's Westside.

Designed by Lloyd Clifton and operated by McCumber Golf, the par-72, 6,124-yard course is known for its wide-open play. Yet it's still a challenging course because the greens are small. The approach to the 15th hole, for example, is a long 436 yards, lined with a number of bunkers that end at a smallish green. The hole is a par 4.

The course is open year-round. Greens fees are $25 Monday through Friday and $33 on Saturday and Sunday, cart included. A cafe sells sandwiches, hot dogs, beer, and mixed drinks. There's a driving range, and lessons are available.

Deerfield Lakes Golf Club
**3825 Deerfield Country Road, Callahan
(904) 879-1210**

Deerfield Lakes, located in the small town of Callahan about 25 miles northwest of downtown Jacksonville, has a lot to crow about these days. Home course of Bubba Dickerson, 2001 U.S. amateur golf champion, it's a par-72, 6,030-yard course with narrow yet forgiving fairways and a number of elevated greens.

The course layout is good for both the accomplished and the beginner. The signature hole is the 5th—a picturesque par 3 over water. Weekend greens fees are $29.50 before 1:00 P.M. and $20.50 after 1:00 P.M. Fees Monday through Friday are $21.50 before 1:00 P.M. and $17.50 after.

The dress code is more relaxed than at most other golf courses. Jeans and T-

If you're looking for a new set of clubs, consider having a set made for you. It's not as expensive as you might think. A local company, Masterfit Golf, can make them for you in four to five days. Plus, the grip size, the length, and the weight of the clubs will be perfect. A fitting takes about 25 minutes. Call (904) 246-3100.

shirts are permissible; cutoffs and tank tops aren't. Tee times are only required on weekends and holidays. You can walk the course during the week but must use a cart on the weekends. A snack bar serves sandwiches, beer, and mixed drinks. There's also a fully stocked pro shop.

Eagle Harbor
**2217 Eagle Harbor Parkway, Orange Park
(904) 269-9300
www.eagleharboronline.com**

Eagle Harbor Golf Club is nature's answer to challenging golf and gracious lifestyles. This Clyde Johnston–designed course gives the visitor a memorable round. Eagle Harbor was selected by *Golf Digest* as a four-star course in the 2000–2001 "Places to Play" edition. Fees are $46.50 Monday through Friday and $65.00 Saturday and Sunday.

Fiddler's Green Golf Club
**13715 Lake Newman Street
(904) 778-5245
www.fiddlersgreengolfclub.com**

Fiddler's Green is a work in progress. Located on the former Cecil Field Naval Air Station on Jacksonville's Westside, the golf course was originally built in 1953 by the Navy Seabees. As part of the wave of base closures several years ago, Cecil Field was handed over to the City of Jacksonville. While most of the facility is being converted into commercial and industrial use, the city has retained the golf course for public use.

An Orlando-based golf course management company that now operates the

CLOSE-UP

Wanted: A Few Good Men (Women and Children, Too)

When it comes to putting together two of Jacksonville's major sporting events, The Players Championship and the Bausch & Lomb Championships, organizers say they could never do it without their volunteers.

The Players Championship uses some 1,500 volunteers every year to quiet the crowds, pick up trash, check tickets, flip burgers, answer phones in the media center, even drive golf carts with disabled fans to special seating areas.

The Bausch & Lomb Championships has a different yet just as critical need for volunteers. Every year organizers of the premier tennis tournament on the First Coast must find some 80 children to work as ball girls and ball boys during tennis matches. These volunteers run after balls during competition and make sure the players are supplied with plenty of cold water and fresh towels. Adult volunteers are also needed at the Bausch & Lomb to usher spectators to their seats, drive tournament buses, and answer questions for guests and players.

In both cases volunteers say they do it for the love of the game and often take a week off work or school in order to attend the event. They return year after year, making both volunteer efforts well-oiled machines. In the case of The Players Championship, adults pay $85 a year for the privilege of volunteering. This fee gets volunteers a job during the golf tournament, as well as a badge for the

course for the city is trying to bring the par-72, 6,222-yard course up to U.S. Golf Association standards. It might take several years. In the meantime, it's not a bad course, especially for beginners—and you can't beat the cost. Weekday greens fees, including cart, are $19 for active or retired military personnel and $21 for nonmilitary. Weekend fees are $26 for everyone.

 Most golfers never see the most exclusive golf club in the city. Pablo Creek Golf Course has only about 200 members, who pay about $100,000 to join. This is where David Duval and Vijay Singh often play to avoid the crowds.

Carts are required only before 1:00 P.M. on weekends and holidays. A snack bar serves food and beer, and a beverage cart cruises the course on Saturday and Sunday. There's also a driving range and practice putting green.

The Golf Club at Fleming Island
2260 Town Center Boulevard, Orange Park
(904) 269–1440
www.flemingislandgolf.com
Opened in September 2000, this semiprivate club features a championship layout designed by Bobby Weed. The par-71 course, offering playing lengths from 4,801 to 6,801 yards, can challenge golfers at every skill level. Fleming Island Golf Club has two PGA golf professionals on staff.

week, and a tournament shirt, hat, and parking pass. Best of all, it lands them a free round of golf on the Stadium Course later in the year, provided they work at least 24 hours in their volunteer position. Most volunteers make sure they do.

At the Bausch & Lomb Championships, ball girls and ball boys get free tennis togs, including shoes, shirt, shorts, and sweatshirt. They also get meals on volunteer days. Ballpersons must be at least 12 years old and able to catch and throw a tennis ball. They also must pass a basic training course held a day before tournament play. As ballpersons, the kids get the best seat in the house and the chance to be up close and personal with the likes of Lindsay Davenport and Serena Williams. But if a player is having a bad day, this can be a double-edged sword. Players have been known to yell at ballpersons, but the kids are coached beforehand not to take this personally.

Older, returning ballpersons land the best matches and work the televised finals.

Officials for Jacksonville's 2005 Super Bowl spent several days huddling at The Players Championship in 2002, studying the tournament's volunteer structure. Super Bowl officials recruited some 7,000 volunteers to work during the week of the game. Benefits for Super Bowl volunteers did not include tickets to the big game, although they did include the opportunity to be a part of all the hoopla.

If you're interested in volunteering for The Players Championship, call (904) 285-7888 for more information. Call early though, because so many volunteers return every year, only a small number of new volunteers are needed.

And if you're interested in volunteering for the Bausch & Lomb Championships, go to the tournament's Web site at www.blchamps.com, where you can download a volunteer application form.

To reach the course, take US 17 south past County Road 220 to Fleming Island in Orange Park. Greens fees are $40 during the week and $50 on the weekend.

The Golf Club at North Hampton
22680 North Hampton Club Way
(904) 548-0000
www.hamptongolfinc.com
This semiprivate course was designed by Arnold Palmer. A par-72 championship design, North Hampton wraps around 10 spring-fed lakes lined with coquina boulders. The wild grasses and rolling hills are intended to give the feel of an old Scottish links course—in sunny Florida.

The Golf Club at South Hampton
315 Hampton Club Way
(904) 287-7529
www.hamptongolfinc.com
Like its sister course, the golf course at North Hampton, the design intent at the South Hampton course is to offer every golfer the appropriate risk-reward situations that challenge the experienced player and offer encouragement to the novice. Sixteen large lakes and more than 60 contoured bunkers, combined with meticulous landscaping, provide players with a superbly conditioned facility. The distinctive layout will test shot-making abilities and require the use of every club in the

golf bag. Greens fees are $55 during the week and $65 Saturday and Sunday.

Golf Club of Amelia at Summer Beach
4700 Amelia Island Parkway
Fernandina Beach
(904) 277-8015
www.summerbeach.com

Designed by PGA Tour veterans Mark McCumber and Gene Littler, this 18-hole course embodies the tranquil beauty of Amelia Island. The meticulously maintained course was the site of the 1998 Liberty Mutual Legends of Golf, a prestigious Senior PGA Tour event that attracted such golfing legends as Lee Trevino, Chi Chi Rodriquez, and Sam Snead. The course winds through majestic palm, pine, and oak trees. A few holes offer views of the Atlantic Ocean.

Golf Club of Jacksonville
10440 Tournament Lane
(904) 779-0800
www.golfclubofjacksonville.com

The Golf Club of Jacksonville is maintained to the exacting standards of the PGA Tour. It'd better be. The PGA Tour, which also operates the famed Tournament Players Club at Sawgrass, runs the 18-hole course. But while the TPC is exclusive—and pricey—the Golf Club of Jacksonville is open to the public and charges reasonable fees. *Golfers Digest* gives the club four stars.

Opened in 1989, the par-71, 6,007-yard course was designed by Bobby Weed, who designed the TPC's Valley Course with Pete Dye. The Golf Club's most picturesque hole is the 12th—a par 4 with water running along the left side of the fairway. The course's most challenging hole is the 11th—a par 4 that traverses two marshes. It's been voted one of the most difficult par-4 holes in Jacksonville.

The course is located on Jacksonville's Westside, about 4.5 miles west of I-295 on 103rd Street. Since this is one of the more popular public courses in the Jacksonville area, reservations are a must. Tee times can be secured two weeks in advance.

Greens fees are $37.50 Monday through Friday and $47.50 on weekends; prices include cart rental. You can practice at a lighted driving range or work on your putting and chipping. The course's PGA pros also give lessons. *NOTE:* Wear a collared shirt, and leave the denim at the hotel.

Hyde Park Golf Club
6439 Hyde Grove Avenue
(904) 786-5410
www.hydeparkgolf.com

For a faint glimpse of old-time Jacksonville golf, hit the links at Hyde Park. One of Jacksonville's older, more scenic courses, it was designed in 1925 by the legendary Donald Ross. Hyde Park has all of Ross's trademark designs: smaller greens and difficult holes down the back nine. The last four holes at Hyde Park are made tougher with a rolling terrain.

The par-72, 6,153-yard course was on the PGA Tour in the 1940s and 1950s as the Greater Jacksonville Open. Hyde Park's most infamous hole is the 6th, or, as it is fondly called, Hogan's Alley. During one pro tournament, it took golf legend Ben Hogan 11 strokes to complete the par-3 hole.

Playing at Hyde Park today is a pleasant affair. The locals who regularly play the course or gather in the lounge for political chitchat reflect the open Southern hospitality found throughout Northeast Florida. Greens fees are $36 on the weekend and $26 Monday through Friday. You can play nine holes during the week for $18. The pro shop begins taking reservations for weekend play on the preceding Monday.

Jacksonville Beach Golf Course
605 South Penman Road
Jacksonville Beach
(904) 247-6184

First opened in 1960, the Jacksonville Beach Golf Course was redesigned in 1987 by Bob Walker, who, along with Ray Floyd, oversaw the redesign of storied Augusta National.

The 6,181-yard, par-72 course is relatively flat but has a fair amount of water

World Golf Village

One of the best things about golf on the First Coast, say avid golfers, is walking around the lake at the World Golf Village and finding the signatures of Hall of Fame members. World Golf Village can best be described as a mecca for golf lovers. Located off I-95 about 45 minutes south of Jacksonville in St. Augustine, WGV hosts the World Golf Hall of Fame and two first-class golf courses: the King and Bear, designed by Arnold Palmer and Jack Nicklaus, and the Slammer and Squire, designed by Sam Snead and Gene Sarazen. There's also a state-of-the-art golf school, the PGA Tour Golf Academy, which features a 2,700-square-foot teaching center located at the far end of the Slammer and Squire range. There are two indoor hitting bays at the academy, eight outdoor bays, video instruction, and three full-time instructors.

The World Golf Village opened in 1998 with two resorts within the complex, an IMAX theater, and a variety of shops and restaurants. The most popular restaurant is the Murray brothers' Caddyshack, founded by actor Bill Murray and his four brothers and named for the golf movie Murray starred in as a deranged greenskeeper. World Golf Village is fully accessible online at www.wgv.com, where you can book not only vacations but also tee times.

hazards. The 14th hole, for example, is a short par 3, but navigating the water surrounding the hole can be tricky. The course is easy to walk, which is what most late weekday afternoon players do. Surprisingly, summer play can be pleasant, thanks to afternoon sea breezes that often blow in from the Atlantic, located about a quarter mile to the east.

Weather permitting, the course is open year-round except Christmas Day. Greens fees for walkers are $15–$21 during the week and $28 on weekends. Fees including a cart are $28–$35 during the week and $42 on weekends. The course offers a teaching academy. The cost ranges from $30 to $50 for a half-hour lesson. There's also a lighted driving range and putting green. Inside the clubhouse you'll find a snack bar and lounge. Also of note: Golf carts are equipped with GPS systems that give players a precise distance to the hole.

Mill Cove Golf Club
1700 Monument Road
(904) 646-4653
www.millcovegolf.com
Located halfway between downtown Jacksonville and the Beaches, off Atlantic Boulevard, Mill Cove Golf Club is one of the best-looking public golf courses in the city.

Designed by Arnold Palmer and opened in 1990, Mill Cove is situated in a heavily wooded area and features gently rolling hills. Unlike many other Florida golf courses, there are few houses located on the fringe of the course. An adjoining nature preserve provides plenty of wildlife.

The 6th hole of this 5,815-yard, par-71 course is perhaps the most challenging. A

Masterfit Golf operates the largest golf range in Jacksonville. It's located on US 1 just north of Racetrack Road. It has 60 tee positions, a big short-game area, and instructional and club-fitting bays.

par 4, it has trees on either side of the fairway. Your second shot needs to carry over water. If you do lose a ball or two, the picturesque setting provides some compensation.

Greens fees during the week are $37 for 18 holes and $20 for 9 holes. Weekend and holiday fees are $44 for 18 holes and $25 for 9 holes, cart included. There's a full-service restaurant and bar.

Oak Bridge Golf Club at Sawgrass
254 Alta Mar Drive, Ponte Vedra Beach
(904) 285-5552

Want to play a private course without busting your budget? Try Oak Bridge, located in Sawgrass, Ponte Vedra Beach's oldest exclusive gated community. Oak Bridge isn't for beginners, however. It's a par-70, 6,031-yard course that has narrow fairways and lots of water.

The most difficult hole is the 7th—a monster par 5 measuring 537 yards from the white tees. Ball placement, especially off the tee, is tricky. If the trees don't get you, the ponds might. For a semiprivate course, the greens fees, including cart rental, aren't unreasonable: $45 Monday through Friday; $55 on the weekends. The course is open year-round.

Walk-ons are welcome, but nonmembers are advised to get tee times in advance. (You can call up to seven days in advance.) Dress requirements are collared shirts, no denim, and no metal spikes. Oak Bridge has a full-service lounge that's also available to nonmembers.

Pine Lakes Golf Club
153 Northside Drive South
(904) 757-0318

As public courses go, Pine Lakes is about as open to the public as it gets. The Northside course, built in 1965, has few pretensions. There's no dress code. There are no golf spike restrictions. You can walk during the week and after 1:00 P.M. on weekends. Best of all, it's a fun, yet still challenging course with lots of trees and water hazards on 15 of the 18 holes. The par-72 course covers 6,265 yards.

The 11th hole offers the biggest challenge. It's a par 4 that ends at an island green—water around the back and along the right side of the hole. For extra fun, try Pine Lakes' unusual seven-acre "aqua" driving range. You hit into a lake. Specially made range balls float to the side, where they are gathered.

The course is open year-round. There's a snack bar with beer and mixed drinks. A beverage cart serves the course only on weekends. Greens fees vary from season to season, so call ahead.

Queen's Harbour Yacht and Country Club
1131 Queen's Harbour Boulevard
(904) 221-1012
www.queensharbourcc.com

Queen's Harbour is a semiprivate course, but you can play there if you're staying at one of the area hotels. Just get the front desk or concierge to make arrangements.

Located in the Queen's Harbour gated community along the Intracoastal Waterway, the par-72, 6,000-yard course has wide-open fairways but plenty of marsh and water hazards. The course's signature hole is the 18th—a par-3 island hole surrounded by water.

The course is open year-round. A snack bar is open to the public. The dining room, however, is reserved for members. A round of 18 holes costs from $50 to $100, depending on the season.

The Tournament Players Club at Sawgrass
1000 TPC Boulevard, Ponte Vedra Beach
(904) 273-3235
www.tpc.com

If you want to play either of the Tournament Players Club's two courses, you have three choices: stay as a guest at the Sawgrass Marriott Resort, become a TPC course member, or hope a member invites you to play.

Hardcore golfing enthusiasts visiting the Jacksonville area will want to play the TPC's stadium course at least once in their life. The 18-hole course is home to The Players Championship every March. The stadium course features one of the most photographed holes in the United States—the famed 17th island. The par-72, 5,815-yard course, designed by Pete Dye, opened in 1980.

Greens fees are seasonal and range from $160 during off-season (summer months) to as high as $324 during peak season. For less money, you can play the TPC's Valley Course, which was designed by Bobby Weed and Pete Dye and opened shortly after the Stadium Course. Greens fees for guests at the Marriott are $103 off-season and $170 in-season.

If you have a room reservation at the Marriott, it's suggested that you make a reservation for either course 30 days in advance.

Windsor Parke Golf Club
13823 Sutton Park Drive North
(904) 223-4653
www.windsorparke.com
Considered by some local golf pros to be Jacksonville's top public course, Windsor Parke is the only nationally rated course in Jacksonville. Open since 1990, the Arthur Hills–designed course is nestled in the tall

Southern pines off Butler Boulevard on the way to Ponte Vedra Beach. The par-72, 6,043-yard course has mostly flat terrain but a fair amount of water hazards as you approach the greens.

The signature 16th hole is a par 3—only 150 yards from the white tees—but the carry to the green is almost entirely over water. The course is open year-round, except Christmas Day. After a round of golf, you can enjoy drinks and appetizers at the 19th hole lounge or dinner at a full-service restaurant.

The club's PGA professional staff offers lessons. The course also has a driving range and putting, chipping, and sand practice areas. Collared shirts and soft spikes are required. Greens fees, including cart rental, are $50 Monday through Thursday and $60 Friday through Sunday.

Located off Butler Boulevard, the course is easily accessible from Baymeadows, Southpoint, downtown Jacksonville, and the Beaches.

FISHING

A fter golf, fishing is the largest sports industry in Florida. According to the Florida Fish and Wildlife Conservation Commission, the state hosts 3.4 million anglers per year, making Florida the No. 1 fishing destination in the United States. In Jacksonville, it's easy to see why.

With quick access to the Atlantic Ocean, miles and miles of sandy beaches, a deep-channel river, and thousands of acres of tidal marshes, the Jacksonville area offers anglers a variety of fishing habitats. There's something for everyone. You can sit at anchor in the mouth of the St. Johns River pursuing the elusive flounder, paddle a kayak around shallow salt marshes searching for tailing redfish, or head offshore for kingfish. There's also excellent freshwater bass fishing on the St. Johns River south of Jacksonville.

For the best fishing in the Jacksonville area, you'll need a boat. If you bring your own, there are ample public boat ramps scattered throughout the area for quick access to either the Intracoastal Waterway or the ocean. If you don't have your own, you can rent a boat or hire one of the dozens of fishing charters available in the area.

Jacksonville also is home to a number of well-known fishing contests, most notably the Bellsouth Greater Jacksonville Kingfish Tournament, billed as the largest kingfishing tournament in the United States.

Before you begin fishing, though, make sure you've got the proper licenses.

FISHING LICENSES

Florida law requires that you obtain a fishing license if you attempt to catch fish for noncommercial use. Nonresidents are required to obtain a saltwater fishing license when saltwater fishing from either a boat or land. Anglers under the age of 16 and Florida residents over 65 are exempt from the law. Residents are allowed to fish from land or a bridge without a license but must have a license when fishing from a boat, unless they are under the age of 16 or over 65. A freshwater fishing license is required for both Florida residents and nonresidents.

Licenses are available at the Duval County Tax Collectors offices (904–630–2000) or most bait shops. For more information call the Florida Fish and Wildlife Conservation Commission regional office in Lake City at (386) 758-0525 or in Jacksonville Beach at (904) 270–2500. The Division of Law Enforcement can provide a complete listing of Florida's regulations of protected species and restrictions on size and number of fish you can keep. Or visit the commission's Web site at www.floridaconservation.org.

It is unlawful to harvest, possess, land, purchase, sell, or exchange the following species of fish: Nassau grouper, jewfish, sawfish, basking shark, whale shark, spotted eagle ray, sturgeon, white shark, sand shark, big eye sand tiger shark, and manta ray.

JACKSONVILLE-AREA FISH

You've got your fishing license in hand, and you've determined where you want to angle. Let's take a look at the many species of fish that inhabit Jacksonville's local waters.

Redfish

Reds are a great fish to catch and eat, making them one of the more popular targets for area anglers. You can land redfish in inland waters or in the ocean, off the beach.

If you're fishing the Intracoastal Waterway and its marshes, the reds feed around oyster mounds and on the flats. In shallow waters, the tail fins of reds will poke out of the water.

The best inland fishing opportunities for redfish are on lower tides in the middle of the day or afternoon. The sun warms the dark mudflats, and the reds are more active. March through December offer the best results for catching redfish.

In recent years, fly fishing for redfish has become popular. Flies resembling shrimp or fiddler crabs are the most often used artificial lures. You can buy them at local fly-fishing shops.

King Mackerel

If you're interested in catching king mackerel, or kingfish, you've come to the right place. Kingfish can be caught off Jacksonville from the surf to the Gulf Stream as far as 80 miles offshore. Kingfish also can be caught off fishing piers.

The king mackerel is a slender, streamlined fish, slightly flattened from side to side with a tapered head. Its color ranges from an iridescent bluish green on its back to silvery sides. Two dorsal fins can fold back in to a groove to enhance speed. They feed on any available food but favor jacks, sea trout, sardinelike fishes, ribbonfish, herring, shrimp, and squid.

The most popular method for catching kingfish is to slow-troll live menhaden shad, also known as pogies, either on a downrigger or free-lined.

King mackerel are a highly sought after gamefish. A challenging catch, they put up a spectacular fight by leaping and skyrocketing out of the water. The best

Local anglers say winter is the best time to fish for redfish in Northeast Florida because the reds are clustered in schools.

season for kings in North Florida is the summer. Kings begin migrating from southern Florida in the spring. As the kingfish move north during the summer months, kingfish tournaments migrate along with them. The annual Bellsouth Greater Jacksonville Kingfish Tournament is held in July.

Kingfish are tasty, as long as they aren't too heavy. They can be cooked or grilled as steaks or fillets. Kingfish more than 15 pounds have a heavy oil content, which makes for a strong "fishy" flavor. However, you can smoke larger fish with appetizing results. Most kingfish hooked off Jacksonville weigh about 20 pounds. The Florida record, by the way, is 90 pounds.

Bluefish

When the bluefish run along the coast during fall and spring, catching them from the beach is a snap—they'll eat almost anything. If you hit a school of bluefish, be prepared to reel them in, one after another. But while the blues off Jacksonville's coast run thick in numbers, they lack the same size as the bluefish you'll find farther north. Most of the blues here are in the one-to-two-pound class.

The bluefish is something of a misnomer, as this species is most commonly a sea green color above, fading to a silvery shade on its lower sides and belly.

Like to fly fish from a canoe or kayak? Then head to the Pellicer Flats west of the Intracoastal Waterway between Marineland and Palm Coast. Anglers call this spot "redfish heaven."

Bluefish eat a variety of small-bodied animals such as shrimp, small lobsters, crabs, and larval fish and mollusks. Adult bluefish are opportunistic feeders, commonly focusing on schooling species such as menhaden, squid, and sand eels. For bait, most locals use dead shrimp.

Bluefish anglers fish from boat or shore along nearly every harbor entrance, town dock, beach, and jetty. Wire leaders are a must. Bluefish are equipped with sharp teeth that can snap through monofilament lines.

Jack Crevalle

Known as the bulldog of inshore waters, the jack crevalle runs between 3 and 10 pounds. When these fighters begin feeding off the top, get ready. They strike like a mad fish and will test any tackle that you own.

The best time for jack crevalle is April through November.

Ladyfish

Often referred to as the "poor man's tarpon," ladyfish perform aerial acrobats when hooked. Like tarpon, they can come out of the water several times before being landed.

Ladyfish can run in numbers. They range from about two pounds to five pounds, and the best months for action are April through August.

Tarpon

If you're in search of real tarpon, Jacksonville's waters aren't your best bet. Southwest Florida, for example, offers better inshore tarpon fishing. That's not to say the area is devoid of tarpon. Anglers going after reds or trout in inshore waters accidentally hook tarpon from time to time. Lucky folks. Tarpon hooked in Jacksonville's inshore waters can weigh anywhere from 25 to 200 pounds. Overall, however, they are very difficult to hook.

Trout

Trout are plentiful in the mouth of the St. Johns River and in the inland creeks off the river and the Intracoastal Waterway.

Local anglers use dead and live shrimp and artificial lures. Like redfish, trout has become a favorite among the growing ranks of local saltwater fly fishers.

The best times of year for trout are from mid-March through mid-December.

Other local species include dolphin, pompano, flounder, and cobia.

WHERE TO FISH

There are basically four different areas to fish in the Jacksonville area, each offering its own distinct fish and fishing nuances: the freshwater rivers mostly to the west of Jacksonville; the Intracoastal Waterway and tidal marshes that stretch north and south along the backside of the Beaches; surf casting from the beach; and deepwater fishing in the open waters of the Atlantic Ocean.

Surf Fishing

Surf fishing in Northeast Florida, indeed throughout Florida, has greatly improved since the state banned the use of large commercial nets near the shore in the late 1990s. Locals report that surf casting has been producing some of the best results in years.

Ocean fishing is great because you don't know what you might catch. Species you might reel in include whiting, redfish, Spanish mackerel, bluefish, trout, pompano, and everybody's favorites, stingrays and catfish.

The most sought-after species in the Jacksonville surf is whiting. In fall the blues run along the beaches in thick schools. You can also catch redfish from time to time. With the disappearance of the nets, your chances of hooking a colorful—and very tasty—pompano has greatly improved.

For the best results, fish on the incoming tide. That's when small bait fish get carried closer to shore, with larger fish following in hungry pursuit. Local anglers prefer dead or live shrimp or cut-up mullet as bait.

Offshore Fishing

On the floor of the Atlantic Ocean, 9 miles off Jacksonville's shore, sits debris from Jacksonville's old Gator Bowl. The debris is testament to Jacksonville's ever-changing skyline. The old cement chunks also have created a wonderful environment *for* fish, and thus a great place *to* fish.

Since there are no natural formations off the coast of Jacksonville, most of the best offshore fishing is done around man-made reefs, such as sunken vessels and the Gator Bowl debris.

Most offshore fishing is done by trolling, and the most common fish caught is the kingfish. Cobia is a fun fish to catch—good eating, too. For the best grouper fishing, try the "Ledge" off St. Augustine.

Other fish commonly caught offshore include bluefish, barracuda, bonito, dolphin, mackerel, mako, marlin, sailfish, tuna, and wahoo. These fish tend to congregate around wrecks: amberjack, barracuda, cobia, grouper, mackerel, permit, snapper, and shark.

FISHING CHARTERS

A1A Watersports
2327 Beach Boulevard
Jacksonville Beach
(located in Beach Marina)
(904) 249-6666
www.a1awatersports.com
The company offers both inshore and blue-water fishing charters. They have dozens of boats and some of the most experienced charter captains in the area. A 50 percent deposit is required to guarantee all charters. For inshore fishing trips, prices range from $225 for a half day to $350 for a full day.

Fun Fishing Charters
17184 Dorado Circle
(904) 757-7550
www.hammondfishing.com
Captain Jim Hammonds covers the St. Johns River, backwater creeks off the Intracoastal Waterway, and the jetties. A Jacksonville native, Hammonds has been fishing since he was five with his dad. He specializes in helping anglers catch red bass, speckled trout, jack crevalle, bluefish, flounder, sheepshead, shark, tarpon, and black drum.

***King Neptune* Deep Sea Fishing**
4378 Ocean Street, Mayport Village
(904) 246-7575
www.kingneptunefishing.com
Captain Scott Reynolds has been taking large groups deep-sea fishing for more than 20 years. His 65-foot deep-sea fishing boat can hold up to 45 anglers. Reynolds will take you 15 to 30 miles offshore in the *King Neptune* and supply you with a rod, reel, bait, and fishing license.

He knows literally hundreds of spots to catch fish either on the natural bottom or artificial reefs, and you may return to dock with a variety of reef fish including snapper, sea bass, or grouper. The *King Neptune* has a galley where you can purchase food, or you can bring your own snacks, beer included. Prices vary. Reservations required.

Mayport Princess Deep Sea Fishing
4378 Ocean Street, Mayport Village
(904) 241–4111
You could call the *Mayport Princess* and the *King Neptune* friendly competitors. Both dock at Monty's Marina in the historic village of Mayport. Captain George Strate has some 30 years experience taking large groups of anglers out into the ocean to deep-sea fish. The *Mayport Princess* is a bit smaller and faster than the *King Neptune* and holds up to 40 people. Captain Strate knows these waters like the back of his hand, including hundreds of the best fishing spots for the cur-

rent water conditions. He too will supply you with a rod, reel, bait, and fishing license. The *Mayport Princess*, however, does not have a galley, so if you want anything to eat or drink while out on the water, bring a cooler. The *Mayport Princess* sails year-round. Prices vary, and reservations are required in advance.

FISHING GUIDES

The Salty Feather
3733 Southside Boulevard
(904) 645–8998
www.saltyfeather.com
The Salty Feather is a full-service fly-fishing center that's been in business since 1994, offering a full array of flies, rods, reels, lines, leaders, fly-tying tools, accessories, gadgets, clothing, books, videos, gift items, and much more. Salty Feather also offers guides for whole- or half-day fly-fishing trips as well as fly-fishing classes year-round.

BOATING AND WATER SPORTS

At times, it seems that everyone in Jacksonville has some connection to the water. On weekends the roads are clogged with big pickup trucks hauling sportfishing boats. You can also tell when there's a good swell hitting the area shores by the heavy volume of cars zipping along with surfboards strapped to their roofs. During the hot summer months, there's usually a procession of people making their way to Jacksonville's beaches.

In fact, it's hard to avoid seeing water in the River City, including the St. Johns River, its many creeks, the Atlantic Ocean, and the Intracoastal Waterway.

If you're planning to visit Jacksonville, you owe it to yourself to experience our abundant natural resources. Fishing enthusiasts can launch their boats at the well-used public boat ramp in Mayport and head out for a day of fishing in the open waters of the Atlantic Ocean. Sailors can enjoy the wide stretches of the St. Johns River south of downtown. Pleasure boaters can ply the scenic Intracoastal Waterway. Surfers, Jet Skiers, and kayakers have miles and miles of potential area in which to play.

If possible, you'll want to experience the Jacksonville area by boat. Many hidden, out-of-the-way sights, especially along the Intracoastal, are accessible only by boat. If you bring your own, don't fret about getting it into the water. There are numerous public boat ramps scattered throughout Jacksonville. If you don't bring a boat, rentals and charters are available year-round.

For those who prefer to experience nature a little closer to the waterline, if not actually in the water, Jacksonville offers some wonderful spots for kayaking, surfing, and swimming. There's even offshore scuba diving for qualified divers.

Jet Skis and other personal watercraft (PWCs) are popular in Jacksonville. You can ride them on the Intracoastal Waterway, the ocean, or the St. Johns River. If you bring your own PWC or rent one while you're here, be sure to inquire about where you can operate them. For example, you can launch PWCs from the beach only at specific places. Once in the water, you must maintain a safe distance from swimmers and surfers.

BOAT AND PWC RENTALS

A1A Watersports
2315 Beach Boulevard, Jacksonville Beach
(904) 249-6666
www.a1awatersports.com
A1A Watersports is located on the Intracoastal Waterway at Beach Marine marina in Jacksonville Beach. A1A has nine powerboats, including a 19-foot bowrider, an 18-foot dual-console fishing boat, and 16-foot skiffs.

A1A Watersports also has six PWCs for rent, including the 50-mph Yamaha WaveRunner XL700. PWCs rent for $60 an hour and can only be used in the Intracoastal Waterway near the marina. A1A is open from 9:00 A.M. until dark, seven days a week year-round.

Dock Holiday Boat Rentals
3108 Highway 17 South, Orange Park
(904) 215-5363
www.dockholidayboatrentals.com
Dock Holiday specializes in renting houseboats—big houseboats. The company has two 41-foot classic Gibson houseboats for rent and also rents 20-foot fishing boats and 25-foot pontoon boats. They do not rent PWCs.

Located at Doctors Lake Marina in Orange Park, Dock Holiday is convenient to the St. Johns River. Owner Monty Murphy says he doesn't allow any of his rental boats to go north of the Buckman Bridge on the St. Johns River because of the swift currents that run through downtown Jacksonville. The boats can be taken as far south on the St. Johns as a renter wants.

Be careful traversing the St. Johns River. The currents in the St. Johns—one of the few rivers in the world that runs south to north—can be treacherous. In some spots currents can clock 8 knots.

Water Sports
250 Vilano Road, Vilano Beach
904-829-0006
www.nflwatersports.com
Water Sports is located in Vilano Beach across the Intracoastal Waterway from St. Augustine. They rent 18-foot fishing boats, pontoon boats, and PWCs.

Water Sports is also the only place in the Greater Jacksonville area that offers parasailing. The cost is $50 to $80, depending on how high up you go. Distances range from 400 to 1,400 feet. PWCs rent for $75 an hour.

SAILING

While sailing isn't as popular as fishing and motorboating in the Jacksonville area, it still has plenty of loyal adherents. There's good offshore sailing in the open ocean waters off Jacksonville's beaches, but making your way out on the St. Johns River can take hours.

If you have the time, a great weekend sail is from Jacksonville to either St. Augustine to the south or Fernandina Beach to the north. You can sail in the ocean or along the Intracoastal Waterway. In Jacksonville most day sailing is done in the St. Johns River south of

downtown, where the river widens considerably.

While staying in the Jacksonville area, why not take sailing lessons? There are two certified sailing schools in the area.

Whitney's Marine
3027 Highway 17, Orange Park
(904) 269-0027
www.whitneysmarine.com
Whitney's Marine, located about 30 nautical miles from the ocean on the St. Johns River in Orange Park, has recently started a sailing school. The Offshore Sailing School, certified by the U.S. Sailing Association, offers lessons from basic sailing all the way to offshore coastal sailing.

Windward Sailing School
1010 Atlantic Avenue, Fernandina Beach
(904) 261-9125
www.windwardsailing.com
Located in Fernandina Beach, about a 40-minute drive from Jacksonville, Windward Sailing School offers basic and advanced sailing instruction and navigational lessons.

If you're already an experienced sailor, you can rent a boat at Windward. They have a CAL 24 and 2001 Hunter 212 available for day sails only. (They aren't for offshore.) They rent for $130 for a half day and $220 for an eight-hour full day.

Two larger boats, a Hunter 28 and a Hunter 31, can be sailed in the ocean. Rents range from $200 for four hours to $500 for two days and one night, with each additional day at $165.

KAYAKING

Jacksonville's waters offer a variety of conditions for the beginner and advanced kayaker. Enjoy the quietude of paddling through the placid waters of a nature preserve. Paddle among the dolphins on a calm sunny day in the Atlantic Ocean. Or catch some of the big, rough surf that hits our shores on a consistent basis.

If you like nature trips, you've got your choice of preserves. Timucuan Ecological and Historic Preserve comprises more than 46,000 acres along Jacksonville's river- and oceanfront. Guana River State Park is a 2,400-acre coastal park located on a barrier island midway between St. Augustine and Jacksonville. Bounded by the Atlantic Ocean and the Intracoastal Waterway, the total Guana tract comprises some 12,000 acres of public conservation and recreational land. (See the Parks chapter for more information on these preserves.)

**Black Creek Outfitters
and Black Creek Guides
10051 Skinner Lake Drive
(904) 645-7003
www.blackcreekoutfitters.com**
Black Creek sells outdoor gear, apparel, footwear, and accessories addressing adventure travel, backpacking, hiking, and kayaking. Outdoor education focuses on coastal kayaking, climbing, and basic outdoor skills. They also offer basic and advanced kayak instruction and guided kayak trips throughout Northeast Florida. (You must be an American Canoe Association certified paddler to rent a kayak for unguided trips.)

Black Creek is open Monday through Friday 10:00 A.M. to 8:00 P.M., Saturday from 10:00 A.M. to 6:00 P.M., and Sunday noon to 5:00 P.M.

**Gecko Latitudes Kayaking
(904) 824-7979, (866) 411-8011
www.geckolatitudes.com**
Gecko Latitudes owner Robert Burks makes no bones about it: He's out to change the way you think about the environment. To that end he'll hook you up with a kayaking ecotour, perhaps one at sunset when the sky is pink, a great blue heron is feeding on fish next to your kayak, and a pair of dolphins are playing hide-and-seek with your paddle in the tannic water. Then he'll reel you in when he slips a microphone into the water and you hear those endangered dolphins whistle, click, and chirp. By the end of your ecotour (be it a tour for women, seniors, school groups, or families

out for a half-day, full-day, overnight, or moonlight trip), you'll care a little more about the environment and wanting to preserve it. Burks operates out of St. Augustine but offers kayaking tours in state parks throughout the region, including Guana, Anastasia, and Washington Oaks.

**Kayak Adventures
Jacksonville Beach
(904) 249-6200
kayakadventuresllc.com**
Kayak Adventures' guides will meet you at Guana River State Park for half-day and full-day trips. They specialize in organizing fly-fishing and light-tackle fishing trips via kayak in waters near Guana. All equipment is provided. The cost for guided kayaking is $50 per person for a half day and $85 for a full day, and the price includes lunch. Fishing trips cost $200 for the first person and $100 for a second. Three-hour kayak instruction is $60 per person. The company accepts all major credit cards except American Express. Reservations are required.

In addition to being an open-water kayak instructor, owner Walter Bunso has special training to instruct and work with the disabled.

SURFING

Although Florida's not known for big surf, the Northeast Florida coastline gets its share of good waves, especially fall through spring. The surf generally goes flat in the hot summer months—that is, until a passing hurricane or tropical storm sends large swells our way.

You can surf anywhere along the Florida coast, but some spots are better than most. Here are the four top spots.

Boat-A-Rama is Jacksonville's biggest boat show. It's usually held in February and features boats, motors, trailers, the latest in marine accessories, and fishing seminars.

If you rent a Jet Ski or other personal watercraft, be careful. While PWCs represent less than 13 percent of registered vessels in Florida, they account for 32 percent of all accidents and 45.7 percent of all injuries, according to the Florida Fish and Wildlife Conservation Commission's Division of Law Enforcement. If you are involved in an accident while riding a PWC, you have an 80.1 percent chance of suffering an injury requiring more than first aid.

The Jacksonville Beach Pier

Located in the heart of Jacksonville Beach, the "Pier" has long been known for its exceptional break. From Third Street, turn east on Fourth Avenue. There's parking and an outdoor shower.

The Pier has a good break for both long and short boarders. One big drawback: When it's breaking well, the Pier can attract big crowds. Inexperienced surfers would be wise to avoid the throngs and surf on the fringe of the crowds.

The Poles

The Poles is unquestionably the best surf break in the Jacksonville area, if not along the entire east coast of Florida, so it can get crowded on big-wave days. It's located just south of the mouth of the St. Johns River, adjacent to Naval Station Mayport.

Unless you have a military pass to get onto the base, access to the Poles is through Jacksonville's Hanna Park. The Poles got its name from the pilings sticking out of the beach dividing the naval base from the park.

Admission to Hanna Park is $1.00 per person. Ask the attendant at the gate for directions to the Poles.

The North Jetties

The beach between Fort George Inlet and the mouth of the St. Johns River, known locally as the North Jetties, also offers ideal surfing waves. The long, gradually sloping beach at Huguenot creates surf that almost always breaks.

Access is through Huguenot Park, which is located off Heckscher Drive east of Fort George Island. Admission to the park is 50 cents per person. A real plus: You can drive on the beach.

Anastasia State Park

Another dependable spot for waves is St. Augustine's Anastasia Park, which sits just south of the inlet. Surf is usually a little bigger here than in the Jax Beach area and often breaks better. Anastasia can be good on any swell direction but can be absolutely epic on an Atlantic storm swell. Anastasia is often ignored by the Jax-based surfers, but it shouldn't be. In general, if you are unsure about where to go, head to Anastasia for some good times.

From St. Augustine head east across the Bridge of Lions and look for the Anastasia State Park signs on the left side of the road. Park admission is $3.25 per vehicle—showers and restrooms provided.

Surf Shops

Aqua East Surf Shop
696 Atlantic Beach, Neptune Beach
(904) 246-2550
(904) 828-4848 (surf report)
www.aquaeast.com
Located on Atlantic Boulevard in Neptune Beach, Aqua East is the largest of the surf shops at the Beaches, with a good selection of clothing and boards. Surfboard and kayak rentals are available.

Austin's Surf Shop
615 South Third Street, Jacksonville Beach
(904) 249-9848
Want to see what an old-fashioned surf shop looks like? Drop in on Austin's in Jacksonville Beach. The selection isn't extensive, but you'll get personalized attention from Austin himself.

Fort George Island Surf Shop
10030 Heckscher Drive, Fort George
(904) 251-3483
(904) 251-WAVE (surf report)
Fort George Island Surf Shop is located on Heckscher Drive on the way to the North Jetties. The shop sells boards and gear and rents surfboards and kayaks. Owner Ray Hetchka is a wealth of local knowledge.

Secret Surf Shop
115½ First Street, Neptune Beach
(904) 270-0526
The latest surf shop to open at Jacksonville's beaches, it's a cozy little shop located next to Pete's Bar. Run by local surfers, the shop sells new and used surfboards, swimwear, and apparel and also has a few boards for rent. A plus: It's just a short walk from the shop to the beach.

Sunrise Surf Shop
834 Beach Boulevard, Jacksonville Beach
(904) 241-0822
(904) 241-0933 (surf report)
www.sunrisesurfshop.com
Known among local surfers as *the* surf shop in the area, this shop carries a good selection of new and used boards and apparel. Sunrise also rents surfboards and body boards.

Surf Camps and Lessons

Saltwater Cowgirls Camp
This popular five-day surf camp held in the summer in Jacksonville Beach is for girls only. The camp consists of beach and water instruction with a strong focus on water and board safety. The camp keeps a 6-to-1 student-instructor ratio. In addition to surf instruction, there's "surf basketball," paddle races, and other fun activities. The cost is $150 if you have your own board and $200 if you need to rent one.

For more information call (904) 242-9380 or (866) 873-3696, or visit www.saltwatercowgirls.com on the Web.

Super Surf Camp
Offered by Sunrise Surf Shop and the City of Jacksonville Beach from June through August, the camp is geared to wanna-be surfers age seven and up. Each session runs for one week, from 8:00 A.M. to noon. Campers learn water safety, first aid, and how to surf. Snacks, drinks, and boards are provided.

For more information or to reserve a spot, call Sunrise Surf Shop at (904) 241-0822.

Surf Contests

The Wavemaster's annual surf contest in Jacksonville Beach is the largest amateur surfing contest in Florida.

About two decades ago the Wavemasters decided to hold a contest in hopes of attracting a bevy of bikini-clad girls and, in the process, raise a little money for local charities. Today that contest has evolved into Florida's largest and most prestigious open amateur surfing contest. This annual contest attracts more than 300 competitors from all over the Southeast and draws thousands of enthusiastic spectators.

WINDSURFING

The best place for windsurfing in the Jacksonville area is The Pond, located at the southern end of Ft. George Inlet and accessible through Huguenot Park. Park admission is 50 cents per person. There is a designated windsurfing-only area within the park.

CLOSE-UP

Manatees

Is it possible to write a story about manatees in the Jacksonville area without calling them "gentle giants"? Those two words have been overused past the point of cliché when describing manatees. So here goes. The test begins now. Can we do it?

Manatees, or sea cows, are aquatic herbivores that live primarily in Florida's warm freshwater, including the St. Johns River. Scientists believe that these slow-moving mammals live for 60 years or more—if they don't get run over by a fast-moving powerboat, that is. The average adult manatee is 10 to 12 feet long and weighs 1,500 to 1,800 pounds. Scientists figure that a 1,000-pound manatee must eat 100 to 150 pounds of food a day. Now that's a lot of plants. Sometimes they get help from the folks who live along the St. Johns River, who've been known to spot a manatee by their dock and run inside for a head of lettuce for the endangered creature to munch on.

Although their eyes are small, scientists believe that these gent ... (oops) sea cows can see pretty well. They communicate with one another by making sounds underwater. To the human eye, most manatees look alike. The only sure way scientists have to tell them apart—if they haven't been tagged—is by the propeller scars on their backs. Virtually every manatee has at least one, older manatees often have more.

Jacksonville isn't the best place in Florida to see a manatee. Crystal River or Homosassa Springs north of Tampa would probably get that designation. But lucky visitors and Jacksonville residents sometimes happen upon a floating gray mass in the St. Johns River, usually when walking on the Southbank Riverwalk near the Duval County school board building.

The Pond is tidal but has no strong currents. It is exceptional on northeast winds and offers sailing for beginners to advanced windsurfers. At mid to low tide, sandbars will emerge—the primary hazard at this spot.

Within Huguenot Park you can gain access to the St. Johns river with gorgelike conditions. Sailable only on a counter opposing wind and tide (east or west wind), the river is very dangerous and unquestionably an experts-only site. Also available at the park is ocean sailing from the beach area. Epic conditions can be had on southeast days (advanced to intermediate) and northwest or southwest days (advanced only). Sailing the beach at Huguenot on a northeast wind is not recommended. There is a large sea jetty, and if you break down, you'll be eating jetty rock.

From I-95 take Heckscher Drive east to Fort George Island. About 2 miles west of the Mayport ferry dock, turn right at the flashing yellow light into Huguenot Park. Look for the sailing area on the south bank of the inlet.

Jacksonville Associated Windsurfers, or JAWS, is the largest area windsurfing club. JAWS is very active in protecting windsurfing access at Huguenot Park and promotes frequent intramural events. JAWS also maintains a local wind line

For decades manatees have flocked to this part of the St. Johns River when the temperature hits freezing, usually in January or February. That's because the Southside Generating Plant next door to the school board building used to discharge water that was about 10 degrees warmer than the rest of the St. Johns. Those 10 degrees made a big difference to a freezing manatee.

But in October 2001 the Jacksonville Electric Authority, which owns the Southside Generating plant, closed the plant down. JEA is selling the prime riverfront property and building a bigger power plant elsewhere. But if you're a manatee, old habits die hard. The gentle gia... (ughhh!) sea cows still swim to this area in cold months, searching for warmer waters. When they don't find them, they often must be rescued by scientists from SeaWorld in Orlando, who have a contract with the state to take in wayward manatees, nurse them back to health if necessary, and then release them back into the wild, usually around Crystal River or Homosassa Springs.

By most counts, there are about 1,000 manatees left in Florida. A debate is raging in the state legislature between boaters and manatee lovers over how best to protect these gentle giants (oh, what the heck!) from death by collision with motorboats. The state stringently enforces manatee speed zones, which slow boaters to a virtual crawl. Violators must appear in court, where a judge will set the fine and possibly include jail time. Some in the boating community feel there are too many regulations relating to manatees, while the environmental community feels there are nowhere near enough protections in place to preserve the dwindling numbers of manatees in Florida. Boaters want to remove manatees from the endangered species list after their numbers climb to a certain level. The Save the Manatee Club (www.savethemanatee .org) is fighting passage of any legislation that would put such a process in place.

number, The Wind Talker, that provides real time updates on wind conditions, including speed, direction, and history. Access to the wind line is limited to JAWS members. Annual dues are about $20 and entitle you to monthly newsletters, parties, events, and the wind line.

For more information about windsurfing in Jacksonville-area waters, check out the JAWS Web site: home.talkcity.com/BoxSeatBlvd/lowjiber/.

KITESURFING

Kitesurfing, also known as kiteboarding, is gaining popularity in Jacksonville, especially along the beaches. It offers the speed of waterskiing, the tricks of wakeboarding, and the carving turns of surfing.

A kitesurfer rides a lightweight board with foot straps while holding an aluminum bar that controls the kite. Jeff

Manatees are difficult to see from a moving boat. A swirl on the surface of the water could indicate a diving manatee. You may also glimpse a manatee's back, snout, tail, or flipper breaking the surface. Listen for the lumbering animals to breathe when they surface.

Weiss, a kitesurfing instructor, says that Jacksonville's beaches are ideal for kitesurfing. "All you need is a 10-knot wind and you're loving life," he says.

Before you run out and try it, however, lessons are highly recommended. For lessons and more information, call Kitemare Kiteboarding at (866) 321–KITE.

SCUBA DIVING

With offshore depths from 40 to 120 feet, natural limestone reef ledges, and a long history of artificial reef building, Jacksonville offers the diver looking for an abundance of marine life and seascapes a great dive opportunity. Visibility can range from 20 to 120 feet, depending on the season (summer is best). For information on dive instructors, retail dive shops, and charters, you can start with the list below.

Atlantic Pro Dive
1886 Third Street South
Jacksonville Beach
(904) 270–1747
www.atlanticprodivers.com
The shop offers classes, offshore charters, retail equipment, rentals, and service.

Divers Supply
9701 Beach Boulevard
(904) 646–3828
www.divers-supply.com
Divers Supply sells and rents equipment, tanks, and accessories; offers certification lessons and basic open-water instruction;

and offers dive trips to freshwater springs in central Florida May through September. Ocean trips to artificial reefs are available during summer.

Offshore Dive Charters
1304 Sixth Avenue North
Jacksonville Beach
(904) 463–3236
www.offshoredivecharters.com
Captain Dan Lindley offers year-round dive trips up to 25 miles offshore in water depths of up to 130 feet. Air tanks are provided.

Scuba Cove Adventures
14603 Beach Boulevard
(904) 223–1300
Located on the western side of the Intracoastal Waterway near Jacksonville Beach, the shop offers instruction, equipment sales and rentals, and dive charters.

ADDITIONAL ONLINE RESOURCES FOR SURF AND WEATHER CONDITIONS

Surf reports
www.fluidgroove.net
www.stksurf.com

Live surf camera
www.jaxsurfcam.com

Conditions in St. Augustine Beach
Surf Station's Web site:
www.surf-station.com

Tides
www.jacksonville.com/weather/tidesnew.shtml

Marine forecast
www.wunderground.com/MAR/AM/435.html

MARINAS

The Intracoastal Waterway running through Jacksonville is busy every fall and

Every fall Jacksonville Beach is the site of an extraordinary parade: the return of the right whales, which visit the area to calve in Florida's warm coastal waters. The endangered right whale is 45 to 55 feet long and can weigh up to 70 tons. Hunted to near extinction before coming under governmental protection in the 1930s, there are only about 300 right whales in existence today.

spring as sailboats and motorboats make their way up and down the Atlantic coast.

Whether you are merely passing through area waters, arriving for an extended stay, or trailering a boat behind your car, a handful of marinas in the Jacksonville area are equipped to handle most any need.

Amity Anchorage Marina
1106 Friendship Drive, Switzerland
(904) 287-0931

If you find yourself sailing or motoring on the St. Johns River well south of downtown Jacksonville and want to spend a night or two in a quiet marina surrounded by the sounds and sights of old Florida, Amity's your anchorage. Just make sure you call ahead. The marina has only 48 slips, most of which are usually occupied by locals.

Best described by its owner as a "quiet marina in the country," Amity Anchorage is a no-frills operation. There's water and power for your boat. There's a bathroom and a shower for you. And you can buy a bag of ice. That's about it. But you can't beat the scenery and the price: 50 cents per foot per night.

Beach Marine
2315 Beach Boulevard
(904) 249-8200
www.jaxbeachmarine.com

So maybe quietude isn't your thing. Beach Marine, located on the Intracoastal Waterway at Beach Boulevard in Jacksonville Beach, offers all the noisy fun you'd expect to find in a big marina: big boats coming and going, some real live-aboard characters, and nearby restaurants and nightclubs.

The marina itself has 170 wet slips. The dock house sells gas and diesel and offers pump-out services. Transient boaters have access to a weight room, sauna, Laundromat, and mail service. You can even get your hair done at Debra's Hair Salon. The cost for transient docking is $1.25 per foot per day.

The Jacksonville Marine Association is a great resource for everything from boat charters to yacht sales. Here's the number: (904) 724-3003.

Several marine-related businesses are located at the marina, including Todd Marine, which has been specializing in engine parts for over 40 years, and Boat Tree, a boat sales and service shop. A1A Water Sports rents personal watercraft and pontoon boats. The phone number is (904) 249-6666.

Mayport Marine
4852 Ocean Street, Mayport
(904) 246-8929

After changing hands several times over the past decade, Mayport Marine is now in stable hands, promises proud new owner Neal Abel.

Located in the working fishing village of Mayport, the marina sits just 2.5 miles from the open ocean, making it Jacksonville's closest marina to the Atlantic. The marina has just 15 slips for transient and overnighters, but its dock can handle vessels up to 190 feet long. The marina also has 230 dry storage slips for smaller boats.

Diesel and gas are available, and there's a live bait shop. A full-service marine shop can do all repairs, including rebuild engines. A deli serves sandwiches, snacks, beer, and ice. The per-day cost is $1.00 per foot.

Palm Cove Marina
14603 Beach Boulevard
(904) 223-4757
www.palmcovemarina.com

Located on the western shore of the Intracoastal Waterway at the Beach Boulevard drawbridge (about 9 miles from ocean), Palm Cove Marina is one of the last full-service marinas on the waterway until St. Augustine, 25 miles to the south. It's just a short cab ride over the Intracoastal into

Want to charter a houseboat? Call the folks at Doctors Lake Marina in Orange Park at (904) 264-0505.

the Jacksonville beaches, where there's plenty of nightlife and good restaurants.

An extensive renovation of the marina was completed in 2000 by its new owner, Jacksonville construction executive Ron Foster. There's new dry storage and docking, and the marina basin, always prone to silting in, has been dredged. The marina has 200 wet slips, a few of which can accommodate vessels up to 100 feet in length. The marina also has dry storage for 500 boats.

Palm Cove offers a full range of marine services, including repairs, fuel, pump-out station, toilets, and a travel lift to pull boats out of the water. There's also a full complement of new accommodations for the sailor: a lounge, bathrooms, and showers. The cost for transient vessels is $1.00 per foot per night.

Tackle, bait, beer, and ice also are available at the marina's store. There are no boat rentals. Palm Cove has an added feature none of the other area marinas has: The excellent Marker 32 restaurant is located on the marina's grounds.

PUBLIC BOAT RAMPS

If you trailer your boat to Jacksonville, you can launch it at any number of public boat ramps, free of charge. Following is a list of some of the more popular boat-launching sites maintained year-round by the City of Jacksonville:

• **St. Johns Marina,** 901 Museum Circle, is located on the south bank of the St. Johns River in the heart of downtown Jacksonville, between the Hart Bridge and the Jax Brewery restaurant.

• **Bert Maxwell,** 680 Broward Road, is located on the Northside just off I-95.

• **Mayport,** 4870 Ocean Street, Mayport, is located near Highway A1A, next to Mayport Marine marina. The Mayport public boat ramp offers the best access to the Atlantic Ocean. There's ample parking for your vehicle and trailer, but it can get especially crowded on the weekends and holidays.

• **Intracoastal,** 2501 20th Avenue at Beach Boulevard, is located in the same basin as Beach Marine marina. This is a great spot for launching your boat for quick runs up and down the Intracoastal Waterway. Parking is limited.

• **Wayne B. Stevens,** 4555 Ortega Farms Boulevard, is located on the Ortega River with quick access to the St. Johns River south of downtown Jacksonville.

• **Arlington,** Arlington Road, is located off Arlington Expressway on the St. Johns River.

• **Hood Landing,** Hood Landing Road at Julington Creek, is located in the extreme southern end of the county. Julington Creek flows into the St. Johns River.

• **Sister's Creek Marina,** 8203 Heckscher Drive, is located in the northwest quadrant of the intersection of the Intracoastal Waterway and the St. Johns River. The City of Jacksonville acquired the site in 1999 and spent several million dollars building new docks and a boat ramp. Sister's Creek is also home to the annual Greater Jacksonville Kingfish Tournament, held in July.

SPECTATOR SPORTS

Jacksonville's miles of ocean and river shorelines and relatively mild year-round climate certainly make for a great playground for everything from golf and tennis to fishing and surfing. But the city also offers a variety of exciting professional and amateur spectator sports for even the most discerning fan, including Super Bowl XXXIX in 2005.

Want to take in an NFL game in one of the league's most modern stadiums? Check out the Jacksonville Jaguars. Want to watch top professional women tennis players compete amid sheltering live oaks? The Bausch & Lomb Championships comes to Amelia Island Plantation every April. Do you want to get an up-close view of the world's best golfers tackling one of the most photographed holes in professional golf? Then The Players Championship in Ponte Vedra Beach is for you. Or maybe you just want to enjoy the small-town pleasures of Saturday-night auto racing? You'll find that at Jax Raceways.

There's more. Jacksonville also has a minor-league baseball team and a minor-league ice hockey team. If you prefer college sports, there's the annual Toyota Gator Bowl and the always entertaining Florida-Georgia game, pitting the football teams of the University of Florida and University of Georgia. Three area colleges—University of North Florida, Jacksonville University, and Edward Waters College—offer plenty of sports action during the school year.

JACKSONVILLE JAGUARS

Football is undoubtedly the king of sports in Jacksonville. And, in recent years anyway, the king in Jacksonville has been the Jaguars. After years of trying to win an NFL team, Jacksonville scored big in 1995, when the league awarded the city one of two new franchises.

Since entering the league the Jaguars have become one of the most successful expansion franchises in the history of the National Football League. The Jaguars have been to the play-offs four times and played in the AFC Championship game twice. The Jaguars won 49 games in their first five seasons, including an NFL-best record of 14–2 in 1999.

The Jaguars play in Alltel Stadium, located near downtown Jacksonville on the banks of the St. Johns River. Formerly called the Gator Bowl, the stadium was completely rebuilt to accommodate a professional team. With 73,000 seats, Alltel is one of the biggest NFL stadiums in one of the smallest cities. While those facts often give team owners heartburn when they're trying to fill the stands, it generally means good news for visitors. There are usually spare seats at Jaguars games, unlike at many other NFL venues. And it gets better. In preparation for the Super Bowl in February 2005, the city and the Jaguars spent millions of dollars to upgrade the stadium and add more corporate skyboxes.

Alltel Stadium is easily accessible by special game-day public buses. There's also ample parking around and near the stadium. You can get ticket and game-day information from the Jaguars' toll-free

Want a good deal on Jacksonville Jaguars tickets? You can usually buy tickets in front of the stadium on the day of a game. If you wait until just after the game has started, you might get a better deal on tickets. **NOTE:** *Under Florida law, someone selling tickets to a sporting event cannot sell them for more than $1.00 over their face value.*

The Long Road to an NFL Franchise

For years Jacksonville's quest for a National Football League team seemed hopeless. The city's overeagerness for a pro team was often used by NFL owners as a bargaining chip to extract better deals in other cities, while the misses only fed Jacksonville's inferiority complex.

But community leaders and fans never gave up the dream. In 1989 yet another partnership was formed to lasso an NFL team. The group, Touchdown Jacksonville, included several prominent Jacksonville businessmen as well as Jeb Bush, now Florida's governor, and Hamilton Jordan, former president Jimmy Carter's chief of staff.

A year later, chances improved when the NFL announced it would expand the league by two teams for the 1993 season. The City of Jacksonville quickly cranked up its acquisition efforts. The city council unanimously voted to spend $60 million to renovate the Gator Bowl should the city be awarded an expansion football team. Jacksonville was one of 11 cities to apply for one of the two expansion teams, and reporters quickly traveled to each of those other cities to size up our chances in comparison.

To beef up its ownership team, Touchdown Jacksonville added several more partners, including Nine West shoe store magnate J. Wayne Weaver. By late 1991 the group, which had selected "Jaguars" as the team name, presented its bid to Commissioner Tagliabue and other NFL officials in New York.

An ongoing labor dispute with players, however, delayed the NFL's selection of the expansion cities until 1993, with play beginning in 1995. Jacksonville's hopes were dashed yet again when city hall balked at spending more money to make further stadium improvements needed to meet NFL specifications.

Eventually the city and Touchdown Jacksonville reached a new lease agreement. But then Weaver, who had became the managing partner, said he'd pursue bidding for the team only if 9,000 club seats were sold in a 10-day period. Unbelievably, the city exceeded the daunting challenge, selling 10,112 club seats. On November 30, 1993, Jacksonville was awarded a franchise team, making it one of the smallest cities in the NFL.

number, (877) 452–4784, or from the team's official Web site, www.jaguars.com.

Tickets are also available on a ticket exchange Web site maintained by the *Florida Times-Union,* Jacksonville's principal daily newspaper. TicketXchange enables ticketholders to sell their tickets online. To access ticketXchange, visit the *Times-Union*'s Web site at www.jacksonville.com. While you're at the site, you can read the paper's extensive coverage of the Jags.

JACKSONVILLE BARRACUDAS

When the NFL and college football seasons are finished and you still need that live-sports action fix, head to the Jacksonville Veterans Memorial Arena and take in some Jacksonville Barracudas hockey.

Affectionately called the 'Cudas, this hockey team will remind you of the little engine that could. It has a winning record in a new league called the World Hockey Association Two (WHA2). The 'Cudas are coached by Ron Duguay, who played in the National Hockey League for 12 years, then married supermodel Kim Alexis. The couple now lives in the Jacksonville area.

The Jacksonville Barracudas are lucky to face-off on home ice in the Veterans Memorial Arena, which has to be the nicest stadium in their league. You can read more about this all-purpose facility in the Arts chapter.

Tickets are extremely affordable and start at $12, and believe us when we say there is literally not a bad seat in the house in the Veterans Memorial Arena. The 'Cudas play a grueling schedule that starts in the winter and continues through the spring and includes 30 home games alone.

For ticket information call (904) 367-1-ICE or check out the team online at www.jacksonvillebarracudas.com, and as the saying goes, "Get hooked on Barracudas hockey!"

JACKSONVILLE SUNS

If you're visiting Jacksonville in the spring or early summer and you enjoy the intimacy minor-league baseball offers, you'll want to catch a Suns games. With about 70 home games each season, you'll certainly have plenty of opportunities.

The Suns are a Class AA Southern League farm team for the Los Angeles Dodgers. The team plays at a cupcake of a stadium called The Baseball Grounds of Jacksonville that seats 10,000.

Suns tickets can be ordered by phone and charged to American Express, Discover, MasterCard, or VISA. Call the Suns office at (904) 358-2846. Ticket orders placed less than one week prior to the game will be left in your name at the will-call window. To make sure you get the best seats available, purchase tickets on the Internet at www.jacksonvillesuns.com. All Internet orders must be placed at least four hours prior to game time.

Regular season ticket prices start at $3.00 to $5.50 for seats in the bleachers or on the grass berm in left field. Reserve seating from $4.50 to $7.50 will get you a seat in right field. Behind homeplate, seats go for these incredibly affordable prices: $7.50 to $10.50. And tickets in a special box right behind the dugout are $15.50 each. Senior citizens age 62 and over and military personnel with an ID get a discount, and children ages 4 to 14 get a $1.50 discount. Play your cards right and you may even catch the famous chicken, a concert, or fireworks. Talk about getting some bang out of your buck!

THE PLAYERS CHAMPIONSHIP

One of professional golf's biggest tournaments, The Players Championship, comes to the TPC at Sawgrass in Ponte Vedra Beach every March. While not one of the major PGA tournaments, The Players Championship does attract top players, including local players David Duval and Vijay Singh, with its multimillion-dollar purse, one of the richest on the PGA tour.

The TPC is best known for its 17th island hole, and each year it is the most popular among spectators. The signature hole is a short-length par 3 with a wide green that narrows to the right side. The right side of the green is protected by a small well-maintained bunker, which sometimes will be a relief to players who come up short of the green. Club selection on this hole is critically important; with the tricky winds of spring, the Championship could be won or lost here. A larger spectator mound has been created behind the green.

For tickets and information, call the tournament office at (904) 285-PUTT or (800) 741-3161. You can purchase tickets online at www.pgatour.com, where you also can take a virtual tour of the TPC Stadium course. The Tournament Players Club at Sawgrass is located in Ponte

The First Coast Soccer Association hosts a big tournament every September called the First Coast Labor Day Soccer Shoot Out. Boys and girls travel here from all over the Southeast to play in the tournament. Learn more about it at www.firstcoastsoccer.com.

Vedra Beach west of Highway A1A and south of J. Turner Butler Boulevard.

THE BAUSCH & LOMB CHAMPIONSHIPS

The Bausch & Lomb Championships at Amelia Island Plantation in April draws many of the world's top women tennis players for nine days of singles and doubles. The tournament has undergone a number of name changes since it began in April 1980, but one thing hasn't changed: It has consistently attracted such top names as Graf, Hingis, Evert, Navratilova, Seles, Sabatini, and the Williams sisters.

The intimate 5,000-seat stadium nestled among live oaks and Spanish moss provides a great setting to watch tennis. For tickets and more details, call (800) 486-8366 or visit the tournament's Web site at www.blchamps.com.

COLLEGE FOOTBALL

The Toyota Gator Bowl is played on New Year's Day at Alltel Stadium. Started in 1944, the Gator Bowl always pits a top team from the Atlantic Coast Conference against either a top team from the Big East conference or Notre Dame. For information and tickets, call the Gator Bowl Association at (904) 798-1700 or visit the Web site at www.gatorbowl.com.

The Florida-Georgia football game is played in September at Alltel Stadium.

The football rivalry is fierce, and the pre- and postgame partying is legendary. It's jokingly referred to as the world's biggest cocktail party.

JU DOLPHINS

For a small liberal arts college, Jacksonville University fields some surprisingly competitive teams, especially in basketball. The JU Dolphins gained national fame in the early 1970s when 7-foot center Artis Gilmore led the team to the NCAA finals. While JU hasn't been able to assemble another team as good as the one Gilmore led, the Dolphins still consistently produce competitive teams.

JU, which competes in the Atlantic Sun Conference, also offers spectators exciting baseball and soccer games. The school only recently added football. For more information and schedules of all JU games, visit the university's Web site at www.judolphins.com. You can get more information about the Atlantic Sun Conference at www.atlanticsun.org.

EDWARD WATERS COLLEGE

The school may be small, but the football team is mighty. EWC is one of the oldest black colleges in the country, but it manages to field one tough little football team and a scrappy basketball team, too. (To learn more about the history of EWC, see the chapter on African-American tourism.) Both teams play a full schedule of games, mostly against other small, predominantly black colleges. For a schedule of Tiger games, call the school's athletic department at (904) 366-2789. By the way, Jacksonville's much-loved former sheriff, Nat Glover, is a graduate of EWC and an alumnus of its football team.

JAX RACEWAYS

Move over football, here comes auto racing. Built in the 1960s, Jax Raceways, north of the airport on Pecan Park Road, holds races three nights a week. Tuesday is amateur night, a chance for anyone to bring a car out to the drag strip and let her rip. Friday night features drag races, mud-bogging, and go-kart races. Saturday is the featured auto racing. It's NASCAR for the drivers who work on their own cars and have day jobs to pay for them. Saturday is the biggest night, drawing about 3,000 fans.

Best of all, you can bring your own coolers. The concession stand does not sell beer, but plenty of people bring their own. For those who don't drink, there is one alcohol-free section in the stands.

On Saturday the preliminary heats start at 7:00 P.M. and racing begins about 8:00 P.M. Admission for adults is $10.00 in the stands and $13.00 in the infield. Military, seniors, and students ages 12 to 17 pay $8.00 for the stands and $10.00 for

Why be a sports spectator? Join the Jacksonville Track Club for fun, fitness, and fellowship. The club hosts a variety of runs all year long, including training runs to get you in shape for the real thing. For more information go to www.jacksonvilletrackclub.com.

the infield. Children ages 6 to 11 pay $3.00 for either the stands or infield. Children under 6 get in free. Call (904) 757-5425 for more information, or go to the Web site at www.jaxracewaysonline.com.

MUG RACE

The annual Mug Race is a 38.5-nautical-mile sail-racing classic on the St. Johns River, from Palataka to Jacksonville, sponsored by the Rudder Club of Jacksonville. For more information, call the RC at (904) 264-4094.

DAY TRIPS 🚗

ST. AUGUSTINE

. . . as we had received an invitation from a friend to visit St. Augustine, which is the Newport of Florida, we thought it a good time to go seaward.

> Harriet Beecher Stowe
> May 30, 1872
> Palmetto Leaves

Ironically, when Harriet Beecher Stowe first visited St. Augustine in 1872, she didn't get there by going "seaward." She traveled south on a riverboat on the St. Johns River from Jacksonville to a settlement called Tekoi, which no longer exists. Then she headed east. "The railroad across to St. Augustine is made of wooden rails; and the cars are drawn by horses," she wrote. Needless to say, it took hours to get there.

Today it will only take you about 45 minutes to get to St. Augustine from Jacksonville, and chances are you'll find it as quaint as Stowe did. She also found it ". . . impressive from its unlikeness to anything else in America . . . and in harmony with its romantic history."

Tourism has become a billion-dollar industry in St. Johns County since Stowe's day with much of those dollars spent in St. Augustine, the oldest permanently occupied European settlement in America. And tourists don't show any signs of staying home. According to the St. Augustine & St. Johns County Chamber of Commerce, some 3.5 million tourists visit the county every year.

If St. Augustine is good for families, its old-world charm is great for couples who enjoy romantic weekend stays in historic B&Bs, dining by candlelight at award-winning restaurants, and moonlit walks along the sea wall by Matanzas Bay.

NOTE: Parking is a problem in St. Augustine, so once you find a parking space, keep your car there as long as possible. Everything you need is within walking distance anyway.

Getting There

You can still get to St. Augustine from Jacksonville by water, but we suggest using the Intracoastal Waterway or the Atlantic Ocean, not the St. Johns River. Once there, try docking your boat at the St. Augustine Municipal Marina, located in the heart of downtown.

Most people, however, drive the 38 miles to St. Augustine from Jacksonville, choosing one of three main highways to get there. The most obvious is I-95 south to exit 95. Turn left at the exit, heading east, until you hit US 1. Turn right onto US 1 heading south, then turn left onto King Street. Follow King Street into the heart of downtown.

Highway A1A is the scenic route to St. Augustine because it runs parallel to the ocean. Take A1A south through Ponte Vedra. Continue south for nearly 40 minutes until you hit Vilano Beach. Turn right at the Vilano traffic light, and head west over the Vilano Bridge. Turn left at the first traffic light, at the intersection of A1A and San Marco, and follow San Marco into the heart of downtown.

The third highway from Jacksonville to St. Augustine is US 1. Take US 1 south for about 40 minutes until you get to the intersection with King Street. Turn left on King Street, and take it into the heart of downtown.

A Short History

We have the Spanish to thank for St. Augustine. They arrived in 1565 led by Pedro Menendez de Aviles and started a small settlement named St. Augustine some 55 years before the Pilgrims landed at Plymouth Rock.

The Spanish managed to keep St. Augustine and "La Florida" for nearly 200 years, despite repeated attacks by the British. By 1695 they'd finished construction of a fort, the Castillo de San Marcos (now the oldest building in St. Augustine), to shelter themselves from those attacks. But the British and U.S.-backed patriots, who attacked La Florida from strongholds in Georgia, finally took their toll. La Florida became a U.S. territory in 1821, a state in 1845.

Enter railroad baron Henry Flagler, who arrived in the 1880s (perhaps after reading Stowe's book) with a big checkbook and even bigger dreams of turning St. Augustine into the American Riviera. He built several grand hotels before losing interest in St. Augustine and moving south to Palm Beach. Those grand hotels are much beloved by residents and tourists today.

In the 1920s St. Augustine became a popular artists' colony, and artists brought a bohemian spirit that never entirely left the city. Pulitzer Prize-winning author Marjorie Kinnan Rawlings felt it. She spent time here in the forties when she wasn't at her home in rural Cross Creek. Countless artists still call St. Augustine home and continue to draw inspiration from the city.

Where to Stay

Bayfront Westcott House
146 Avenida Menendez
(904) 824-4301, (800) 513-9814
www.westcotthouse.com
Built in the 1880s for Dr. John Westcott, this pink Victorian house has two beautiful porches overlooking Matanzas Bay. Sleep late and enjoy your breakfast on the second-floor porch. Each of the nine rooms is brimming with antiques as well as such modern amenities as a king- or queen-size bed, private bath, cable television, and telephone.

Best Western Historical
2010 North Ponce de Leon Boulevard
(904) 829-9088, (800) 528-1234
www.jalaramhotels.com
This is a good place to stay with the kids. It's not exactly in the heart of downtown, but it's within walking distance (6 blocks) of the historic district. There's a nice pool to cool off in after a long day of touring. Amenities include a free continental breakfast and cable television.

On the first Friday of every month, St. Augustine art galleries host ArtWalks. The galleries stay open until 9:00 P.M. so that you can stroll between them and enjoy wine, cheese, live music, and art.

Casa de la Paz Bed and Breakfast Inn
22 Avenida Menendez
(904) 829-2915, (800) 929-2915
www.casadelapaz.com
This 1915 Mediterranean-style home has been totally renovated with elegant antiques. Choose from one of seven rooms overlooking the sailboats moored in Matanzas Bay or the inn's quiet Spanish court yard. Casa de la Paz enjoys a great location in downtown St. Augustine. You'll also enjoy breakfast in the inn's lovely sunroom.

Casa Monica Hotel
95 Cordova Street
(904) 827-1888, (800) 648-1888
www.casamonica.com
This 138-room hotel is, as they say in Italy, *deluxo*. Franklin Smith, a Boston architect who founded the YMCA, designed it in 1888. The hotel closed during the Depression and remained closed for some 30 years until the county bought the building in 1968 and turned it into a courthouse. By 1997 St. Johns County had built a new, modern courthouse, and hotelier Richard Kessler bought the Casa Monica for $1.2 million. He gutted the sixties courthouse interior and created a premier, AAA four-diamond hotel in the heart of St. Augustine. This is where the king and queen of

Spain ate lunch during their visit in 2001. (Their tight schedule did not permit an overnight stay.) The decor is Moorish Revival, and amenities include an outdoor pool; a whirlpool spa; an exercise room; a four-star restaurant, 95 Cordova; and a rooftop garden and pavilion that resembles a sultan's tent. Best of all, walk outside the hotel's front door and you're in the thick of things, directly across the street from the heart of old St. Augustine.

Coastal Realty
(800) 587-2287

Try something new—stay in a fully furnished condo in St. Augustine Beach. It's not as costly as you'd expect, plus with a full kitchen you can cook some of your meals if you so desire. Many of the condos are within walking distance of the ocean and include amenities like tennis courts and pools. Lots of local real estate companies specialize in both long- and short-term rentals; Coastal Realty is just one of them. For more rental companies, check out www.staugustine.com, the award-winning Web site for the local newspaper, the *St. Augustine Record.*

Attractions

Castillo de San Marcos, St. George Street, and the Spanish Quarter Village Downtown Historic District

The Castillo de San Marcos, now operated by the National Park Service, is a must-see. The building is made from coquina blocks extracted from a quarry in what is now Anatasia State Park. Built by the Spanish, the fort was finished in 1695. Once Florida became a state, the Castillo was renamed Fort Marion, and it is there that Seminole Chief Osceola was held prisoner for a time before escaping. When you leave the Castillo, walk down quaint St. George Street, the oldest shopping street in St. Augustine. Stop at the Spanish Quarter Village, 29 St. George Street,

and see the living history museum, a tiny version of Colonial Williamsburg. Here you can get a feel for a Spanish colonialist's life in the early 1800s: A blacksmith makes wrought-iron pot handles, a señora feeds her goats and tends her garden, and a carpenter makes furniture.

Lightner Museum
75 King Street
(904) 824-2874
www.lightnermuseum.org

The Lightner is full of beautiful and interesting objects from the early 19th century, from antiques to mechanical musical instruments to costumes to toys. There's also a stained-glass room featuring the work of Louis Tiffany. The three-story museum building is itself a work of art. The former Hotel Alcazar was built in 1887 by Henry Flagler and designed by the same architects who designed the New York Public Library. The collection now housed within its walls belonged to Chicago publisher Otto Lightner, founding editor of *Hobbies Magazine,* who purchased the Alcazar in 1946. (He's also buried there.) The Alcazar's former indoor swimming pool and casino are now full of shops and the Cafe Alcazar, which is a great place for a tourist time-out.

Potters Wax Museum
17 King Street
(800) 584-4781
www.potterswax.com

Talk about a St. Augustine institution, Potters Wax Museum has been open for well over 50 years. There are 160 wax figures here, from George Washington to Britney Spears. The folks here like to say their museum is a great way to learn history, face to face with the people who lived it. If you've never been to a wax museum, this one is well worth the price of admission. Chances are you'll tour it with a group of children on a field trip who may not be too familiar with President John F. Kennedy but can sure recognize Michael Jordan.

Ripley's Believe It or Not! Museum
19 San Marco Avenue
(904) 824-1606
www.ripleys.com
This is the place to see freaks of nature, such as a two-headed or a six-legged cow (both stuffed). The two extra legs on the six-legged cow, by the way, grew out of its back. There's also cool stuff like the world's largest moving Ferris wheel made out of Erector sets—lots of them. Believe it or not, Ripley's says that its all-time most popular exhibits are two fertility statues from West Africa that are practically guaranteed to get a woman pregnant. (Those statues go on tour and aren't always at the museum.) In short, if you grew up reading Ripley's in the Sunday comics, you'll enjoy it here.

St. Augustine Alligator Farm
Highway A1A South
(904) 824-3337
www.alligatorfarm.com
Here it is. Your chance to get up close and personal with an alligator. There are more than a thousand alligators here, and some are absolutely huge because they've been enjoying "three squares" in captivity for a while. The running joke in St. Augustine is that if a hurricane comes ashore and knocks down the fences surrounding the alligator farm, watch out. Make sure you take in one of the entertaining programs by staff naturalists, who are full of fun facts about alligators, as well as the farm's extensive collection of birds, snakes, and other reptiles. See our Kidstuff chapter for more on the Alligator Farm.

St. Augustine Lighthouse and Museum
81 Lighthouse Avenue
(904) 829-0745
www.staugustinelighthouse.com
You can't miss it. The black-and-white-striped St. Augustine Lighthouse is one of 30 lighthouses still standing in Florida—one of only six in the state open to the public. Climb the 219 stairs to the lantern room and enjoy great views of the

Atlantic Ocean, Intracoastal Waterway, and St. Augustine. A museum in the restored lightkeeper's house chronicles the history of this faithful lighthouse and the role it played in Florida's maritime history. There's also a dynamite gift shop with all sorts of nautical "stuff" for sale.

Where to Eat

Columbia Restaurant
98 St. George Street
(904) 824-3341
www.columbiarestaurant.com
The Columbia is located in the heart of the historic downtown area, and somehow it just feels right to eat Spanish/Cuban cuisine in this ancient Spanish town. Sip a glass of sangria in a quiet garden courtyard before your meal of classic chicken and rice, steak, seafood, or paella. The crusty bread and black bean soup are also winners.

Conch House Restaurant and Lounge
57 Comares Avenue
(904) 829-8646
www.conch-house.com
If the Conch House was located in Key West, you'd expect to see Jimmy Buffet sitting at the bar. This is a casual, fun, tropical sort of place with tiki huts and a large wooden deck overlooking the scenic Salt Run. Dine indoors while still enjoying the waterfront view and Caribbean cuisine, including seafood. The lounge features a very popular two-for-one happy hour during the week.

Like to sail? Take a day trip on a tall ship called the Schooner Freedom, *a replica of a 19th-century blockade-runner that used to frequent the waters around St. Augustine. There are day and evening cruises. Call (904) 810-1010 for reservations. The* Freedom *is based at the public marina in downtown St. Augustine.*

Gypsy Cab Company
828 Anastasia Boulevard
(904) 824-8244
www.gypsycab.com
Gypsy Cab Company has been a fixture in St. Augustine for decades—sort of a Steady Eddie. It's a popular lunch spot, serving unusual salads and soups and fish dishes, and it's also a good choice for dinner. The restaurant is located just blocks from the St. Augustine Alligator Farm and the St. Augustine Lighthouse.

Enjoy wine? Then you may want to tour the San Sebastian Winery in St. Augustine. The actual vineyards are miles away in Central Florida, but at the winery in downtown St. Augustine, you'll see how wine is made and you can also buy a bottle of vino.

Manatee Cafe
525 Highway 16, #106 Westgate Plaza
(904) 826-0210
www.manateecafe.com
If you like healthful cuisine prepared with filtered water and organic fruits and vegetables, don't miss this restaurant. It's open only for breakfast and lunch, but the owners do a powerful job of making both those meals memorable. Order eggs in a pita with a fresh salad and homemade dressing, a breakfast burrito, Cajun-style chicken, or a homemade pizza, to name a few specialties. For dessert try a piece of homemade Key lime pie or a homemade cookie of the day. Yum-yum.

95 Cordova
95 Cordova Street
(904) 810-6810
www.95cordova.com
This is St. Augustine's premier restaurant, located in the city's premier hotel, the Casa Monica. The readers of *Folio Weekly* magazine voted it the best restaurant in St. Augustine in 2001. The restaurant prides itself on combining fresh, local

ingredients in new, masterful ways, which means guests enjoy specialties like a beef-steak tomato stack, semolina-crusted calamari, and curried chicken salad.

Opus 39
39 Cordova Street
(904) 824-0402
www.opus39.com
Looking for fine dining in the nation's oldest city? Look no further. Diners have two choices at Opus 39: a three-course prix fixe menu or a five-course prix fixe "tasting menu." Each contains delightful choices like vanilla-infused Maine lobster or beef tenderloin on a bed of potatoes. The choices change constantly, depending on the freshest ingredients available. The wine list is fun, too—full of selections from small California wineries in and around Napa, Sonoma, and the Russian River. Creativity abounds here, from the open kitchen in front of the entrance that warmly greets guests to the art by local artists displayed on the walls. Even wine sales are a mark of the owners' creativity. That's because a city ordinance prohibits sales of alcoholic beverages within 100 feet of a church. Since a Methodist church sits directly across the street from the restaurant, the owners get around the law by inviting all guests into a "wine boutique" in back of the restaurant, 101 feet from the church. Guests enjoy a wine tasting and a chance to buy the wine their waiter will later bring to the table.

O'Steen's Restaurant
205 Anastasia Boulevard
(904) 829-6974
There are those who say that the fried shrimp at this restaurant are the best in Northeast Florida. Ditto the Minorcan clam chowder, which is beloved by many as a local delicacy. The Minorcans, by the way, came to St. Augustine as indentured servants, and their descendants still form a small core of the city's population. Their tomato-based clam chowder certainly lives on, and you can almost taste the history in every bite. Plan to arrive at

O'Steen's as early as possible; there's always a wait, and the restaurant doesn't take reservations. Stick it out—you won't be disappointed.

Take a Tour

Anastasia State Park
1340A Highway A1A South
(904) 461-2033
www.myflorida.com
This is one of Florida's most popular state parks. Much of it used to be a coquina quarry for the Spanish during colonial times. Huge blocks of coquina were cut from the earth and hauled by slaves over to St. Augustine to build structures such as the Castillo de San Marcos. Park naturalists give guided tours of the Spanish quarries and also of the park's salt marsh. You can also take a self-guided tour through the oak hammock. Call about a month in advance to book a quarry walk.

Flagler's Legacy Tours
Flagler College
(904) 829-6481
This is your chance to see the inside of Henry Flagler's once-famous Ponce de Leon Hotel, now Flagler College. Beautiful woodwork from the 1880s remains, as does original Tiffany windows and ornate murals. There's also a small museum featuring paintings and artifacts from the hotel period. Your college-student tour guide will give you a whole new perspective on Henry Flagler. Tours are held April 30 through September 1.

Ghost Tours of St. Augustine
(888) 461-1009
A city as old as St. Augustine is bound to have its share of ghosts. Harriet Beecher Stowe wrote about St. Augustine's ghosts in *Palmetto Leaves.* She interviewed an elderly man during her 1872 visit who told her the city cemetery was particularly haunted. Ghost Tours of St. Augustine will take you there during a 90-minute walk-

ing tour that begins nightly at 8:00 P.M. Many companies give these ghostly tours. It's hard to say which one is best, since much of the experience depends on the theatric ability of your tour guide. There are also family ghost tours designed not to scare the wits out of your children.

St. Augustine Sightseeing Trains
(800) 226-6545
www.redtrains.com

St. Augustine Trolley Tours
(800) 397-4071
www.oldtowntrolley.com
These trolley-trains are a great way to get around town, especially in the heat of summer. Tour guides/drivers will tell you interesting St. Augustine stories while driving you through narrow streets and lanes. You can get off and on when you please, and one ticket is good for three consecutive days. Buying a ticket at either one of these companies is a good vacation investment.

Up for an adventure? Try parasailing. Three people can literally fly side by side at the same time. And fly you will, up to 1,400 feet into the blue. Call (904) 819-0980 to book your trip.

MARINELAND

9600 Ocean Shore Boulevard, Marineland
(904) 460-1275, (888) 279-9194
www.marineland.net
Located 20 minutes south of St. Augustine, Marineland was the world's first oceanarium when it opened in 1938. The owners built it primarily as an underwater movie studio, and classics like *Tarzan of the Apes* and *Creature from the Black Lagoon* were filmed here. But the oceanarium's real mission became known when the public started to visit. Tourists loved the place and literally flocked here for a chance to see marine life up close. In its

Bridge of Lions

For more than 20 years now, St. Augustine residents have been arguing over how best to rebridge the gap over the Matanzas River, a gap currently spanned by a rapidly aging Bridge of Lions.

The Bridge of Lions, which opened in 1927, is a much-photographed, much-loved St. Augustine landmark—it's also outdated. The reason this matters in a city filled with operational antiquities is because the bridge plays a vital role as a transportation link between downtown St. Augustine and the northern part of Anastasia Island. Yet the bridge is suffering from structural problems and no longer meets safety requirements.

In 1998 bridge lovers banded together and formed a group called Save Our Bridge. Members scored a major coup when they got the Bridge of Lions listed on the National Register of Historic Places. They feel that there's no better gateway into or out of the nation's oldest city than the stately drawbridge with its four tile-roofed towers, antique light poles, and proud Italian-marble lions standing guard. The bridge, they say, is especially picturesque when decked out in Christmas lights or adorned with American flags waving from every light post. A larger, more modern span, they argue, would forever alter the landscape and only serve to dump more traffic into the already crowded, narrow streets of downtown St. Augustine.

The opposition is not moved. Many opponents live on Anastasia Island and have to use the bridge every day to reach the mainland. They know all too well how frustrating it can be when the Bridge of Lions closes abruptly because the ancient drawbridge gets stuck in the "up" position. These are the people who must wait in long lines of traffic for the bridge to reopen, only to find themselves late to work, late to class, and in a foul temper.

heyday in the fifties and sixties, up to half a million people visited Marineland every year, making it the biggest tourist attraction in Florida at the time. The oceanarium is listed on the National Register of Historic Places.

But slowly things started to change. I-95 opened, making it faster and easier for tourists to bypass Marineland and drive farther south to the newly opened SeaWorld and Disney World. Tourist dollars drained away, and by the eighties the resort was struggling to keep its head above water. The park's owners filed for bankruptcy in 1998, and part of the resort was eventually acquired by the Trust for Public Lands and part by an Atlanta developer. In 2000 the foundation that owned the oceanarium filed for bankruptcy and was bought by the same Atlanta developer who had bought part of the resort.

Marineland then returned to basics and tapped into the one resource that made it so famous in the first place: the oceanarium. Guests were allowed to scuba or snorkel in the oceanarium for the first time. They were also allowed to swim with

Opponents argue that there's nothing historic about the Bridge of Lions. As far as they're concerned, the fact that it's listed on the National Register of Historic Places only means someone did a good job filling out a lot of paperwork. They want the state to build a new, higher, fixed-span bridge over the Matanzas River.

In 1999 state transportation officials all but ended this debate when they announced plans to "rehabilitate" the Bridge of Lions. Three years later, when construction plans were finalized, St. Augustine residents finally learned just what "rehabilitate" means: As little as 5 to 10 percent of the original 1927 bridge will actually be saved and restored. The rest will be new construction made to look just as the bridge looked when it opened in 1927. This has given new life to the opposition, which argues that the state is basically building a new bridge and therefore should make it as modern as possible.

So far, the state is pushing ahead with plans to rehabilitate the bridge, but there may be a problem. Work was set to begin in August 2004 at a cost estimated by state engineers of about $57 million. At this writing the project was to include installation of a temporary two-lane bridge just north of the existing Bridge of Lions, which would keep traffic moving during the lengthy rehabilitation.

But the lowest bid was nearly $20 million more than state estimates. The reason, says the state, is because the price of steel and concrete worldwide has doubled of late due to skyrocketing demand. So now the state must decide what to do next: reject all bids, spend more to build a new bridge than budgeted, or make changes in the project that could affect the final look of the rehabilitated bridge. Whatever the choice, one thing is certain given the history thus far: The decision is likely to generate more controversy.

the park's dolphins. Today Marineland is back on the road to solvency, focusing on a more intimate family experience that larger theme parks cannot offer.

Getting There

Marineland is about 75 minutes south of Jacksonville. The easiest way to get there from Jacksonville is to drive south on I-95 until you reach exit 93, which is State Road 206. Turn left, heading east on 206,

and eventually drive over the Intracoastal Waterway to Highway A1A. Turn right, heading south 6 miles until you reach Marineland. The park is open every day except Tuesday from 9:30 A.M. to 4:30 P.M.

What to Do

A trip to Marineland is like a trip back in time to Florida in the fifties or sixties. For starters, children will love the dolphin show, which includes a chance to pet a dolphin and hold out a fish to feed one. Kids will also enjoy watching the sea lion show and learning about the park's nine African penguins.

The more adventurous will want to scuba dive or snorkel in Marineland's 450,000-gallon reef oceanarium. It's home to more than 500 marine creatures, including a 100-pound black drum, two stingrays, and three rare sea turtles. The oceanarium is 18 feet deep and is continuously fed by seawater from the Atlantic. Wave to your family and friends as they watch your underwater adventure from the park's observation window (and take great pictures, too).

Finally, don't miss the chance to swim with the dolphins. It's one thing to sit in the stands and watch them perform aerial tricks, quite another to be in the water rubbing their backs. At Marineland's Dolphin Encounter, you'll don a wet suit and send dolphins on a variety of fetching tasks. One quickly realizes just how intelligent dolphins truly are.

AMELIA ISLAND

Getting There

Some say the best thing about Amelia Island, 32 miles northeast of Jacksonville, is getting there. Getting there means a chance to drive the Buccaneer Trail (aka SR 105/A1A), one of the most scenic two-lane highways in the South. Put on the Jimmy Buffet tunes and wind your way along miles of pristine marshes, thick oak hammocks, and tiny marinas. You'll see snowy egrets and, if you're lucky, a great blue heron. You'll also cross a number of bridges, where local folks line up with rod and reel to fish some of Florida's finest waters. This is as good as it gets in Northeast Florida.

To get to the Buccaneer Trail from downtown, take I-95 north to the Heckscher Drive/SR 105E exit (124A). Turn right, heading east onto Heckscher Drive (the Buccaneer Trail), and follow it for about 30 miles until you reach Fernandina Beach.

Once you get to Fernandina, the main town on Amelia Island, you're just half a mile, as the crow flies, to Georgia. Stroll along Centre Street and enjoy the shops and restaurants. Amelia Island calls itself the birthplace of the modern shrimping industry, so be sure to check out the shrimp boats on the dock, and enjoy some boiled, fried, or grilled shrimp or another local delicacy, a grouper sandwich.

A Short History

Frenchman Jean Ribault is the first European credited with landing on Amelia Island. Since he arrived in May 1562, he named the island "Isle de Mai." But the French didn't hold on to it for long. In 1565 Pedro Menendez, headquartered in St. Augustine, wiped out the French, claimed the island for Spain, and renamed it Santa Maria. Spain held on to it (and to Florida) for nearly 200 years, until the English took over in the 1700s. The English named it Amelia Island after King George II's daughter.

In 1783 Britain gave Amelia Island, and all of Florida, back to Spain, and from 1783 to 1821 Florida was a mighty unstable place to live. Amelia Island is proof of that. This tiny island changed hands at least three times as Spain tried to hang on to it. U.S.-backed Patriots took over for a short time, as did a Scotsman named Sir Gregor MacGregor and even Mexican rebels (i.e., pirates).

Pirates/smugglers had their heyday here in 1807, when President Thomas Jefferson signed the Embargo Act, stopping all foreign imports, especially from Britain and France. Pirates, working from the natural deepwater port of Fernandina, found a lucrative trade breaking that embargo. Life calmed down a lot for

Amelia Island residents when Spain ceded Florida to the United States in 1821. Forty years later, in 1861, the Confederate States of America took control, but only for a year.

Local historians have nicknamed Amelia Island the Isle of Eight Flags because of the eight flags that flew here: Spanish, French, English, Patriot, Green Cross of Florida (Gregor MacGregor), Pirate, Confederate, and, finally, U.S. Pirates, by the way, are said to have buried a still unfound treasure on Amelia "beneath an oak that is pierced by a hanging chain." If you find it, let us know.

Where to Stay

If you're staying the night on this 13-mile barrier island, two world-class resorts— Amelia Island Plantation and The Ritz-Carlton, Amelia Island (see the Resorts chapter)—offer accommodations. There are also a dozen or so B&Bs. Our list is by no means conclusive, but it will help you start planning your stay.

Amelia Island Williams House
103 South Ninth Street
(904) 277-2328, (800) 414-9258
www.williamshouse.com
To many people the Williams House is everything a bed-and-breakfast inn should be: a historic home from the 1850s, beautifully decorated from top to bottom and filled with antiques. The inn has won all sorts of awards, including designation as a Historic Landmark Site, the highest honor awarded by the Florida Department of State, because the owners keep it in such great shape. You should see this inn at Christmastime, when it turns into something out of a Dickens novel. There's a lot of history here; for instance, Jefferson Davis, president of the Confederacy, is said to have stayed at the Williams House around the same time it was also a stop on the Underground Railroad.

Elizabeth Pointe Lodge
98 South Fletcher Avenue
(904) 277-4857, (800) 772-3359
www.elizabethpointelodge.com
If you think you're in Cape Cod, we forgive you. This oceanfront inn looks more New England than Florida, which only adds to its appeal. There are 25 rooms, all with a private bath and all decorated in a maritime theme. A beautiful porch overlooks the ocean, complete with lots of very comfortable rocking chairs. The breakfast here is truly delicious, always featuring fresh fruit, pastries, and something hot such as eggs—plus you can gaze at the ocean while you eat. The owners are so good at what they do that they run a school on the premises to teach would-be innkeepers how to run an inn or a B&B.

Florida House Inn
20 and 22 South Third Street
(800) 258-3301
www.floridahouse.com
Built in 1857, this is the oldest hotel in Florida—and it's charming. It once had 25 rooms and no indoor plumbing, but today all 15 rooms have a private bath, some complete with claw-foot tubs. In deference to the inn's past, some of the rooms still have working fireplaces, and you can still rock on the inn's wide porches or sit in its shady backyard—a cool, quiet oasis anytime of day. The Florida House also operates a popular restaurant in the dining room, which serves delicious home-style Southern cooking. There's also a fun little bar downstairs, reminiscent of an English pub. Pets are welcome here, and this is also a great place to rent scooters to tour Fernandina Beach.

Greyfield Inn
Cumberland Island
(904) 261-6408
www.greyfieldinn.com
Greyfield is located on Cumberland Island, Georgia, the barrier island just north of Amelia, across the Cumberland Sound.

ℹ️ *Looking to rent a condo on Amelia Island? There are a number of realty companies to serve your needs, and the Amelia Island Chamber of Commerce will help you find them. Go to www.islandchamber.com for information.*

You're likely to walk past Greyfield's business office as you stroll around Fernandina. A private ferry, the *Miss Lucy,* docks at the Fernandina Beach Harbour Marina and is one of only a few ways to reach the island. Cumberland Island is where John Kennedy Jr. and Carolyn Bissette got married. It's part national seashore, part privately owned. The Kennedys had their reception at the Greyfield Inn, a beautiful old white house built in 1900 for Thomas Carnegie's daughter. His granddaughter, Gogo Fuller, a jewelry artist, now operates the inn. Staying here is a special experience, a chance to live like old money in a bygone era. The meals are four star and so are the accommodations, plus Greyfield offers Cumberland Island as its playground. Book your reservations early. People make plans months in advance for a chance to stay here. With reservations, you can also visit Greyfield for dinner or for a day trip.

Harbor Hampton Inn and Suites
19 South Second Street
(904) 491-4911
www.hamptoninnandsuites.net
This hotel enjoys a great location in the heart of downtown across the street from the marina. There are 122 units—61 rooms, 61 suites. Amenities include a free continental breakfast that will keep you charged most of the day, a nice swimming pool overlooking the Fernandina Harbour Marina, and an exercise room. Suites come equipped with stoves, microwaves, and refrigerators. The hotel also offers meeting space for up to 125 people. When making reservations at the Harbor Hampton Inn,

make sure you're booking at the hotel near the marina, not the Hampton Inn on the beach in Fernandina. There's a big difference. Best to book directly with the hotel's front desk to avoid any problems.

Attractions

Amelia Island Lighthouse
Lighthouse Circle
Built in 1838, this is the oldest lighthouse still standing in Florida. It's currently closed to the public, but you can drive up and see this little white gem, which is smaller than the St. Augustine lighthouse because it was meant to guide ships in the Fernandina River and Cumberland Sound, not ships in the ocean. It has weathered hurricanes and a move from Georgia and is now located in a residential neighborhood on Egan's Creek.

Amelia Island Museum of History
233 South Third Street
(904) 261-7378
www.ameliaislandmuseum.org
Located in the old Nassau County Jail, this is the place to learn the history of Amelia Island, from the Timucuans to modern day. Knowledgeable guides will fill you in on all the facts during guided tours of the museum or walking tours of the historic district. The walking tours, which require 24-hour advance notice, are especially fun because guides take you inside several churches and historic homes.

Centre Street Historic District
Fernandina Beach
Centre Street, the main shopping street in Fernandina Beach, runs through a 50-block area of downtown that's listed on the National Register of Historic Places. As you stroll along Centre Street, notice the redbrick buildings dating back to the 1870s, which once housed Fernandina's general stores and businesses. Off Centre Street there is an amazing collection of Victorian architecture. Fernandina became

downright respectable once it got rid of its pirates. By the 1800s Northern tourists flocked here on steamships direct from New York City to vacation.

As you stroll along the side streets, enjoy the gingerbread adorning the mansions and cottages, especially on North Sixth and South Seventh Streets. Be sure to walk inside the Florida House Inn on South Third, the oldest surviving tourist hotel in Florida, and the white clapboard First Missionary Baptist Church on South Ninth, the oldest African-American church in the state. Fernandina's heyday was short-lived, however. Once Henry Flagler arrived in St. Augustine in the 1880s, he decided to build a railroad south from St. Augustine to Key West, leaving Fernandina Beach literally off line. But historians say that decision may have actually saved many of the Victorians in Fernandina, which otherwise could have been razed in the name of "progress."

Fort Clinch State Park
2601 Atlantic Avenue
(904) 277-7274
www.myflorida.com
Fort Clinch is located on the northern tip of Amelia Island, with the Atlantic Ocean to its east and a coastal hardwood hammock to the west. It's the only state park on Amelia Island that offers camping. The federal government built the fort in 1847; 14 years later, at the start of the Civil War, Confederate troops took control of it. But they didn't stay long. In 1862, one year after they arrived, General Robert E. Lee ordered his soldiers to withdraw because he needed them elsewhere. After the Civil War, Fort Clinch didn't see much action until 1898, when it was called to duty for several months during the Spanish-American War. Today reenactors dress up as Union soldiers the first weekend of every month and live like garrison soldiers in 1864—they maintain the fort, cook their own meals, and take turns on sentry duty. There are also Confederate garrison reenactments on selected weekends in March, April, and October. (Dates may vary, so

call ahead.) Besides the fort itself, there's an entire state park to explore with its nature trails, fishing pier, and beachfront. The beach here, by the way, is a favorite place to find sharks' teeth.

Activities

Kayak Amelia
(904) 251-0016, (888) 30-KAYAK
www.KayakAmelia.com
Looking for an adventure? Hop in a kayak and see Amelia Island from the water. You'll feel like a Timucuan as you paddle through the marshes and slip silently by wading egrets. The guided trips include paddling instructions for beginners, all the equipment you'll need, and knowledgeable guides to answer your natural history questions. All you need to bring is the sunscreen.

Amelia Island is famous for its bird-watching. Spring and summer bring the most colorful visitors, including painted buntings, summer tanagers, and our favorite, roseate spoonbills.

Kelly Seahorse Ranch
7500 First Coast Highway
(904) 491-5166
www.kellyranchinc.com
Saddle up and ride through the surf on horseback. These guided group rides are slow and safe enough for beginners. You'll see lots of island creatures on your trip, especially as you wind your way through a coastal hammock. Reservations are a must.

Schooner Voyager
Fernandina Beach Harbour Marina
(904) 321-1244
This replica of an 1840s sailing ship docks in downtown Fernandina at the foot of Centre Street. It looks like something out of *Mutiny on the Bounty* with its 100-foot

gaff-rigged sails. Take a two-hour tour of Cumberland Sound by day, or, better yet, take the tour at sunset.

Every December the bed-and-breakfast inns on Amelia Island, along with several historic churches, offer a Christmas tour. It all looks like something out of a Dickens novel, plus the inns serve up some holiday music and refreshments.

Windward Sailing School
1010 Atlantic Avenue
(904) 261–9125
www.windwardsailing.com
Fernandina is a great place to learn to sail. A mild climate and steady winds make it possible to sail year-round, plus the natural deepwater port means that beginners never have to lose sight of land. A retired naval commander runs the school, which is certified by the American Sailing Association. Beginners can learn to sail in a weekend with one four-hour classroom session Friday evening and two consecutive all-day sails on Saturday and Sunday. There's also a bareboat class, which leaves the dock Friday evening and returns 48 hours later on Sunday. Students spend the entire time on the water. The advanced bareboat class takes that concept a step further and includes nighttime sailing instruction.

Where to Eat

Beech Street Grill
801 Beech Street
(904) 277–3662
www.beechstreetgrill.com
In the mood for grouper encrusted in toasted macadamia nuts with a dollop of curried citrus cream and mango salsa? Or how about local shrimp stuffed with crab and covered in black-eyed gravy with cheese grits and collard greens? Meals like

these have made this award-winning restaurant famous. Don't bother trying to get in without a reservation, though.

Florida House Inn
22 South Third Street
(904) 261-3300
www.floridahouseinn.com
Experience real Southern cooking served boardinghouse style. It's all the fried chicken, mashed potatoes, and biscuits you can eat. Wash it all down with sweet tea, a true southern tradition. This restaurant is popular with locals, especially firefighters, so you know it's good.

The Grill
The Ritz-Carlton
4750 Amelia Island Parkway
(904) 277-1028
Whet your appetite on some spicy pickled vegetables with blue crab and crisp wonton. Move on to oysters glazed in a Southern barbecue sauce vinaigrette. It's difficult to decide on an entree, but how about shrimp with a peanut-chili sauce? To make the evening extra interesting, eat in the kitchen (with special reservations) and watch the split-second timing it takes to create these award-winning meals. (See the Resorts chapter for more on a seat in the kitchen.) The Grill, if you haven't guessed, is the headquarters for fine dining on Amelia Island. One of only four AAA five-diamond restaurants in Florida, it's located on the ocean at The Ritz-Carlton, Amelia Island Resort.

Joe's Second Street Bistro
14 South Second Street
(904) 321-2558
www.joes2ndstreetbistro.com
This cozy little restaurant is located in the heart of the historic district in a restored house that dates back to the days when Theodore Roosevelt was president. You can eat inside by the fireplace or outside in a charming courtyard next to the fountain. Either way, the menu is filled with popular, well-prepared dishes like grilled

New York strip steak with three sauces: roasted shallot and bacon butter, Gorgonzola butter, and glacé de viande. There's also a nice selection of pastas, such as linguine with shrimp and scallops in a white-wine sauce, and fish dishes, such as grilled mahi-mahi with jalapeño cheese grits and roasted sweet pepper sauce. Whatever you choose, you're sure to leave the table satisfied.

Le Clos
20 South Second Street
(904) 261-8100
Taste some delicious French Provençal food, mix it with a romantic 1906 cottage bathed in candlelight, and you have all the ingredients for a lovely dinner. The chef was trained and worked in France, and it shows. She does amazing things with seafood. Reservations are a must because this cottage is intimate.

O'Kane's Irish Pub and Eatery
318 Centre Street
(904) 261-1000
www.okanes.com
You'll feel like you're back in Ireland with the menu here, which features such classic Irish dishes as shepherd's pie and corned beef and cabbage. There's American food, too, like fried shrimp and burgers. Kids eat free every Monday and Tuesday, and there's live music in the pub every Wednesday through Sunday evening.

OKEFENOKEE NATIONAL WILDLIFE REFUGE

Visitor Center
(912) 496-3331
Why travel halfway around the world to visit someplace exotic when you can drive 45 minutes northwest of Jacksonville to the 400,000-acre Okefenokee Wildlife Refuge? Located on the Florida-Georgia border, this stark, watery landscape looks like the land where time began. All that's missing are the dinosaurs, which are actually here in a sense in their American alli-

gator descendants. The Okefenokee is the largest swamp in North America and was saved for posterity in 1937 by President Franklin Roosevelt, who made it a wildlife refuge. It was once a major hunting ground for the Creeks and Seminoles, who named it "land of trembling earth" because small trees and bushes tremble when you stomp on the swamp's shaky peat bog islands.

Getting There

There are three entrances to the swamp, which is roughly 40 miles long and 20 miles wide. The east entrance, near Folkston, Georgia, is the easiest to reach from Jacksonville. Take I-95 north from downtown to I-295. Take I-295 heading west, and get off at the US 1 exit. Turn right onto US 1, and head north through Callahan and Hilliard until you reach Folkston. In Folkston, turn left onto SR 121/23 and head south for 7 miles to the east entrance.

What to Do

There are three major things to do in the Okefenokee Swamp: boat, view wildlife, and camp. For starters, stop at the visitor center at the east entrance for free brochures and information to help you enjoy your visit. Then drive the 9-mile loop road at the east entrance to get an idea of what the park is all about. Chances are very good that you'll see an alligator or two on this drive. You'll also pass the camping and picnic areas.

Kayaks, canoes, and motorboats can be rented in the park near the east entrance through Okefenokee Adventures (866-THESWAMP; www.okefenokee adventures.com). Take your own boat tour of the swamp, or take a guided half-day, full-day, or overnight boat trip with Okefenokee Adventures. For a real adventure, camp overnight within the swamp on one of seven designated overnight platforms that sleep up to 20. Just don't roll off! Alligators are plentiful around these platforms because, unfortunately, they've learned that they're good places to find food. There's also a campground on terra firma operated by the U.S. Fish and Wildlife Service, which you can return to after your half-day or full-day boat tour. To make camping reservations call (912) 496–3331.

The swamp water looks like iced tea because it's full of tannin, a compound derived from decaying tree bark. In its deepest spot, the water in the swamp is only about 9 feet, and in the summer it can be far less than that. Ninety percent of the water in the Okefenokee comes from rainfall, and when there's a drought the swamp dries up. Forest fires become a big problem, and paddle trails become unnavigable.

As you boat in the swamp, try to see some of the sites, such as the Suwannee Canal, dug by the forest industry in the late 1800s in an attempt to drain the swamp. Walk around Billy's Island, former home of Seminole Billy Bowlegs, and enjoy the bald cypress trees. Learn what life was like in the swamp before the Civil War at the Chesser Island Homestead, built by William Chesser in 1858.

But it's the wildlife that most people come to the Okefenokee to see. The swamp is home to Florida black bears, bobcats, otters, raccoons, opossums, and alligators. It's also a well-known haven for birds, with frequent visits from such rare species as ospreys, bald eagles, red-cockaded woodpeckers, and great blue herons. There are some 50 species of fish in the refuge and more than 600 species of plants.

ICHETUCKNEE SPRINGS STATE PARK

**State Road 238, Fort White
(386) 497–2511**
Floating in an inner tube down the Ichetucknee River makes for one of the best day trips around, plus it's a unique North Florida experience—best shared with friends and family on a hot July day, when just walking across a parking lot to your car makes you swelter. That's when you know it's time to head to Ichetucknee Springs. The name is Native American, and it's said to mean "pond of the beaver." We've never seen any beavers while tubing down the Ichetucknee, but they're probably around somewhere. The water in this crystal-clear aquifer-fed river is 73 degrees year-round. There's just no better way to cool off on a very hot day; in fact, you may find yourself downright chilly by the end of your run.

The concept is simple: Rent a big inner tube, jump in the water, and relax. The current will carry you down river, giving you plenty of time to enjoy the scenery, which includes lots of interesting cypress trees, cliffs, and swamps. Bring a mask and snorkel—you'll see lots of fish—or just lay back in your inner tube and enjoy looking at the treetops.

If you plan to travel down the Ichetucknee any time of year besides summer, we recommend that you do it in a wet suit or a canoe. We also recommend that you start early. To protect the river, park officials limit the number of people who can tube each day. Only 2,250 people are allowed to tube the river from the midpoint, and just 750 people are allowed to tube the entire length of the river on a daily basis. Be nice to the river while you are in it. Don't leave behind any trash, and don't destroy the vegetation. If a lot of damage occurs, park officials will further limit the number of people who can tube down the river.

Getting There

From Jacksonville, take I–10 west to the US 90 exit. Follow US 90 to Lake City and SR 41. Follow SR 41 south to SR 47 south. Follow the signs, which will lead you straight to the park. It takes about 90 minutes to get to the Ichetucknee from Jacksonville.

There are two park entrances, a north entrance and a south entrance. Most people use the south entrance in the summer. Park your car and carry your tube to the tram, an open-air bus that takes you through the woods to the midpoint launch area, where you can jump into the water and begin your float. The trip from the midpoint area to the end point, where you must get out, takes about 90 minutes. Another tram will take you from this area back to your car in the main parking lot. The tram from the midpoint costs $3.25 per person; children under age five are free. You pay this fee when you enter the park.

If you want to tube the entire river, remember that you need to arrive early because only the first 750 people are allowed to do so. It takes about three and a half hours to float the entire length of the Ichetucknee, and the setup is a bit complicated. You need to have a driver drop you and your tubes off at the north entrance. Then the driver must take the car to the main parking lot at the south entrance. A shuttle van will return the driver to the north picnic area to rejoin his or her party if necessary. At the end of your full-river float, a tram will take you back to your car in the south parking lot. It costs $4.25 per person to float from the north entrance; children under age five are free. One more planning note: The latest you can start your float from the north entrance is four hours before sunset.

Tube Rental

Nothing is rented inside the park. You have to stop and rent your tubes and/or snorkel gear from vendors outside the park entrance, or bring it all from home. But don't worry. These vendors are not

It seems that every time you go tubing on the Ichetucknee, you see some poor soul who's dropped his or her car keys in the water while floating down the river. Needless to say, this is a huge drag. Keep your car keys around your neck, pinned inside your bathing suit, or hidden in a key holder somewhere around your car.

hard to find. Just look for the roadside shops with hundreds of huge black and yellow inner tubes and rubber rafts. Some vendors are cheaper than others, but not by much. The vendors will tie the tube to the roof of your car, and you don't have to drive the tubes back at the end of the day. The vendors come to the park and get them.

Where to Stay

The easiest way to overnight near the springs is to camp. There aren't any hotels nearby, just farm country. Ichetucknee Springs is a day park only, so there are no camping facilities within its boundaries. The closest state campground is 12 miles away at Oleno State Park. Call (386) 454-1853 for reservations.

Where to Eat

There is a large concession stand inside the park at the south entrance, but the lines are usually long and the food is nothing to write home about. It's best to pack a picnic lunch and eat at one of the many picnic tables inside the park. There are also grills—just remember to bring the charcoal. Large groups may want to reserve a covered picnic pavilion. Call (386) 497-4690 for reservations.

RELOCATION

N ow it's time to change hats. With this chapter, we take off our tour guide hat and don our chamber of commerce hat. Consider this chapter, and all the ones to follow, part of an Insiders' relocation guide—helpful information to make your move to Jacksonville that much easier. We write this relocation guide with pleasure because Jacksonville truly is a special place to live.

One April morning I (Marisa) walked with my family to the beach, where my four-year-old daughter frolicked in the surf. The water was chilly by Florida standards, about 68 degrees, but the sun warmed our backs. "I love this!" Ana cried, repeatedly. "It's cold and warm at the same time!"

Who wouldn't love it? There wasn't a cloud in the bright blue sky, the seas were calm, and a pod of dolphins crested the surface of the water before us. This is why we live in Florida, my husband and I said to each other, for the beach and weather. In addition, we think we're more active here than if we lived up north. And we're not the only people who believe that. *Men's Fitness* magazine ranks Jacksonville the 18th fittest city in America. While other folks in other cities are busy being couch potatoes, *Men's Fitness* says Jacksonville residents are outside running and biking and burning up calories.

The other main reason for living here is work: We've always been able to find the job we want and need in Jacksonville. Other people must realize this, too, because according to *Expansion Management* magazine, Jacksonville was the hottest city in America for business relocation as of January 2002.

When we moved here over a decade ago, we were overwhelmed by the size of the city and the number of choices in neighborhoods. Each neighborhood seemed to offer its own unique attractions, and it was difficult to decide just which one was right for us.

To save other people that frustration (and the gas it takes to drive all over Jacksonville!), my coauthor and I start the relocation section of this book with an overview of neighborhoods and real estate.

ARLINGTON

If you want to live on the river but don't have gobs of money, Arlington is a good place to look. Chances are, you'll be able to buy an older cinder-block home with a killer view that you can renovate. There is a lot of waterfront property in Arlington, which is surrounded by the St. Johns River to the west and north and the Intracoastal Waterway to the east. Fort Caroline National Park, site of the oldest European settlement in America, is nestled in the heart of Arlington. Jacksonville University is also located here, as is Jones College. Small but busy Craig Airport serves corporate jets and private planes, and Tree Hill Nature Preserve is a large natural park in a suburban setting.

Arlington was one of the first suburban neighborhoods in Jacksonville, so it has long played a role in the city's housing history. It enjoys a central location 10 minutes from downtown and 20 minutes from the Beaches. And since Arlington is generally an older neighborhood, it's full of stately

---

i *The State of Florida offers a homestead exemption to Florida residents who own and occupy a home by January 1 of any given year. The exemption is $25,000 off the assessed value of your home. In most counties, you must renew this exemption annually.*

oaks that provide welcome cool shade during Jacksonville's long, hot summer.

Although there is an abundance of older cinder-block ranch homes in Arlington, there are also many newly developed communities in East Arlington around Fort Caroline and Monument Roads. Some lovely tree-filled neighborhoods like Hidden Hills (yes, there are actually hills!), with homes built in the late eighties and early nineties, are surrounded by good schools and convenient to shopping centers.

WEST BEACHES

West Beaches is one of the fastest-growing areas of Jacksonville. It's called West Beaches because it is geographically located west of the Intracoastal Waterway, about a 10- to 15-minute drive to the beach, depending on traffic. This is where you can buy a brand-new three-bedroom, two-bath home with a two-car garage in the low $200,000 range.

If you want trees, West Beaches is generally not the place to look. Developers have been known to clear-cut many of these neighborhoods in order to construct rows of new homes without any of those pesky trees in their way. The West Beaches development of Queen's Harbour is an exception to this no-tree trend. It offers beautiful upscale homes with plenty of trees on man-made canals. Homeowners can park their boat out back and, through a series of locks, motor their way from their backyard to the Intracoastal.

West Beaches homes are generally new and conveniently located to downtown, Southside, and the Beaches. They are also convenient to many new shopping centers, which are cropping up in their wake. West Beaches has several new schools to accommodate the growth in the neighborhoods. It takes about 20 minutes to drive to downtown Jacksonville from here, often in heavy rush-hour traffic. There are also many new apartment communities in West Beaches, offering everything from efficiencies to townhouses.

Got a question about city services? Call (904) 630–CITY. "One call does it all," as the city likes to say.

THE BEACHES— ATLANTIC, NEPTUNE, AND JACKSONVILLE BEACHES, PONTE VEDRA AND SAWGRASS

Insiders know that the beach is where it's happening, baby! Now it must be said up front that both authors of this *Insiders' Guide* live at the Beaches, so we are not impartial. But living at the Beaches is like living in a small town near a big city. You can work in the big city (Jacksonville) and enjoy all the opportunities it has to offer, then come home to your small town, where it's not unusual to walk or ride your bike to shops and restaurants. Plus the greatest park in the world, the Atlantic Ocean, is at the end of the street, often just a walk or a bike ride away.

The Beaches, as Jacksonville's beach communities are collectively known, are made up of Atlantic Beach, Neptune Beach, Jacksonville Beach, and Ponte Vedra. Ponte Vedra is actually outside the Jacksonville city limits in St. Johns County, but because it is such a bedroom community, Jacksonville all but claims it as its own. Although Atlantic, Neptune, and Jacksonville Beaches are technically within Jacksonville's city limits, they are still cities unto themselves, each with a separate police force and their own elected city officials. Beaches residents pay taxes to the City of Jacksonville, and Jacksonville, in turn, gives a portion of that money back to the beach communities. Children who live at the Beaches and go to public school attend Duval County schools.

It's a different story for Ponte Vedra residents, who are governed by the St. Johns County Commission, which meets in St. Augustine. Taxes are fractionally less in St. Johns County, and schoolchildren in Ponte Vedra attend St. Johns County

i

If you are a Duval County resident, you can vote in Jacksonville. To register to vote, go to a drivers license office, a public library, or to the Supervisor of Elections Office downtown. Call (904) 630–1410 for more information.

schools. Still, because of geography, Ponte Vedra residents are often closer to parts of Jacksonville than they are to St. Augustine.

Sawgrass is the name of a large subdivision in Ponte Vedra Beach. It's confusing sometimes, because some people think that Sawgrass is actually a city on a map. It's not. The Stadium Course at Sawgrass in Ponte Vedra Beach is where The Players Championship, a large golf tournament, is played every year.

The Beaches is also entertainment headquarters for much of Northeast Florida. Many popular nightclubs are located here, and in spring and summer you can count on a festival, fair, or outdoor concert almost every weekend. And it's only going to get better. The City of Jacksonville is in the process of building a new pier in Jacksonville Beach, which will be another entertainment headquarters for the Beaches.

Beach living offers an abundance of lifestyle choices. Perhaps you're looking for an elegant gated community like Marsh Landing in Ponte Vedra, where homes are priced from the high $400,000s to more than $4 million. Maybe an older cinder-block ranch house in the low $200,000 range in Neptune Beach better fits your budget. Perhaps a wood-shingled beach cottage that looks like something straight out of a Maine village is more your style. A number of these "cottages" in Atlantic Beach cost $500,000 and up. As a rule, the closer to the ocean or even the Intracoastal, the higher the price of the house.

The Beaches is also home to one of the city's two naval bases, Naval Station Mayport. It is located adjacent to the

quaint fishing village of Mayport, where working shrimp boats line the docks. The St. Johns River Ferry, popularly called the Mayport Ferry, will take you and your car across the river to scenic Heckscher Drive, also called the Buccaneer Trail. The Buccaneer Trail takes you to Amelia Island (see the Day Trips chapter).

NASSAU COUNTY/AMELIA ISLAND AND FERNANDINA BEACH

Head north of Jacksonville along I-95 and you'll hit Nassau County, home to Amelia Island—a place known around the world for its beautiful golf and tennis resorts and wide, sandy beaches. It has also become a popular destination for wealthy Midwesterners who want to own a second home, be it a house or condominium, in Florida. Consequently, there are a number of very upscale residential communities on Amelia Island. Fernandina Beach is the largest town on Amelia Island; its downtown is listed on the National Register of Historic Places because of its many well-preserved Victorian homes. Fernandina Beach is full of bed-and-breakfast inns, restaurants, and recreational activities, including Fort Clinch State Park. It also plays host to a shrimp festival every year that attracts thousands of visitors. Life got a lot easier for many Amelia Island residents with the opening of a Harris Teeter grocery store conveniently located near Amelia Island Plantation, a popular year-round resort community.

NORTH JACKSONVILLE, FROM EAST TO WEST

North Jacksonville runs roughly from 20th Street north to the Nassau County line and from I-295 on the west almost to the Atlantic Ocean. It's a vast area that includes lots of pretty marshes, new housing developments, and attractions like the

Anheuser-Busch Brewery and the Jacksonville Zoo and Gardens. The eastern portion of this area also includes two of Jacksonville's most popular playgrounds: Huguenot Memorial Park and Little Talbot Island State Park.

Like the West Beaches area of Jacksonville, North Jacksonville is a growing corner of our city. Communities like Oceanway, New Bern, and San Mateo are growing fast as housing developments and strip malls find their way to North Jacksonville. The ever-expanding Jacksonville International Airport is located here, as are two growing business parks: the International Tradeport and Imeson Industrial Park. North Jacksonville is about a 15-minute drive to downtown.

North Jacksonville also includes remote communities like Black Hammock Island, once the haunt of local fishermen only. That's changing as new homes find their way to Black Hammock Island, which, as the name suggests, encompasses a lot of beautiful marshland.

THE URBAN CORE

For a long time, Jacksonville's urban core largely comprised poor African-American communities and downtown office buildings, but that's changing. At this writing, the urban core is a hotbed of real estate activity as developers take advantage of downtown riverfront property and older buildings ripe for renovation. New projects include the $36-million Berkman Plaza, a riverfront apartment and town house community. The town houses sell for more than $600,000, while a one-bedroom apartment with a river view rents for about $950 a month. Right next door local developers are spending $860 million to turn a former shipyard into an upscale retail and residential community complete with riverfront condominiums. It's still hard to buy a cup of coffee in the urban core come the weekend, when all the Monday-through-Friday businesses have closed, but city leaders hope that as more people move to

downtown Jacksonville, more shops and restaurants will open to take care of their needs.

SPRINGFIELD

Historic Springfield is the largest residential historic district in Florida, with wide tree-lined streets and architecturally distinguished houses. Trouble is, you have to be an urban pioneer to live here. Springfield used to be Jacksonville's premier neighborhood, but over the years it fell into disrepair, and once-beautiful Victorians became rooming houses and crack houses. Today preservationists are taking back Springfield house by house. Located just north of the downtown business district, Springfield is the sort of place where you can buy a tumbledown wooden Victorian for about $60,000, with city aid. Renovation costs are significant because in many cases the entire house needs to be rebuilt, but often the folks buying these houses are handy and do a lot of the work themselves.

Want to work for the City of Jacksonville? Check out the job listings on the city's Web site, www.coj.net.   ℹ️

RIVERSIDE AND AVONDALE

Even for the residents of these charming Westside neighborhoods, it is hard to tell where Riverside ends and Avondale begins. So people often just refer to this area collectively as Riverside Avondale. It's bordered to the west by Highway 17 and to the east by the St. Johns River. It lies between I-10 to the north and the Ortega River to the south. Riverside and Avondale are both well-established neighborhoods with old historic homes and majestic oak trees draped in Spanish moss.

Riverside often attracts young professionals who want a short commute to

Habitat for Humanity

Champagne corks popped in 1989 as workers at the new Jacksonville branch of Habitat for Humanity celebrated their first year in operation. HabiJax, as it is called here, built three homes that year, a modest yet glorious beginning for a group that since has built more than a thousand homes for low-income families in Jacksonville. Along the way, HabiJax has received commendations from the U.S. Department of Housing and Urban Development as a model for other communities to follow.

Using donations and volunteer labor, HabiJax builds homes at below-market cost. Then it sells those homes with interest-free mortgages to low-income home buyers, who generally have been unable to buy a home of their own. Home buyers, who often are single mothers with full-time jobs, must put down $500 and log 300 hours of sweat equity building their own home. It's a formula that has paid off for HabiJax, which has a long waiting list of local residents who dream of owning a HabiJax house.

HabiJax attributes much of its success to strong partnerships with local groups like the Northeast Florida Builders Association. The two paired in 2000 to build Fairway Oaks, an entire subdivision of 101 homes built in just 17 days. It was a feat never before accomplished by a Habitat for Humanity group in the United States, and former president Jimmy Carter, a driving force behind Habitat for Humanity, spent a day framing a house to help ensure that it would happen. Corporations donated money to buy materials and provided an army of volunteers to help build. Local

downtown Jacksonville. The houses range from modest duplexes and small apartment complexes to magnificent estates on the river. Riverside is also a medical hub, with the St. Vincent's Medical Complex and numerous medical offices near the hospital. Publix, a large Florida-based grocery store chain, recently opened a grocery store in the heart of Riverside, so many residents can now walk to the market. Numerous shopping areas in Riverside feature some of the city's best restaurants and art galleries.

In Avondale, a little farther west, homebuyers are restoring big old brick homes from the fifties to their original grandeur. Like Riverside, Avondale has its own collection of small shopping districts and quaint streets. Both neighborhoods enjoy a small-town charm in the shadow of a big city, with numerous public parks, tennis courts, and softball and soccer fields.

ORTEGA

Ortega is synonymous with "old money." It sits on a peninsula in the St. Johns River, with the St. Johns to the east and another

restaurants donated food to feed everyone, and the builders supplied trained carpenters and other tradespeople with the expertise to quickly frame a house. Before it was transformed into Fairway Oaks, the neighborhood was called Golfbrook Terrace and was well-known to police as one of the most dangerous housing projects in the city. Today the sound of children playing tag on the sidewalk has replaced the sound of gunfire.

The partnership with the Northeast Florida Builders Association has worked so well for HabiJax that the two joined forces again in 2002. This time they built 40 homes in a month. HabiJax would like to do more big projects, but the big parcels of land needed for such projects are not easy to come by. The majority of HabiJax homes have been built one by one in Jacksonville's urban core, where the city has knocked down dilapidated, abandoned crack houses and given the land to HabiJax to build new homes. The group's signature one-story, three-bedroom house with living room, dining area, and front porch dot many a street in the city's urban core.

Besides building homes for those who need them, HabiJax serves another important purpose. It creates a sense of community—not just in Jacksonville but also beyond. For instance, low- and middle-income volunteers rub elbows with the city's elite at building sites, laying tile and painting walls. College students spend their spring breaks building HabiJax homes. Churches sponsor homes, with church members raising the money, organizing the build, and supplying the labor. Wealthy families sponsor homes in the name of a deceased loved one. Retirees who own an RV travel the country to build homes. Almost everyone who volunteers to work on a HabiJax home is touched by the experience almost as much as the family who will eventually live in it.

smaller river, the Ortega, to the north and west. The Florida Yacht Club and Timuquana Country Club form the social hub of this community, which also happens to be where many of Jacksonville's current movers and shakers grew up. Many attended private schools in this Westside neighborhood and worshiped at the same churches. *Worth* magazine once ranked Ortega 46th among the nation's top-50 wealthiest neighborhoods. Homes run from average ranch-style homes to stately waterfront mansions. If you approach Ortega from the north, you will need to drive across a narrow two-lane drawbridge over the Ortega River. The bridge is a relic from the 1920s.

WESTSIDE

There's an old saying in Jacksonville that "the Westside is the best side," and that may be so. Much of the Westside, an amorphous area on the west side of the city, is largely rural. But growth is heading west in the form of huge residential neighborhoods, strip malls, and office parks. The former Cecil Field Naval Air Station, closed by the federal government in 1993, is located on the Westside. The navy gave Cecil Field's 17,224 acres to the City of Jacksonville, and the city has been working tirelessly ever since to attract businesses out that way. It's paying off. A portion of the old base is now called the Cecil Commerce Center, and Florida Community College at Jacksonville plans to open a campus there in the future.

The Westside is a large community starting just north of I-10 and stretching south to Clay County. It's bordered on the east by I-295 and continues west to Baker County and east to Riverside. Other neighborhoods on this side of town include Ortega Forest, Ortega Hills, Lakeshore, Cedar Hills, Murray Hills, and Normandy. Argyle Forest and Chimney Lakes are two large Westside neighborhoods bordering Clay County. They each offer affordable single-family homes, schools, bike paths, shopping centers, and restaurants.

SOUTHSIDE

Centrally located, the Southside is bordered by Arlington to the north and east, St. Johns County to the south, and San Marco and I-95 to the west. The Southside is literally in the middle of it all. This is where the University of North Florida is located, as well as Tinseltown, a popular new entertainment district; Southpoint, an area of office parks and hotels that many consider to be a second downtown; and the Avenues Shopping Mall. The Southside has a wide range of housing opportunities, including the most apartment complexes in the city, which are predominantly grouped around Baymeadows Road. The Southside also offers luxury gated communities such as Deerwood. Southside residents enjoy easy access to the Beaches (about 20 minutes away) via J. Turner Butler Boulevard and easy access to I-95, which can take you to downtown Jacksonville in about 20 minutes, depending on the traffic.

SAN MARCO

San Marco is one of Jacksonville's prettiest neighborhoods. Some of the homes here sit on the river, but most are snuggled into great tree-lined streets. For those of you familiar with the Washington, D.C., area, San Marco reminds a lot of people of Chevy Chase, Maryland. The houses are nicely sized, often brick, frequently two-story—and expensive. San Marco enjoys a convenient location to downtown Jacksonville; it's only about a five-minute commute. A popular shopping district here is full of shops, restaurants, and nightclubs, even a movie theater.

SAN JOSE, EPPING FOREST, BEAUCLERC, AND MANDARIN

San Jose, Epping Forest, Beauclerc, and Mandarin lie south of San Marco. This is another fast-growing part of the city, and each of these communities has luxury homes along the river. Farther inland, the homes are older, modest, and generally larger single-story ranch-style houses. The Bolles School, the city's premier private school (Jeb Bush's son was a student here) is located in San Jose on the St. Johns River.

Mandarin is one of the fastest-growing residential communities in Jacksonville, with thousands of people moving into its quiet, shady neighborhoods every year. It was largely farmland until the late 1960s, when developers discovered the area. Now there are far more cars than there ever were cows in Mandarin. To its west, Mandarin is bordered by the St. Johns River. To its south lies St. Johns County with the neighborhoods of Julington Creek and Fruit Cove.

Mandarin has strong schools, churches, and synagogues, as well as many strip malls and shopping centers. It's rich in history, and it is here that Harriet Beecher Stowe once owned an orange grove.

Thanks to the efforts of the Mandarin Historical Society, much of the area's history is remembered in the Mandarin Store and Post Office, an old country store that was once the heart of the area. Mandarin is located about 30 minutes from downtown Jacksonville in rush-hour traffic.

ORANGE PARK/CLAY COUNTY

South of Ortega, outside the Jacksonville city limits, lies the popular community of Orange Park. At first glance, Orange Park appears to be nothing more than suburban sprawl, but get off the main highways and into some neighborhoods, and you will see lovely tree-lined streets full of homes that are generally less expensive than those in Jacksonville. Orange Park is located in Clay County, which includes many other popular municipalities, such as Green Cove Springs, Keystone Heights, Penney Farms, and Middleburg.

New Florida residents must apply for Florida tags and car titles within 10 days after they begin working, apply for a homestead tax exemption, or enroll their children in school. Proof of Florida insurance is also required before the tags can be issued.

Many people live in Orange Park and commute some 30 minutes or so to work in Jacksonville. Many an Orange Park neighborhood is also filled with families whose father and/or mother works at NAS Jacksonville, just to the north. The St. Johns River borders the east side of Orange Park, and there are some lovely riverfront homes over that way. Orange Park is home to St. Johns River Community College, the Orange Park Shopping Mall, and the Orange Park Kennel Club, to name a few standouts.

EDUCATION

Education isn't Jacksonville's strong suit. The city's public school system has been troubled for years, operating under a court-ordered desegregation plan for more than 30 years until it was lifted in 2000, and the options for postsecondary education are limited.

But the education outlook is not entirely bleak. Jacksonville has some excellent private elementary and high schools for those who can afford them. There's also a growing number of Christian schools for those who prefer a religious-based education. Meanwhile, the city is busy trying to improve the public school system.

In this chapter we'll look at local colleges and special postsecondary schools, the public school system, and private secondary schools.

COLLEGES AND UNIVERSITIES

If you're interesting in attending a four-year college in the Jacksonville area, there's a relatively young but growing state university and three small liberal arts colleges, including a historic African-American school. If it's a community college you seek, Jacksonville has one of the largest community colleges in the country. Florida Community College at Jacksonville offers a wide range of degree classes and a multitude of special job-training programs at campuses conveniently spread throughout the city.

Edward Waters College
1658 Kings Road
(904) 470–8000
www.ewc.edu
Edward Waters College is a historically African-American four-year private col-

lege. Founded in 1866 by the African Methodist Episcopal Church, the school is located on the city's Northside in one of its most blighted neighborhoods.

With about 1,300 students, the school has five academic divisions: Arts and Sciences, Business Administration, Education and Human Services, General Studies, and Continuing Education. Annual tuition is about $7,500.

In recent years Edward Waters has struggled financially. The school has received donations from major corporations, including $200,000 from Pepsi Bottling Group, as part of a $25 million capital campaign begun by EWC President Jimmie Jenkins. EWC also has received nearly $700,000 in grants from the U.S. Department of Housing and Urban Development, aimed at revitalizing area homes and businesses.

Since Jenkins arrived at the historic school in 1997, enrollment has quadrupled, a football program has been started, and a cosmetic overhaul of the campus has gotten under way.

Flagler College
74 King Street, St. Augustine
(904) 829–6481
www.flagler.edu
Founded in 1968, Flagler College is a four-year private nondenominational college located in historic downtown St. Augustine. The college occupies the former Hotel Ponce de Leon, built in 1888 by oil magnate and Florida developer Henry M. Flagler. Eight of the college's structures are designated as historic buildings; some are adorned with murals by American painters Martin Johnson Heade and George W. Maynard.

With about 1,800 students, the college offers a 22-to-1 student-teacher ratio. Flagler features 19 major courses of study and 14 minors leading to baccalaureate degrees. The most popular majors are business administration, sport management, graphic design, communication, and political science.

Flagler is accredited by the Commission of Colleges of the Southern Association of Colleges and Schools. Sixty percent of the students come from Florida, with the remainder hailing from 44 other states and foreign countries. Tuition is about $7,400.

Florida Community College at Jacksonville
101 West State Street
(904) 633-8100
www.fccj.org

Florida Community College at Jacksonville, referred to locally as FCCJ, opened its doors as Florida Junior College in 1966 with 2,000 students. Today FCCJ is the 10th-largest community college in the United States, with more than 55,000 students enrolled in degree or continuing education courses.

Based on enrollment figures, the most popular degrees are standard associates of arts, followed by associates of science in nursing and computer information sciences. In-state tuition is $57.90 for each credit hour.

FCCJ has five campuses and four training centers throughout Northeast Florida and serves as a feeder school to Florida's four-year universities. In Florida, students who receive an associate in arts degree from the state community college system are guaranteed acceptance into the state university of their choice, such as the University of Florida in Gainesville and Florida State University in Tallahassee.

FCCJ offers 58 associate of science degree programs and 52 vocational and technical certificate programs. Over the years the community college has worked closely with Jacksonville businesses to design training programs to meet the city's workforce needs. The Donald Zell Urban Resource Center at the main downtown campus provides customized work-

force training in all facets of business. Consequently, FCCJ offers strong business and health care programs as well as computer sciences and the culinary arts.

There are more than a half dozen campuses and centers conveniently located all over the city. Besides the main downtown Jacksonville school, FCCJ has three primary satellite locations: the Kent Campus, located on Roosevelt Boulevard on the Westside; the North Campus, located 8 miles north of downtown; and the South Campus, located on Beach Boulevard about 8 miles west of the Atlantic Ocean.

In 2002 FCCJ expanded its job training capabilities when it opened the $25 million Advanced Technology Center adjacent to its downtown campus. The tech center includes training programs in four key areas: information technology, biotechnology, advanced manufacturing, and transportation technology. These are the emerging sectors targeted by Jacksonville economic development officials. For a tour of the Advanced Technology Center, call (904) 598-5600.

Jacksonville University
2800 University Boulevard North
(904) 256-8000
www.jacksonville.edu

Founded in 1934 by local businessmen, Jacksonville University has maintained strong ties to the business community. In 2000 the school completed one of the largest capital campaigns in city history by raising $60 million. The campaign got a major boost with a single $20 million contribution from the Davis family, founders and principal owners of the Jacksonville-based Winn-Dixie supermarket chain.

JU is located on a picturesque campus on the St. Johns River in the Arlington section of the city. With 2,200 students, it boasts a low, 14-to-1 student-faculty ratio. Annual tuition is about $18,000.

JU offers undergraduate and adult degree programs as well as graduate programs. JU is best known for its nursing

Catch a concert by the UNF Jazz Department. The jazz bands there are ranked some of the best in the nation.

school, school of education, biology and marine science programs, and its school of fine arts. It offers master's degrees in teaching and business administration and professional programs in engineering, dentistry, law, and medicine. JU also offers a well-regarded executive MBA program that many area businesspeople have completed. There's also a Weekend Studies program, with classes on Friday evening, Saturday, and Sunday, that is popular with many Jacksonville professionals.

The school fields competitive teams, especially in basketball and baseball. Its football program is the only nonscholarship football program in the state.

University of North Florida
4567 St. Johns Bluff Road South
(904) 620-1000
www.unf.edu
The University of North Florida is one of Florida's fastest-growing four-year state universities. The school, founded in 1965, doesn't offer nearly the number of degrees and programs as Florida's bigger, better-known institutions—University of Florida in Gainesville and Florida State University in Tallahassee—but UNF is adding programs and expanding its facilities yearly. In 2001 UNF opened a $22 million Fine Arts Center. A science and engineering building opened in 2004.

The 1,300-acre campus, located off Butler Boulevard in Jacksonville's bustling Southside, opened in 1972 with 2,027 stu-

Former two-term mayor John Delaney, who spearheaded the Better Jacksonville Plan, is now the president of the University of North Florida.

dents. Today UNF has more than 13,000 students and 46 undergraduate degree programs in addition to 23 graduate degree programs and comprises five colleges: Arts and Sciences, Business Administration, Education and Human Services, Health, and Computer Sciences and Engineering. Most students (80 percent) live off campus.

The most popular majors at UNF are business management, education, and health professions. UNF also has a respected jazz program.

Like most of Florida's other public colleges and universities, UNF's in-state tuition is (relative to other states) modest. Annual tuition and fees for Florida residents in 2004 were $2,900. For out-of-state students, tuition and fees were $13,300. Room and board added approximately $5,500.

SPECIAL SCHOOLS AND PROGRAMS

Florida Coastal School of Law
7555 Beach Boulevard
(904) 680-7700
www.fcsl.edu
The Florida Coastal School of Law, Jacksonville's only law school, opened in 1996 with 140 students. Several years later, the private law school achieved accreditation. Today the school has nearly 500 students, many of whom attend part-time. Annual tuition is $20,300.

Florida Technical College of Jacksonville
8711 Lone Star Road
(904) 724-2229
www.flatech.edu
Founded in 1984, Florida Technical is a private two-year junior college that offers students technical training in computer programming and computer-aided drafting and design. The school also offers diplomas in network administration and C++/JAVA and Oracle programming.

Jones College
5353 Arlington Expressway
(904) 743-1122
www.jones.edu
Jones College is a specialty four-year private college that offers bachelor of science and associate in science degrees with majors in computer accounting, information systems, marketing, management, medical assistant, and other business-related fields. The school has about 600 full- and part-time students.

University of Phoenix
8131 West Baymeadows Circle
(904) 636-6645
www.online-university-information.org
University of Phoenix, a private school, offers BA degrees in administration, management, marketing, and accounting and BS degrees in information technology and health-care services. MBAs are available in some areas. Phoenix also offers many courses and programs online.

Webster University
6104 Gazebo Park Place South
(904) 268-3037
www.webster.edu/jack
Webster University was founded as a liberal arts college in suburban St. Louis in 1915; its graduate division was established in 1967. The Jacksonville campus, located near Avenues Mall at the intersection of I-95 and US 1, opened in 1993. The university also offers both master of arts (MA) and master of business administration (MBA) programs in various fields of business, management, education, the liberal arts and science, and the fine arts.

PUBLIC SCHOOLS

Duval County Public Schools
1701 Prudential Drive
(904) 390-2000
www.educationcentral.org
Duval County Public Schools is a sprawling school district. With 126,000 students,

For information regarding Duval County's magnet school program—schools focusing on specific interests, needs, and talents—call (904) 390-2082.

it is the sixth-biggest school district in the state of Florida. Some of the performance measures aren't encouraging. Among Florida's seven large urban school districts, Jacksonville had the highest dropout rate in 2003.

Duval County Public Schools comprises 103 elementary schools, 24 middle schools, 17 high schools, 2 academies of technology, 3 exceptional student centers, 5 special schools, and 6 charter schools that operate throughout the county.

There are, of course, many bright spots in Duval's public schools, including Stanton College Preparatory School, which was rated the best public school in America in 2000 by *Newsweek* magazine. That same year, Paxon School for Advanced Studies in Jacksonville was rated seventh. Both schools ranked so high on the strength of two academically rigorous programs: International Baccalaureate, where the curriculum is based on international standards, and Advanced Placement, which allows students to earn college credit in high school. Another Duval County public high school also made *Newsweek*'s list: Douglas Anderson School of the Arts tied for 346th out of the 472 schools ranked.

All public school students in Florida must pass the FCAT, Florida Comprehensive Assessment Test, in order to advance to the next level. All students in grades 3 through 10 take the FCAT reading and math tests in the spring of each year. All students in grades 4, 8, and 10 take the FCAT writing test, while students in grades 5, 8, and 10 take the FCAT science test.

Magnet Schools

Many of Duval County's best and brightest high school students attend Stanton College Preparatory School, an all-honors public magnet school named the best public high school in the nation in 2000 by *Newsweek* magazine. Paxon School for Advanced Studies, another all-honors public magnet school, earned the seventh spot on that same list. Both schools provide a rigorous academic program of advanced academic courses, and students are clamoring to get in. About 1,500 high school students attend Stanton (www.stantoncollegeprep.org), and there's a waiting list about that long for others who want admission. In fact, Paxon started its academic magnet program in 1999 in response to the demand for more seats at Stanton.

Both schools offer the International Baccalaureate program—a two-year comprehensive liberal arts education for academically talented and highly motivated students. Stanton's IB program is one of the largest and most successful in the world. In 1999 the IB class was ranked first in the nation out of 257 high schools and second in North America out of 370 high schools for the number of IB diplomas awarded (104). The IB program puts nearly impossible demands on students, who always seem to rise to the challenge. For instance, there's no kicking back for seniors in the IB program. They must take IB English Literature; Calculus, or IB Math Studies; Foreign Language V; IB Science; IB Contemporary History; an elective; and an IB class on research and critical think-

The magazine studied a total of 22,500 public high schools. (See the Close-up for more information about these exceptional public high schools.)

After reading up on Duval's public schools, some relocating families have bought homes in St. Johns County. Communities like Ponte Vedra and Julington Creek are close enough to Jacksonville to make for a reasonable commute but are still within the St. Johns County public school district. That school system is smaller than Duval's and therefore, some believe, less problematic.

Jacksonville's public schools offer special programs to students who are physically or mentally handicapped, sensory impaired, and emotionally disabled, as well as those who are gifted. Currently more than 24,000 exceptional students are served in 18 programs.

To register your children in public school, go to the school and show documentation that you're a current resident. You must also show a birth certificate and an up-to-date shot record. Children must also have had a physical in the last 12 months.

PRIVATE SCHOOLS

Jacksonville has a number of excellent—albeit some quite pricey—private schools,

ing. And if that's not enough, all students are also encouraged to participate in after-school activities like sports, band, or the debate team.

If Stanton College Prep is the quintessential Duval County high school for right-brain thinkers, then Douglas Anderson School of the Arts (DASOTA) is its left-brain counterpart. Students with an exceptional talent for creative writing, dance, theater arts, visual arts, or instrumental and vocal music can audition for a spot in DASOTA. Entry into Douglas Anderson is just as competitive as at Stanton and Paxon, and the waiting list is just as long for students who don't get in on the first round. At DASOTA (www .educationcentral.org/dasota) talented students explore the arts in depth. They travel and perform in an award-winning jazz band, dance in recitals and musicals, and display their artwork all over town.

Douglas Anderson students must earn a total of 28 high school credits, four more than are required for graduation in Florida. Students can take honors and advanced-placement courses and must take a minimum of two classes each day in the arts. They can take more arts classes each day in the upper grade levels as graduation requirements are met.

Duval County's magnet school program began after a 1972 court order mandating that the county desegregate its schools. After several misstarts the county finally arrived at the magnet school idea and opened Stanton, its first magnet school, in 1981. Many magnets, including Stanton, are located in economically disadvantaged neighborhoods. Still, students from all over the city flock to these schools because of the programs offered.

ranging from pre-K through high school. The growth in the number of private schools, particularly religious-affiliate schools, has been partly the result of the troubled public system. For younger students there's a wide choice of church-affiliated, Montessori, and special schools with a very specific focus.

The Diocese of St. Augustine operates a number of parish schools, which usually have long waiting lists. Many begin with some sort of preschool program and continue through eighth grade.

You can get a list of all the private schools in the area from the Florida Department of Education's Office of Choice at (800) 447-1636 or (850) 245-0502. We've listed some of Jacksonville's

secondary private schools to give you an idea of the options available.

Arlington Country Day School
5725 Fort Caroline Road
(904) 744-0466
www.acdsjax.net

Founded in 1954 as an elementary school, Arlington Country Day School added a high school in 1995. The school is known for its small classes, from preschool through grade 12. In 2003, 37 of the school's 52 graduates earned either academic or athletic scholarships to colleges or universities.

Despite its small student population, in recent years ACDS has developed a powerhouse of a basketball program.

The school's varsity team has been ranked among the top high school teams in the country.

Bishop Kenny High School
1055 Kingman Avenue
(904) 398-7545
www.bishopkenny.org
Founded in 1952, Bishop Kenny High School is a four-year Catholic preparatory school with 1,600 students. Ninety-nine percent of the 2003 graduating class went on to college, 71 percent of them to a four-year college. More than half the school's 84 faculty members have master's degrees.

The Bolles School
7400 San Jose Boulevard
(904) 733-9292
www.bolles.org
Located on a beautiful riverfront campus in Jacksonville's San Jose area, the Bolles School is considered by many to be the city's premier private preparatory school. The school is popular among Jacksonville's business elite.

Bolles was founded in 1933 as an all-boys military school on the banks of the St. John's River. In 1961 the school dropped its military status, and it began admitting girls in 1971. Today Bolles has more than 1,800 students in classes from pre-K through grade 12 at five campuses. Bolles's upper-school campus is located in San Jose. The middle school—Bartram Campus—is located nearby. Bolles also operates a lower-school campus in Ponte Vedra Beach.

Students from 25 different countries and 17 states are enrolled in the Bolles boarding program. For foreign students, Bolles offers an English-as-a-second-language program. In addition to its excellent academic reputation, Bolles has some of the state's top athletic programs. Alumni include Atlanta Braves infielder Chipper Jones.

Episcopal High School
4455 Atlantic Boulevard
(904) 396-5751
www.episcopalhigh.org
Episcopal High School is Jacksonville's other top private prep school. It actually begins with grade 6 and continues through grade 12. Episcopal is located on a scenic 58-acre riverfront campus. It has excellent athletic facilities, including a heated pool.

Providence School
2701 Hodges Boulevard
(904) 223-5270
www.prov.org
Christian schools, based on the popular Catholic school concept, are now growing in popularity in Duval County. Providence begins with preschool and continues through grade 12.

Trinity Christian Academy
800 Hammond Boulevard
(904) 596-2400
www.tcajax.org
Founded in 1967, Trinity Christian is affiliated with Trinity Baptist Church. Accredited by the Florida Association of Christian Colleges and Schools, it's located on a 148-acre campus in West Jacksonville just off I-10. An athletic powerhouse, especially when it comes to high school football, Trinity offers classes from kindergarten to grade 12.

University Christian School
5520 University Boulevard West
(904) 737-6330
www.ucschool.org
Affiliated with University Baptist Church, University Christian is an extremely diverse private school that begins at the kindergarten level and continues through grade 12. Another athletic powerhouse, its football and basketball teams often beat the local private and public school competition.

CHILD CARE 🧸

With more than 400 licensed child care centers in this city, taking care of kids while mom and dad are at work is big business in Jacksonville. And that's not even counting the hundreds of state-licensed day care homes or the hundreds of churches citywide with child care programs that open their doors to everyone.

Jacksonville offers plenty of child care choices, which can make the task of finding the provider that's right for you seem daunting indeed. Fear not. Jacksonville offers something unique to help provide focus and demystify your search. It's called the Jacksonville Children's Commission, which (among other things) operates a citywide child care resource and referral program. This service will help you find child care that's right for you and your family.

We've included a few of the larger child care centers in this chapter to help you start your search. But parents still need to do their homework—visit a number of potential caregivers and check up on them with the Licensing Unit of the State of Florida's Department of Children and Families at (904) 723-2064. The Licensing Unit will tell you whether the child care provider you are checking out has been cited by the state or if there are a number of client complaints against them.

There's nothing more agonizing for parents than putting their children in day care. Taking advantage of the available resources, however, can make some of those child care choices easier.

RESOURCES

Duval County Child Care Directory
(888) 708-5700
Consider this directory your bible for child care in Duval County. Updated every year, the book lists most child care centers in the city by zip code. Many home day care providers are listed there, too. You can pick up one of these books for free at the Duval County Library nearest you, or you can get one from the Jacksonville Children's Commission. If you are moving here from out of town, this directory will definitely make your child care search a lot easier.

Jacksonville Children's Commission
Child Care Resource and Referral Program
421 West Church Street, Suite 201
(904) 630-6408
www.jaxchildrenscommission.org
Heaven sent—that's how many Jacksonville residents feel about the Jacksonville Children's Commission. This mostly city-funded agency was established in 1994 to help children of all age groups and income levels thrive in Jacksonville. The commission wears many hats. It can help low-income families register their preschool children in Head Start programs and can help middle- and upper-income families find child care providers. It operates a toy-lending library that's open to all and provides travel grants to, for example, members of a high school marching band who want to perform at the Rose Bowl.

Here's how the Child Care Resource and Referral program works: The commission operates a comprehensive database with information on child care centers, family day care homes, church programs, after-school programs, summer camps—you name it. Call the commission and arrange an interview. A counselor will be assigned to your case, and using the database the counselor will match your needs with the appropriate local services. You will receive a list of potential providers as well as a thick folder full of reading material designed to help you succeed in your child care search. If you don't find the child care you need the first time around, you can return to your counselor for more help. Best of all, it's free.

CHILD CARE PROVIDERS

Bank of America
Child Development Center
9000 Southside Boulevard
(904) 464-3902
www.brighthorizons.com
Mothers who work on the sprawling Southside campus of Bank of America can drop their kids off at the Child Development Center on the way to the office. At lunch these same moms can get some exercise as they walk to the center to eat with their kids. When work is over, there's no harrowing drive through heavy traffic to race to the day care center before closing time. Instead moms drive to the other side of campus and pick up their children before heading home. Why can't all employers offer on-site day care facilities like this?

Chappell Child Development Centers
8400 Baycenter Road
(904) 739-1279
www.chappell-school.com
Founded in 1958, Chappell is one of the oldest and biggest child care centers in Jacksonville. The first school was a kindergarten started by LaDauskie Harward Chappell. Her daughter, Katheryne Chappell Drennon, took over the company in 1979 and expanded into corporate child development centers. In 1984 she opened the country's first privately owned, freestanding, nonsubsidized child care center

The YMCA of Florida's First Coast offers great after-school care and summer programs for children at all of its locations. Call (904) 296-3220 for information.

in an office park setting in Deerwood. Today Chappell has six child care centers in Jacksonville, including one at each of the Florida Community College of Jacksonville's four primary campuses: Downtown, North, South, and Kent. Chappell also has operated child care centers on-site at numerous Jacksonville businesses, including Johnson & Johnson, Blue Cross and Blue Shield of Florida, AT&T, IBM, and the Jacksonville Jaguars.

Magellan Academies
10550 Deerwood Park
(904) 646-9596
www.magellanacademies.com
Do you work weekends? Saturday nights? Then check out Magellan Academies, which offers two locations, the Southside location listed above and a second location at the intersection of Philips Highway and Baymeadows Road. Magellan will also take drop-ins, so if your child care provider calls in sick for the day, you have a backup. The staff here tries to make the time your child spends in day care as rewarding as possible. They take field trips, offer dance and karate classes, and even teach a foreign language.

UNF Child Development Research Center
University of North Florida
4567 South St. Johns Bluff Road
(904) 620-2372
www.unf.edu/dept/cdrc
The University of North Florida offers a child development center on campus that also serves as a teaching facility for student teachers. Your child will get expert care here, as well as plenty of attention from earnest young students eager to work with children. The learning environment is excellent, and children thrive here. Many learn to read and write earlier than they normally would. There's only one problem: This child development center is very difficult to get into and the waiting list is long, so be sure to have a backup plan.

YMCA Riverside Center
221 Riverside Avenue
(904) 355–1436
www.firstcoastymca.org/yates
Want your child to learn to swim? Take him or her to a YMCA Child Development Center like the one listed above. The YMCA takes advantage of the pools at most of the centers to teach your child how to swim. Kids love the change of pace, and parents love the fact that their

Looking for child care over the long Christmas vacation or any other vacation for that matter? We highly recommend the minicamps at the Museum of Science and History. Call (904) 396–7062 for details.

children are learning a very valuable skill while in day care.

HEALTH CARE AND WELLNESS

R est assured. If you get sick while visiting Jacksonville, you will get some of the best health care available. The city is blessed with some internationally renowned health care facilities, such as the Mayo Clinic, where researchers are conducting a major study of Alzheimer's disease; Wolfson Children's Hospital; and Nemours Children's Clinic, a medical and surgical specialty clinic.

We also have a Ronald McDonald House across the street from Nemours, where families with sick children can stay for extended periods of time. For emergencies, Shands Jacksonville provides Level 1 trauma care for patients in 19 counties in Northeast Florida and South Georgia. It's one of just six Level 1 trauma centers in Florida.

Meanwhile, there's been plenty of movement and change among Jacksonville's hospitals. A merger between two of the biggest medical centers—Baptist and St. Vincent's—was untangled, and as the city continues to grow, hospitals are expanding as fast as they can.

HOSPITALS

Baptist Medical Center
800 Prudential Drive
(904) 202–2000
www.e-baptisthealth.com
Baptist Medical Center is one of the largest health care providers in Jacksonville. Under the umbrella of Baptist Health, a faith-based health system, the Baptist Medical Center is actually a collection of health care facilities rather than a single hospital.

The Baptist health system offers a full range of medical and surgical specialties, including adult and children's emergency centers, cardiovascular care, comprehensive cancer services, and a full complement of women's and children's services. Other specialized medical services include wound care, psychology and psychiatry, and pulmonary care.

Baptist Medical Center's primary hospital is a 538-bed facility conveniently located on Jacksonville's Southbank. If you are driving south on I–95 through Jacksonville, you can see the hospital to the left after you cross the St. Johns River. The Southbank center also includes the Baptist Cancer Institute, which provides medical oncology, surgical oncology, and radiation therapy services.

Baptist Medical Center Beaches is a 90-bed full-service hospital located in Jacksonville Beach. It serves the Jacksonville beaches and surrounding communities. The hospital also has a 24-hour emergency department with 26 beds, 6 operating suites, and 8 maternity suites, with more planned.

To the north of Jacksonville in Fernandina Beach, Baptist operates the Baptist Medical Center Nassau, a 54-bed full-service community hospital that serves Nassau County and Southeast Georgia residents. Services include an emergency department, four-bed critical care unit, five-bed maternity unit, and three surgical suites.

Baptist also owns and operates Wolfson Children's Hospital, a major 178-bed regional referral hospital for children that is adjacent to the main Southbank hospital. It is the only children's hospital serving

Northeast Florida and Southeast Georgia. Besides providing a full range of pediatric medical care, Wolfson also has a 48-bed neonatal intensive care unit for critically ill newborns.

If you visit Wolfson, be sure to check out the unique 660-foot-long Kids' Walk—a suspended covered walkway over I-95 that connects Wolfson to Nemours Children's Clinic.

In addition to the full-service hospitals, Baptist also operates 17 primary care health centers located throughout neighborhoods in Duval, Nassau, and St. Johns counties.

Brooks Rehabilitation Hospital
3599 University Boulevard South
(904) 858-7600

Brooks Rehabilitation Hospital is a 127-bed not-for-profit hospital that specializes in treating patients with brain injury, strokes, spinal cord injury, and comprehensive orthopedic problems. It is the eighth-largest rehabilitation hospital in the country.

Brooks is located at the corner of Beaches and University boulevards, next door to the Memorial Hospital.

The Mayo Clinic
4500 San Pablo Road
(904) 953-2000
www.mayo.edu

The renowned Mayo Clinic in Rochester, Minnesota, opened its first satellite facility in Jacksonville in 1986 on land donated by the late J. E. Davis, Jacksonville's legendary businessman and one of the founders of the Winn-Dixie supermarket chain. The Mayo Clinic's century-old mission is to conduct medical research, provide medical education, and meet the health care needs of adults.

Like its counterparts in Minnesota and Arizona, Mayo in Jacksonville is a multispecialty outpatient clinic. Mayo is known for its team approach, where specialists from many different areas consult together for the benefit of the patient. Consequently, Mayo refers to its staff physicians as "consultants."

Baptist Medical Center operates the Pavilion Inn, a hotel inside the hospital for families of patients. Call (904) 202-1680 for reservations.

Over the years, the Mayo Clinic has greatly enhanced Jacksonville's reputation, especially as the number of influential people visiting the city for treatment continues to grow. The Jacksonville Mayo Clinic has attracted such well-known patients as the Reverend Billy Graham and Lady Bird Johnson, as well as wealthy individuals from Latin America and the Middle East.

In addition to providing standard medical care, Mayo Clinic Jacksonville also offers a range of special services. An executive health program for harried CEOs combines a resort package of golf, tennis, or spa with a physical exam. Mayo operates four primary care centers in Jacksonville, St. Augustine, and Kingsland, Georgia, for easy doctors' visits. At the Jacksonville clinic, Mayo also operates a nicotine dependence center and a sleep disorders center.

If you want to be treated at the Mayo Clinic in Jacksonville, you can make your own appointment. The clinic also welcomes physician referrals. Patients who need hospitalization are admitted to nearby St. Luke's Hospital, a 209-bed facility that affiliated with the Mayo Clinic in 1987. But that's set to change. As we went to press Mayo was still awaiting final state regulatory approval to build a 215-bed hospital on its campus after it sells St. Luke's. St. Vincent's has agreed to buy it.

Memorial Medical Center
3625 University Boulevard
(904) 399-6111
www.memorialhospitaljax.com

Opened in 1969, Memorial is now one of Jacksonville's largest full-service community hospitals, with 273 beds. The hospital was acquired in 1995 by Nashville, Tennessee–based HCA Inc.

More recently Memorial completed a $34 million expansion to meet the growing number of patients coming through its doors. Among the additions, the hospital increased its emergency room bays from 20 to 34; added another cardiac catheterization lab, creating a total of three; and expanded the number of outpatient surgery rooms from six to eight. Memorial also installed a new MRI unit.

Memorial is one of the few hospitals in Northeast Florida to perform PET scans, a noninvasive procedure used to detect early heart disease.

Nemours Children's Clinic
807 Nira Street
(904) 390-3600
www.nemours.org
Located on the Southbank across I-95 from the Baptist Medical Center complex, Nemours Children's Clinic has more than 60 pediatric specialists on staff. The specialist physicians at Nemours treat more than 38,000 children each year. Nemours is funded by a trust set up by the late Alfred I. duPont, one of Jacksonville's most generous benefactors. DuPont died in 1935, and the Children's Clinic was established the following year. In his will, duPont wrote, "It has been my firm conviction throughout life that it is the duty of everyone in the world to do what is within his power to alleviate human suffering. It is, therefore, natural that I should desire, after having made provision for the immediate members of my family and others whom I have seen fit to remember,

that the remaining portion of my estate be utilized for charitable needs."

DuPont's desire lives on at Nemours, where children with severe medical conditions get treatment regardless of their family's ability to pay. Every year Nemours receives earnings from the trust, which has large holdings in two of Northeast Florida's biggest public companies, the St. Joe Co. in Jacksonville and Florida East Coast Industries in St. Augustine.

Shands Jacksonville
655 West Eight Street
(904) 244-0411
www.shandsjacksonville.org
Shands Jacksonville, affiliated with the University of Florida in Gainesville, is Jacksonville's only teaching hospital. It also provides the majority of care to the city's poor and indigent.

Shands Jacksonville was created in fall 1999 when Shands HealthCare of Gainesville bought and merged two financially ailing hospitals—University Medical Center and Methodist Hospital. The hope has been to keep an academic medical center in Jacksonville's growing metropolitan area. But, financially speaking, the merged hospitals have had a difficult time.

Still, the city, State of Florida, and Shands Gainesville all express a willingness to keep Shands Jacksonville operating because of the vital role it plays in serving the area's health care needs.

Shands houses Jacksonville's only top-level trauma center, which serves patients from 30 counties. It has the only dedicated stroke center of its kind, which has reversed the effects of strokes in many patients.

St. Luke's Hospital
4201 Belfort Road
(904) 296-3700
www.mayo.edu
St. Luke's Hospital is a not-for-profit, nondenominational hospital conveniently located near the intersection of I-95 and Butler Boulevard. It offers general acute-

St. Luke's Hospital in Jacksonville is known for offering the best food of any local hospital. Patients order their meals over the telephone just like they were ordering through room service at a hotel. Consequently, patients can have lobster tail for breakfast or scrambled eggs for dinner.

care services and specializes in medical and surgical procedures

St. Luke's has been providing health care to Jacksonville residents since 1873, when it opened as Florida's first private hospital. The hospital has come a long way from its original two rooms and four beds.

Today St. Luke's is a 289-bed facility located in the city's bustling office district. In 1987 St. Luke's affiliated with the Mayo Clinic, located 9 miles to the east. St. Luke's is the admitting hospital for Mayo patients. Sixty-three percent of its patients are 65 or older, and the hospital treats a higher proportion of patients with complex and severe problems than any other hospital in Jacksonville.

As part of changes taking place among Jacksonville's medical centers, St. Luke's is slated to be sold to St. Vincent's Medical Center after the Mayo Clinic builds its own hospital on its grounds.

St. Vincent's Medical Center
1800 Barrs Street
(904) 308-7300
www.jaxhealth.com
St. Vincent's Medical Center is located on the west bank of the St. Johns River in the Riverside section of Jacksonville. The 528-bed hospital is a full-service tertiary care center and it was named one of the nation's top 100 hospitals for cardiology in 1999.

St. Vincent's is a faith-based, nonprofit health system serving the health care needs of North Florida and South Georgia. It was founded by the Daughters of Charity in 1916 to provide health services to the sick and the poor. Now St. Vincent's is a member of Ascension Health, the largest Catholic health system in the United States and the successor organization to Daughters of Charity National Health.

As previously noted, St. Vincent's is expected to purchase St. Luke's Hospital from Mayo Clinic Jacksonville and assume operation as a new, smaller 145-bed hospital.

Orange Park

Orange Park Medical Center
2001 Kingsley Avenue
(904) 276-8778
www.opmedical.com
Located in suburban Clay County, Orange Park Medical Center is a 219-bed hospital offering a full range of services, from emergency care and wellness to psychiatric and diagnostic.

Opened in 1974, Orange Park Medical Center is owned by Nashville, Tennessee-based HCA Inc. The hospital recently opened an $8 million addition for its expanded women's health and pediatric services.

St. Augustine

Flagler Hospital
400 Health Park Boulevard
(904) 819-5155
Named after famed Florida industrialist Henry Flagler, this sprawling medical center comprises 440,000 square feet of medical space on a 75-acre health park conveniently located on US 1.

Flagler Hospital is a full-service medical complex offering emergency care, oncology, maternity, pediatrics, and a center specializing in women's health care. The complex was recently expanded to include an eight-story Patient Tower; larger birth, pediatrics, and intensive care units; a new oncology center; and an expanded heart and lung center.

MENTAL HEALTH SERVICES

Mental health facilities are often included in many of Jacksonville's hospitals. In this listing you'll find some of the facilities that provide comprehensive and specialized care.

Executive Physicals

Life changes when you get to be a CEO. You fly first class, you sign checks for many millions of dollars, and you no longer have the time or inclination to sit in a waiting room reading old, tattered copies of *Sports Illustrated* as you wait to see a doctor.

Enter the Executive Health Program at the Mayo Clinic in Jacksonville, a one- or two-day checkup tailored to meet the demands of busy corporate executives. With an executive physical, you don't wait to see a doctor, the doctor waits to see you. The program began over 10 years ago and since then has become so popular that it's now copied by clinics throughout the state.

Here's how it works: You arrive at the Mayo Clinic the day of your appointment, where employees who will shepherd you through the process greet you virtually at the front door. There are no forms to fill out or questionnaires to answer. All that pesky paperwork was completed back at the office and sent in ahead of time. Shortly after you arrive at the Mayo Clinic, you change your clothes and a battery of testing begins: blood samples, urine samples, a stress test, X-rays, vision tests,

hearing tests, colonoscopies—you name it. This is your chance to get tested without a wait and, best of all, to find out the test results before you leave the clinic. This is also your chance to meet with some of the best doctors in the country to discuss your health and well-being. And if a problem is found while you're being poked and prodded, you will see a specialist about it during this same visit.

Mayo officials say that 18 to 20 corporate executives go through the executive health program each day. Between tests, these bigwigs can sit in an office to read a newspaper, call their secretary for messages, and log on to a computer to check e-mails. It's the best medicine money can buy, and it comes with an executive price tag: $2,200 to $4,600. Mayo says that about 3 in 10 patients pay for the program themselves because this sort of checkup is not usually covered by health insurance. But more and more companies are picking up the tab because a healthy executive is a good investment. Convenience is also a good investment for busy corporate executives, who know all too well that time, as they say, is money.

Baptist Behavioral Health
800 Prudential Drive
(904) 202-2000
www.e-baptisthealth.com
Part of the Baptist Medical Center complex, Baptist Behavioral Health provides psychiatric and psychological care and outpatient services.

Child Guidance Center
5776 Saint Augustine Road
(904) 448-4700
www.childguidancecenter.org
From four locations throughout the city, Child Guidance Center offers outpatient counseling and psychiatric care services to children up to 18 years of age. The

center also offers on-site family counseling and intensive crisis-intervention programs.

The other three locations are at 1110 Edgewood Avenue West (904-924-1550); 1100 Cessery Boulevard, Suite 100 (904-745-3070); and 6316 San Juan Avenue, Suite 41 (904-783-2579).

Hope Haven Children's Clinic
4600 Beach Boulevard
(904) 346-5100
www.hope-haven.org
Hope Haven, a not-for-profit facility, provides a range of psychological testing for children, including attention deficit disorder, or ADD. Hope Haven also offers speech therapy.

Hope Haven first opened in the late 1800s to provide medical care for children suffering from tuberculosis. By the 1930s the facility had expanded its care to include the growing number of children afflicted by polio. In the 1980s the board decided to shift Hope Haven's focus again in order to meet the evolving developmental needs that families face when raising children in our contemporary society.

To schedule an appointment, you first have to provide some patient information over the phone. A caseworker will call back on a first-come, first-served basis.

Mental Health Center of Jacksonville
3333 West 20th Street
(904) 695-9145
The Mental Health Center has been operating in Jacksonville since the mid-1960s. The facility provides outpatient medication management and offers 24-hour emergency services. There's a stabilization unit for patients who are admitted for inpatient care.

The Mental Health Center, as well as the Mental Health Resource Center, is operated by Renaissance Behavioral Health Systems, a not-for-profit company that provides administrative, accounting, and data-processing services to a group of affiliated health care service providers.

Mental Health Resource Center
11820 Beach Boulevard
(904) 642-9100
Like its sister facility, the Mental Health Center, the Mental Health Resource Center offers crisis stabilization services as well as inpatient and outpatient case management services. The Mental Health Resource Center also has a children's unit for treating children under age 18.

You can call Renaissance Behavioral Health Systems to determine which of the facilities would best serve your needs. The phone number is (904) 743-1883.

Ten Broeck Hospital
6300 Beach Boulevard
(904) 724-9202
www.tenbroeckjax.com
Ten Broeck Hospital offers some of the most comprehensive mental health services in the city. Opened in 1999, this 99-bed mental health hospital has a full range of inpatient, partial, outpatient, and residential services for children, adolescents, families, adults, and seniors. Patients are referred to Ten Broeck by physicians, psychologists, social workers, community mental health centers, schools, courts, hospitals, social services, and managed care organizations.

Ten Broeck is known for its adolescent psychiatric inpatient program, which utilizes the medical model of treatment to treat adolescents (ages 12 to 18) who are experiencing problems with psychiatric illnesses and/or emotional disorders. This program is designed to provide the highest level of direct patient care possible, including physical, social, spiritual, medical, and psychotherapeutic treatment interventions.

Ten Broeck also offers highly structured programs for adults who are chemically dependent.

Looking for a holistic physician or dentist in Jacksonville? We recommend you pick up a free copy of Natural Awakenings *magazine at the library. The ads inside will steer you in the right direction.*

HOSPICE CARE

Community Hospice of Northeast Florida
4266 Sunbeam Road
(904) 268-5200
www.communityhospice.com
Hospice Northeast Earl B. Hadlow Center for Caring is a 24-bed residential facility that includes two beds for respite care. The facility is named after the late Earl Hadlow, a longtime prominent Jacksonville banker.

The center is a collaboration between Community Hospice of Northeast Florida and Shands Jacksonville Hospice and Palliative Care. The mission of Community Hospice is to provide quality, compassionate care to terminally ill patients and their families. Care is available in a variety of settings: at home, in a long-term care facility, in an assisted-living facility, in a hospital, or at the Earl B. Hadlow Center for Caring.

For in-home hospice services, call (904) 268-5200.

ALTERNATIVE CARE

Alternative treatments such as chiropractic, acupuncture, aroma therapy, homeopathy, massage, biofeedback, and even psychic healing have been gaining wider public followings in the United States in recent years. The *New England Journal of Medicine* reports that one-third of Americans use at least one kind of alternative therapy.

You'll find ample providers of alternative medical care in Jacksonville. Here are just a few of the clinics that offer natural and holistic medicine:

Atlantis Medical Center
412 Second Street, Jacksonville Beach
(904) 242-0774

The Complementary Care Center
7563 Philips Highway, Suite 206
(904) 296-9355

Holistic Health Center
1173 Ponte Vedra Boulevard
Ponte Vedra Beach
(904) 285-8802

AIDS AND HIV SERVICES

According to the state Department of Health, Florida ranks second in the nation for the number of reported adult and adolescent HIV/AIDS cases and third in the nation for pediatric cases (children under the age of 13). AIDS is the #1 cause of death among African Americans in Florida who are 25 to 44 years old. Here are a few of the organizations that offer related care and case management in Jacksonville:

Duval County Health Department
HIV/AIDS Specialty Care
1833 Boulevard, Suite 500
(904) 798-4810
www.dchd.net

Lutheran Social Services
4615 Phillips Highway
(904) 448-5995
www.lssjax.org

Northeast Florida AIDS Network
1045 Riverside Ave, Suite 110
(800) 376-6326
www.nfanjax.org

SENIOR LIVING

With a median age of 33, Jacksonville doesn't have a huge senior citizen population like some South Florida cities do. Still, many people are now discovering what navy folks learned a long time ago: Jacksonville is a great place to retire. The weather is warm, outdoor recreation is plentiful, housing is affordable, and the number of resources and opportunities for seniors grows every day. In short, Jacksonville helps seniors maintain active, independent lifestyles for as long as they are physically able.

One of the best things about retiring here is that the city of Jacksonville really appreciates its seniors, especially for their volunteer contributions. The Adult Services Division of the City of Jacksonville offers numerous programs for seniors of all income levels. And with your city on your side, the whole process of aging can be so much easier and successful.

In the late 1980s Jacksonville established a Special Events Advisory Council for Senior Citizens. The group, composed partly of people over age 60, is a think tank of sorts, charged with coming up with ideas for programs and events that seniors would like to attend. Since some of the members are themselves senior citizens, they have a pretty good idea of what they'd like to see happen here. Many of the group's ideas have been put into action, such as the Jacksonville Senior Games, the Mayor's Walk for Senior Wellness, the Mayor's Fish-a-Thon, and a Senior Expo.

After talking with a number of senior citizens, we came up with a top-10 Insiders' list of the best reasons for seniors to live in the River City. By no means is this list exhaustive, but in our opinion it contains some of the best things about retiring here.

In the end, we think you'll agree that Jacksonville's quality of life doesn't stop at age 65. Growing old is never easy, but living in Jacksonville makes those elder years a little less difficult.

TOP 10 REASONS FOR SENIORS TO LIVE IN JACKSONVILLE

1. **Senior discounts.** From a round of golf to a round of food, Jacksonville seniors love their discounts. We've got a good line up on some places to go to save money.

2. **Learning never ends.** Jacksonville University is a good place to go for senior educational programs. So are area museums, hospitals, and libraries.

3. **City programs.** City Hall takes care of Jacksonville's seniors with a host of special programs and events, from the mayor's annual Christmas party to an annual luncheon honoring senior volunteers.

4. **Senior centers.** The City of Jacksonville operates 22 senior centers throughout the city where seniors can get lots of social interaction as well as a nutritious, hot midday meal for just pennies. A city van will pick you up and take you to the center for just $1.00. And while you're there, enjoy programs galore to keep you busy.

5. **Volunteer opportunities.** Jacksonville needs its senior volunteers! City Hall will match volunteers over age 55 with just the right volunteer opportunity.

6. **Travel and wellness clubs.** Local hospitals and tour companies host clubs for seniors that take regular bus trips to nearby points of interest.

7. **Health care.** From physicians who make house calls to the Mayo Clinic, Jacksonville offers a full range of health care options for seniors.

8. **Retirement communities.** Jacksonville's retirement communities offer a full range of services for the elderly, from independent living to assisted living to skilled nursing. We've picked our top three Insiders' favorites to tell you about.

9. Senior publications. The River City offers a variety of free publications for seniors that are chock-full of information and articles.

10. The beach. No top-10 list of anything in Jacksonville is complete without a listing for the beach, our greatest natural resource. Children of all ages, from 1 to 100, enjoy keeping active with walks on the beach.

Senior Discounts

Alhambra Dinner Theatre
12000 Beach Boulevard
(904) 641-1212
www.alhambradinnertheatre.com
Seniors age 60 and over get a 10 percent discount off the price of their ticket at this popular dinner theater. The discount is offered every night of the week except Friday and Saturday. Be sure and make reservations for the Alhambra; it's frequently sold out.

Cummer Museum of Art and Gardens
829 Riverside Avenue
(904) 356-6857
www.cummer.org
Every Tuesday from 4:00 to 9:00 P.M., the Cummer offers free admission. The Cummer hosts special art exhibitions, such as Toulouse Lautrec: Artist of Monmartre, featuring lectures for seniors. These seated gallery talks are popular with many seniors, who can't stand for long periods of time anymore. They're usually free with the price of admission and include plenty

The State of Florida is looking for volunteers of all ages to become "Ambassadors for Aging." To learn more about this grassroots program that helps increase awareness of the contributions of elder Floridians, contact the Department of Elder Affairs in Tallahassee at (850) 414-2004.

of information about the current special exhibition as well as free refreshments. Call the Cummer for a calendar of events, and while you're at it, ask about becoming a volunteer docent at the museum.

Jacksonville Zoo and Gardens
8605 Zoo Parkway
(904) 757-4462
www.jaxzoo.org
Seniors age 65 and older save 10 percent on all zoo memberships. Daily admission prices are also discounted for seniors to $6.50, and the zoo offers behind-the-scene tours for seniors. Just make your reservations ahead of time. There are a number of volunteer possibilities for seniors here as well, from docents to assistant animal keepers. Volunteers are also needed for special events, community outreach, and more. Call (904) 757-4463, ext. 176, for information on volunteering.

Piccadilly Cafeteria
200 Monument Road
(904) 725-5777
www.piccadilly.com
There are four Piccadilly Cafeterias in Jacksonville, and they are all very popular. The one listed above is near the Regency Mall and is one of the busiest. It's located about 20 minutes from the beach and about 20 minutes from downtown. All Piccadilly Cafeterias offer a 10 percent discount off the total price of a meal for seniors Monday through Wednesday from 2:00 to 5:00 P.M. There is also a Piccadilly Cafeteria at the Avenues Shopping Mall.

Sundays at Jacksonville University
2800 University Boulevard North
(904) 256-8000
Students from the College of Fine Arts at Jacksonville University perform Sunday afternoons during the school year, usually in the school's intimate Terry Concert Hall. Ticket prices are low, and the quality of performances is high at these Sunday events, which are popular with seniors. Single tickets are about $7.00, and there are discounts for groups. Seniors say that

these concerts make them feel young again as they relive their college days with a return to campus life.

Theatre Jacksonville
2032 San Marco Boulevard
(904) 396-4425
www.theatrejax.com
Jacksonville's official theater has been serving up quality community theater productions since 1919. The shows are chosen carefully and are usually a popular mix of musicals and dramas. Seniors enjoy a $5.00 discount off ticket prices for Thursday evening and Sunday matinee performances.

Windsor Parke Golf Club
13823 Sutton Park Drive North
(904) 223-4653
www.windsorparke.com
Challenging: That's the name of the game at Windsor Parke Golf Club, which is conveniently located on Jacksonville's Southside between downtown and the Beaches. Seniors play a round of golf for $30, which is about half what it costs everyone else to play. The Seniors Bonus program is only available Monday through Thursday most of the year. From February to May the senior discount is available on Tuesday only. Call ahead and reserve a tee time; Windsor Parke, which was designed by Arthur Hills, is a popular place to golf.

Late-Learning Programs

Elderhostel
(877) 426-8056 (toll free)
www.elderhostel.org
From Amelia Island to St. Augustine, Northeast Florida offers a variety of Elderhostel opportunities for seniors. Jacksonville University is often the locale for an Elderhostel program; so are area hotels and resorts. Headquartered in Boston, Elderhostel offers educational and travel experiences for seniors worldwide. To request a catalog of upcoming courses,

The Temporary Loan Closet at the Independent Living Resource Center lends medical equipment to those who qualify. Call (904) 399-5668.

call the number above or log on to get the same information. Your local Duval County Public Library carries current Elderhostel catalogs; ask for them at the information desk.

College of Lifelong Learning
Jacksonville University
(904) 256-8000
www.ju.edu
There really is something for everyone at Jacksonville University's College of Lifelong Learning, which offers both credit and non-credit courses. The credit programs can lead to a college degree and are offered through the Adult Degree Program. The noncredit classes are offered by the Continuing Education Department and include everything from foreign languages to pottery to golf to computers. Seniors love it!

Community Education Programs
Duval County Schools
(904) 390-2000
Select Duval County schools have been designated "community schools" in Jacksonville, which means they offer continuing education classes in the evening. Seniors over age 60 receive a $5.00 discount off the registration price. Courses vary from school to school, but this is a good opportunity to study a foreign language or learn about computers. The courses fill up quickly, so register early at the community school nearest you. (Duval County schools are listed in the white pages under the heading "Schools.")

You can ride city buses for free if you're 60 or older by showing a Transit Identification Card. To get this picture ID, call (904) 630-0995.

City Programs

Community and Senior Center Services Program
1805 Flag Street
(904) 630-0928
www.coj.net/comm/asdcentr.htm

The City of Jacksonville operates 22 well-loved and well-used senior centers all over town. These are places seniors can come during the day to meet other retirees, play cards and bingo, exercise, eat a hot meal, or take a computer class. Every center offers additional classes like painting, knitting, line dancing—you name it. Many of the centers hold monthly—in some cases weekly—dances for seniors. The list of activities, which also includes day trips, is long; call the senior center nearest you and ask for a calendar of events. Or access a calendar at the Web site listed above. By the way, seniors often go home with free delicacies from local grocery store bakeries. The bakeries jettison the baked goods that haven't been sold after a certain date and hence aren't completely fresh. Instead of throwing it all away, many stores contribute it to the local senior centers, which we've listed below.

Arlington Senior Center
1078 Rogero Road
(904) 723-6142

Beaches Senior Center
281 19th Avenue South
(904) 241-3477

C. T. Brown Community Center
4415 Moncrief Road
(904) 764-8752

C. T. Joseph Community Center
6943 Buffalo Avenue
(904) 765-7522

The State of Florida operates a 24-hour crisis abuse hotline for the elderly. To report abuse call (800) 962-2873.

L. D. Clemons Community Center
55 Jackson Avenue
(904) 693-4918

Louis Dinah Senior Center
1805 Flag Street
(904) 630-0728

Hammond Community Center
3312 West 12th Street
(904) 786-8554

J. S. Johnson Community Center
1112 Jackson Street
(904) 630-0949

Lane Wiley Senior Center
6710 Wiley Road
(904) 783-6589

Lincoln Villa Community Center
7866 New Kings Road
(904) 765-2654

Longbranch Senior Center
4110 Franklin Street
(904) 630-0893

Mallison Community Center
441 Day Avenue
(904) 387-3682

Mandarin Senior Center
3848 Hartley Road
(904) 262-7309

Mary L. Singleton Senior Center
150 East First Street
(904) 630-0995

Maxville Community Center
10865 Pennsylvania Avenue
(904) 289-7157

Moncrief Community Center
5713 Teeler Avenue
(904) 764-0330

Mt. Carmel Terrace (kosher)
5846 Mt. Carmel Terrace
(904) 737-9075

Oceanway Community Center
12215 Sago Avenue West
(904) 751-2375

Riverview Community Center
9620 Water Street
(904) 765-7511

Twin Towers
619 West 44th Street
(904) 924-5343

Westside Senior Center
1083 Line Street
(904) 630-0724

Woodland Acres Senior Center
8200 Kona Avenue
(904) 725-0624

Foster Grandparent Program
150 East First Street
(904) 630-5450
www.coj.net/comm/asdfoster.htm
This is one of the city's best volunteer programs. Seniors are assigned to programs like Head Start or the Police Athletic League, where they mentor and tutor at-risk children and children with special needs. Seniors are asked to spend up to 20 hours a week working with children. In return, seniors get a small tax-free stipend for their work, transportation reimbursement, special training, a lunch allowance, a physical exam, and the knowledge that they can change the life of a young person.

Independent Living Program
1093 West Sixth Street
(904) 630-0966
www.coj.net
The city's Independent Living Program provides respite care for caregivers, giving them a chance to get out of the house for a break while a volunteer takes care of their homebound loved one. It's also a good place to go if an elderly person needs help finding medical care, food stamps, or transportation. This program serves low-income residents, and its goal is to keep these residents living independently for as long as possible. If you need assistance cleaning your house or doing your grocery shopping (or you know someone who does), call the Independent Living Program. Caseworkers will assess your situation and send in the volunteers to help if you qualify.

Mayor's Special Events for Senior Citizens
117 West Duval Street
(904) 630-3450
www.coj.net
The City of Jacksonville honors its seniors with a variety of programs and activities promoting recreation and outreach. The mayor's office hosts more than a half dozen of these events, which are open to the public and extremely popular. There's a country store in the fall; safety and security seminars every spring and summer presented by the Jacksonville sheriff's office; and Summertime Fun in the Sun day trips to places like Savannah and Silver Springs. Senior Games are held every October, and a Senior Expo is held every spring. The city also provides transportation to all these events from senior centers and senior residences all over Jacksonville.

Retired and Senior Volunteer Programs (RSVP)
150 East First Street
(904) 630-0998
www.coj.net/comm/asd/rsvp.htm
Do you have two hours a week to donate to the Jacksonville Public Libraries or five hours a week to cook at the local homeless shelter? Whatever your available time and whatever your interest, RSVP will help you find the volunteer opportunity that's right for you. Some of the work can even be done in your home!

Volunteering is a great way to make a difference in the community and enrich your own life at the same time. RSVP volunteers do not need to be retirees; they just need to be age 55 or older.

Travel and Wellness Clubs

Club 55+
St. Vincent's Medical Center
(904) 308-7357
www.jaxhealth.com/Club55
Club 55+ is a wellness and travel club that's offered by St. Vincent's Medical Center. Members pay a one-time fee of $30 per person or $40 per couple to join. Membership entitles you to a free meal (lunch or dinner) for a guest if you are staying in the hospital. It also provides pharmacy discounts at the hospital as well as discounts at the gift shop there. Members can get help filling out their insurance forms or getting papers notarized for free. They also receive a newsletter in the mail. Best of all, the club organizes day trips by bus to places like Savannah, Mt. Dora, and St. Simons. Club 55+ members don't meet every month but often get to know one another on these trips.

> **i** *Need transportation to one of the city's senior centers? Call (904) 630-0801 to arrange a pickup.*

Destinations Unlimited Tours
9951 Atlantic Boulevard
(904) 722-8100
www.destinationsunlimitedtours.com
Destinations is a tour bus company that's hit on a great marketing tool: It runs Senior Travel Clubs all over town. Seniors attend a monthly meeting and hear talks about upcoming points of call. Destinations runs trips up and down the Eastern Seaboard, as well as right here in Florida. Even if they don't take the bus trip, seniors enjoy getting out for the meeting and hearing about the trips. The company operates a 24-hour travel hotline

(904-399-2770), which lists a long calendar of upcoming trips as well as the latest on the travel club meetings.

Senior Friends
Memorial Hospital Jacksonville
(904) 391-1320
Senior Friends is a wellness and travel club for members age 50 and over. This is an active group of about 1,000 members who pay $15 per person or $25 per couple annually. That fee entitles members to a quarterly newsletter that's packed with opportunities. Senior Friends sponsors day trips to unusual locales, such as Cirque du Soleil in Orlando. Members attend health fairs, enjoy free health screenings, and participate in monthly potluck luncheons at the hospital with speakers, such as an elder-law attorney. They take monthly trips to local restaurants called Chat & Chews, which are great opportunities to get to know one another. Senior Friends also receive discounts at Memorial Hospital's outpatient pharmacy. Some events are weekly, such as card games and volunteer opportunities.

Memorial is located on the Southside; it also operates a chapter of Senior Friends for Beaches residents. This chapter is located at San Pablo and Beach Boulevard at the Memorial Health Care Center. For information about events at the Senior Friends Beaches chapter, call (904) 858-7509.

Senior Publications

Senior Services Directory
7563 Philips Highway, Building 100
Suite 110
(904) 296-1304
www.heritagepublishinginc.com
The City of Jacksonville and a local company publish a free directory every year that's chock-full of phone numbers and

information for seniors. Pick one up at one of the city's 22 senior centers, or contact the publisher for your free copy.

Seniors Housing Guide
9838 Old Baymeadows Road
(904) 997-0899
www.SeniorHousingGuide.com
This little glossy, about the size of a *Reader's Digest,* is worth its weight in gold. It's an advertising vehicle for virtually every senior housing community in Jacksonville, from independent living to nursing care facilities. Best of all, it's free; you can pick one up at your local library.

Retirement Communities

Fleet Landing
One Fleet Landing Boulevard
Atlantic Beach
(800) 872-8761
www.fleetlanding.com
Located in popular Atlantic Beach, Fleet Landing is just a walk away from Jacksonville's wide sandy beaches and the Atlantic Ocean. In fact, it's not uncommon to see residents enjoying a brisk walk to the beach through a lovely tree-lined Atlantic Beach neighborhood. Fleet Landing started as a continuing care community for navy retirees but has since expanded to include everyone. It's located next door to Naval Station Mayport, with its Post Exchange, commissary, and medical facilities.

The quiet, gated community offers 320 living units, including independent cottages, patio homes, and apartments. Residents gather for meals and socials at the "O" Club, as in Officers' Club. Health care services are available at the on-site health center, and there's a fully equipped physical therapy department on campus. If you need some help with day-to-day liv-

The City of Jacksonville hosts the Senior Games every year to encourage and celebrate fitness in anyone over age 50. Call (904) 630-7392 to find out how you can volunteer or, better yet, participate!

ing, Fleet Landing offers an assisted-living residence called Leeward Manor. There's also a skilled nursing wing and a memory-impaired unit for Alzheimer's patients.

NBA Cypress Village
4600 Middleton Park Circle East
(904) 223-4663
www.cypressvillage.com
Cypress Village's 120-acre campus is centrally located on Jacksonville's Southside, right next door to the Mayo Clinic Jacksonville. A shuttle bus regularly takes Cypress Village residents to the clinic, so they never have to worry about how they'll get to their doctors' appointments. Cypress Village residents pride themselves on their active lifestyles, whether it's fishing in a well-stocked campus lake or building a model train set with a hobby group. An 18-hole golf course, Windsor Parke, borders the facility and is a favorite golfing locale for residents who enjoy Windsor Parke's senior discount. Residents can live in a house, which they own, or a high-rise apartment. Cypress Village also offers assisted living or skilled nursing care for residents who need help recovering from an illness or operation before returning to their homes. Cypress Village has partnered with the Mayo Clinic to provide residents with a state-of-the-art Alzheimer's facility, which has a research association with Mayo Jacksonville so that patients benefit from the latest in medical care.

Westminster Woods on Julington Creek
25 State Road 13
(904) 287-7300
www.westminsterretirement.com

King of the Colada

Ninety-year-old Ricardo Gracia loves to recall the past—particularly 1954, the year he invented the piña colada.

Wait a minute, that drink had an inventor? Wasn't there always a piña colada? Besides, how do you know Gracia, who still works as a sommelier at Cafe on the Green at the Sawgrass Marriott Resort, really came up with the idea? Well, here's his story. You decide.

First, some background. In 1950 Elizabeth Taylor married playboy Nicky Hilton, heir to the Hilton Hotel chain, touching off a Hilton/Hollywood heyday that would last for years. Although Taylor and Hilton divorced within months of their marriage, Hilton International Hotels became a popular playground for Hollywood stars.

Enter Ricardo Gracia, a dapper 36-year-old bar manager at the first Hilton International Hotel, the Castellana, in Madrid. He loved his job because, after all, tending bar was in his blood. He'd been born above his grandfather's bar and restaurant in Barcelona in 1914, where he used to play among the bottles, mixing concoctions, when he was just a toddler.

In 1954 the Castellana was "party central," and each guest, upon arriving at the hotel, was greeted with a complimentary Coco Loco—a rum drink mixed with coconut milk and cream of coconut and served in half a coconut. An integral part of these drinks were the coconut cutters, who'd scramble up tall coconut trees each day to cut down the necessary number of coconuts needed for arriving guests, then slice open the hard-shelled seed.

One day management fired the coconut cutters after a labor dispute, and bar manager Ricardo Gracia found himself with a huge problem: how to make and serve the hundreds of Coco Loco welcome drinks the hotel had become famous for without the coconuts. Not only did he need the coconut milk, but a simple glass seemed so unworthy of the Hilton panache. Gracia turned to the pineapple. He told his team of bartenders to substitute pineapple juice for the coconut milk and serve the drink in half a hollowed-out pineapple. That worked for a while, until Gracia and his bartenders began experimenting with all the leftover fruit. Within weeks Gracia was blending a new concoction of crushed pineapple, pineapple juice, cream of coconut, and rum. He threw in some crushed ice because another bar-

---

Affiliated with the Presbyterian Church, this 75-acre, tree-filled campus is located on the banks of Julington Creek. Westminster Woods was the first continuing-care retirement community in Jacksonville when it opened over 40 years ago, and it's still going strong. This facility offers 350 living units ranging from villa homes and garden apartments to assisted living, skilled nursing, and Alzheimer's care. There's also a health care and physical therapy facility located right on campus.

tender, Monchito, was using it with great success in a drink of his own that he called a pineapple freeze.

Such was the piña colada's humble beginnings, a start so ho-hum it's hard not to believe Gracia's story is true. There was no copyright, no money, and no fanfare. The piña colada just sort of evolved at the hands of Ricardo Gracia and his team of bartenders. In short order, though, the drink took off, and Gracia brought in 26 blenders so that his bartenders could keep up with demand—up to 1,000 piña coladas a day. Somewhere along the line, Gracia decided that his new drink needed a name. Piña, which means "pineapple" in Spanish, seemed logical; someone suggested colada, which means "strained" in Spanish, and thus the drink was christened.

Gracia worked for Hilton Hotels for 36 years, at more than half a dozen properties worldwide. Everywhere he worked, he introduced the piña colada, and it was always a sensation. He served it to movie stars, millionaires, famous singers, and renowned artists. He often had his picture taken with the luminaries, and he still carries those photographs with him today in a well-worn scrapbook. There's Ricardo with Ava Gardner, Errol Flynn, Vic Damon. And wait, look at that picture of Marilyn Monroe wrapped in a black lace teddy. "I served her a piña colada in San Juan," said Gracia. "Joe DiMaggio joined her down there. I asked him for a photograph of Marilyn, and he gave me this." That photo looks like it could fetch some money on eBay.

Looking back, Gracia says he's made millions of piña coladas, not millions of dollars from inventing the drink. He'll still mix one for you at Cafe on the Green. It comes in a tall glass with a piece of fresh pineapple, a strawberry, a straw, and a little paper umbrella. Not exactly like the old days, but the drink holds its own. Take one sip and you know that a master prepared it: The texture is perfect, creamy not frozen, with no big chunks of ice or pineapple.

Gracia tried retirement for three months after he and his wife moved to St. Augustine in 1987, but he longed to be serving drinks again and took a job at the Sawgrass Marriott just as it was opening. He's been with them ever since as a sommelier, which is interesting because this former bon vivant may have invented the piña colada, but he no longer drinks them. These days his favorite drink is a quiet glass of Bordeaux. It's more suited, he says, to his memories.

The dining room sits on Julington Creek, and residents enjoy sitting near the picture windows in this lovely room and watching the boats go by. They also like to watch their neighbors fish or shrimp from the dock. (One resident even docks his boat out back!) Westminster Woods likes to say that it's the most affordable continuing-care retirement community in Jacksonville. It's certainly one of the prettiest.

JOB MARKET 💼

The St. Johns River, the beaches, the golf courses, the neighborhoods, the restaurants, the entertainment—all make Jacksonville a great place to live and visit. But that's not all the city has to offer. In recent years Jacksonville has become a job-creating machine. During most of the 1990s, the region averaged about 12,000 new jobs each year, which helped push the total population of the greater Jacksonville area over the one million mark in 1999.

Local economists say the strong job growth likely will continue for the foreseeable future as more companies relocate to the area to take advantage of Jacksonville's relatively low cost of doing business. An added bonus: Florida has no state income tax.

Historically, Jacksonville's economy has been anchored by the military, transportation, and financial services (banking and insurance). The U.S. Navy has two active bases in Jacksonville: Naval Station Mayport is the homeport for the aircraft carrier USS *John F. Kennedy*. Naval Air Station Jacksonville is home to the Naval Air Depot, or NADEP, an aircraft maintenance facility. With more than 3,800 civilian workers, NADEP is one of the region's largest industrial employers.

As a gateway to Florida, Jacksonville has long had vibrant transportation and distribution industries. CSX Railroad is based in Jacksonville. Landstar Systems, a progressive trucking company that utilizes technology to coordinate shipments, moved its corporate headquarters from Connecticut to Jacksonville and employs 200.

The Port of Jacksonville, which encompasses three deepwater terminals, produces 45,081 direct and indirect jobs in Northeast Florida and $1.3 billion annually in economic output.

While banking and insurance aren't as prominent as they once were in Jacksonville, they still account for some of the city's top employers, including Blue Cross and Blue Shield of Florida (9,500 employees) and the Florida headquarters of Bank of America (5,500 employees).

Jacksonville's economic development officials aren't resting on their laurels, however; the city continues to be aggressive in its efforts to woo new businesses and industry. The Economic and Development Commission is generous (some would say too generous) when it comes to offering incentives to attract new companies. An incentive package could include tax breaks, grants, infrastructure, job training, land, cash, and other perks. When you couple incentives like these with the city's strong quality of life—affordable housing, a dependable military economy, and good weather—many companies find Jacksonville hard to resist.

More recently, large customer-service call centers have sprouted up throughout the area, employing thousands of workers. America Online employs 1,600 at its new call center facility on the Southside near the University of North Florida. BellSouth, the Atlanta-based telecommunications company, opened a technical service center in Orange Park and hired 1,000 workers.

It's no wonder *Expansion Management* magazine ranked Jacksonville as the No. 1 "Hottest City" in America for business relocation in its January 2002 issue. The city has been ranked among the top 10 for four consecutive years and is the only U.S. city to be ranked No. 1 twice.

While wages range across the board—from several million for top CEOs to the minimum wage of $5.15—the typical job in Jacksonville averages about $33,000 a year. That job might be found in financial services, manufacturing, or health services, including insurance. Jacksonville also has a large business services market, which includes call centers, computer programming, data processing, and accounting. Retail work and construction jobs remain strong as do child care and teaching positions in both public and private schools.

MAJOR JACKSONVILLE COMPANIES

Following is a list of some of the city's bigger companies with large operations in Jacksonville.

Alltel Corp.
www.alltel.com
Alltel Corp., a Little Rock, Arkansas–based telecommunications and information processing company, entered Jacksonville in the early 1990s with the acquisition of Computer Power, a major mortgage processing company. Alltel is the corporate sponsor of Alltel Stadium, where the Jacksonville Jaguars play.

Anheuser-Busch Companies
www.anheuser-busch.com
The big beer maker has one of its two Florida breweries in Jacksonville. It's located on the Northside. Beer made at the Jacksonville facility is distributed throughout the southeast.

AOL Time Warner
www.aol.com
Among other things, a division of AOL Time Warner provides computer online services and has a large customer service center in Jacksonville near the University of North Florida.

Bank of America Corp.
www.bankamerica.com
The mega bank mergers over the past decade resulted in the disappearance of Barnett Banks, a century-old name in Jacksonville and once the largest bank in Florida. Barnett merged with NationsBank of Charlotte, North Carolina, which then merged with San Francisco–based Bank of America. Bank of America's Florida operations are based in Jacksonville, where the company employs 5,500 persons. Bank of America has a campus near the Avenues Shopping Mall and even operates its own small Duval County school for children of employees.

Jacksonville now has three Fortune 500 companies headquartered here: CSX Corp., Fidelity National Financial Inc., and Winn-Dixie.

BellSouth Corp.
www.bellsouth.com
This Atlanta-based telecommunications company, already a major employer in the Jacksonville area, boosted its presence with the opening of a 1,000-worker technical service center in Orange Park.

Blue Cross and Blue Shield of Florida
www.bcbsfl.com
Blue Cross continues to be the largest writer of health insurance in Florida. In Jacksonville, where it is based, the insurer has offices next to downtown and in a sprawling suburban campus on the city's Southside. Blue Cross employs 9,600 workers in Jacksonville.

Convergys Corp.
www.convergys.com
Convergys, a customer care and billing company, operates a large telemarketing operation in Jacksonville.

CSX Corp.
www.csx.com
Jacksonville is the major center of operations for CSX Railroad. All train movements are tracked and monitored at a state-of-the-art control center in Jacksonville. CSX Corp. moved its corporate headquarters from Richmond to Jacksonville in 2003.

The Jacksonville Chamber of Commerce has relocation packets for those planning to move to the area. To get a copy, call the chamber at (904) 366-6600 or visit the chamber's Web site at www.myjaxchamber.com.

Fidelity National Financial Inc.
www.fnf.com

Fidelity National Financial is the nation's largest title insurance company with some 50 percent of the market and annual sales of $7.7 billion. After its purchase of Alltel's Information Services division, Fidelity relocated its corporate headquarters from Santa Barbara, California, to Jacksonville in 2003. It employs about 1,500 workers in Jacksonville, mostly data processors.

Johnson & Johnson
www.jnj.com

The company that's often rated the best employer in America makes its Vistakon contact lenses here in the River City.

MPS Group
www.mpsgroup.com

MPS is an information services and professional staffing company for the accounting, legal, technology, and health care industries.

Northrop Grumman Corp.
www.northgrum.com

The giant aerospace company operates aircraft maintenance facilities in St. Augustine and at Cecil Field, the recently converted former naval air station.

Looking for a job in Jacksonville? Robert H. Johnson has written a book called How to Find a Job in Jacksonville. *Updated twice a year, this job-hunting manual contains current information on job openings and career possibilities in Jax. It's available on Amazon.com.*

ParkerVision Inc.
www.parkervision.com

ParkerVision, a homegrown technology company, has developed a new technology, billed as a major advancement for sending and receiving the radio signals used in everyday appliances such as TV remote controls and automatic garage door openers.

PSS World Medical Inc.
www.pssd.com

PSS was a local success story. A scrappy entrepreneur founded the medical supply company in the late 1980s and built it into a billion-dollar enterprise. But the torrid growth rate took its toll, and the company ran into financial problems.

The St. Joe Co.
www.joe.com

Among Jacksonville companies, the St. Joe Co. has one of the most storied pasts. St. Joe is the descendant of a collection of companies owned by Alfred I. duPont, heir to the Delaware dynasty. DuPont moved to Jacksonville at the turn of the 20th century. He (and later his brother-in-law, Ed Ball) began buying up banks, railroads, paper mills (in Port St. Joe, Florida, hence the name), and more than one million acres of land. Today St. Joe's new management, led by former Disney executive Peter Rummell, has shed the old-line industrial holdings and is focusing exclusively on real estate development. In particular, the company is building upscale residential communities along the Gulf of Mexico in Florida's Panhandle, where St. Joe owns most of its land.

Stein Mart Inc.
www.steinmart.com

Jay Stein grew up in Mississippi and came to Jacksonville in the 1960s to attend the Bolles School. After college he entered the family retail business, founded by his grandfather. As Stein expanded the stores, he decided to relocate the headquarters to Jacksonville. Today Stein Mart sells designer clothes at discount prices and has more than $1.4 billion in sales and 261 store locations throughout the United States.

Winn-Dixie Stores
www.winn-dixie.com

Jacksonville-based Winn-Dixie is one of the largest supermarket chains in the United States and one of the city's biggest private-sector employers with a workforce of 13,000. Winn-Dixie was founded in the 1920s by four Davis brothers. The Davis family, which still owns more than half the shares of the publicly traded company, is one of Jacksonville's biggest charitable givers. The supermarket chain has stumbled in recent years as aggressive competitors have moved into its markets, but new management has been busy trying to turn things around.

JOB-RELATED RESOURCES

Jacksonville-area chambers of commerce are quite active and helpful to those looking to relocate or start up a new business. Here's a list of possible resources to help you in your search.

Amelia Island/Fernandina Beach Chamber of Commerce
(800) 226-3542

This business group supports the fast-growing Amelia Island and Fernandina Beach area of Nassau County.

Clay County–Orange Park Chamber of Commerce
(904) 264-2651

This business group supports Clay County and Orange Park, Jacksonville's neighbors to the southwest.

Want to improve your computer skills? Check out the classes at Florida Community College of Jacksonville's Advanced Technology Center (ATC). Call (904) 633–8100 for information.

Florida Times-Union
(904) 359-4111

The newspaper runs classified employment ads. The Business News section covers the comings and goings of local companies.

Jacksonville Better Business Bureau
(904) 721-2339

The BBB can provide information on local companies, such as whether they've had consumer complaints or regulatory action taken against them.

Jacksonville Business Journal
(904) 396-3502

This journal provides good weekly coverage of Jacksonville's business and industry.

Jacksonville Chamber of Commerce
(904) 366-6600
(904) 366-6620 (relocation info)

The dominant business group in Northeast Florida, the chamber maintains loads of resource materials and economic data.

Other Area Chambers of Commerce

Jacksonville Beaches Chamber of Commerce
(904) 249-3868

Ponte Vedra Beach Chamber of Commerce
(904) 285-0666

St. Augustine Chamber of Commerce
(904) 829-5681

Jacksonville's Economic Outlook

To get a good fix on the strengths of Jacksonville's economy and where it might be heading in the coming years, *Insiders' Guide* posed some questions to John Godfrey, one of the region's top economists. Godfrey, former chief economist with Barnett Banks (now part of Bank of America), is the principal economist with Florida Economic Associates in Jacksonville.

Q: How would you describe Jacksonville's economy? What is its backbone?

A: Jacksonville's economy is growing more rapidly and is also more stable than the nation as a whole. We are adding more jobs at a more rapid pace; we also seem to weather economic downturns much better than the rest of the nation does. This should not be a surprise, given the backbone of the region's economy. We have a large defense sector in Naval Air Station Jacksonville and Naval Station Mayport, and we are an attractive place for corporations to expand and relocate, particularly those involving back-office operations. This is a natural outgrowth of Jacksonville's historically large banking and insurance operations. We are also a significant transportation hub.

We have the port, we have rail transportation, and we have significant over-the-road and airline facilities. This shows up not only directly in the transportation services but also in the willingness of companies to set up distribution centers in Jacksonville, from Publix Super Markets warehouses to Baccardi Rum, Budweiser, and Toyota.

Q: Is Jacksonville overly dependent on any one industry or sector?

A: No. Jacksonville has a good balance, which provides overall stability.

Q: What kind of economic growth has Jacksonville experienced through the 1990s and into the new millenium?

A: Defense has probably been one sector that has not grown; it's solid, but it hasn't grown. Everything else has grown steadily.

Q: If you had to compare Jacksonville's economy with another city or cities in the United States, which ones would they be?

A: One that certainly comes to mind would be a blend of Atlanta and Charlotte—Atlanta with its transportation and distribution sectors and Charlotte with its financial services. Neither of them has a port, however, which makes Jacksonville unique. This can be a disadvantage when it comes to growth, however, because it's very tough to expand our port to the east. Atlanta can expand—has expanded—to the north, south, east, and west of its railroad and trucking hubs. An East Coast seaport city like Jacksonville suffers a disadvantage in that it can't expand east, but it can sure put goods on boats and send them regularly to Puerto Rico.

Q: **In terms of employment, what sort of annual growth rates do you expect to see through 2005 and 2010?**

A: I would expect to see Jacksonville generating between 3 and 4 percent job growth per year, and that's an average for good times and bad times.

Q: **If Jacksonville's economy has an Achilles' heel, what would it be?**

A: The most vulnerable area in our economy is the defense sector. NADEP, at NAS Jacksonville, where military aircraft from all over the world are repaired, is the largest industrial employer in the city. That's the kind of thing that some base closings could impact. We could also be vulnerable if we don't get a new aircraft carrier at Naval Station Mayport if the USS *John*

F. Kennedy is reassigned to Japan. We could also be vulnerable at Kings Bay (Georgia) Nuclear Submarine Base if the government decides to phase out some of its nuclear subs and Trident missiles. Part of what makes us vulnerable is that these are not private corporate decisions that could be changed by offering state and local incentives. It's kind of tough to provide such incentives to the military.

Q: **What's the best-kept secret about Jacksonville's economy?**

A: I've spent much of my professional career extolling the virtues of the Northeast Florida economy, so I've tried to make sure there weren't any secrets.

Q: **Is the Jacksonville Metro area a good place to start a business?**

A: It's a superb place to start a business for a number of reasons: the cost of doing business here is less than in most places, the cost of rental space is less, and the cost of building something new is less. There's still adequate space around the city to accommodate a wide variety of businesses. Comparable housing prices are a lot less here than in some other parts of the country. Plus, we have a good lifestyle here.

WORSHIP

Churches are everywhere in Jacksonville. So are synagogues, temples, and mosques. Whatever your religious or spiritual needs, chances are you'll find the right house of worship in Jacksonville. There's even plenty of variety within denominations.

Religion and prayer are present in many aspects of daily life in Jacksonville. For example, Insiders know not to plan big meetings on Wednesday night because that's when many Baptists—the predominate denomination in Jacksonville—attend services. Many public meetings and major events, such as the inaugural Jacksonville Jaguars game, begin with a prayer from a member of the local clergy.

Indeed, the region has a rich religious history. The French Huguenots, whose Protestant beliefs didn't sit well with Catholic Europe, fled for the New World in 1562. They settled a small community on the St. Johns River in what is now Jacksonville. Spanish explorers celebrated the first mass in the New World in what is now St. Augustine.

Many of Jacksonville's Protestant churches trace their origins back to the 1800s. Black churches, both downtown and on the Northside, are centers for community life and often the places where change begins in Jacksonville's black community. Bethel Baptist Institu-

tional, established in 1838, is one of the oldest churches in the city. (See the African-American Tourism chapter for more on its history.)

Following is a look at some of Jacksonville's religious and spiritual offerings.

BAHA'I FAITH

The local Baha'i Faith community consists of about 150 people throughout Duval County. Baha'is, who follow the teachings of the religion's founder, Baha'u'llah, and believe that humanity is one single race, strive for the unification of one global society. They promote the abandonment of prejudice, equality of men and women, elimination of extreme wealth and poverty, and universal education. In keeping with followers of the faith around the world, Jacksonville Baha'is hold feasts every 19 days, which is the length of the Baha'i "month."

Baha'i houses of worship are open to the public. Devotional programs are simple, consisting of prayers, meditations, and the reading of selections from the sacred scriptures of the Baha'i Faith and other world religions. The Jacksonville Baha'i center is located on the city's Southside at 2140 South St. Johns Bluff Road (904–646–9813). Worship services are held Sunday at 10:00 A.M.

BAPTIST

There are numerous Baptist churches in Jacksonville—conservative, liberal, predominately white, and predominately African-American. The Jacksonville Baptist Association (904–727–6800) is a good resource of Baptist churches. The association can help you find the church that best fits your spiritual needs.

Every spring around Easter, the City of Jacksonville sponsors a Blessing of the Fleet. Anyone with a boat can motor over to Metro Park or the Landing (locations vary from year to year) for a communal blessing. Go to www.coj.net for the exact date and time.

Here are two of Jacksonville's most prominent Baptist churches: The first, a historic African-American church, is the oldest; the second is the largest.

Bethel Baptist Institutional Church
215 Bethel Baptist Street
(904) 354-1464

Bethel Baptist, the oldest church in Jacksonville, was organized in 1838 for the religious activities of Jacksonville's black community. During the Civil War it also served as a hospital but was destroyed during Jacksonville's Great Fire of 1901. The church building is on the National Register of Historic Sites.

Bethel Baptist is led by father-son pastors Rudolph McKissick Sr. and Rudolph McKissick Jr., two of the most influential members of the city's black community.

First Baptist Church of Jacksonville
124 West Ashley Street
(904) 356-6077
www.fbcjax.com

The First Baptist Church of Jacksonville has had a long and influential presence in downtown Jacksonville. Established in 1838 as the third church in the city, First Baptist's first church was destroyed by the Great Fire of 1901.

A new house of worship—Hobson Auditorium—was built in 1903. It served as the primary worship center until 1976, when the Ruth Lindsay Auditorium was built. A larger auditorium was constructed in 1993 and seats 9,200.

Today First Baptist Church of Jacksonville is one of the largest churches in the country, with some 25,000 members. The church's downtown campus covers 9 square blocks and 14 buildings. Known as the "Miracle of Downtown Jacksonville," First Baptist continues to grow, bringing in 900 new members each year.

Led by Pastor Dr. Jerry Vines, First Baptist broadcasts its Sunday services live on the local NBC affiliate, WTLV Channel 12.

BUDDHIST

Jacksonville is home to Tibetan and Vietnamese styles of Buddhism. The Northeast Florida Buddhist Association, comprising mostly Vietnamese Mahayana Buddhists, has more than 500 members. The group meets weekly at its Jacksonville temple (904-781-4183). Jacksonville is home to more than 2,600 Vietnamese, making it the 48th-largest concentration in the United States, based on 2000 Census data.

For followers of Tibetan Buddhism, there is the Karma Thegsum Choling Jacksonville, founded in 1986 (904-389-6885).

CATHOLIC

The Catholic Church has long historic ties to Northeast Florida. The oldest continually operating parish in the United States is the Cathedral Basilica in St. Augustine. It was established in 1565—55 years before the Pilgrims landed at Plymouth Rock—when Spanish explorers celebrated mass. In fact, the city of St. Augustine is named after the feast day of St. Augustine, the day the Spanish first sited La Florida.

The famed Santa Fe Trail originated here. It was from St. Augustine that Franciscan missionaries began the trek north and west to spread Catholicism. It also was here that the first Catholic schools and hospitals were opened.

In the 1880s the Sisters of St. Joseph order opened a school for black children. Today St. Joseph Academy High School in St. Augustine is one of the longest-operating schools in Florida.

The Diocese of Saint Augustine embraces 17 counties spanning the

There are two Catholic bookstores in Jacksonville: Queen of Angels in Mandarin and Our Daily Bread in Jacksonville Beach.

 CLOSE-UP

Family Fun at First Baptist Church of Jacksonville

Competing for the attention of today's young families can be a daunting task for clergy. There's a long list of distractions: television, video games, movies, ball games, and school. What's a ministry to do?

The folks at First Baptist Church of Jacksonville decided it was time to compete on their own home turf. In order to minister to more families and their children, First Baptist, the city's largest religious congregation with 25,000 members, has built a state-of-the-art, four-story, 12,000-square-foot Children's Building and Welcome Center on its downtown campus.

The new center, which cost $16 million, functions as a big entertainment center with a specific theme: to teach youngsters in a friendly, fun way about God and the Bible. Designed by former Disney World designer Bruce Barry, it's the closest thing to a Christian theme park we have in Jacksonville. Each of the four floors features a different biblical theme geared to children of all ages. On the second floor, for example, two 350-gallon saltwater tanks full of ocean creatures with a walkway between them depict Moses's parting of the Red Sea.

And forget about stairs or elevators. What child won't enjoy a slide that delivers kids from the third floor to the second floor? The entrance to the spiral slide looks like the mouth of a giant whale. Sound familiar? Yep, it's the biblical tale of Jonah and the whale.

Elsewhere in the building, a time machine "transports" children back to biblical times, where they can act out stories from the Bible in full costume dress. A large performing arts theater features Christmas pageants. A children's store on the second floor sells Bible-themed goodies like stickers and stamps. "Our goal is to minister to families," said Assistant Pastor Lewis Howard. "This facility allows us to do that."

The Center for Family Ministry is used for First Baptist's large Sunday school classes, as well as its Wednesday-evening musical classes. The center is open to all visitors. The church wants its new Center for Family Ministry to function as the gateway to First Baptist's sprawling complex, including one of the country's largest church auditoriums. "Our doors are wide open," Howard said. So head on over and check it out.

northeast section of Florida from the Gulf of Mexico to the Atlantic Ocean. It covers 11,032 square miles and serves about 143,000 registered Catholics in 24 parishes.

The Diocese of Saint Augustine Catholic Center is located at 11625 St. Augustine Road, Jacksonville. For more information call (904) 262–3200 or visit their Web site at www.dosaonline.com.

CHARISMATIC CHRISTIAN

There are numerous charismatic, non-denominational churches in Jacksonville. New ones keep opening all the time, tucked away in little strip shopping centers throughout the city. Check the yellow pages under "Churches" for an up-to-date listing.

EPISCOPALIAN

The first Episcopalian congregation in Jacksonville began in 1834 and is now housed in St. John's Cathedral, mother church for the city's Episcopalians. The first St. John's burned to the ground in the Great Fire of 1901.

In its 50-plus years as a cathedral, St. Johns has chosen to remain downtown, still perched atop Billy Goat Hill and serving as a beacon of light for city residents. The Cathedral Foundation's high-rise residences and Meals-on-Wheels program continue to provide quality care for the city's elderly.

There are 24 Episcopalian churches in the Jacksonville area. For more information call the Episcopalian Diocese of Florida, based in Jacksonville, at (904) 356-1328.

HINDU

The Hindu Society of Northeast Florida's temple is located in Orange Park. There are an estimated 800 Hindu families living in the Jacksonville area. Many are immigrants from India and work in professional positions, such as health care and computer sciences.

The society plans to build a bigger temple in Jacksonville once a suitable location has been found. For more information, call (904) 269-1155.

ISLAM

Islam, one of the fastest-growing religions in the world, also has a growing presence in Jacksonville. Northeast Florida has the third-largest Palestinian population in the United States.

Founded in 1978, the Islamic Center of Northeast Florida (904-646-3462) is the city's largest mosque. It is led by Iman Al-Hajj Hafiz Muhammad Zaid Malik. All Muslims are welcome to use the Islamic Center building, which holds daily prayers. Muslims believe in all of God's prophets, including Jesus Christ. However, they believe that Muhammad was the last and final prophet.

The Islamic Center has founded the Al-Furqan Academy next to its mosque on St. Johns Bluff Road. The academy, which serves about 60 students, is named after a chapter in the Quran, the holy book of Islam. Al-Furqan means "criteria to judge right from wrong."

Meanwhile, across the St. Johns River in the predominately African-American section of Jacksonville, the American Muslim Society has a smaller mosque. The Jacksonville Masjid (904-387-6910) was founded more than 25 years ago. It has about 70 members.

JEWISH

Jacksonville has a thriving Jewish community of about 7,000 persons, centered in Mandarin. There are three large synagogues in Jacksonville and one at the Beaches.

**Jacksonville Jewish Center
Conservative Synagogue
3662 Crown Point Road
(904) 292-1000
www.jaxjewishcenter.com**
The Jacksonville Jewish Center (Conservative) is the oldest and largest of the area

synagogues, with some 1,000 families. Located on Crown Point Road in Mandarin since 1976, this is the third home for the congregation. The first synagogue, which was called B'nai Israel, formed in 1901 on Duval Street in downtown Jacksonville. The congregation moved to Third and Silver Streets in Springfield in 1928 and changed the name to the Jacksonville Jewish Center.

Today the Jewish Center occupies a 35-acre campus that includes many recreational facilities, an Olympic-size swimming pool, indoor basketball court, nature trail, duck ponds, one indoor and three outdoor playgrounds, volleyball courts, and a large gazebo. The synagogue also has the Solomon Schechter Day School, which has classes from pre-K through grade 8.

Following are the other synagogues in Jacksonville:

Beth-El (Orthodox)
288 North Roscoe Boulevard
Ponte Vedra Beach
(904) 273-9100

Congregation Ahavath Chesed (Reform)
8727 San Jose Boulevard
(904) 733-7078

Etz Chaim Synagogue (Orthodox)
10167 San Jose Boulevard
(904) 262-3565

PRESBYTERIAN

First Presbyterian Church (118 East Monroe Street) dates its founding to March 2, 1840, with its charter as the Presbyterian Church of Jacksonville by the Territorial Legislature of Florida. Obadiah Conger, a retired New England sea captain, carried the charter by horseback to Jacksonville. It is probable that the small congregation was meeting prior to that date, but this cannot be confirmed. In any event, the church is one of the oldest spiritual congregations in the city.

UNITARIAN/UNIVERSALIST

Unitarians are a diverse religious community, welcoming people regardless of race, religious background, ideological outlook, gender, family status, sexual orientation, or ethnic heritage.

Founded in 1906 and active in the civil rights movement, the Unitarian Universalist Church of Jacksonville (904-725-8133) now has about 340 members. The church's current house of worship, at 7405 Arlington Expressway, was designed by noted Jacksonville architect Robert C. Broward and built in 1966.

MILITARY

Ask many World War II–era folks what they know about Jacksonville, and chances are a fair number of them will say they served time here in the navy or knew someone who did.

For many of us, Jacksonville conjures up images of aircraft carriers and destroyers, helicopters and fighter jets, and navy families running across the tarmac to smother dad with kisses upon his return from a six-month deployment.

Jacksonville is home to two major navy bases: Naval Air Station Jacksonville (NAS Jax) and Naval Station Mayport (NAVSTA Mayport).

NAS Jax is home to numerous helicopter and fixed-wing aircraft squadrons. It's also where navy aircraft and ground support equipment from all over the world are repaired. At the Naval Air Depot, Jacksonville, or NADEP, 3,800 civilian employees (many retired navy) fix it all—from a flat tire on a Seahawk helicopter to a complicated electronic circuit board on an F-16 fighter jet. NADEP is the largest industrial employer in Northeast Florida.

NAVSTA Mayport is homeport for 22 ships, including the USS *John F. Kennedy,* an aircraft carrier referred to by some as "Big John." NAVSTA Mayport is also home to a large helicopter engine repair facility.

About an hour up the road, near St. Marys, Georgia, is Naval Submarine Base Kings Bay. Kings Bay, as the locals call it, is homeport for two large submarine squadrons and 10 Trident ballistic missile submarines.

Another military location in the heart of Jacksonville doesn't usually get much attention. It's the U.S. Marine Corps Blount Island Command, which maintains 13 pre-positioned ships—supply ships that are always loaded with ground-defense systems and ready to deploy at a moment's notice. Pre-positioned ships carry enough supplies and equipment in their holds to allow troops to engage in several weeks of warfare anywhere in the world. In 1990, during Operation Desert Storm, the Blount Island Command played a key role in the war effort by shipping tons of military supplies and hardware overseas.

The Coast Guard also plays a vital and growing role in Jacksonville, responsible for everything from port security to making sure that certain shrimpers use turtle exclusion devices on their nets. Its most visible base is located in Mayport.

According to the navy, the economic impact on Northeast Florida and Southeast Georgia from these four bases combined is $6.45 billion. There are more than 227,000 people associated with these bases, from active-duty personnel to reservists, retirees, civilian workers, and their respective families. Put another way, 20 out of every 100 people you will meet in Northeast Florida and Southeast Georgia will have some connection to the U.S. Navy or the U.S. Marines.

Finally, the navy is proud to offer this fact: More than 20,000 navy personnel and marines donate literally hundreds of thousands of volunteer service hours to the Jacksonville community every year. These volunteers do it all, from building HabiJax houses to speaking to scout groups and mentoring at-risk kids.

Without a doubt, the navy and the marines are important to Jacksonville—and residents know it. Jacksonville appreciates its military community and looks forward to ever-growing associations in the years ahead.

Most of the amenities described in the following listings are available exclusively for active and retired military personnel and their families.

NAVAL AIR STATION JACKSONVILLE

(904) 542-2345
www.nasjax.navy.mil

In 1939 Jacksonville residents voted in favor of a $1 million bond issue to purchase 3,896 acres of land for Naval Air Station Jacksonville, making it the only military installation in the nation established by a direct gift of the people. The first pilot landed at NAS Jax on September 7, 1940, before the runway was even finished. In short order, three runways were built here, along with a small aircraft repair facility that would one day become the very big Naval Air Depot, Jacksonville (NADEP). Today NADEP is the largest tenant command at NAS Jax and the largest industrial employer in Northeast Florida. All kinds of navy aircraft and support equipment from around the world are repaired at NADEP. In addition, numerous helicopter and fixed-wing aircraft squadrons are based at NAS Jax. The base is also home to Patrol Squadron Thirty (VP-30), which is the navy's largest aviation squadron and the only "Orion" Fleet Replacement Squadron, which prepares and trains U.S. and foreign pilots and air crew and maintenance personnel for further operational assignments.

NAS Jacksonville is birthplace of the Blue Angels, the navy's precision flying team. Captain Butch Voris, a highly decorated navy pilot, started the Blue Angels here in 1946. The team flew in its first air show at Craig Airfield in Jacksonville, winning first place. The Blue Angels are now based in Pensacola but return to Jacksonville almost every year to perform in the annual Sea and Sky Spectacular. (Check out the Annual Events chapter for more on this popular air show.)

Marina at NAS Jax
(904) 542-3260

There's lots happening at this on-base marina, located on the banks of the St. Johns River. You can rent almost any type of pleasure boat, from kayaks and canoes to sailboats, bass boats, and Boston Whalers with an outboard motor for fishing. For navy personnel who own a boat, the marina offers slips, moorings, and dry storage on a daily, monthly, or yearly basis. This is a great place to take a sailing or safe-boating class or enter a bass-fishing contest. The Ship's Store sells bait and fishing tackle as well as ice, drinks, sandwiches, and that all-important Florida fishing license. If you're caught on the water without one, you could be fined. **NOTE:** You have to pass a safe-boating quiz before you can rent a boat at the marina.

NAS Jacksonville Golf Club
(904) 542-3249

NAS Jax has 27 holes of championship golf on base for golfers of all ages and skill levels. There are two very pretty, well-maintained courses here—a par-72, 18-hole course and a par-35, 9-hole course. Group or private lessons are available at NAS Jax Golf Club, and on Friday afternoon, navy women get together for a golf clinic; the cost is $10 per clinic. Several golf tournaments are played at this club, including the annual Southeast Military Invitational Golf Tournament in May and the Navy Birthday Golf Tournament in October.

RV Park at NAS Jax
(904) 542-3227

NAS Jax operates a small but lovely RV park on base overlooking the St. Johns River. There are a total of 25 sites, 8 with sewer, water, and electric and 4 with water and electric. The rest are "primitive," but there's a new shower and bathroom facility here, so primitive camping isn't that primi-

---

Every year hundreds of military folks participate in the Navy Run at NAS Jax. It features a 10K competitive run and a 5K noncompetitive walk. The race starts when a cannon is fired from the base weapons department.

tive. Make your reservations early, because this RV park fills up fast. Full-hookup sites are $13 a day or $80 a week. Campers must check out after 14 days.

Jax Air News
(904) 542-3531
www.JaxAirNews.com
This free, award-winning weekly publication is devoted solely to all that is happening at NAS Jacksonville. It's the best way to keep in touch with everything that's going on at this large base. It's also a good way to keep up to date with changes in the U.S. Navy. Check it out!

NAVAL STATION MAYPORT

(904) 270-5011
www.nsmayport.navy.mil
Most people understand that Naval Station Mayport is a busy seaport, but they don't realize that it's a busy air facility as well. Twenty-two ships are homeported here, including the granddaddy of them all, the aircraft carrier USS *John F. Kennedy*. Caroline Kennedy christened the ship in 1967. The airfield can accommodate any aircraft owned by the Department of Defense, and there are more than 100,000 helicopter and fixed-wing flights from here every year. The airfield is also a popular place with thousands of military personnel, who hop aboard military flights as passengers. In addition to ships' crews and their squadrons, Naval Station Mayport hosts a large maintenance facility that repairs Seahawk helicopter engines.

The current Naval Station Mayport grew slowly from its beginnings in 1939. It was used during World War II then deactivated after the war until 1948. Once reactivated, the base grew steadily, often expanding to accommodate bigger ships and planes. The harbor was dredged deeper, more acreage was added to the base, and runways were extended. Today Naval Station Mayport employs nearly 12,000 active-duty military personnel and covers 3,409 acres.

Mayport Golf Club
(904) 270-5380
Located on the grounds of Naval Station Mayport, this golf club features an 18-hole, par-72 course. Thanks to a recent multi-million-dollar renovation, the course is in its best shape in years. Towering oak and palm trees line the fairways, which sit between the Atlantic Ocean and the Intracoastal Waterway. The course is open from 7:00 A.M. to 7:00 P.M. except in the winter, when it closes at 6:00 P.M. After a round of golf, check out NAVSTA Mayport's version of the 19th hole. It's called Bogeys, and it features a special happy hour Wednesday through Friday from 4:00 to 6:00 P.M.

The USO Center at 2560 Mayport Road is open to all military personnel and their families. It offers activities, hospitality, or just a place to go. The center is open from 9:00 A.M. to 9:00 P.M. Monday through Friday and 9:00 A.M. to 6:00 P.M. Saturday. Call (904) 246-3481 for more information.

Nature Trails
(904) 270-5226
Naval Station Mayport is located on some of Jacksonville's prettiest property. If it were not a navy base, Mayport would be full of pricey oceanfront and marshfront homes. Mindful of its stewardship, the navy has set aside some of this marshland and created three nature preserves with boardwalks and nature trails. The areas are located just outside the main gate and behind Ribault Bay housing at the end of Assisi Lane. All the trails are open to the public.

Walk along the boardwalk just outside the main gate to see bald eagles, ospreys, wood storks, and pelicans. Fishing is allowed from the boardwalks and from platforms at each of these nature trails. It's nice to visit the trails at the end of the day, when the sun has receded a bit and

many marsh residents are looking for an evening snack. Just bring plenty of bug spray no matter when you go; in Florida, marsh and mosquito are synonymous.

The Navy Lodge at Naval Station Mayport
(904) 270-5011

This Navy Lodge is a wonderful little secret. Essentially it's a modern 52-room oceanfront hotel located on the base. If you are active duty, a reservist, a retiree, or a Department of Defense employee on orders, you can make reservations to stay at the Navy Lodge. If you are a civilian sponsored by an active-duty member, a reservist, or a retiree, you can stay here, too. Make reservations early, because even though the hotel is something of a secret, enough people know about it to fill the place up almost every night. Amenities include microwaves, refrigerators, and coffeemakers in every room. Some rooms also have fully equipped kitchens with utensils and dining areas. Local telephone calls are free, and there are hair dryers, free coffee, HBO, and clock radios in every room. Stay on the second or third floor for a view of the ocean. The first floor has a lovely view of the sand dunes. Best of all is the price: A room here goes for about $50 a night.

Mayport Mirror
(904) 270-7817
www.mayportmirror.com

Like its counterpart at NAS Jacksonville, the *Mayport Mirror* covers all the news that's fit to print at Naval Station Mayport. It also has the latest navy news, too, making this weekly a must-read for navy personnel and their families as well as reservists and retirees.

NAVAL SUBMARINE BASE KINGS BAY

(912) 673-2000
www.subasekb.navy.mil

With 16,000 acres and 9,000 active duty, reserve, and civilian personnel at work here, this is a huge base. It's located in Camden County, Georgia, which, thanks to the U.S. Navy, is one of the fastest-growing counties in the state. The base opened in 1978 and was originally planned as the forward refit site for just one submarine squadron, Squadron 16, then operating out of Spain.

But in no time at all, powerful Georgia politicians like then Senator Sam Nunn, a member of the Senate Armed Services Committee, helped garner more money and more prestige for the new base in his home state. In 1980 Kings Bay was named the homeport for the Atlantic Fleet of Trident ballistic submarines. This sparked a massive, nine-year, $1.3 billion construction program. Crew-training facilities had to be built, as did nuclear weapons handling and storage facilities, submarine maintenance and repair facilities, and facilities for all the personnel who would be living and working on base.

The first Trident nuclear submarine, the USS *Tennessee,* arrived in 1989. Nine more Trident subs, all named after a state, arrived after that. In the end, construction of Kings Bay was the largest peacetime construction program ever undertaken by the U.S. Navy.

Kings Bay is one of the navy's prettiest bases. Four thousand of its 16,000 acres are protected wetlands, making the base home to wood storks, alligators, and all sorts of swamp critters.

Navy Lodge at Naval Submarine Base Kings Bay
(912) 882-6868

With 26 rooms, this modern motel is smaller than the Navy Lodge at Naval Station Mayport. It also does not enjoy an oceanfront location, but in terms of price (currently $41 per night) and convenience (located right on base), it's hard to beat. Amenities include kitchenettes in every room, with a microwave and small refrigerator. There's free coffee in your room, free HBO and Disney on the cable, and free local calls. If you want to rent a movie, you can do that at the front desk and play it on the VCR in your room. The rooms fill up fast, so be sure to make reservations early. The Navy Lodge is open to all active-duty personnel as well as reserves and retirees. Civilians who are sponsored by active-duty personnel, reserves, or retirees can stay here as well.

U.S. MARINE CORPS BLOUNT ISLAND COMMAND

There are no tourist opportunities at this command, but we mention it so that you know what goes on here. Located next to Jacksonville's Blount Island port terminal, the 725 marines and civilians who work at this military command maintain 13 prepositioning ships. These supply ships stand always ready to sail to hot spots anywhere in the world. They are loaded with war machinery and humanitarian-aid and troop-support supplies. Several of the ships stay in Jacksonville; the rest are docked elsewhere but come here for routine maintenance. If the president of the United States needs to send troops into battle at a moment's notice, these ships will quickly meet them at the nearest port, carrying up to a month's worth of supplies. This command (and the port of Jacksonville) played a huge role in Operation Desert Storm, ferrying supplies to the Middle East.

COAST GUARD GROUP MAYPORT

(904) 778-0846
www.uscg.mil/d7/units/grumayport
Tiny, but mighty. That's a good way to describe the United States Coast Guard's

The Trident Lakes Golf Club at Naval Submarine Base Kings Bay is open to the public select weekends of the year. Call (912) 573-8475 for information.

presence in Jacksonville. Coast Guard Group Mayport is the umbrella organization for several coast guard units based in this area, the largest of which is the Marine Safety Office. This unit is responsible for rescuing stranded boaters and fishermen at sea. It covers a large territory ranging from St. Catherine's, Georgia, to Port Malabar, Florida, and encompasses 240 miles of coastline and 40,000 square miles of ocean. This territory also includes inland waterways, like 161 miles of the St. Johns River and a portion of the Intracoastal.

The Marine Safety Office uses four ships, or cutters, to help rescue stranded boaters. The cutters are based at Coast Guard Base Mayport, a tiny, six-acre facility located on the St. Johns River right next door to Naval Station Mayport. You will pass this base if you ever drive out Mayport Road to catch the St. Johns River Ferry.

Since it is now part of the Department of Homeland Security, the U.S. Coast Guard is also responsible for protecting the Port of Jacksonville from a terrorist attack. This, as you can imagine, is a tall order. The coast guard won't reveal much of its port protection protocol, but some things are public knowledge. For instance, foreign ships heading to our port must now give several days advance notice of their arrival so the coast guard can board the ship at sea for inspection. Also, no boats are allowed near cruise ships entering or leaving our port. If a boater violates

It is worth the drive to St. Marys, Georgia, just to see the Trident submarine docked in the dirt outside the main entrance to Naval Submarine Base Kings Bay. The sub is so huge, it's jaw-dropping.

Firebase Florida

It's all here: the command and control bunker, the machine gun emplacements, even the sandbags—6,000 of them.

Welcome to Firebase Florida at Camp Blanding, a composite firebase typical of the kind used in Vietnam between 1965 and 1973. The firebases were small, isolated enclaves in the middle of nowhere, safe havens from the enemy for platoons or even a battalion. They were also used as jump-off points for further operations or for forward observations of the North Vietnamese.

The Vietnam Veterans of North Florida spent 10 years planning and building Firebase Florida after the Museum Society at Camp Blanding asked them to build a memorial symbolic of the Vietnam experience. The veterans decided that a firebase would be perfect, but only after much deliberation. "We were isolated out there in a sense, and the only thing you owned was the perimeter of the firebase," said Sergeant Bill Wilder, a former marine and a Vietnam veteran. "That was really the only secure place; you never really were secure outside the wire."

Firebase Florida is part of Memorial Park at Camp Blanding, about an hour south of Jacksonville. It's located in a large field formerly used for training purposes back when Camp Blanding was a busy training facility for the U.S. Army. There's also space in the park for monuments and displays honoring the men and women who served in Korea and Desert Storm. Desert Storm veterans have donated tanks and other transportation equipment. Korean War veterans in Florida have yet to leave their mark.

At the heart of Camp Blanding is a museum dedicated to the World War II

that protection zone, he or she will have to answer to the coast guard.

Another unit of Coast Guard Group Mayport is called HITRON Jacksonville. This unit is actually based far from the water on the western side of Jacksonville at Cecil Field. HITRON Jacksonville uses force from helicopters to stop drug traffickers on the high seas. Its members also help protect the Port of Jacksonville from terrorist attack.

Finally, Coast Guard Group Mayport also operates a factory of sorts at its Mayport base responsible for maintaining and reconstructing the big, colorful navigational buoys that help keep boaters on course. Some of the buoys also measure water temperature and wind speed and provide other nautical information to the coast guard.

MILITARY MUSEUMS

Camp Blanding Historical Museum and Memorial Park
Route One, Starke
(904) 682-3196
This museum, open to the public, houses a collection of weapons as well as a replica of a World War II army barracks. There are also lots of photo exhibits,

experience. Nine infantry divisions trained at the camp between 1940 and 1943. In 1943 soldiers heading out to fight in both Europe and the Pacific also began to train here. The Camp Blanding Museum is dedicated to the men who headed off to war from Camp Blanding, some never to return again.

The museum houses all sorts of World War II–era weapons from the United States, Germany, and Japan. There's also a small replica of a World War II barracks, complete with a pot stove, bunk beds, and those infamous green army blankets that were never soft and cuddly but always mighty durable and warm. Mannequins dressed in a variety of officer and enlisted man uniforms tell a silent tale about what life was like at Camp Blanding for the thousands of men who trained here during World War II.

There is no charge to visit the Camp Blanding Museum or Firebase Florida, across the street from the museum in Memorial Park. Both are open almost every day from noon to 4:00 P.M.

Back at Firebase Florida, crowds of schoolchildren gather. The firebase has become a popular field trip destination, and it's not uncommon to see students or scouts playing with a 105 Howitzer set up inside the sandbag perimeter, a typical cannon from a firebase in Vietnam.

The veterans who built Firebase Florida are proud of the living memorial they've created. It was dedicated on Memorial Day 2000 to the men and women who died in Vietnam and also to those who survived. Organizers hope that veterans who've had a hard time talking about their experiences in Vietnam will visit the firebase and find it therapeutic. Most of all, organizers believe, Firebase Florida will help keep alive the fact that American servicemen and women fought proudly in Vietnam for freedom and their country.

medals, and uniforms. The museum is open daily from noon to 4:00 P.M. and admission is free. (See the Close-up above for more information.)

St. Marys Submarine Museum
102 St. Marys Street West
St. Marys, Georgia
(912) 882-2782
www.stmaryssubmuseum.com
During World War II, U.S. submarines—manned by less than 2 percent of U.S. sailors—sank more than 50 percent of enemy ships. This museum, open to the pubic, is dedicated to them, and to all members of the "Silent Service," past and present. Located in St. Marys, Georgia, near Naval Submarine Base Kings Bay, the Submarine Museum is only a 45-minute drive north of Jacksonville. Opened in 1996 in an old city-owned building, the museum has grown to include two floors and 4,500 square feet of space. By far, the biggest draw here is the museum's operational "Type 8" periscope, which raises up through the museum's roof for a great view of the quaint fishing village of St. Marys. Museum officials say it is the only periscope in the southeast open to the public for general viewing—unless, of course, you're lucky enough to climb aboard a submarine. There is also an old

sonar system console on display as well as the ballast control panel and a ship's atmosphere control panel. All these panels are from the USS *James K. Polk*, one of the 41 original Trident submarines, which was decommissioned in 1999. Also of particular interest at the museum are drawings from several 1940s-era submarine training manuals. Crewmembers had to memorize the drawings of various submarine systems and pass a test in order to be qualified to work aboard a sub.

The museum is also very proud of its research library, which contains information on hundreds of submarines world-wide, including foreign subs. There's also a movie about life aboard a submarine and computer-interactive kiosks with sub information from the present all the way back to the USS *Holland*, the first submarine recognized by the U.S. Navy. Be sure to stop in at the museum gift shop before you leave, where you can buy a boat patch for just about every submarine from World War II to the present. The museum is open daily except Monday. Admission is $3.00 for persons ages 19 to 62, $2.00 for active-duty and retired military and anyone ages 63 to 99, and $1.00 for children ages 6 to 18. Call in advance for a group tour.

MEDIA 📺

Staying informed in Jacksonville isn't difficult, even for the visitor or new-comer. There's a ready supply of mainstream and alternative print and electronic media to help you find out what's going on. Whether you're interested in local politics, sports, arts and entertainment, the weather, or the business climate, chances are good you'll find it in Jacksonville's mix of newspapers, radio stations, TV stations, and Web sites.

While Jacksonville has a rich news history, in recent years the city and its surroundings also have become popular locations for the filming of feature films. John Travolta filmed *Basic* at the old Cecil Field Navy Base in 2002, and John Sayles filmed *Sunshine State* on Amelia Island in 2001.

DAILY NEWSPAPERS

Financial News & Daily Record
10 North Newman Street
(904) 356-2466
www.jaxdailyrecord.com
The *Financial News & Daily Record* reports on Jacksonville's business and legal communities. Published since 1912, the *Daily Record* is where you'll find all the city's legal notices.

In recent years the paper has expanded its coverage to include more profiles and feature articles dealing with the business, legal, and real estate industries in Jacksonville.

The *Daily Record* is published Monday through Friday. You can buy a copy at most bookshops and newsstands. Many nonlegal types read it faithfully for the daily gossip or Heard on the Street column that appears on the front left side of the paper. Sometimes the gossip is even correct!

Florida Times-Union
One Riverside Avenue
(904) 359-4111
www.jacksonville.com
Founded in 1883, the *Florida Times-Union* is Jacksonville's only major daily newspaper. If you're a newspaper reader, the *Times-Union,* locally known simply as the *TU,* is your best source for all-around news items in the Jacksonville area.

With a daily circulation about 175,000 and Sunday circulation about 230,000, the *Times-Union* is the seventh-largest daily newspaper in Florida. The *Times-Union* is owned by Augusta, Georgia–based Morris Communications Corp. (In the spirit of full disclosure, Morris Communications Corp. also owns the Globe Pequot Press, publisher of the *Insiders' Guide* series.)

The *Times-Union* covers local politics, business, entertainment, and sports and is a frequent winner of state journalism awards, which, given Florida's strong newspaper industry, is an impressive accomplishment. The *Times-Union*'s free Web site has received numerous national awards for an online news site since it was first launched in 1998.

After the city won a National Football League team, the *Times-Union* beefed up its sports department to provide the type of in-depth coverage required for a major professional sports franchise. The daily also provides comprehensive pro and amateur golf coverage. If you plan to do any fishing during your stay in the

---

i

For the latest on what companies are planning to relocate or expand in Jacksonville, insiders swear by Times-Union *business columnist Karen Brune Mathis, who appears in the business pages daily.*

Ron Littlepage, Jacksonville's Populist Voice

You could say that Ron Littlepage, opinion columnist for the *Florida Times-Union*, has the best journalism job in Jacksonville. Littlepage himself chuckles at the notion. "It's close," he admits. "But I think the outdoors writer has the best job because he gets paid to go hunting and fishing all the time."

Such are the priorities of Littlepage, who really would prefer to be fishing for flounder than fishing for an exclusive that will shake up City Hall. Still, Littlepage manages to write about the environment a lot anyway, which means he's not usually stuck behind a computer all day. He's often out gathering information for a column, be it from a boat on the St. Johns River or monitoring the antics at a school board meeting.

Littlepage's column is a staple for many local readers, who thumb through the newspaper each day to the back page of the Metro section to see what he's writing about. His column usually appears every Tuesday, Thursday, Friday, and Sunday, but it's often driven by subject matter. If he has nothing to write about on one of those days, readers may have to wait until he does. For fans, it's worth the wait. They like how he champions the underdog, disagrees with the status quo, and frequently criticizes City Hall. City leaders from the mayor down have found themselves the target of his keyboard, and it usually makes for a rotten day when one of their policies is the subject of a Littlepage column. Constituents start calling; so do other reporters—and soon enough that public official finds him- or herself on the defensive.

Oddly enough, Littlepage sometimes finds *himself* on the defensive, especially when angry readers call to disagree with what he's written about. "I get branded a liberal a lot," he says. "Of course in this conservative area, it doesn't take much to be branded a liberal." At times like this, Littlepage makes it clear that his opinions are his own and do not represent the opinions of the newspaper. "That's what the editorial page is for," he says, and frequently, on any given issue, a Littlepage

Jacksonville area, check out *Times-Union* outdoor columnist Joe Julavits. During the week he provides quality updates on where the fish are biting. Julavits's excellent feature stories appear every Sunday.

For weekend events and entertainment, check out the paper's Friday edition for comprehensive lists of live entertainment, movie reviews, and other happenings.

For more detailed coverage of Jacksonville's communities, the *Times-Union* publishes seven different twice-weekly neighborhood papers, such as *Shorelines*, covering the Beaches communities; *River City*, covering the north Jacksonville neighborhoods; and *County Line*, which covers Clay County and Orange Park.

column and a *Times-Union* editorial are light-years apart.

Littlepage has been writing his column since 1989. Before that he was the newspaper's assistant managing editor, a job he loved—and hated. He begged his bosses for a change. He was sick of the endless meetings and the budgets and wanted to return to the reason he got into journalism in the first place: to help be a catalyst for change. Littlepage says that he most enjoys writing about Jacksonville's natural resources, from the St. Johns River to the Timucuan Preserve. "We have so much to offer here," he says.

When Littlepage and his wife, Mary, entertain out-of-town guests, they try to provide a sampling of some of Jacksonville's natural areas. "I take them out in a kayak into our marshes and creeks," he says. He also likes to take guests fishing and hiking. His favorite fishing spots are top secrets, but they're generally in the marshes off Sister's Creek north of Heckscher Drive. A favorite hiking spot is in Clay County near Green Cove Springs in an area called Bayard Point, near the Shands Bridge.

Littlepage hails from deep in the heart of Texas. He talks with a twang and has created an alter-ego character called Jimmy Ray Bob (married to Sissy Lou), who occasionally makes it into his columns. Jimmy Ray is forever eating boiled peanuts and expounding on the Florida political scene from gubernatorial to local mayoral races. Consequently, Jimmy Ray appears a lot during the political season when Littlepage uses him as a "change of pace."

True to his roots, Littlepage believes that Jacksonville is just getting too big, and he's sad to see it happening. He's not much of a big-city person and prefers to think of Jacksonville as a town of neighborhoods, each with its own distinct flavor, from the fish camps up on the Northside to the fancy homes in San Marco. "It's a good mix," Littlepage says.

Littlepage is modest about the power of his pen. He only hopes his strongly opinionated columns on local issues increase people's awareness, gets them more involved and talking about issues. "If they're not reacting to it in some way," Littlepage says, "then I've probably chosen the wrong subject."

You can read Littlepage's columns before you get to town online at www.jacksonville.com.

St. Augustine Record
One News Place, St. Augustine
(904) 829-6562
www.staugustine.com

The *St. Augustine Record* has been chronicling the news in the Ancient City and St. Johns County for more than a century. The *Record* is owned by Morris Communications Corp., just like its sister publication the *Florida Times-Union.* Daily circulation is 18,000.

The *Record* recently left its longtime home in downtown St. Augustine for an ultramodern facility on the outskirts of town that includes a day care center for employees as well as an Internet cafe. The newspaper needed to expand to a new headquarters so it could better cover fast-growing St. Johns County. The *Record* also hosts a popular award-winning Web site, which features stories from the daily newspaper as well as general travel information about St. Augustine. It could be argued that more people look at this Web site every day than read the actual newspaper.

WEEKLIES AND BIWEEKLIES

Beaches Leader
1114 Beach Boulevard, Jacksonville Beach
(904) 249-9033
www.beachesleader.com
If you're interested in what's happening at Jacksonville's beach communities, you'll want to pick up a copy of the *Beaches Leader.* Published since 1963, the *Beaches Leader* and its sister publication, *Ponte Vedra Leader,* focus exclusively on the communities of Atlantic, Neptune, Jacksonville, and Ponte Vedra Beaches.

The newspapers cover local politics, crime, sports, and entertainment. The *Beaches Leader* also carries good fishing reports from local fishing captains. For those hunting for Beaches real estate, the *Beaches Leader* runs classified ads of homes for sale and for rent. It's also a good place to find area garage sales on the weekends.

The *Beaches Leader* and *Ponte Vedra Leader* are published every Wednesday and Friday; you can buy them at newsstands, at drug and grocery stores, and through home circulation.

Florida Star
5196-C Norwood Avenue
(904) 766-8834
www.thefloridastar.com
Jacksonville's largest black publication, the *Florida Star* has been published since 1951. The *Florida Star* is a statewide weekly newspaper with a circulation of 5,000 and a readership of 10,000, according to the Audit Bureau of Circulations. The *Florida Star* covers all the news that is relevant to Jacksonville's black community—business, human interest, and entertainment as well as politics and education. The *Florida Star* is sold at 135 locations, including Publix and Winn-Dixie grocery stores and Walgreens Drug stores, mostly in the predominantly African-American sections of the city.

Folio Weekly
9456 Philips Highway
(904) 260-9770
www.folioweekly.com
Folio Weekly, which bills itself as Northeast Florida's news and opinion magazine, is the area's spunky alternative paper. *Folio Weekly* often runs stories and opinions you won't find in the mainstream media. The tabloid-size paper also features movie, arts, and music reviews.

For visitors and residents alike, *Folio Weekly*'s comprehensive entertainment listings, movie reviews, and book reviews are indispensable. *Folio Weekly* also runs the most extensive personals listings of any publication in the area.

Forty-five thousand copies of the paper are distributed free every Tuesday throughout Northeast Florida, from Fernandina Beach to St. Augustine. You can find your free copy at most public libraries, bookstores, and coffee shops and at many restaurants. Also look for it on newsstands.

Jacksonville Business Journal
1200 Riverplace Boulevard
(904) 396-3502
www.jacksonville.bizjournals.com
The *Jacksonville Business Journal* provides weekly news and commentary on the area's businesses and industries. Regular columns cover such topics as health care, marketing, real estate, and high technology. The *Business Journal* also publishes an annual *Book of Lists*, a comprehensive compilation of the city's major

companies and firms. Editors contribute daily business reports to local television and radio stations.

Ponte Vedra Recorder
100 Executive Way, Ponte Vedra Beach
(904) 285-8831
As its names suggests, the *Ponte Vedra Recorder* covers the upscale community of Ponte Vedra Beach. As chronicler of Ponte Vedra's social scene, the weekly newspaper is generally full of stories and photos of the latest soirees.

The *Ponte Vedra Recorder* is published every Friday. You can buy a copy at newsstands and supermarkets or subscribe to get your copy in the mail.

MAGAZINES

Arbus
415 Park Avenue
(904) 353-0100
www.arbus.com
This is Northeast Florida's arts and business magazine. But don't be fooled; it's not a business magazine like the *Jacksonville Business Journal*. This magazine covers the business of art. The magazine always features a cover story on a prominent local or regional artist, and it carries stories about the latest exhibitions at area art museums such as the Cummer. *Arbus* also covers music and offers a comprehensive calendar of upcoming art and entertainment events. It's published every other month and is given away free at area newsstands and in coffee shops, sandwich shops, and some restaurants. Don't miss this color glossy. The ads are often as enlightening as the stories. We certainly look forward to it.

Jacksonville Magazine
534 Lancaster Street
(904) 358-8330
www.jacksonvillemag.com
Published since 1983, *Jacksonville Magazine* is the area's oldest city magazine.

Regular editorial features include personality profiles, restaurant spotlights, travel, local history, and current events. *Jacksonville Magazine*'s regular columns cover personal finance, health, real estate, fashion, and a newsmaker Q&A. Each issue offers a two-month calendar of events and a dining guide listing more than 100 area restaurants. *Jacksonville Magazine* is published monthly and is distributed to 60,000 readers. It can be purchased at newsstands, supermarkets, and bookstores or by subscription.

Water's Edge
One Riverside Avenue
(904) 359-4583
www.waters-edge.com
Water's Edge is one of Jacksonville's newest magazines. The oversize glossy features articles on homes, interior design, gardening, restaurant reviews, and profiles of interesting personalities and their homes in the coastal South. *Water's Edge* is published bimonthly by the *Florida Times-Union*. It's available at bookstores, select Publix and Winn-Dixie supermarkets, the lobby of the *Florida Times-Union* building at One Riverside Avenue, or by subscription. *Water's Edge* will remind you of *Southern Living* magazine—only bigger!

SPECIAL-INTEREST PUBLICATIONS

Entertaining You
5571 Playa Way
(904) 743-7440
This weekly entertainment newspaper carries features and reviews of upcoming movies, theater, dining, music, and nightlife in the Jacksonville area. *Entertaining You* is distributed free every week. It's available at public libraries, convenience stores, and drug stores. It's a great place to find discount coupons for upcoming events and free passes to movie screenings.

First Coast Parent
P.O. Box 51023, Jacksonville Beach
(904) 346-0045
The *First Coast Parent* is a monthly news-magazine distributed free throughout the area. It features monthly columns on parenting, health, and book reviews. Each issue also includes a calendar of events for parents and children. It's available at many public libraries, convenience stores, and bookstores. Some moms swear by it!

Golf News
10 North Newman Street
(904) 356-2466
www.golfnews-southeast.com
Distributed free each month, *Golf News* covers both professional and amateur golfing in Northeast Florida and Southeast Georgia. The publication carries articles about local courses and profiles of area golfers, as well as the latest information on golf tournaments.

H Magazine
One Riverside Avenue
(904) 359-4058
www.jacksonville.com
Published monthly by the *Florida Times-Union, H Magazine* is all about your health. The magazine offers regular columns like Ask the Experts and Focus on Fitness, as well as monthly features like Organ Donations and Surviving Breast Cancer. Many doctors, surgeons, and medical specialists advertise in this free glossy, so if you're looking for a physician, this is a good place to start. *H Magazine* is free in news boxes around the city as well as at your favorite public library.

Natural Awakenings
P.O. Box 54465
(904) 997-6677
www.naturalawakenings.com
From Chinese medicine to discovering the ancient healing traditions of the Shamans, this free monthly magazine covers it all. The editors of *Natural Awakenings* say it's

the premier publication to turn to on the First Coast for information on how to improve the quality of your life physically, mentally, emotionally, and spiritually. You can pick up a copy of *Natural Awakenings* at your local library.

Neighborhoods
117 West Duval Street, Suite 305
(904) 630-2969
Neighborhoods magazine may be produced by the City of Jacksonville, but don't hold that against the publication. This is not your typical government-issued propaganda piece.

The glossy monthly magazine features profiles of Jacksonville's many neighborhoods and its people, as well as news items and updates on the city's massive $2.2 billion Better Jacksonville Plan. It also has a pretty good calendar of upcoming events that's worth checking out.

You can pick up a copy of *Neighborhoods* magazine at public libraries and City Hall.

Women's Digest
12620-3 Beach Boulevard
(904) 350-0807
www.womensdigest.net
If it's of interest to women, you'll find it in the pages of *Women's Digest*. This free monthly tabloid is available at the library and in various news boxes around the city. There are good stories inside like "Who's Keeping the Arts Alive in Jacksonville?" and "Family Fun Outings on the First Coast." The ads are just as much fun to look at as the stories themselves!

TELEVISION

As in most other growing cities, Jacksonville's television news coverage is very competitive, especially after the Federal Communications Commission allowed media companies to own more than one television station in any given market.

Now Clear Channel Communications and Gannett Broadcasting each own two television stations in Jacksonville. Regardless of the changes, experts say local television news in Jacksonville continues to outperform its market size of 52. In other words, the quality of television news in Jacksonville is above average.

WAWS Fox 30
11700 Central Parkway
(904) 642–3030
www.fox30online.com
Owned by Clear Channel Communications, WAWS is the local FOX affiliate. It's also the home for your favorite UPN shows after 11:00 P.M. FOX delivers its signature newscast at 10:00 P.M. as well as additional newscasts throughout the day. It also operates a popular interactive Web site that often includes viewer opinion polls based on news stories seen during its newscasts.

WJCT TV-7
100 Festival Park Avenue
(904) 353–7770
www.wjct.org
WJCT is Jacksonville's Public Broadcasting Station. This is where you'll find such national shows as *Masterpiece Theater, Austin City Limits, The NewsHour with Jim Lehrer,* and *Sesame Street.* Local programs aired on WJCT include *Jacksonville Exchange Week in Review* and *Florida Crossroads.*

WJEB TV-59
3101 Emerson Expressway
(904) 399–8413
www.wjeb.org
WJEB is a noncommercial educational affiliate of the Trinity Broadcasting Network, the world's largest Christian television network. WJEB has provided Jacksonville and its surrounding areas with quality Christian and educational programming since 1991. This is a very popular station in town.

Jacksonville's television stations each have a UHF or VHF number assigned by the FCC. They also have a different number assigned by the local cable franchise. For instance, CBS-47 appears on channel 47 if you're using the rabbit ears but cable channel 6 if you're on cable.

WJWB TV-17
9117 Hogan Road
(904) 641–1700
www.wjwb.com
WB-17 is the Warner Bros. affiliate. It doesn't run any locally produced news programs, but it does air a selection of popular syndicated programs as well as popular WB programming such as *The Gilmore Girls* and *Dawson's Creek.* Channel 17 is owned by Media General, a communications company based in Richmond, Virginia. In May 2004 WJWB was the No. 1 WB affiliate in the country.

WJXT TV-4
1851 South Hampton Road
(904) 399–4000
www.news4jax.com
As the former longtime CBS affiliate, WJXT has been the news leader among Jacksonville TV stations for decades. Its main anchor team—consisting of two news anchors, weatherman, and chief sportscaster—has been together longer than any of the other anchor teams in the city and has developed a strong following.

In 2002 WJXT's parent company, Post-Newsweek, opted to discontinue its CBS affiliation and strike out as an independent station. As an independent, WJXT management has promised to increase its local news offerings, along with syndicated sitcoms in its prime-time lineup. It's a bold experiment, but the station is confident that it will come out on top.

Check out the weekly journalists' round-table discussion of the week's headlines every Friday morning at 9:00 on public radio's WJCT 89.9 FM. It's a good way to stay on top of local current events.

WTEV CBS-47
11700 Central Parkway
(904) 642-3030
www.cbs47.com
WTEV is the city's new CBS affiliate and a sister station to WAWS. Clear Channel Communication didn't skip a beat when it acquired the CBS affiliation in July 2002 after WJXT gave it up. WTEV airs CBS programming as well as a host of local news shows that are produced by the same news team that does the local Fox news.

WTLV/WJXX
1070 East Adams Street
(904) 354-1212
www.firstcoastnews.com
Local stations WTLV (NBC) and WJXX (ABC) merged their news operations in 2000 to bring viewers one local news team called First Coast News. The same anchors and reporters are seen on both stations in newscasts. Gannett owns both stations and carries the different network programming that belongs to each affiliate; just the local news teams are the same. The merger of the two stations was a bold television experiment, but it has worked out well for both stations. Today WTLV is the station to watch (and beat) at 11:00 P.M. for local nightly news.

RADIO

Whatever your taste in music or talk show host, you'll likely find what you want over Jacksonville's airways. While country and western is the predominant musical format, there is plenty of choice should you be more interested in oldies, urban, alternative, or classical music.

ADULT CONTEMPORARY
WSOS 94.1 FM
WEJZ 96.1 FM
WMXQ 102.9 FM

ALTERNATIVE
WPLA 93.3 FM

CHILDREN
WBWL 600 AM

CLASSICAL/EASY LISTENING
WJCT 89.9 FM
WKTZ 90.9 FM

COUNTRY
WQIK 99.1 FM
WGNE 99.9 FM
WROO 107.3 FM
WAOC 1420 AM

NEWS/TALK/SHOPPING
WJXR 92.1 FM
WOKV 690 AM
WVOJ 970 AM
WJGR 1320 AM

OLDIES
WKQL 96.9 FM

RELIGIOUS
WNCM 88.1 FM
WJFR 88.7 FM
WECC 89.3 FM
WNLE 91.7 FM
WBYB 100.3 FM
WBGB 106.5 FM
WAYR 550 AM
WIOJ 1010 AM
WROS 1050 AM
WSVE 1280 AM
WCGL 1360 AM
WZAZ 1400 AM
WOBS 1530 AM
WQOP 1600 AM

ROCK/CLASSIC HITS

WWRR 100.7 FM
WFYV 104.5 FM

SMOOTH JAZZ

WJSJ 105.3 FM
WSJF 105.5 FM

SPORTS

WFXJ 930 AM
WZNZ 1460 AM
WGSR 1570 AM

STANDARDS

WJAX 1220 AM

In case a hurricane hits Jacksonville, have plenty of batteries ready for your portable radio. There's a good chance local television stations will be knocked off the air for several days, depending on the severity of the storm.

TOP 40

WAPE 95.1 FM
WFKS 97.9 FM

URBAN

WJBT 92.7 FM
WSOL 101.5 FM
WHJX 105.7 FM
WEWC 1160 AM

INDEX

ABOUT THE AUTHORS

MARISA CARBONE

Marisa Carbone is a TV reporter and producer who enjoys spending her free time traveling the Northeast Florida region in search of good restaurants, good shops, and the area's rich history.

A graduate of Columbia University's School of Journalism, Marisa has worked as a TV producer at CNN in Atlanta and WNBC in New York City. She arrived in Jacksonville in the late 1980s. Marisa currently works as a reporter for the local FOX and CBS affiliates. She has two children.

PHOTO: FAVORITE STUDIOS

JOHN FINOTTI

When John Finotti moved to Jacksonville in 1989 to work for the *Florida Times-Union*, he figured he'd spend two, maybe three years in Northeast Florida before pushing on to a bigger newspaper in a bigger city. It didn't take long before he was rewriting those plans.

The ability to live near the ocean—and on a reporter's salary—changed his mind about leaving any time soon. As a beach resident, John has become an avid year-round surfer—even donning a full wet suit, booties, and hood in the winter months to brave Northeast Florida's surprisingly chilly ocean waters. John also enjoys fishing, whether he's pursuing elusive flounder off the jetties at the mouth of the St. Johns River, gliding along salt marshes in his kayak, or standing knee-deep in the surf.

As a freelancer, over the years John has written for the *New York Times, BusinessWeek,* and other publications. In 1998 after nine years at the *Times-Union,* he left to become a staff writer for *Florida Trend,* an award-winning statewide magazine based in St. Petersburg. John is now a principal in Access Corporate Communications.

PHOTO: FAVORITE STUDIOS

HELP US KEEP THIS GUIDE UP TO DATE

Every effort has been made by the authors and editors to make this guide as accurate and useful as possible. However, many things can change after a guide is published—phone numbers change, facilities come under new management, etc.

We would love to hear from you concerning your experiences with this guide and how you feel it could be improved and be kept up to date. While we may not be able to respond to all comments and suggestions, we'll take them to heart and we'll also make certain to share them with the authors. Please send your comments and suggestions to the following address:

The Globe Pequot Press
Reader Response/Editorial Department
P. O. Box 480
Guilford, CT 06437

Or you may e-mail us at:

editorial@GlobePequot.com

Thanks for your input, and happy travels!